ALL BUT MY SOUL

Abuse Beyond Control

Chuck Cean,
Keep up the good work
all my best.

Jeanne I. King, Ph.D.

Jeanne King

Mind Matters Publishing

First published in 2001 in paperbound by Mind Matters Publishing, Scottsdale AZ.

Printed in the United States of America

9 8 7 6 5 4 3 2 First Edition

The information contained in this book is not intended as a substitute for psychological counseling or as a source of legal advise; instead its purpose is to serve as an educational resource on family violence and legal domestic abuse.

The domestic violence to the author and her children referenced in this book is contained in public court records. The court proceedings are also within the public domain and are contained within the same court records. The facts of this story are in the public domain for anyone to review.

Library of Congress Control Number: 00-092045

King, Jeanne I., 1952

All but my soul: abuse beyond control / Jeanne I. King, Ph.D.

    p.   cm.

Includes bibliographical references.
ISBN 0-9706763-2-8   (pbk)

    1. Family Violence. 2. Wife Abuse. 3. Child Abuse.
    4. Victims of Crime. 5. Abusive Men. 6. Title.

Books from Mind Matters Publishing are available for textbook/course adoptions and are sold at bulk discounts to qualifying community and educational organizations. For further information visit our Website **www.AllButMySoul.net** or call **(888) 782-0723**.

To Whom It May Concern

To Whom It May Concern:

In August 1997, I became aware of the plight of the Blumenthal children through my involvement with HEAR MY VOICE /Protecting Our Nation's Children.

I referred the children's mother, Jeanne King (Blumenthal), to reputable individuals and organizations I hoped could secure a physically and psychologically safe outcome for her three sons in this protracted custody litigation. These contacts, and others, have expressed great concern about the potential danger posed by husband/father Lewis Blumenthal but have found their hands tied by the subterfuge of Lewis' legal counsel with the apparent consent of the judge.

As Executive Director of Children Remembered, I have followed the evolving patterns in this case that appear to expose three vulnerable boys and their mother to an increasingly precarious situation. **I am reminded of the Nicole Brown Simpson/Simpson children tragedy.**

My impression of Jeanne King is a women who has placed her life in jeopardy in order to protect her children. It is remarkable to me that she has maintained her sanity and dignity through the many years of physical abuse during the marriage and psychological abuse that has followed during these years of endless divorce and custody proceedings.

The judicial and social welfare systems that are supposed to protect vulnerable children are being manipulated to the dangerous disadvantage of the Blumenthal boys. Jeanne King has explored every lawful option available. This is clearly a case that needs a courageous, highly skilled and experienced, committed legal expert who understands the nuances and implications of domestic violence on a wife and children, and who is free of the local interdependence of the rich and politically connected in the Chicago community.

I implore you to review the materials provided by Jeanne King and accept the case for the sake of Bradley, David and Marc Blumenthal and endangered children everywhere. **Do not let Jeanne King become another Nicole Brown Simpson. Do not let Bradley, David and Marc become orphans or murder victims.**

Sincerely,

Evelyn Eman Delmar
Executive Director
Children Remembered
April 17, 1998 (Reprinted)

This book is dedicated
to my three sons,
Bradley, David and Marc,
for your courage, your patience
and the wisdom of your innocent hearts;
and
to All who have been violated
by a loved one or by a professional.

Contents

Illustrations

Part Three   Abuse Is A Choice
              For Adults Only

Acknowledgments

I never thought that writing about the most painful experience in my life could yield an experience more satisfying than ever imaginable; but it did. For this, I am most deeply grateful to our Creator. I am honored to have received that which came through me in writing *All But My Soul: Abuse Beyond Control*.

I am thankful to my teachers and coaches, both past and present, for their knowledge, wisdom and guidance. Deepak Chopra, for showing me how to evoke the healing response from within, helping me identify a "toxic relationship" and teaching me the value of embracing my desires. Wayne Dyer, Marianne Williamson and Doreen Virtue, for guiding me through audio tapes in listening to my inner voice and the wisdom of the infinite. The many authors whose work I have recently embraced and from which I have grown. Drs. Dutton, Walker, Jacobson, Gottman, Wilson, Ms. Jones, Ms. MiCarthy and Captain Snow's contributions to the body of literature on domestic violence have helped me put the pieces of my life experience with family abuse into perspective.

I am ever so grateful for having the opportunity to have worked with the wealth of talent and resources that contributed to the creation of this manuscript. Justin, for seeing that there was "a book in me," and coaching me in allowing it to flow out. Katie, for suggesting that I could "let the book write itself." Marika, my editor, for providing insights on grammar and giving your loving support in keeping me focused on the bigger picture of our lives. Mei Wei, my design consultant, for your artistic input in guiding me through the typeset and your creative skill in designing the cover, and for your heartfelt devotion to helping victims of domestic violence.

I remain in awe, with full appreciation, for the fortitude, tenacity and discipline that I managed to bring forward in writing and producing *All But My Soul*. The inspiration and human support that came to me along the way clearly helped make this possible. My gratitude to Tim, for your encouragement and wisdom and for inspiring my courage and commitment to writing *All But My Soul*. Jo, for your sensitive reflections in which you always reminded me to follow my heart and stay on track. Paul and Roberta, for your kindness, support and generosity. Lisa, Mary and Sam, for your friendship and unwavering, unconditional love during the most difficult phase of my life.

My patients, who have shown me that transformation and healing occur from within and to whom I am most grateful to have been a part of your journey toward health and happiness. My dear mother, for her acceptance of my being myself. My beloved father, for teaching me loving compassion and inner strength. Lew, my exhusband, for giving me the opportunity to know the distinction between violating and honoring others. And finally, all of the people who supported me in breaking the cycle of abuse in family and in court.

My blessed children, for showing me a source of infinite devotion within me, and within themselves, and inspiring all of us with pure love. Bradley, David and Marc, you have given me memories that have molded the meaning of my life.

Preface

B attered women, breaking out of abusive relationships, show up in all shapes and forms. There are those that run in the middle of the night and those that go before their abusers come home for dinner. There are those who flee with babies in diapers and those who wait until the children are in college. There are those who leave without their children and many who have no children. Then, there are some who are denied contact with their children and can't even say good-bye.

They are rich; they are poor. Some are educated and some are not. They are black, white, yellow and many of mixed origin. These women are of all faiths and religious orientations, some believing in God and many without this belief.

There are as many versions of this story as there are people living it. But there are only a few key themes that characterize this particular syndrome. They are clear, distinct and when they are yours, you know it. You may not admit it to yourself or to others, but on a primal level you are aware of your being violated, and it hurts. You know you are in danger and so you run.

You are one of the "four million women" who are abused every year. You fall into the "fifty per cent of women" who are beaten during marriage. You know the potential of greater risk to you by your abuser *after* you leave, but you can no longer live in direct contact with his current escalating abuse. Your present danger is real, as it is for many. So you flee to avoid being battered further today and to avoid being compromised by domestic violence forever. You are not alone. "Every fifteen seconds" a woman is assaulted by a current or past intimate partner.* (cited in Campbell, 1997; Walker, 1979; Wilson, 1997).

This is my story of how I came to grips with being abused and how I ultimately salvaged my life. As a communicator, a facilitator and a healer, I am compelled to give back to the community of women trapped in the same nightmare that eroded my life. I have much to offer in the form of psychological insight, basic information and human understanding and support. My words and experience may very well resonate with your pain. My intention is to assist you in ushering yourself into a life of peace, dignity, respect, health and pure happiness. This is your birthright. It is yours to recreate.

---

* See Appendix A for **Statistics on Family Violence**

Introduction

For years as a practicing psychologist, I wanted to write a book. I always had a way with words as a small child and young Latin scholar. My patients often said, "Dr. King, you should write a book." I was enjoying the work I was doing so much that it didn't appear essential to my making the contribution to humanity that I desired at the time. I imaged it would come when I was drawn to do so.

I was helping people resolve chronic medical conditions and recurring psychological problems through teaching self-regulation. I had become such an excellent coach, my patients and peers noted how I could teach the control of physiological processes to anything that was breathing. It was my passion, and it had become my excellence.

It was the silver lining inside a personal cloud that I have only recently fully understood. My self-regulation skills were an outgrowth of a personal encounter with pain management. I was practicing "doctor heal thyself" for the sake of survival after a cervical spine injury resulting from a domestic assault by my husband. The incident had involved our oldest son as well.

In my plight with the domestic violence in our home, I reached out and the family violence transformed into severely cruel litigation abuse. I had reached a point of exhaustion and, one day, was lamenting over my predicament with the audio film producer who made the self-regulation tapes I created for my patients. As he listened, he suggested I might benefit in telling our story on tape.

He brought me to an individual who had experience with documentary films. The film producer listened to me for an hour. At some point, as it was all flooding out of me, he said, "We must get you on video." The next week we made a four hour documentary film. It was cathartic for me to put this whole story on one recording. We edited the film down to a 45 minute video, entitled *Domestic Violence Transformed into Litigation Abuse,* and circulated it.

The video film caught the interest of a producer in Chicago who hosted a television talk show. The producer made two more videos of our story and entitled the films *Court-Sanctioned Domestic Violence.* In this television talk show series, I told my story along with the input of numerous specialists. These included: a domestic violence court advocate, a specialist in treating perpetrators, a specialist in treating victims of abuse, an activist in children's rights and two local divorce attorneys familiar with the court system.

This movie was subsequently used in a graduate level course in domestic violence at the Illinois School of Professional Psychology in Chicago. A female graduate student called me after watching this film and said, "I can't believe what I have seen in your story. This is my story, only not as severe." She added, "I learned so much and feel so relieved to know that this absurdity was not just mine." She was grateful to know that she was not alone.

It was then that I realized I was coming closer to writing a book. I knew there would be no better way for me to reach the millions of women in this predicament. Why, because there are too many and most are in hiding with themselves and/or with society. In a book I could intimately, boldly and directly connect with victims in innocence, those in denial and those not knowing where to find answers.

I initially wrote *All But My Soul* to tell my story for my children's future understanding and for the benefit of the millions of battered women and abused children, afflicted with and entrapped by family violence. However, writing this manuscript provided an unexpected and additional benefit. It was exhilarating for me to allow a sixteen year nightmare to gush forward spontaneously, effortlessly and most amazingly within a hundred days. It gave me significant insight into how we got where we are and provided an emotional release which had a healing effect on me.

After writing my story, I decided to research the professional literature on domestic violence. To my surprise, I learned that family violence is a full field of study in psychology. My review of the literature revealed that our family is a classic text book case. This discovery was like living the symptom picture of a cancer and suddenly the reality of the diagnosis sinks in. While I knew all along that we suffered from toxic abuse, the recognition of all its elements – from the subtle to the blatant – was most humbling. There is no doubt I was lost somewhere between my trance of victimization and an ignorance of this sub-specialty discipline in my own profession. The impact this information had on me was sobering; it brought about a profound awakening.

I have inserted some salient bits of academia into *All But My Soul*, sometimes where it is relevant to the chronology of our story and mostly at points where the insights became apparent to me. A further elaboration on domestic violence myths, facts and basics are contained in the Appendices. Seeing our life in the context of professional literature may enlighten other victims in the understanding of their own predicament. Those familiar with the domestic violence syndrome will recognize our circumstances as self-evident, in which case the information insertions will serve to augment or reinforce an appreciation of this silent insidious social dysfunction.

My intention is to assist victims and those who can be of service in the interruption of the cycle of violence before it gets out of hand and beyond control. It is my mission to contribute to the liberation of victims and to their wholeness and potency. It is my hope to touch women and children trapped in abuse and serve as a catalyst for their empowerment and peace.

Jeanne King, PhD.

Jeanne King, Ph.D.

December 9, 2000

Dearest Bradley, David and Marc,

I have written this book for your understanding when you are mature enough to appreciate it. The contents of *All But My Soul: Abuse Beyond Control* will put much into perspective.

Our not having these years together has nothing to do with you or me. I would never turn my back on you. You are good sons – you are the best. And you have an excellent, strong and healthy mother who is eternally committed to your welfare.

I learned, as I am sure you recognized, that seeking our remedy for abuse through divorce court served to keep all of us in the abuse cycle. Abuse is about control, and the litigation fueled your father's determination to continue fighting for control.

Your Dad had decided he was going to "get rid of your Mom" long ago, after I spoke out about the hitting in our home. Since then I recognized the more I struggled against being pushed out of your lives, the less contact we had. Today my calls to you do not get through at your home. We have not heard each others voices for over three months. I know this is not your choice and I want you to know it is not mine, either.

I did not leave you; I held on until there was no more contact, and then I stopped being abused. I wait for you, always. Until we connect, know personal strength comes from within.

I love you, Bradley, David and Marc, and I believe in each of you. You remain in my heart, my thoughts and my prayers everyday.

My Love Forever,

Mom

Mom

PART ONE

Family Violence:
Child and Spousal Abuse

CHAPTER 1

Abuse from the Beginning

In the Beginning

Husband's Criticism and Father's Jealously

Baby's Injury; Father's "Accident"

Paying the Price for Good Advice

My Cloudy Vision

I long to be with my children. *God gave me the most blessed gift of three healthy sons, and today their father denies us direct access to one another. My children mean as much to me as my next breath. It feels like a part of my being has been ripped out of my life to be placed on hold, until God only knows when. I am doing all that is humanly possible to come to grips with and comprehend our tragic, irrational predicament.*

Perhaps you're reading this because you, too, have awakened to a similar situation or you know someone headed in this direction; or possibly because you have a loved one locked in family abuse. Maybe you feel a mysterious, unavoidable tug to see how this can happen. The story is unbelievable, though meticulously true.

My children and I have been torn apart and have not see each other for seven months. It is November 1999, and our desire to connect remains with each passing day. My youngest son, Marc who is age 10, has written me asking, *"Mom why can't we see you and how can we get you back."* He goes on to say, " *Mom, I'm just tearing apart from not seeing you."* The children's father, Lew, has informed numerous individuals – including our children – that I abandoned my sons and have made no attempt to be in contact with them. Nothing could be further from the truth. Lew actually pushed me out of our children's lives and drove me out of my community, after abusing us for over sixteen years.

I feel Marc's innocent and desperate wanting to know what happened to Mommy and why he can't see Mommy, and I am compelled to document the true story. If Lew or his court agents won't allow my children to know it today, it will be available for their future. I feel it is wrong to tell children a parent abandoned them and lead them to believe the parent did not want to or is not allowed to be a part of their lives. I believe this causes a primal wound in children, of not being wanted by the natural parent or questioning a healthy parent-child bond. Children then see them-selves through this wound, which compromises their growing self-esteem and creates a fragile sense of self. My children deserve to know the truth, if not for a healthier childhood, for a more normal and healthy adulthood. I am driven to tell this story for my own children and for all children who are abused.

If I can help one abused child and his or her abused mother – a battered wife – in writing this book, then my re-living our pain to share this story will be a service well worth it. I know if some publication like this would have been available to me years ago, my children would not have remained in family violence, nor locked in child abuse today.

My three sons and I are victims of domestic violence. I am a refugee of 14 years of well-documented physical and emotional abuse to myself and a witness of ongoing child abuse to my three sons: Bradley, age 15; David, age 12; and Marc, age 10. It is hard for me to believe that our abuser was able to take his vengeance to such an extreme: severing me, the protective parent, from our abused children. Here's how it evolved.

An Abuse Dynamic Forms

Nearly sixteen years ago, Lew and I were planning our wedding. We were sitting in a small room in his two bedroom apartment in a low rent neighborhood in Chicago, across from Michael Reese Hospital were he was employed, as an attending physician. It was January, 1984 and the air was cold, with the feel of winter in the apartment. I was dressed in my nightgown with my hair in a neatly rolled bedtime bun on top of my head. We were arguing about who would attend the reception ceremony honoring our wedding. The bickering between us escalated into a fight, resulting in his pulling my hair by the bun to the point of pain. The discomfort to my scalp and head was startling; and his action of pulling my hair until I cried was so shocking that I was unable, at the time, to process what had happened.

I went to sleep. Upon awaking the next morning, I couldn't get close to Lew until I had sorted out what had occurred. I was a few months pregnant with our first child, Bradley, and I think I would have done anything to make what Lew did okay so as not to upset the pregnancy. I recall rationalizing with myself that his actions and my reaction were like two children fighting. It seemed weird, but I would not let myself get intimidated by it. I rationalized the fight as reflective of how I saw our relationship developing. We interacted like two siblings merely having fun, except when he was criticizing me, which was far too often for a healthy growing relationship.

Lew is a small framed man, 5' 10", and at that time he weighed about 145 pounds. He has small shoulders and, relative to my size, Lew was not intimidating. At 5' 7" and weighing about 125 pounds, my body stature was solid and athletic, providing me a physical presence equal to his. He was, in fact, the smallest man I had ever been romantically involved with. It was his teeth and his refreshing smile that I found appealing. On the day we met near the swimming pool at the East Bank Club in July 1983, I saw Lew as a fairly attractive man with a zest for life, coupled with a respect for hard work.

I did not expect to become romantically involved with Lew, as he was not my typical attraction. What I liked about him was the friendship that immediately evolved, and bloomed with belly breaking laughter and loads of carefree fun and frolic. Lew was actually a rebound companion for me, as I was getting over the break up of a seven-year relationship. I knew that he was partially involved with someone else, and so it made our getting to know each other safe for me. I didn't really have to worry about whether he like me or not, because I wasn't concerned or interested in his long term attraction to me. So, a playful friendship evolved. While it seemed pure at its inception, it was seriously clouded with too much pot and partying.

We were ages thirty and thirty-one at the time of our courtship, I being a year older than him. I saw him like a buddy, smaller, younger and not the threat that a lady sometimes feels when you meet the man that knocks your socks off. No, he was just a lot of fun, until I learned about the tyrant within who emerged behind closed doors. At the time I envisioned myself with a much more handsome and masculine looking man, to which I had been accustomed. I was a quite attractive young lady, with high cheek bones, classic features and an inviting smile. My body was in proper proportion and turned many heads on many beaches. When I met Lew I was an accomplished scholar, having recently completed my Ph.D. in psychology. I was an excellent student, with an appreciation for academics, education and professional success.

Lew was an obstetrician gynecologist by profession, and was always eager to give the impression that he knew more about my body than I. Having children had been my childhood dream since about age three. I recall telling Lew that I was concerned that I was unable to conceive, because I had been sexually active for many years without using birth control, and had never once got pregnant. I attributed this to having erratic menstrual periods. Lew determined he would show me that I was ovulating and I could conceive.

Knowing this wouldn't happen, I went along with our unprotected sex. A courtship and a romance with sexual intimacy and personal experiment emerged.

Lew became one of these dates that never left. He kept coming back day after day, and within two months he was at my apartment more then his own. We took an exotic romantic vacation and partied until we both dropped. Lew helped me rediscover my carefree self, the one I had buried in my prior relationship. Shortly after our return from this vacation, we were walking down the street near my apartment on Dearborn Avenue in Chicago. It was cold outside, with winter setting in, and I walked bundled and sick. I told Lew that I was nauseous and couldn't get a hold of myself. I felt my environment spinning and was completely out of sorts. He said, "You're pregnant, unless you prove otherwise!"

Lew insisted on me giving him a urine specimen to take to his lab for analysis to determine if I was, in fact, pregnant. The results came back positive, and he exclaimed with excitement that a "bambino" was there. He and his lab friend enjoyed the news and subsequently broke the word to me. I was stunned, excited, exhilarated, delighted, but profoundly scared as I realized that "first comes man, than comes baby," and I had done it backwards. I had no pre-intention of marrying Lew, but here I was pregnant with his baby.

We spent days deliberating what next. Lew wanted me to abort the pregnancy. I withdrew from him and decided I needed to sort this out on my own, as his choice did not feel right to me. I sought counsel with my gynecologist, Dr. Alan Charles, and of course my Mom. I left the conversation with Dr. Charles hearing him say, "If you have an abortion, it could interfere with conception in the future." That's all I could remember from our dialogue and that was enough for me. There was nothing I wanted more than a child and I wasn't going to do anything to interfere with my having one. Then in a meditation, I got a knowing that to abort this pregnancy was to kill life, and there was no way I could do that. So my decision was made; now I had to figure out what to do with Lew. On some level, I felt guilty that I saw no room for negotiating in this decision, but I could not process it any other way. I felt like it was my decision as it was happening in my body. I told Lew that I could not abort the pregnancy, and I let it go at that. I truly expected nothing from him; I only wanted him to stop badgering me to abort the baby.

Lew then pulled back from me to do his own personal sorting. After visits with his family and friends, he came back talking about marriage. I wasn't ready for that commitment, so I called my Mom to hashed it over with her. My oldest brother, Lou King, had made that mistake of getting his girlfriend pregnant before getting married and it didn't work out for him. I did not want to follow his foot steps, but I couldn't abort the pregnancy. I think I would have been happy to have had the pregnancy without marrying Lew. Lew, on the other hand, said he felt obligated to marry if I kept the pregnancy. He recounted a discussion he had with his father in which he was trying to decide if he and I should get married. Lew said that his Dad, Papa, had said, "How would you feel if she was with someone else?" Lew told me that feeling made him decide that he wanted to marry me, and so he proposed. My head was in such a cloud with the surge of pregnancy hormones that I did not know how to respond. So, once again, I pulled back to sort and sift, but the cloud wouldn't part for me to see clearly the right thing to do. It felt appropriate to get married, as we were from similar backgrounds and seemed to be falling in love, but intuitively and privately I was uneasy about marrying Lew.

*   *   *

The pregnancy hormone surge cascaded and we visited his family with our news of pregnancy and decision to marry. The family celebrations came left and right and, before I knew it, his mother was planning our wedding and reception. I became the honored mother-to-be and the reticent bride. After the incident of pulling my hair over the planning, I started to notice many signs of something that felt wrong to me, but I didn't understand what it was. I had no label for it and no direct personal backdrop from which I could understand what was going on. All I knew was that I was marrying a very critical man, who appeared intense and inappropriate in his expression of anger. I did not realize the enormity of what this meant at that time.

I hated his criticism, but thought I could deal with it. I was accustomed to men bad-mouthing women, as my father did the same to my mother. Dad picked on Mom implying that she was not smart, competent or capable; but it was subtle, and nothing like the way Lew did it. Lew was methodical and relentless about his criticism. He would come to my apartment, with lists in his hands of all the things that I had done wrong, or that he wanted me to change, or that he thought I should change to be a better human being. I found myself living on the defensive in order to hold my own. It would have been acceptable for him to have one or two items from time to time to critique. Then I could have heard it, processed it and used it to better myself if appropriate. However, it was Lew's habit to show up with a litany of what I later came to call "let me count the ways in which I hate you."

It was everything from, "You were late for me and I have been waiting for you." to "Your shoulders are too big." He was right about my tardiness as I had already gained a reputation for being late, but I had never heard anyone pick on my body the way Lew did. He told me that my arms and shoulders were too big and, as I filled out during the pregnancy, he began to call me "moose." I remember going into the bathroom, crying, just to regain my composure. When I talked to my doctor about how sensitive I thought I was becoming, he said pregnancy does that to a woman. He assured me that this would pass.

As I have come to understand abusive battering, emerging out of the perpetrator's vulnerability, I believe Lew's masculinity was threatened by my shoulders being almost broader and with more athletic definition then his. It was the main part of my body that he picked on, until I grew to hate my shoulders myself. I went from being proud of my upper body to never wearing anything that revealed my shoulders and didn't realize, at the time, how this was happening.

I was aware that the verbal and emotional abuse around my body escalated as the pregnancy progressed, and had convinced myself that its impact had more to do with my pregnancy related sensitivity. In reviewing the family abuse literature today, I have learned that battering onset during pregnancy is a common theme. Some authors attribute it to the abuser's jealousy over the infant attracting their spouse's love and the fear of perceived abandonment. I am beginning to recognize that the escalation of the abuse pattern may also be related to the batterer's fear of losing domination over his victim. The pregnancy brought out a source of pleasure in me and commitment from me that was beyond Lew's control. This was not comfortable for him, and I did not know control was an issue.

*   *   *

Lew and I made many life changes in the months to follow. My life change inventory score, according to the Holms and Rhea Stress Profile, peaked to the max. In a matter of months, I had changed my marital status, my residence, my employment and had gained over 35 pounds. Then we became a family of three, rapidly.

Bradley's arrival into the world set a record, according to Lew, as the fastest delivery witnessed. Within an hour and a half I went from one centimeter to being fully dilated, and I was told to stop the breathing and suck in; no pushing was necessary. Bradley was making a rapid bursting entrance into the world. It was up there with the most joyous experiences I've ever known. Bradley and I bonded immediately. Within seven days, I was running around our new home in Lincoln Park in my college gym shorts, totally in love with our new arrival. Just being near him, smelling his baby sweetness, made me high.

Bradley was a beautiful baby, so much so that people would stop me on the street, enamored by his striking and radiating beauty. He had the deepest baby blue eyes and the most classic pure angelic features. When Bradley was around nine months, I recall looking at him one day as we were lying on the bed resting and seeing such an angelic quality come forth that I was moved to call him "Angel" and, as a nickname, I later referred to him as "Ang." When I would call Ang every cell in my being would resonate with pure happiness. And when he heard me release this high pitched sweet singing sound, his little arms and legs would flutter in glee. It was very sweet and the family started to pick up on it and also called Bradley "Ang." Then, I started calling him "Angel One." I referred to him with this nickname more than using his birth name Bradley.

At some point, I started calling him "Bradley One." This was too much for Lew, as he would interrupt my calling out "Bradley One" with his saying "Bradley Two." It was the first time I realized that he was really jealous of Bradley. I remember this awareness leading me to wanting to assure Lew that he was ever so important to me in a way that was sacred and un-replaceable by anyone or anything. I wanted him to know how special he was and not to feel in competition for my attention with Bradley. I wanted him to feel it and to also appreciate my loving bond with Bradley as though it was an investment in our child's future, something that he too would reap the benefits of in years to come.

However, somehow no matter how hard I tried to balance my affections, it was never enough for Lew. He was always wanting more, or demanding that it be delivered in a different way. Even saying hello in the "wrong tone" became cause for Lew's unpredictable outbursts. Yet I never knew what the right manner was, because it was always changing and appeared to be more a function of how Lew was feeling. This was most obvious to me in his reaction to the meals I was preparing. I had brought a love and talent for cooking to our relationship. A favored dish, like Shrimp Creole, was sometimes met with delight and sometimes blasted with disapproval, if any food boxes, bags or remnants of packaging for the side dishes was discovered in the kitchen by Lew. What I couldn't understand about his disenchantment was that he was the one, of the two of us, who found pleasure in frozen pizzas. I soon recognized the food I served was not the issue.

The "un-pleasable" spilled over into many areas. Most perplexing was his emerging sexual fetishes and demands. In my effort to celebrate his arrival and out of my true joy to see him walk through the door, I'd welcome him with an erotic willingness to make love. Invariably this resulted in our having much sex. But what used to be superb oral sex now became inadequate, because with it came his newly expressed resentment of my unwillingness to swallow his semen. I had enjoyed many sexual romances, but never had any man ever requested or demanded that I do that. Lew repeatedly said, *"If you really loved me,* you would want to swallow it." From his perspective, I did not love him because I didn't want to gulp down his semen. I wondered why he cared what I did with the semen long after he released it. Lew was obsessed with my discrete discharge of his bodily fluids from my mouth. His resentment over this grew and became the subject of continuous teasing and badgering me. He was relentless, and it was disgraceful – even spilling over into his asking whether my friends "swallow." At the time, I dismissed his obsession as a peculiar gynecologist desire, yet I could not understand his unwillingness to honor my personal limits.

My greetings, our gourmet meals and the romance served to light the fire, but it was a glow replaced with rage when I showed my affections toward our baby. I remained frustrated in dealing with Lew's jealously, but was determined not to let it interfere with my bonding with Bradley. I recall curling up in a semi-walk-in closet, many times, to hide while I breast-fed Bradley. I hoped it would minimize Lew's lashing out with anger during moments of intimacy with my infant. It only bought us time.

I recognized that Lew seemed to derive pleasure at finding fault with things about me, Bradley and about our growing bond. As long as he was in this mode, I was on the defensive, eagerly trying to jump the hoops before me to please him, whereas he was deriving a sense of empowerment. I felt these interactions as tension-making for me, and knew they were making him feel good. At some juncture, I thought it was unhealthy that he feel good as he was creating scenarios in which I felt bad. I decided to try other ways to reassure Lew that he did not have to compete with Bradley. I tried to show him that my love for him would not be replaced by my love for Bradley. But nothing I did accomplished this. Lew's ongoing berating, belittling and demeaning me and my involvement with Bradley deepened as Bradley grew, and the outbursts of violence and anger became more unpredictable.

I rationalized Lew's fury in my mind by telling myself his actions and jealously were because Bradley came so soon in our relationship, prior to our establishing a solid base as a couple. I felt partially responsible for the "quick" family and what this took away from Lew, as I was part of the pregnancy. My owning part of his jealousy only made me feel more guilty and more paralyzed in my ability to create anything different between us. In retrospect, I realize that his jealously was his alone and was merely an expression of the abuse and control issues, which came to the forefront more vividly in the years to come.

Family Violence Unfolds

Around December of 1985, when Bradley was 17 months, Lew, Bradley and I were shopping in Ace Hardware store in Lincoln Park. After being there for about 20 minutes, Lew wanted to leave and swiftly tried to hurry us out of the store. We had completed our purchases. I was holding our bags and Lew said, "Let's go." We were in the housewares section and Bradley was standing in front of the little dishes and house nick-nacks that were eye level for him. He was merely browsing with appropriate curiosity. I could see he was enjoying the colors and shapes of the objects and was unaware of his father's sense of urgency to exit.

Bradley continued, engaged in his delight, and Lew grabbed his little arm. In a firm and angered voice, Lew said, "We're leaving." Bradley hadn't made the transition as quickly as Lew, and was still fixated on the objects that had captured his attention. Lew took hold of his little arm tighter and yanked it so hard that Bradley was startled out from his gaze. Bradley let out a painful cry and, like a limp noodle, he yielded to follow his father's direction. As we all exited the store and walked down the street to the parking garage, I was haunted with a fear and knowing that something was wrong.

When we got to the car, I attempted to put Brad in the car seat and could see that his little arm was dangling, inverted and locked at the elbow joint. I was sure something was wrong when I attempted to remove his little jacket and saw he could not move his arm. The pain in his face and his cry concerned me at a level deeper than I could comprehend at the moment. I knew that Lew had hurt him, and this both frightened and enraged me. I insisted on taking Bradley to the hospital to get an x-ray.

Lew and I drove Bradley to Michael Reese Hospital where Lew was employed, and we walked into the back entrance, bypassing Admissions. We went directly into the cast room where we met Dr. Charles Slack, an orthopedic surgeon. Dr. Slack had been a colleague of Lew's and had served as a physician to me over the years. Dr. Slack examined Bradley's arm and brought him into the x-ray room to x-ray his arm. Following the evaluation, Dr. Slack determined that Bradley's elbow was dislocated and required casting and immobility for several weeks. Dr. Slack put Bradley's arm in a full arm cast from his shoulder to his little wrist and placed it in a sling. Bradley remained in this cast for six weeks.

My heart was aching as I watched my child's arm being put in a cast and deep down inside knowing that the way this happened was not my child's fault, but instead was Lew's action of forceful exertion. I tried to explain the event to Dr. Slack and noticed how

Lew was cutting me off and could sense the awkwardness it posed for Dr. Slack. I did not try to pursue blame of the event, as my child's well-being was most paramount in the moment. I remember little Bradley sitting in my lap as the Doctor prepped him for casting. I felt Bradley's fear, but knew we would make it through this.

I was relieved to know that Bradley's arm was healing as it lay immobilized in the cast. We spent extra time getting ready for bed, changing clothes and eating. Just about everything we did was with focus, and a certain amount of deliberation, to insure protecting Brad's arm and keep the cast clean. Bradley was a quick learner and rapidly figured out how to negotiate the world around his full arm cast. I was so proud of what a trouper he had become. But for weeks I struggled with trying to come to grips with how this happened, and my means for doing so didn't serve me.

I repeatedly initiated discussions with Lew in which I voiced my belief of his being too forceful with Brad in the hardware store. I suggested that finding another way to evoke compliance and cooperation would serve us all. One evening in my effort to get my point across, I waited until Lew was comfortable and, as we were lounging in the family room after Bradley had gone to bed, I expressed my opinion.

"You pulled his arm too hard," I said. "He's just a little baby." "If you pull it hard enough so it causes injury, that's too hard." I suggested, "There could have been another way to get compliance, to get cooperation with the child still hanging in, lingering and looking at the dishes."

"Oh no," Lew claimed, "I pulled and Brad pulled the other way."

But, I knew Bradley didn't pull the other way because I was watching. I saw Bradley yanked forcefully without time to respond.

These discussions frustrated me, angered Lew and led to greater denial of his role in the incident and Bradley's resulting injury. Lew convinced himself that the incident was Bradley's fault and routinely told his friends and family a recount of the "accident" that he had come to believe. When we would go to a party, people would ask what happened to Bradley's arm. Before I could get a word out Lew would say, "I was trying to get Brad to leave the hardware store and Brad just pulled in the opposite direction." For extra drama on some occasions, Lew reported that Brad fell to the floor and demanded going in the opposite direction. Lew would usually close with a comment of how "these things happen when children don't listen."

Lew's belief about this event started to bother me, and I recognized that if he saw it this way, it could and would most likely happen again. Since we were accustomed to dealing with our personal problems in the family, I addressed this over an intimate family discussion with Lew's mother and father along with Lew. As I reflected on the story, I was filled with tears, partly for my child and out of my own personal frustration. Lew's mother and his father both adamantly told me, *"These things happen in families."* From this time on I began feeling I was in the wrong family, but I didn't know how I was going to get me and my child out.

*   *   *

My physical strength and mental clarity had been compromised since Bradley's infancy. I attributed it to normal postpartum, breast-feeding my child and sleep deprivation, typical of having a nursing infant in one's life. I flowed with my loss of stamina and mental fog, believing it would pass. I didn't recognized it at the time, but I suspect my cloudy vision may have weakened my inner strength to trust my instincts and hold to my convictions concerning our family matters. Instead my time, energy and attention was consumed in efforts devoted to basic survival.

I went back to practicing meditation routinely as a way of getting through the day. Morning meditation helped me deal with the short nights and broken sleep, giving me a feeling of having some semblance of restoration. Occasionally an afternoon meditation, which I managed to slip in while Bradley was napping, would help me deal with the afternoon lag of my dragging engine. All of my resources were placed in taking care of Bradley and just getting me through the day. I don't know if Lew realized that my health was failing because, after that second meditation, by the time he got home I would have dinner on the table and we could enjoy some time together, unless of course if we were struggling with our differences.

As Brad recovered and his cast was removed, our little family began preparing for a long-desired vacation to see the Halley's Comet in Tahiti, which Lew and his college roommate had dreamed about and planned for years. With my health lingering and still not understanding why, I continued to take the path of least resistance and go with the flow. That is, I looked to maintain the stability of our home, the continuity of our family and simply took one day at a time, hoping that my strength would return. In preparing for our trip, Lew and I had another run-in that stopped me in my tracks to wonder why was I with this man.

It was the Spring of 1986 and we were packing to go on the trip to Tahiti. Lew wanted to bring some cocaine, which he routinely enjoyed recreationally, when he had unstructured time on his hands. We fought about his use of cocaine, but this time I was adamant in telling him not to use it. We were sitting in our bedroom, on the second floor of our townhouse. I had suitcases on the floor, and we were organizing our belongings for the trip.

"Taking cocaine out of the country would not be wise," I said. "You could get caught coming back into the country with an illegal substance and this would seriously hurt your stature as a doctor."

Lew blew me off and told me that I ought not get into his business. He wanted my support of his taking the cocaine, but I refused to give it.

My unwillingness to condone his taking the drug led to his pushing me onto the bed, where I landed on my back. He threw his body against mine and pinned my arms down and out as far as they would extend. Sitting on my abdomen, he continued holding me down. I had been in this posture many times, pinned to the wall with my arms extended out further than I knew they could stretch. This is what usually happened when I was not in support of something he wanted or did not anticipate an "unexpressed" need of his. I would be pinned to the wall until I cried, at which point he would usually release me to fall to the floor. This time I struggled, trying to wiggle my way out and push him off of me. In my effort to escape his grip, my glasses fell off my face and broke in our struggle. I cried and Lew let me go.

I was numb after this incident and couldn't get close to Lew for several days. I don't know how I brought myself to gather Bradley and me up for this trip, but I know I felt so phony the whole time we were there. Lew, on the other hand, seemed fine and acted as though nothing had happened. As time passed and I felt the warmth of friends, I engaged in our group outing. The periods of time between the numerous altercations were so good that it made comprehending the violence difficult. I was riding a roller coaster with Lew, which I have since learned is called the "cycle of violence." (See Appendix B for an elaboration on the **Cycle of Violence**.)

At some point, I actually recall Lew trying to convince me that the incidents were not happening. On many occasions I would have bruises on my arms, resulting from his grip and bracing restraint. But after the bruise would fade and heal, he would tell me that it never happened. He would say, "Jeanne, *It's in your mind*. You know I didn't bruise you." At some juncture I recall having our discussions about the bruises when I still had one, so as to prove my point, and Lew's response to this was, "You just bruise too easily."

*   *   *

My condition of daily fatigue and fuzzy thinking worsened as did Lew's envy over my relationship with Bradley. Lew expressed wanting to have another child, as he said, "one for him." Lew told me he thought I was giving too much to Bradley and that having another child would be good for Bradley as it would spread out my attention. All of this seemed like nonsense, but my undiagnosed condition had progressed so that all I could think of was how wonderful I felt when I was pregnant and how much I desired to feel that way again. I also had always wanted three or four children and rationalized with myself that if Lew and I had this second child, he would not be as jealous of Bradley and there would not be such brutal fighting.

Although, I hadn't gotten over Bradley's arm and Lew's distortion of the facts, I so desperately wanted stability with my failing health that I was willing to go with the flow so as not to rock the boat. I actually recall reflecting on my brother's broken leg that he suffered as a child and somehow rationalized that accidents do happen in childhood. But deep in my soul I knew Bradley's injury was not an accident; it was a crime. Had I have had the strength and clearer thinking, I may have acted on it then.

I consented to have the second child, but we could not conceive. I saw my obstetrician and he told me that my thyroid was not functioning properly and sent me to an endocrinologist. I had an evaluation with Dr. James Sheinin and learned that my thyroid was practically not functioning at all. He diagnosed me with Hashimoto's hypothyroidism. He helped me understand that this was the reason that I felt like I couldn't turn my motor on in the morning and could barely make it through the day. The Doctor explained that this is why my thinking was so unclear. He also told me that this condition can make you feel depressed, because an under-active thyroid depresses the working of the central nervous system.

I mistakenly started to confuse my physical condition with my social reality of being a victim in an abusive relationship. The personal degradation resulting from being pinned down, restrained and bruised interrupted my happiness and depressed me. I didn't realize it, at the time, how Lew's assaults and my remaining in the relationship with him eroded my self-esteem. After the doctor's diagnosis, I attributed the blues' to my thyroid condition.

When Lew learned of the results of my thyroid screen, he said, "I have never in all the years of my practice as a physician ever seen anyone's thyroid screen that low." I recall his words, "You are off the chart." I was both devastated and elated by this news. On the one hand, I now had a real condition, for which I was told I would have to be medicated for the rest of my life and I hated the idea of having to be on any medication indefinitely. Yet, on the other hand, I had the chance of getting my energy and my life back.

My mother had Hashimoto's hypothyroidism and I was informed that my predisposition was genetic. Hashimoto's hypothyroidism is an auto-immune disorder, in which the immune system fights against the body's own parts. Hashimoto's hypothyroidism is linked to pregnancy and, as I understand it, the immune system attacks the thyroid in response to the foreign matter in the body. My thyroid, the object of attack, had become so severely inactive it was amazing that I was even getting through the days during the last two years. In retrospect, I'm not surprised that I developed this condition as it was certainly a tumultuous time in my life. Symbolically, I believe that my body was alerting me to the war ahead and my engine was petering out so I would get off the road; but I was too weak and too stubborn to listen.

Immediately I was placed on Synthroid, and within 10 days my energy started to come back, my thinking became clearer and I was feeling absolutely wonderful. Bradley and I enjoyed long days in the park and I still had lots of energy left for Lew. Sometime within the first month of my feeling great, I became pregnant with my second child, David.

As I write this book, I recognize that I had been living in a stupor. I can see that Lew displayed the signs of a classic abuser, and I was feeding myself the rationalizations that bind a victim to an abusive relationship. I had never seen abuse before, at least not like I was experiencing, and could never have imagined what was ahead of me by remaining in the relationship with Lew.

Signs and Signals of an Abuser

How to Identify a Potential Batterer

- Jealousy
- Controlling behavior
- Quick involvement
- Unrealistic expectations
- Isolation
- Blames others for his problems
- Blames others for his feelings
- Hypersensitivity
- Cruelty to animals or children
- "Playful" use of force in sex
- Verbal abuse
- Rigid sex roles
- Jekyll-and-Hyde personality
- Past battering
- Threats of violence
- Breaking or striking objects
- Any force during an argument

If your partner exhibits more than three of these warning signs, there is a strong potential for abuse in the relationship. Without effective early intervention, abuse can escalate in severity and sometimes lead to death (or other devastating consequences). If you believe you are in danger, please call:

National Domestic Violence Hotline
800-799-SAFE

All Calls are handled in strict confidence.

"How to Identify a Potential Batterer" from K. J. Wilson, *When Violence Begins at Home.* © 1997 Copyright by K. J. Wilson, Ed.D. Reprinted with permission from Hunter House, Inc. Publishers. (parenthetical added)

> *"Abusers may mentally reconstruct the act (of violence) in order to blame the victim for having provoked the aggression."*
> (Dutton, 1995, p. 49)

CHAPTER 2

Child Abuse and Wife Assault

Abuse During Pregnancy

"One More Kiss Mommy"

Cervical Spine Injury

Lew's History of Abuse

Over the course of the next year, it became obvious to me that I was in an abusive relationship, which I could no longer deny, excuse or rationalize away. I was in the mid-trimester of my pregnancy with David during the Spring of 1987. Lew and I were in our family room on the second floor of our Lincoln Park townhouse, planning our next vacation. I recall it being a weekend, in which we had time to play, plan and fight. Lew wanted to go on a vacation that involved our leaving the country, as he had been wanting to do for the last two years. Lew was accustomed to taking exotic vacations and enjoying them immensely. It was such an important part of his life that he would plan the next vacation while on the return flight of a vacation. He lived from vacation to vacation, and convinced me that it was important to his well being to offset his rigorous work schedule and the demands of his job.

I loved these vacations, but was unwilling to venture too far away during and immediately after pregnancy. I believed that pregnancy was a vulnerable time and, should I require any medical attention, I wanted it in an American hospital, not some foreign country where I could not speak the language nor trust the medical interventions available to me. I also felt that pregnancy was a time of inward attention and direction, in which I wanted my resources directed to and for the baby's development, not scattered across the world. I privately practiced specific visualizations, as the baby was forming its body parts. I saw this as my job during these critical months. Lew, though he was an obstetrician, didn't see it the same way.

On this particular day he was trying to convince me to take a trip that I felt was in conflict with the growing pregnancy and my body's resources. He did not want to hear about my "excuses" as he labeled my unwillingness to comply. He became angered by my not wanting to go with him.

"You are robbing me of my life pleasures," he said.

"No," I replied, "I am giving you a pleasure that you and I both wanted, and I simply can't do both at the same time."

I explained to Lew that we were making a family and it was going to involve some concessions on our parts. I tried to tell him that this was a limited time in our lives and, once done, we could enjoy his former vacation life style. I saw us going nowhere with this and encouraged him to go on his own, but he insisted on getting me to want to go with him.

There was no way I could budge on compromising the pregnancy and, the next thing I knew, he was pushing me to the ground and holding me to the floor. In his frustration and anger, he grabbed my legs and pulled me up the full flight of stairs to the third floor upside down. I was terrified, feeling my body being dragged up the stairs feet first. With each stair I felt a thump hit my lower back, as he pulled me up the stairs, stair by stair. As the stairs were hitting me harder and faster, I thought I was going to lose the pregnancy. I felt the impact on my spine, where the baby was situated. Terrorized by this, I then heard Lew screaming.

"I'm going to break your back," he shouted. "I'm going to break your back!!!"

I burst into tears and he yanked me up to the third floor landing and let my legs go. I knew it was over and I had to get out of this relationship, unless Lew changed. I could not comprehend how Lew's life profession was about supporting a pregnancy and he was compromising his own. It was clear to me that he was another person in that moment of violence.

Concerned about the pregnancy, I went to see Dr. Alan Charles, my obstetrician, to make sure that all was well. I told him what had occurred, and he clearly appeared to be in a bind as to how to assist me in my marital dilemma and with the violence in our family. Lew and Dr. Charles were long term friends, colleagues and now business partners. Dr. Charles heard of Lew's abuse to me and listen with sincere concern. Dr. Charles had been my gynecologist long before I knew Lew, and I was certain that I wanted him to deliver the baby. However, he was prepared to do the delivery as a professional courtesy to Lew. His office had not been billing me for any prenatal care, and I was under the impression from Lew that he would deliver the baby as a professional courtesy. I knew of the possibility of my leaving Lew, and did not want Dr. Charles showing up for the delivery contingent upon my relationship with Lew, so I paid him under the table for the delivery and asked him to promise me that he would not tell Lew that I did so.

Bradley was 21 months old and David was a few months before birth. I made a commitment to myself that I would figure out how to get us out after the baby was born. Somehow it seemed safer on the unborn baby to wait. I did not want to run while pregnant, as I felt too vulnerable. I had no family that I was close to near me, and didn't feel strong enough to wander off on my own, with my small child and unborn baby. I spent many weeks recoiling from Lew, and realized that the intimacy was fading for me. Whereas Lew appeared happy, especially after an altercation, and faulted me for our distance when I could not get close in the aftermath of a violent fight. He began telling me something was wrong with me as I was becoming cold and unaffectionate.

Months later, in July 1987, my oldest brother Lou King lost his son Brian in a horrible automobile accident. Brain was thrown from a moving vehicle during an accident, resulting in a head injury from which he never recovered. The days in the hospital were extremely tense for my family and the ultimate death of Brain was the most traumatic event in my family's history. Brian was the first grandchild in the King family, and his loss had the most horrific impact on my brother, his ex-wife Vonnie and my parents. My family insisted that I not travel for the funeral. They knew how Brian's death was affecting me and them, and we all feared that bringing us all together would be incredibly upsetting for me. They did not want me to compromise this pregnancy. My brother told me to stay home and promise him that I would name the baby after Brian. And so I did. As my brother and my parents mourned the loss of Brian, I re-evaluated my need to leave Lew. Suddenly my problems seemed so petty compared to my brother's loss. I started thanking God that I had a healthy son and another one on the way.

My energies went into preparing for the birth of my second child and helping Bradley welcome our new arrival. We purchased another crib and decorated Brad's room for two little ones. I set up the baby's infancy crib and changing area near our bedroom and bought the sweetest little clothes for his first few months. September 14, 1987, I went into labor with my second son whom I named David Brian Blumenthal. David was 8 pounds and 4 ounces of pure sweet silky delight. He was a strong, solid baby with the softest skin I've ever known. He was so baby sweet, that I thought he was too baby-like for his mature name, so I called him "Baba Dee." This became his name for many years. Baba Dee had an even temperament and an excellent disposition, and he learned how to cope with adversity at a very early age. As much as I tried to prepare Bradley for David's arrival, Bradley longed for me to take him back to the hospital. Bradley was to David relative to me, as Lew was to Bradley; that is, extremely jealous. So Bradley and I would go out for special outings, like museums, parks and Moms and Tots when

David was napping, but he wanted nothing to do with caring for David.

*　　*　　*

Weeks after I returned from the hospital with David, Lew started working on me to go on vacation. I knew my body was not ready for a trip, but I allowed his insistence to outweigh my body's messages for mending and recovery. We packed up our little family and went to an indoor water park in Canada, where we partied and played for many days. I was only two months postpartum. David was an avid nursing baby. He loved being breast-fed, and I loved nursing him. I was up in the middle of the night nursing David, then again in the early morning running with Bradley, my active three year old, trying to keep up with his boundless energy. Throughout the day I did my best to be the companion for my playful and demanding husband, who had me going down fifty foot water slides all day long and making love until the wee hours of the night. After several days of this, I felt my body say "no more." When we arrived home, I crashed with pneumonia which left me bedridden for five weeks.

After getting the diagnosis of pneumonia, I made a personal decision that I would never again put Lew's entertainment before my health. It was the beginning of my commitment to set appropriate boundaries for myself, which merely led to an intensification of our fighting about what, when and how we would play. As I was recovering from the pneumonia, I cared for David along with some help from a wonderful woman by the name of Marie. Even with this help, my repeated lifting of David was too much for my weakened tissues, and ultimately my wrists gave in. I was diagnosed with carpal tunnel syndrome, and my lower right arm and hand were placed in a splint for many weeks. I recall many days of lying on the bed with David, having to roll into him to nurse him because I was unable to lift him to bring his little body up to my breast.

Bradley had started nursery school, which gave me a rest period during the day. Eventually, I recovered and regained my health. I was fortunate to have the flexibility in my professional commitments to allow me to use my spare time to restore my strength. After David and Bradley's birth, I had taken about seven months off from my psychology practice and then gradually went back to work two afternoons per week. I had actually selected my profession, during undergraduate school, partly because of the flexibility it gave me – knowing I wanted to raise a family.

February 1988 was my most happy month with our little family. Bradley was socializing and becoming quite industrious, and David was blossoming beautifully. David and I went to a photographer and had a picture taken together, and the contentment of that day radiated from both of us. My memories of the abuse receded into the background during this blissful month. But then came March 1988 and it all started again.

It was one of those evenings when the children and I were on our own, as Lew was out delivering a baby. Bradley and I had gone through our evening bedtime ritual. This consisted of his bath, brushing his teeth and reading to him in our rocking chair which was in his room on the third floor of our townhouse. We would top the evening off singing "ah..ohm." Invariably Brad would fall off to sleep in my lap with me singing and rocking, and then I'd place him in the crib. I placed Bradley in the crib and left him sleeping soundly.

I went downstairs to my bedroom with David, and he and I laid on my bed while I nursed him. We both dozed off, and then I changed sides to complete his feeding before putting him down for the evening. Lew came home and closed the front door louder than normal as he entered. The sound must have awakened Bradley, as I heard him call out, "One more kiss, Mommy."

"One more kiss, Mommy," Bradley uttered again.

Lew stormed up to the third floor where Bradley was and smacked him so hard I could hear the hit from the second floor.

Bradley burst into tears and was crying for the longest time. Lew came down the stairs to the second floor and entered the bedroom where I was nursing David. I got up to go upstairs to Bradley and Lew wouldn't allow me to go to him. He kept me in the bedroom with David, and eventually Bradley fell back to sleep. I could not talk to Lew nor could I sleep through the night with him in the bed with me.

Lew left early in the morning, and I immediately went up to check on Bradley. Bradley was lying in the crib with Lew's hand print in a reddish blue bruise across Bradley's face. I was stunned, outraged and sickened by the bruise on my child's face. Bradley crawled out of the crib and into my lap, and I held him in our rocking chair. The anger built up in me as I looked at his bruised face and I said, "That's it, we're going." I spent the entire day deciding if we should go to the police or just leave Lew without any notice. As I deliberated back and forth, I took some photos of Bradley's face.

Either of the options I was considering would have been best, but instead I decided to wait until Lew came home, hoping that when he saw the actual bruises on Bradley's face that he would recognize the abuse I kept trying to point out. I thought the least that would come from doing this was that I would have given myself the chance to tell him why I could no longer stay with him. The best outcome I hoped for was that he would see what he had done and be moved to change his violent outbursts and abuse toward us. I was wrong; I was dreaming. My decision came out of my desire to keep the family together and an innocent love I still had for our abuser. My motives were pure and ever so unrealistic.

*   *   *

When Lew came home, I gave him time to settle in and walked into the bedroom to talk to him. I said, "What was done to Bradley last night was not discipline; it was abuse." I told him that when you leave marks on a child as was done that you cross a line, and I could not live with that.

David was lying on the bed in the room with us. He began crying and, when I picked him up to hold him, Lew grabbed David out of my arms and threw him several feet back onto the bed. I was stunned to watch my six month old baby flying from Lew's grip and hit flat on the bed.

"Don't you tell me how to raise our, my, kids," Lew said with anger and in a vicious tone. I was speechless and he throw me to the ground and held me to the floor. Lew sat on me, startling my torso, and spread my arms out as far as they could reach. He continued holding me down, stretching my arms further out, yelling inches from my face.

"I'm going to break your neck ... I'm going to break your neck ... I'm going to break your neck," Lew hollered, each time getting louder and louder, and with escalating vengeance.

I started to struggle to throw him off of me. As I moved my body, he yelled even louder and gripped me tighter. I don't know how long we were there; it seemed like forever. I was absolutely terrified, and then I fell into tears. This time he didn't let go, and I kept sobbing. I don't know when or what caused him to break lose; my next memory is having no movement in my upper body.

I was taken to Michael Reese Hospital and admitted for 10 days. They placed me in cervical traction, and I was treated for an acute spinal injury, which was subsequently diagnosed by Dr. Charles Slack as two degenerative discs (between vertebrae C: 5 and C: 6 and C: 6 and C: 7) precipitated by the trauma. Within hours of my admission, the police were at my hospital room door. A female officer took a full report and, with compassion, elicited the whole story from me as I laid there in tears. She told me that I had to get out of the relationship. She said, "It will never change; it will only get worse."

I kept hearing her words as I laid motionless in traction during my ten day stay at the hospital. I spent hours planning how I was going to escape, but knew I needed first to get my children. The doctor placed me on medications for pain, muscle spasms and inflammation. The nurses were extremely kind and everyone knew the awkwardness of my being there, given that Lew was an attending physician at that hospital and I had told them the whole story of what led to my hospitalization – including Lew injuring me *and* Bradley. I spoke on the phone with my Mom when they released me from the cervical traction, and to a female physician friend who had been a resident physician with Lew. This women had previously confided in me that she once left an abusive husband. I was seeking her support and she confirmed what the police had told me.

I did not hear from Lew the whole time I was in the hospital, although I knew he was there almost daily making rounds with his patients. I knew that he was concerned that I might tell people how I got there. In the past he always wanted to keep this family secret quiet among his doctor friends.

Rabbi Tabashnick from West Suburban Congregation, which Lew attended when growing up, came by to see me. I told him that it was over between me and Lew and I couldn't go back to live with him. He pulled up a chair near my bed and talked to me for the longest time about family, giving Lew a chance, getting a therapist for the abuse. He was relentless.

"Jeanne, You have two small children," said Rabbi. "You owe it to all of you to try everything you can to *save the family*."

I told him that Lew was not amenable to therapy for this condition, and pointed out that he was in denial about it. The Rabbi said this is why he needed the therapy. He gave me the name of a psychologist that was also a rabbi, and said it may make it easier to establish a rapport with Lew given the combined professions.

I was released from the hospital with orders for physical therapy and the continuation of medication for pain, spasms and inflammation. I began physical therapy three times per week, and it became the highlight of my week. It was a place I could go for comfort and relief. I had very limited mobility in my upper body. I could not even lift my arms to comb my hair, and putting on a shirt over head was out of the question. Mornings were my best and, as the day worn on, I could not even lift a cup of tea without pain. I could not lift pots as the weight was far to much for me, so I resigned from cooking and most everything in the kitchen.

Being re-united with the children was wonderful, and in my condition I recognized I could not pack us up and go anywhere. I was truly helpless; physically and emotionally quite wounded. I asked Marie to stay on for longer hours until I healed, and she was a saint. She was so kind to both me and my children. I wouldn't have made it without her.

I hated Lew for what he had done to me and could not face him without tears welling up in me. I wanted just to be done with him. I vacillated between emotional pain and anger. I had never in my life felt as violated as I had been by Lew on the night that led to my injury. In retrospect, I believe that the relationship stopped here. Lew was angered that I may have revealed our "personal matters" to hospital staff, and didn't seem to care much about my condition. There was no apology, no remorse, nothing other than a sense of indifference mixed with self-righteousness. His unwillingness to acknowledge what he had done to me and how he had hurt me seemed to make my injury even more painful. It took two years before I could get an apology from Lew about this incident.

*   *   *

I called Dr. Kanter, the psychologist/rabbi that was recommended to me at the hospital, and went in to see him. I told him the whole story and showed him the photographs of Bradley and some others that I had taken over the years. It was obvious to him that Lew needed to be there. He told me to bring Lew and I told him that I didn't think I could get him to come in. Dr. Kanter said, "I'll call him and get him in here." So I left it to him and he managed to get Lew to go in for individual sessions and sessions with me.

After about the third session in which we were there together, Lew told us about a long history of abuse to his sisters and himself by his mother, Cita. Lew was crying as he vividly recalled Cita beating Ingrid, the younger of his older sisters. He said she got it the worst and told us of belt beatings, being locked in closets and numerous other stories of cruel abuse. As I watched him cry, I felt sorry for him and realized that he was a victim of the very thing I was trying to flee from. I had heard Lew tell about some of this before, but this was the first time I felt his pain. I thought to myself, if he could allow himself to be so vulnerable and honest here, maybe he was ready to address the issue of abuse, in which case we had a chance of salvaging the marriage and keeping the family together. Dr. Kanter established some of what he called "ground-rules" for our therapy. He said to Lew, "You are not to hit your wife and children." And Lew looked at him like a child looks at an authoritative parent.

Intergenerational Transmission of Violence Theory, also known as the "Cycle of Violence Theory," states that *"violent behavior is learned within the family and bequeathed from one generation to the next."* The theory holds that *"children who are victims of child abuse or who witness violent aggression by one spouse against the other will grow up and react to their children or spouses in the same manner."* (Wallace, 1996, p. 17)

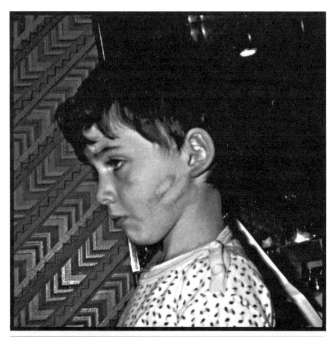

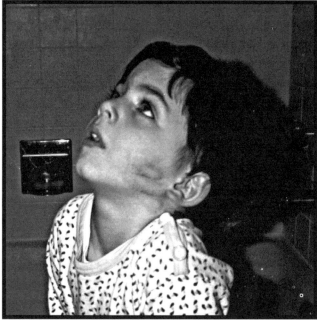

Marks of Child Abuse: Facial Bruises, March 1988

CHAPTER 3

Emotional, Verbal and Psychological Abuse

Doctor Heal Thyself

Verbal Abuse to Intimate Core

Abuse Is the Family Tradition

Child Becomes Target

Mommy as Supervisor and Peacemaker

Attacking Character and Security

B eing in therapy with Lew kept me in the marriage, and I became open to the possibility of his changing and our staying together. My days were filled with child care and regaining mobility in my neck and upper body. I struggled with neck and shoulder pain that was so uncomfortable I could not focus to get much of anything done. I lived on medication just to get through the day, and physical therapy was my source of solace and hope.

After three and a half months of this "half-life," as I called it, I decided that there had to be another way for my body to heal. I longed to be pain-free, and started researching alternative methods for recovery. A physician friend of mine recommended that I try a retreat in Lancaster that was totally devoted to replenishing the body, normalizing tissue and evoking the healing response from within. I realized it was exactly what I needed and so set forth to make the arrangements.

I scheduled my trip for the exact week that Lew was scheduled to go on his annual ten day Canadian fishing trip with his father. I figured this was one week out of the year that he would not give me a hard time doing something for myself. I made arrangements for the children's care, having Marie sleep at our house. Bradley and I made singing tapes of Mommy singing to him and David in my absence. Lew left for his trip first, and then I flew out the next day. I spent seven days surrendering to the most incredible healing experience I have ever known. Major breakthroughs occurred for me during the course of this week. I received rigorous detoxification and purification treatments, along with healing therapies of the ancient yoga traditions. By the end of the week, I was able to turn my head with complete rotation on both sides. I still had pain and remained on my medication for muscle spasms and inflammation for some time after, but the level of pain had significantly decreased.

The mending and purification process continued for a few days after my return home, leaving me fatigued and in need of rest. Then, on the fourth day, a window opened and I was a different person. There was a level of well-being throughout every part of my body and my spirit was vibrant, whole and pure. I was truly happy, blissful and radiating that contentment coming from within. I remained this way for about a month. It was life-changing, mind boggling and beyond words. I was so happy that I welcomed having another baby. Marc, my third son, was conceived out of this joy that I could no longer contain. It was in me and out of me at the same time. The degree of happiness that abound within me may have been witnessed, but was never directly spoken about. It was too sacred and special to verbally flaunt; but I know others observed that I was different.

Within the next month, I learned that I had indeed conceived Marc. Lew was not as excited about this pregnancy as I, but in time we both began to look forward to Marc's arrival. Baba Dee was 10 months at the time and Bradley was beginning pre-kindergarten at Parker School in Lincoln Park. Baba Dee and I took Bradley to his activities, while little Marc flourished growing inside of me. The pregnancy hormones relaxed the muscle spasms and my neck and shoulder pain practically disappeared, at least until shortly after Marc was born.

During the full course of my pregnancy with Marc, I became vigilant in maintaining the health regimen that I learned at the clinic. The benefits were commutative and convinced me that I could regulate my body. I began to walk my talk and lived what I had been teaching my patients about pain and stress reduction. This personal experience led me to a finer understanding and appreciation of my professional practice and a clear enhancement in my ability to teach biofeedback, meditation and self-regulation which had been the primary focus of my clinical practice for years.

Automatically, I began attracting more patients with chronic medical disorders associated with pain, stress and anxiety. I became a magnet for people wanting and needing to learn meditation and self-regulation for symptom reduction and the resolution of their long and life-limiting conditions. My professional stature grew during this period and I became active in the professional biofeedback associations. This expertise and commitment led to my being elected president of the Biofeedback Society of Illinois and serving as the Chair of its Ethics Committee. Lew was superficially proud of my accomplishments, so long as they did not interfere with his position in the spotlight, nor appear to bring me too much pleasure or self-sufficiency. He seemed to enjoy sharing my accomplishments with other people, as though they were feathers in his cap, but behind closed door his support was more like pulling teeth.

As the months progressed in my pregnancy with Marc, I realized that my knees could no longer weather carrying two babies, one inside and one out, in a three story townhouse. Lew and I recognized that we also needed more space for our new arrival. So, I started looking for a new nest for our growing family. Within a matter of months we located a home that fulfilled our desires in Northbrook, a northern suburb of Chicago. I recall the day we first walked into the house. Lew and I were standing on the landing on a bridge overlooking the family room, which was called a "great room," and I felt like I was in a sanctuary. I looked at Lew and said, "I think this is it." We went out for a bite to eat and both came to the same conclusion about the house. We purchased it and moved in the following month.

Our therapy stopped during this period, and I became aware of another form of abuse budding in our relationship. Most people call it verbal abuse, but I felt it as character assault. I started to notice it sometime during my pregnancy with Marc. Lew and I would have some discussion about any matter, and if I was not in support of his desire, his wishes, his preferences or opinion, I was indeed at risk. Instead of pinning me to the wall, as had been his practiced method of dealing with our different perspectives, he blasted me with a litany of verbal abuse and personal assassination. He would say, "You're un-appealing, un-desirable, un-attractive, un-sexy, un-lovable ... UN UN UN ..." until I would shake. He'd hit me with more UN's than I knew were in the English language, and then run through the sequence again and again. It would leave me with a hole in my heart.

These encounters happened almost every other week. Generally they would occur in the bedroom after the children had gone to sleep, and unfortunately these abusive rounds would make falling asleep most difficult for me. It would then take days for me to have contact with him after one of his verbal attacks, but Lew on the other hand was happy and wanting sex the next day. He could not understand my withdrawal from him, and this then became a point for further verbal abuse.

Marc was an active baby in utero, as his movements would awaken me at night, especially on the evenings of Lew's "violent oral verbiage," as I referred to it. Laying in the bed next to Lew sleeping, I wondered how I could be with this man who obviously hated me. Memories of my neck injury flooded me during these long evenings and I felt so much personal degradation being next to someone who had injured me. I would toss and turn, until he would leave the room to finish his nights sleep in his "on-call" home office. Within moments of his departure, I'd surrender into comfort and sleep like a baby.

My unwillingness to sleep with Lew became the next bone of contention, and we spent many evenings fighting about this. What was hard for me at the time was that I was not sure what was keeping me up. Was it the current verbal abuse or the memories from the past? I wasn't sure. In my effort to sort this out, I attempted to open the discussions around his leaving the bruise on Bradley's face and subsequently putting me in the hospital with a neck injury. I had hoped to gain some inner peace and a sense of personal reconciliation with an apology. But, of course, there was none. In fact, at this juncture, Lew was in complete denial that he had left bruises on Bradley's face. He said, I imagined it; it never happened. Even more puzzling was Lew's re-creation of the cause of my hospitalization and cervical spine injury. He was attributing my hospitalization to my childhood gymnastics, yet I had never had any neck problems or cervical spine injuries other than that which came immediately after the physical altercation of March 1988.

I saw the relationship deteriorating once again and knew we needed further help. I began to feel undesirable when I was with Lew and this deepened the ocean between us, as I was losing my desire for intimacy with him. I couldn't comprehend the verbal assaults, because I knew objectively that his expressed words were not true. In the mirror I was still quite attractive, slender weighing 120 pounds (when I wasn't pregnant), personally appealing, very bright, extremely sexy, yet I could no longer feel any of this when we were together.

So I insisted that we go back to see Dr. Kanter. I made the appointment and we went to see him at his suburban office in Skokie, not too far from our new residence. As we walked in the door he greeted us, and his first words were his expressed appreciation for the most recent patient that Lew had sent him. The Doctor and Lew would "shop-talk" a bit about the patient, and somehow Dr. Kanter would shift the discussion to our therapy. But, the dynamics had dramatically changed. With Lew feeding the Doctor patients, I saw the therapeutic process digress into superficial "chat sessions." I recognized that Lew's making referrals to the Doctor sabotaged the therapeutic process, initially underway when we saw him after my hospitalization. Lew's vulnerability and initial self-confrontations around his abuse to us was replaced by his "I'm okay, so what are we here for" attitude and his sense of personal control.

*   *   *

Now here I was surrounded by 6,000 square feet of the American dream; two absolutely beautiful children and one inside of me that I was falling in love with, and a growing successful professional practice. On the other hand, there was my marriage partner who oozed self-righteousness and an unrelenting need to control all of us at any cost. I had lost faith in the therapeutic intervention and started searching elsewhere for remedy of our family problems. Lew and I had both come from families in which you air your laundry in communion with the family circle, and so I set out to orchestrate a family discussion regarding my unresolved issues.

We invited Lew's father, Papa, and his mother, Cita, over for dinner and enjoyed a lovely meal and some light play with our children. Then the adults communed in our living room, and many significant truths were revealed. I told Papa and Cita that I was having a hard time getting over Lew's causing my neck injury and his bruising Bradley's face. Again, they supported one another in their effort to convince me in believing *"these things happen in families*." These were their exact words, but I could not allow such a message to register in me. It made no sense.

With tears in my eyes, I asked Papa, "Do you hit her (meaning Cita) when you are upset about something?" He was without words, and I recall Cita giving some kind of response, of which I could not bring myself to internalize. She almost gleefully and in laughter recollected some incidents in their family which, on the surface, seemed like what was happening in ours, but the male/female roles were reversed. However, I was so full of my own emotion, I gained little from the interaction. What did stick with me is a clear appreciation of the fact that Lew had come from a backdrop similar to what was manifesting in our home.

Many things made sense from here, and I understood my unexpressed feelings concerning the way Cita had treated my children over the years. Cita is a fairly attractive woman, who was in her late sixties or early seventies at that time. She had more armor and external camouflage than I had ever known before. On the outside one would see her as vivacious, friendly, of good will, playful and confident. But when she was angry or when things were not going as she desired, she was harsh and brutal, sometimes exposing a violent edge. What came through was a demeanor of one willing and capable of hurting an innocent and helpless animal. Routinely, when our children were not behaving in harmony with her wishes, she would say with piercing vengeance, "I'm going to make you *black and blue*." There were many times when these words even punctured my own heart as I witness them flung at my children.

Seven days after Marc's exquisite May 4, 1989 entrance into the world, we were gathered in my home preparing for his "Bris." The caterers delivered lavish trays of excellent food to celebrate this momentous occasion. I was running back and forth between the kitchen and dining room, getting the serving area just so for our arriving guests. Marc, whom I called "Marci" was in his infant crib, Baba Dee was having his morning nap and Bradley was tailing Mommy as we laid out the food and party accessories. My little Ang was so happy on this day as he was helping me set up for Marc's Bris and the celebration to come. In his childlike innocence and with enthusiasm and delight at the unfolding feast on our dining room table, he reached his little hand and plucked an olive, quickly to disappear in his mouth. Before I could say, "Wait for the guests," Cita had smacked my child's hand so hard that it startled us both. Bradley fell into tears and I was speechless and felt as wounded as he. There was no bruise, only a red sting; but, more importantly, there was no moment of human correction, instead there was simply a violent outburst. This seemed wrong to me.

Following the Bris, I discussed Cita's smacking Bradley with Lew. I got no response, so I brought my concerns directly to Cita. She vehemently told me that she had the right to treat her grand-children in whatever fashion she felt was appropriate. I knew that we would never agree on this one, and it was not worth arguing with her. I had recalled numerous occasions when Lew's sister, Marlene, spoke of her displeasure with Cita's abrasiveness with her own children. The grandchildren from both of Lew's sisters collaborated what I had witnessed and expressed similar distaste for these actions.

*   *   *

My days fluctuated between delight with the children, frustra-tion with Lew and pride in my professional growth. While I was getting stronger and was clearly more grounded, our family unit was crumbling from within. The dinner table became the battlefield, and my little Ang spent many meals in the line of fire. Dinner used to be something we did together as a family. Lew sat at one end of the table and I at the other. Bradley had his seat to my right in front of the sliding glass doors and David sat directly across from Bradley on my left. Marci was in my lap or in his high chair directly to my right so I could feed him easily. I am a lefty.

I would bring the meal to the table and we would all begin to eat and visit. Lew directed the flow of conversation and the direction of the stones that he carried from within. Generally, it would begin with Lew finding fault in something concerning me or Bradley, which would eventually escalate in some form of violent verbiage or action and someone leaving the table. Night after night of this, I started to recognize that Bradley could do nothing right from Lew's point of view. Lew routinely made sure that Bradley knew that he was moving in his chair too much, not eating everything on his plate, talking too loud or messing the table. Actually Ang was doing everything that children do, but was being criticized, penalized and assaulted for all of it.

Lew repeatedly told him he was "stupid," he was a "brat," constantly berating him. There was no positive correction given to motivate Bradley to be other than what he was. There was only verbal and physical slaps that Bradley could not connect to "right action," or that which was desired by Lew. Instead, I could see my child's fresh, creative, inner strength turn to self-doubting, vulnerable, shameful impotence. He could do nothing right in Lew's eyes, and his behavior began to match this expectation, just as my feeling of being unappealing when I was with Lew matched his declaration of the same.

In my effort to help my child offset what was developing at the dinner table, I decided to involve him in an activity that would nourish his strength and foster a sense of self-expression and personal pride. I took Bradley to a music teacher and discovered that he had a natural talent for playing the piano. We began private piano lessons, and as I saw his pleasure and commitment grow, I sought out to purchase a piano so he could play daily in our home. We spent $4,000 on the most beautiful piano and situated it the room I came to know as the sanctuary. I can remember sitting on the sofa nursing Marci, while Bradley gleefully played for us. We listened to him for hours, and he became a real star.

Two months after Marc was born, my body recovered from the pregnancy and he and I were doing wonderfully. I knew he would be my last baby and so I hung onto the infancy days, making each one more special than the next. However as soon as the pregnancy hormones were out of my system, the neck and shoulder spasms returned. Many people thought it was a function of my having two babies in diapers and all of the lifting associated with their care. Nonetheless, with this pain came the memories of Lew's abuse to me, which compounded the discomfort. I struggled with neck and shoulder pain on and off for over four years, having episodes of no upper body mobility for up to six weeks at a time. The flare-ups and my set backs appeared to be associated with travel, carrying heavy suitcases and children's equipment and seasonal house cleaning. Eventually, I learned what to avoid in order to keep the pain to a minimum. Instead of being focused on changing Lew as I had been doing before, I shifted my attention to integrating everything I could that made a difference in making me pain-free and walked the talk everyday until I became consistently asymptomatic.

I continued to assume the role given to me in our therapy, that being the live-in supervisor in order to keep physical altercations between Lew and the children to a minimum. Lew and I had made an agreement shortly after our first few visits with Dr. Kanter that I would take the liberty to step in with him and the boys when I saw him beginning to lose his cool. So, if a child was acting out or being non-compliant and Lew was exhibiting frustration bordering on striking, I could step in and say, "Lew back off, let me take over here as you look like you are close to losing it." Interestingly, this intervention and agreement worked, at least for a few years.

While there was progress here, the verbal battering to me and Bradley never stopped and I gave up trying. Whenever Ang got assaulted verbally, I'd take him aside in Lew's absence and console him, trying to reassure him that he was a good person inside, no matter what was said or done. For myself, I simply withdrew emotionally from Lew, indefinitely. So instead of having days of distance between verbal beatings, I never really came back. I lived emotionally detached from Lew, and when he'd verbally blast me, I disassociated. My body was in the room, but I took myself out of the interaction. Often this would cause an escalation of his verbal abuse and character shots, which led to my swiftly exiting the room. I had become so commitment to maintaining my own personal integrity, I became unwilling to let myself be showered by his toxic blasts. My mere exiting the room soon became a new subject of further fighting. It seemed to anger him that I was unwilling to remain as his target.

I had been deriving significant benefit from regular meditation practice, and from here I rebuilt my shattered sense of self from the inside. Glimpses of my prior post retreat well-being started to show up on a pretty regular basis. Lew didn't like that I could go into a an empty room, sit and do "nothing" and come out feeling great. Something about that infuriated him. So this became our subject to pick on Mommy. My daily quiet time became, from Lew's point of view, "Mommy robbing him and the family of time," even though I scheduled this time when most everyone, including Lew, was involved in something else. In retrospect, I realize that Lew's problem with my meditating probably had more to do with Lew's need to control my time and the fact that the benefits I was deriving from meditation were also beyond his control.

Whenever he needed or wanted to badger me verbally, naturally he focused on the meditation. Suddenly I was a "weirdo" involved in weird practices, when they brought me stability and contentment in my home. However, these same practices were held out as something to be proud of when it came to talking about me as the "Biofeedback Doctor" to his family and friends. The contradiction was confusing to me, but didn't seem worth my exploring. I simply played the meditation down, and said it was something I was doing for my back. The children, on the other hand, enjoyed Mommy's meditation. David and I practiced breathing quietly before going to bed, and it had a very soothing effect on him.

I knew that Lew's calling me a "psychotic weirdo," as he often said with such cruelty, was just his opinion. Not being an evangelist-type in my home, I had no need to explain myself or try to convert his thinking; it simply didn't matter anymore. My indifference to his opinion led to assaults of a different kind. August 1990 through August 1991 became the year of financial and economic insecurity. When Lew was not in total and full control of our lives, and for him that meant my life too, he would hit me with the following line, "*I'll show you what it is like to have nothing, just wait and see.*" I heard this more often than anything else. It became Lew's sword and he used it like a daily mantra. Eventually, I started to believe him and took his threat seriously. Since my cervical spine injury, he had been denying me access to any cash from our family money. I decided that it was time for me to quickly complete mending my neck and shoulder, and build a foundation in my business to support me and the boys, as I felt the carpet being pulled from under my feet.

I spent the next year developing the Biofeedback and Stress Reduction Program and started marketing it to hospitals. It was such a success, that I was certain I could run my own clinic and offer this service to my patients. After a full day with the children and a shaky evening with Lew, I would begin working after everyone went to sleep. I spent hours generating a business plan, a marketing strategy and drafting articles for publication. My after-hours career was extremely exhilarating and rewarding for me. Keeping these hours kept me out of Lew's line of fire and away from his continuous ridicule.

A turning point occurred in which I recognized that I didn't have time to build the career foundation before leaving, and I could no longer fool myself that Lew was going to change. He reverted back to becoming physically abusive to me and the children, and Bradley started mirroring Lew by rigorously badgering and battering Baba Dee.

Emotional Abuse Maintains the Threat of Physical Abuse

Abuse is "any attempt to control, manipulate, or demean another individual using physical, emotional, or sexual tactics" (Wilson, 1997, p. 8).

Physical Abuse is the use of physical force to control or demean another person. Dr. Wilson lists the following acts of physical aggression and violence, exemplifying physical abuse: pushing, pulling, slapping, hair pulling, choking, shoving, kicking, spitting, restraining, arm twisting, pinning partner to wall, sitting or standing on partner, punching with a fist, burning, shooting, stabbing or attacking with an object or weapon.

In *When Men Batter Women*, Drs. Jacobson and Gottman point out that once a women has been physically abused in which violence has been established as a method of control, emotional abuse often keeps the battered woman in a state of submission and subjugation.

The use of ongoing verbal or emotional abuse becomes a method of psychological control. In *Trauma and Recovery*, Dr. Herman notes that the systematic, repetitive infliction of psycho-emotional trauma is intended to instill fear and terror, promote a sense of helplessness, destroy the victim's sense of self (in relation to others), and engender enslavement and entrapment in the abusive relationship.

Examples of **verbal and emotional abuse** include; threatening to use violence, name calling, criticizing, humiliating, insulting, yelling, controlling access to money, interfering with partners personal liberties, preventing partner from working, controlling partner's use of time, manipulating with lies, threatening suicide, threatening to take custody of children, and using children as confederates against their other parent.

J. Herman, *Trauma and Recovery*, 1992; N. Jacobson and J. Gottman, *When Men Batter Women*, 1998; K. Wilson, *When Violence Begins At Home*, 1997.

CHAPTER 4

More Verbal Licks
and Manly Punches

Batterer's Role Reversal

Verbal Abuse: With Escape and Where There Is None

Halloween Punch and the Witnessing Children

Upper Middle Class Families Have Abuse Problems, Too

It was time to investigate my options, so I sought counsel with a divorce attorney. I told him the entire story to date, and we reflected on some possible courses of action for me to take. In his office I was comforted that there would be a way for me to get away from Lew, but when I returned home I started thinking of how it would feel to follow through with divorce. It occurred to me that if Lew could be as vicious to me as he was when he was married to me and in a "partnership" with me, allegedly to love me, how would he be in relation to me when we were at war. Just the thought of this scared the hell out of me. I saw no end to how he could harass me if he were going all out as I knew vindictive husbands to do in divorce. It was hard enough being his friend, I wanted no part of being his enemy. So I put the idea of immediate divorce on the back burner and went back to protecting the children and building my career.

Fortunately for me, Lew became absorbed in a new business venture that shifted his focus onto himself and away from me. He spent months determining if he would join a partnership with one of his colleagues, and when he decided that he preferred to remain as his own boss and take in a junior partner, he began setting the wheels in motion for this venture. His days were long and completely void of contact with our immediate family. He would leave the house at 6:30 or 7:00 AM, return late in the evening, and was on the phone often until midnight. While he was busy, I was getting my life back and the children were doing very well.

Lew's parents planned a momentous vacation for all of their children and grandchildren, in celebration of their 50th anniversary, on a Caribbean cruise where we brought in the New Year of 1993. It was our first time to have this kind of gathering and it proved to be helpful in rekindling what was dying in our marriage, due to the distancing and abuse. However, weeks after this flame was re-lit, its radiant glow faded for me.

Immediately after our return home from the cruise with the family, Lew dove right back into his work. He was getting ready to build a new office and was trying to decide what designer to use. He asked me what I thought of Bobbie Packer, a woman that had done some work for us in our home. Initially, I hesitated and had no response because I wasn't completely confident in her. I indicated that she doesn't do commercial work and basically said nothing further, at least at that point. In sorting it out, I thought someone with more background in commercial design and decorating might be more to his advantage, and therefore I did not favor Bobbie for the office job. Over the week I also recalled that Bobbie's promises seemed to be unfulfilled. She had committed to getting some curtains for our living room almost six months earlier and we were unable to move this relatively minor work forward, yet when Lew talked of doing his office suddenly she was available evenings and weekends. Privately, I thought of her as "big buck Bobbie."

A week later I was more clear about my feelings in response to Lew's question about Bobbie Packer. It was a Monday morning before he left for work around the second week in January. I said, "I finally understand why I have not been positive about Bobbie doing your office." I mentioned that I had given some thought to it and it occurred to me why she wouldn't be my first choice. I explained my impression of Bobbie, concerning her lack of follow-through in our home and little experience in commercial, and why I felt she would not be good for the job. I shared my thoughts with Lew in a friendly and concerned way, because I honestly didn't want Bobbie to just take Lew for a ride. Although I felt it, I did not say that I sensed the potential for her taking advantage of him. He had such tunnel vision about this project that I didn't think he was evaluating her objectively.

None of my comments were not taken well by Lew, and he may have picked up on my underlying beliefs that were not shared. His response was, "If you had anything constructive to say, why didn't you say it last week when I asked for your opinion." I said that I had hesitated because I knew I wasn't in favor of Bobbie, but hadn't clearly formulated my reason. Then, I went on to say that it is clear to me now.

"Well it's too late," he said with fire in his words and meanness in his demeanor. It was as though he was saying back off, mind your own business, I'm going to do what I want, so butt out. Yet, what bothered me here was that he was spending all of our savings and planning to take out a loan for over $100,000 to do this job. I felt it was my place to have a vote in such a major investment of our resources. Lew was not of the same opinion and we started fighting. He became meaner and nastier to me.

I said, "You are being foolish here to discount me by the fact that I responded to your inquiry of 'What do I think of Bobbie?' one week later." It was the first time I responded directly to what I was observing as I was observing it. I was pointing out my truth concerning how his conduct appeared to me. While it may not have been the nicest way to say it, what followed was not to be believed.

Lew ran me upstairs, pushed me in the master bathroom against the glass shower door and held me there, fiercely and firmly. I was scared by this time, but felt more strength about standing up for myself.

"Don't pin me down," I said clearly and firmly. And he gripped harder.

I held my arms out to move him away so I could pull away from being pinned to the glass door. I was concerned that I might go through the glass. Holding my arms out, and extending my hands against his shoulders resulted in struggle between us. My nail, as he says, touched him. In a fury he ran away and said I scratched him.

Meanwhile I thought the fight was over, but I was wrong. Next thing I know the police are at my front door, because Lew called them saying that his wife was "attacking" him. Lew showed them some nick on his upper neck and the police told me it looked like a shaving nick and they laughed at one another in front of me. I could see that they were amused by this incident.

They asked, "Is there a gun in the house?"

"Yes," I said, "and I want it removed."

I told them where the gun was, and Lew became quite upset because it was in a place where he kept his marijuana. Lew claimed that I was trying to get him into trouble over the drugs, yet I was only concerned about the gun in light of his erratic conduct of calling the police. It was absurd to me and further revealing of his unpredictability to declare that he was an abused husband, given our long history of his physical abuse to me. Lew carried on with the police and they left, without the gun. It took me a few days to come to grips what Lew had done.

A few hours after this incident Lew's mother called to speak to me. I was in such a state of shock that he had the police in our house, trying to play victim, that I decided not to call her back because I was afraid that she would realize how upset I was and I did not want to disclose this outrageous story. I assumed I would cool down and it would be best to return her call at that time. Two days passed and Lew and I still did not speak. Talking to his mother seemed even more difficult, so I held off at least until Lew and I started talking.

By Thursday, which was three days after her call, Lew and I talked and I tried to call Cita on Friday, but of course it was too late. This tardy call-back resulted in distance between the family and myself that lasted for almost six months.

Lew proceeded with his work venture of building his office with Bobbie and I recognized that my opinion didn't matter, so I backed off and let it go. I decided it was his business and his job and, since it brought him great pleasure, it would probably work out fine. Having him happy and involved in his thing served me well, as it allowed me to tend to my business without his constant ridicule.

*   *   *

Spring came along and with that was another vacation. Unfortunately this meant he would not have his work to focus on for the week, leaving me lame duck and back in the line of fire. We went to Disney World with the children and decided to have an evening for just the two of us. It appeared to unfold as a romantic evening. But before our "toast" of gratitude toward and with one another was complete, he managed to railroad me with an oral sword.

"I think our relationship is improving," he said; "but you have some serious problems." He went on to tell me how "weird" I was because of my practice of meditation. He claimed that I had a personality defect of being able to be "self-absorbed" and could focus "too intensely" on my work projects ... and for this I should consult a psychiatrist.

My ability to focus and exercise discipline in pursuing my interests had been an asset of mine all of my life, and now Lew was labeling it as my liability. I recognized he saw it this way because this skill of mine brought me personal excellence and success in my endeavors. Lew could not tolerate my experiencing my own competency or pleasure in anything that he did not control or which did not originate from him.

I realized that this was not a loving toast; it was old Lew back again. I pushed the wine glass away from in front of me, picked up my purse, said good bye and walked out of the restaurant, leaving him at the table. I just couldn't listen to him talk this way anymore. I walked for hours and eventually took a taxi back to the hotel later that evening.

*   *   *

Months later, Lew realized that the best way to critique me and blast me with his verbal assault was in a place where I could not walk away, so he chose to use the moving vehicle as the stage for sharing. We were driving home from a party that his mother had for the whole family at their country club in Oak Park. The children were dressed so sweetly all in matching shirts. We took great pictures of them, and everyone shared in the delight. I was warm and giving to his family and was very happy that his mother and I had finely broken the ice and interacted with love. We all seemed to have such a nice evening, and I felt this was a big step.

On the way home in the car, Lew wanted to discuss our next vacation, which he had brought up weeks before. He wanted to go on an exotic trip involving three locations, staying at each for a few days. I was not in favor of that kind of trip because our children were still too young to adapt well to many transitions. I did not think I was ready for this kind of trip either, because I was concerned with how my neck would hold up in such travel. I was still having flare-ups of immobility in my neck and pain radiating down my right arm when we traveled, and Lew was well aware of this. I very gently explained my hesitation to Lew and he blew up at me saying how I don't care about his needs, etc. When, in fact, I was considering the trip for weeks since his bringing it up because of his needs, not because of my desire; and I had just come from a family gathering in which I was there mostly for him and his need for me to be close to the family. His statement made no sense in the context of all of this. Nonetheless, Lew managed to get it all out.

"You are a terrible person," he said. "You are asocial, un-available, undesirable, unappealing, self-absorbed and a terrible mother." Over and over, on and on, and all of this while our children were in the back seat of the car.

When I got home I was shaking. I sat down and wrote him a letter that said he should think of the garbage that comes flowing out of his mouth before it pours forth so automatically. I mentioned how God may have wanted him to reflect in this way, and it would be beneficial for him to do so during his next silence. Lew was having a second throat surgery due to a growth near his voice box. Following his surgery, he was instructed not to speak and was directed to experience verbal silence. I saved this letter and so did he. I believe it hit square between the eyes. It was the last time for a long while that Lew was so outrageously verbally abusive to me. I think this note, in the face of his health problems, finally drove the message home that I could not tolerate his verbal abuse any longer.

*   *   *

At this juncture Lew was well aware that neither physical nor verbal abuse was acceptable, but this was not sufficient to prevent it. Shortly after Lew had recovered from his surgery and his concerns about his throat were for the most part behind him, we regressed to where we were five years ago. Bradley was beginning the forth grade and I wanted him to have a study area of his own. It was a Saturday and Lew was busy, so I took the three children out to buy furniture for Bradley's room. After shopping for several days prior to this for the best set at the best price, I selected a nice quality group-ing from The Board Room Kid's store. The set cost over $1,500 and seemed to be a good long term investment.

As I was involved in purchasing the furniture, Brad was climbing on the beds and jumping off onto other beds. I corrected him a number of times and was busy trying to get us out of the store. When we got to the car I scolded him and told him how upset I was that he had been so disrespectful of the people's property in the store. I said I would not receive the new furniture under these conditions. We talked about the importance of respecting other people's property and appreciating things that one receives. I insisted that he show me this understanding before we could receive the furniture. He knew that punishment and correction for his behavior was coming. We agreed that he would remain in his room for one full day, which included that evening and all the next day. During this time he was to think about the idea of appreciation for what people do for you and respect for other people's property. He was very willing to follow my instructions.

I informed Lew of the incident, and he agreed to support the punishment. Later, it occurred to me that the next day was Halloween, and I had a foresight that it might cause a problem. Brad woke up in the morning and realized that his conduct the day before cost him Halloween trick-or-treating. Initially Bradley was upset, but I was able to get him to, once again, respect and appreciate the punishment. He was in him room writing me a little letter about appreciation and respecting other people's property.

I asked Lew to support me in the follow-through of the punishment and explained that I believed that it was important for Bradley to know that we mean what we say. However, Lew wanted to go "trick-or-treating" with the kids. He approached me in front of Bradley and said, "Since it's Halloween, let's let Bradley's punishment end now so he can go trick-or-treating." Then all of Bradley's commitment to the punishment was gone and he jumped on the wagon with Lew, and suddenly Mommy was the bad woman keeping him in time-out. I said to Lew, "We talked about this," and I asked him to come to another room to discuss it away from Bradley.

We went upstairs to our bedroom. Lew was wearing a costume mask hat of a monster and I asked him to remove it. "Would you please take the mask off," I said "because it's hard for me to tell you what's bothering me while you're wearing that mask." He did not want to take the mask off and wouldn't even lift it up to talk with me. So we sat there arguing about the mask, while also talking about Bradley and the time-out.

Lew became rather pompous and huffy with me, which I could not understand. He stood up and would not have anything to do with my request to follow our original plan with Brad. As Lew exited the room and walked downstairs, I started to feel insecure around his becoming angry. I walked down the stairs following him, wanting to make it better for Lew. I knew that he was the one missing trick-or-treat and realized that it meant as much to him as it did to Bradley.

"You go trick-or-treating with David and Marc, and Bradley can stay home with me," I said. In my excitement of not wanting to disappoint Lew, some saliva came out of my mouth as I eagerly repeated, "Please, Lew, please take David and Marc trick-or-treating and I'll keep Bradley with me."

Lew looked at me with vengeance, and the next thing I know he hummed a major spit cocked up from the back of his throat like a pig in an alley. I could hardly believe he did that. I was stunned.

I first withdrew, backing up one or two stairs, then went forward to go around Lew. I was flooded with disgust and anxiety. I saw David standing in the foyer at the foot of the stairs and I wanted to go to him to bring us both away from the stairs. As I was coming down the stairs, Lew pulled his fist back and punched me in the upper arm like a man punches another man. Poor David was watching Lew punch me. I then heard Marc in the background screaming, hysterically. Marc was terrified, and the screaming and wild emotion continued to escalate. Lew then came at me once again, with his arm pulled back and his hand locked in a tight fist ready to punch me again. I remain shocked, but clearly seeing what's coming.

"Lew, look at yourself," I said firmly. "Look at your hand." "How can you do this?"

He froze and turned his head to look at his own fist cocked to punch me, and then brought his arm to his side.

Momentarily, I thought Lew caught hold of himself, but I was wrong. I started to walk away from him and he ran after me, so I rushed to the telephone to call the police. Lew wouldn't let me get to the phone. He grabbed me, held me to the floor and I couldn't budge. As I remained on the floor, like I used to be held to the wall, I called out, "Bradley, call the police!" The children were screaming and I don't really recall much of what happened, other than there was lots of excitement and emotional fear. Somehow I got out from under him and hit the emergency signal on our alarm. Shortly after the police came to the house.

I was shaking and scared and so were the children. The police took reports from each of us separately. One of the officers asked if there was a gun in the house. I told him "yes" there was, and I pleaded with him to remove it from our home. Lew did not want them to do that. We had much discussion around the gun and finally Lew agreed, in front of the officer, to let me hide the gun until things cool down. My fear with this plan was, if he insisted on getting the gun back before I felt secure with him, we could get in a fight over the gun. I explained my concern to the officer and he observed Lew getting huffy, with some mean undertone, over my fearful communications concerning when I "will" return the gun at his direction. The officers looked at one another and they separated Lew and I, and then they converged privately. The officers came back into the bedroom and insisted upon removing the gun from our home and they also took Lew's bullets.

I could tell that the officers saw what I was feeling about Lew being controlling and potentially dangerous. They gave me an information packet on domestic violence, and had me sign a document that I had received the material. It was the first time I had ever seen anything in print that described what was going on in my home. One of the officers sat with me in the kitchen and I felt his heart open to me. He gave me the name of someone in the police department and urged me to seek guidance regarding the domestic violence.

The next day my arm turned black and blue. I was repulsed by the fact that I had another bruise from Lew's abusive behavior and loss of control. The next week was my scheduled annual medical with Dr. Sheinin who had been my internist since my thyroid condition was diagnosed. I was sitting in an exam room undressed with a little cloth gown wrapped around me. After the nurse completed the preliminary portion of the exam, Dr. Sheinin came in for my physical. He was listening to my heart with a stethoscope and his eye caught the bruise on my arm. As he was examining my body, he asked how I got bruised. I started telling him about the incident that led to my bruise, and the tears came rushing forward. I could not stop crying and I could not stop talking. I told Dr. Sheinin the whole story of what had been happening in my home to myself and my children.

Dr. Sheinin was incredibly sympathetic. He shared much with me that day which, made me recognize that we all have our "lot" and that how we deal with it is our challenge – our job. He urged me to find the best divorce attorney in the city and do what I needed to protect myself and the boys. He suggested that it would be wise to go back to the police and have the police take a picture of my arm. I felt as though a weight was lifted from me after having this talk with him. It was the first time I had so completely revealed our family "secret" to anyone. I was surprised that I had the courage to be so open with Dr. Sheinin, because he was the Head of the Medical Department at Michael Reese. So, of course, he knew Lew well. But this did not seem to matter to either of us. Dr. Sheinin saw the reality of my situation, and that seemed to be all that was important.

From his office, I walked over to an appointment that I had scheduled on Monday following the Saturday incident, with a divorce law firm, Rinella and Rinella. I walked into their office, filled out a standard form and then met with an energetic female divorce attorney. I told her the story of my marriage and how I was trying to get my business off the ground. She said that it certainly looked like divorce was on the horizon for me, but I would be better postured for the proceedings if I was financially self-sufficient. She assured me that she would be available to assist me when I was ready to begin. In the meantime, she encouraged me to keep records of abuse to me and the children.

Hesitantly, but with a knowing what I was doing was right, I went back to the Northbrook Police Department. I hated being there as it felt sleazy to be to there under these conditions. Nonetheless, I told them I wanted to show the officer my arm and the bruise that emerged out of the incident in our home. I was taken into a small room, and the officer took two Polaroid photographs of my arm and said that he was going to make a supplemental report to the one taken at our house the day of the incident.

When I got home, I visited with Lisa, a woman whom I had employed to work in my home. Lisa is a Jamaican lady who was in her 50's at the time – a woman of great virtue, patience and compassion. I actually hired Lisa for childcare on my working days and for light house keeping at other times. However, she turned out to become more for me and my children. She was a trusted confident and source of support for the next six years. Lisa took pictures of my arm as well. It was embarrassing to have her do this, but I was desperate to come out of the closet. Imagine having your employee calling you "Dr. King" and taking pictures that looked like they came from the ghetto. I started to realize that it can happen to anyone and that social stature did not make me immune to domestic violence.

Who Are the Battered Women?

Battering, for decades, has crossed all boundaries: age, size, economics, educational level, professions and social roles ...

In *The Battered Woman,* Lenore Walker provides a clear and accurate picture of who the battered woman is, contrary to the stereotypical image* most of us hold of women who are battered. Dr. Walker says:

"The battered woman is pictured by most people as a small, fragile, haggard person who might once have been pretty. She has several small children, no job skills, and is economically dependent on her husband. It is frequently assumed she is poor and from a minority group. She is accustomed to living in violence, and her fearlessness and passivity are emphasized above all. Although some battered women do fit this description, research proves it to be a false stereotype.

Most battered women are from middle-class and higher-income homes where the power of their wealth is in the hands of their husbands. Many of them are large women who could attempt to defend themselves physically. Not all of them have children; those who do do not necessarily have them in any particular age group. Although some battered women are jobless, many more are highly competent workers and successful career women. They include doctors, lawyers, corporation executives, nurses, secretaries, full-time homemakers, and others. Battered women are found in all age groups, races, ethnic and religious groups, educational levels and socioeconomic groups. Who are the battered women? If you are a woman, there is a 50 percent chance it could be you!" (Walker, 1979, pages 18 -19)

---

* See Appendix C on **Myths and Facts about Family Violence** for similar myths and surprising facts about battering.

CHAPTER 5

It Is Domestic Violence, Now What?

Marital Therapy Is Not Treatment for Abuse

Blind Blood Can't Help, Either

My Dad's Diagnosis

Blaming Children for the Abuse to Them

I knew I was being abused, but did not know how to stop it nor stop how it was affecting me. I had become impotent with my paralysis around being able to change this dynamic. With my public disclosures and personal admission that I was a victim of domestic violence, I became driven to seek appropriate intervention. The question before me was where do I find it. I had been practicing as a clinical psychologist for over twelve years, during which time I encountered numerous trauma and stress-related medical disorders. I had cultivated an expertise that was becoming second nature for me out of which my patients were deriving significant benefit. However, I had never seen domestic violence in progress, nor had I been exposed to it in my training. I didn't even know which of my colleagues to ask for a referral in this area of social, personal dysfunction.

I started to reach out beyond my immediate professional circle of the psychophysiology community and was led to numerous clinicians in family and conjoint therapy. In interviewing these individuals, I was informed that someone who specializes in domestic violence and family abuse would best serve our family. So I set out to find a domestic violence specialist. Over the years, I had established a good relationship with the children's pediatrician, Dr. Gerald Levin, whom I had frequently asked for recommendations of health and medical care. Dr. Levin was well aware of the abuse in our family, as it seemed that on each of our regular visits I had been reporting and lamenting on the most recent episode of child abuse in our home. He always listened to me with compassion and this time when I reached out, he had his secretary supplying me with two names within 20 minutes.

I called both of the people given to me and made an appointment with one of them within days of the initial phone contact. The group was called Center of Contextual Change, and their orientation primarily drew upon a family systems perspective. The head therapist, Mary Jo Barrett, M.S.W., claimed to specialize in abuse counseling. She provided me with a long resume of her public speaking engagements and publications on abuse. I had noticed that her primary focus was sexual abuse and expressed some concern whether physical violence was within her domain of expertise.

In our first interview, I told her of the incident of October 31, 1993 and, with the bruise still on my arm, I showed her the resulting mark. I mentioned to her that I was aware of Lew's obtaining my telephone records of every phone call placed from my office during the month preceding the incident on Halloween. In relaying this to her, I recognized that Lew's seemingly irrational rage was internally driven. Mary Jo helped me see that Lew may have suspected I was having an affair, which led to his securing my phone records and harboring insecurity about our relationship.

While I was not having an affair with a man, and had not during the course of our marriage, I was having an affair with the idea of not having to be dependent on Lew. I was deriving private pleasure from a sense of self-sufficiency, evolving out of my growing professional accomplishments. At this point, I was not aware of how Lew's perception of my independence contributed to his personal vulnerability, nor did I have a clear understanding of how this related to his brutality. I simply knew it was connected, but I did not know how or why.

Mary Jo and I digressed in our discussion, looking at the earlier years of domestic violence in our family. I described our background history detailing many episodes of abuse which had occurred over the years, both between Lew and myself and Lew and the children.

After the initial session, I still had not made up my mind as to whether this was the appropriate therapy for Lew and I. I decided to see her for three sessions, with Lew involved in the intervention, first before making up my mind. It is not uncommon in psychotherapy to experiment with a few sessions in making a determination if a therapist selection is appropriate. However, I think my desperation and sense of urgency was leading here. In hindsight, I recognize that I really didn't need the three sessions, as I had already seen enough evidence that her expertise did not match the needs of our family. Nonetheless, I was so comforted that someone finally heard me, I continued on with the intervention with Lew, reassuring myself with Mary Jo's promise that she was an abuse specialist. Mary Jo and her associate, Jeff Levy, worked with the two of us together, and in the initial sessions they both taught us much about the abuse dynamic.

While we sat in their little office, Mary Jo and Jeff drew diagrams on their blackboard detailing an altercation, showing the beliefs, feelings and actions of both the perpetrator and victim. Finally, Lew and I had some concrete context to communicate about what was happening so automatically in our home. This was good, but this is where the therapy stopped. Our sessions progressed with Lew and I coming into their office week after week, bringing up the most recent incident of abuse, looking at it, and diagramming it. Period.

I recognized early on that Lew was using Mary Jo's abuse model as a vehicle to contextualize each altercation so as to push the burden of accountability onto me and the children. I now realize that his interpretation of this intervention furthered his perpetuating the battering cycle, and my internalization of the information enabled it. I started to hear Mary Jo's message that the violence and assaults grew out of vulnerability in the abuser, not out of power. She truly helped me see that Lew struck out when he was feeling vulnerable. Still living from the victim mentality, I assumed it was my job to help Lew not feel vulnerable. So I allowed myself to shoulder what was not mine, as I became invested in trying to reassure Lew that he didn't have to hurt us to be important to me or himself. This went nowhere other than maintaining the cycle, because now I had even more ownership of Lew's choice-making than before.

From Lew's point of view, all the blame for his outbursts could be rationalized as appropriate responses to, what he came to term, "provocation." So there was no ownership of his actions, no new options and no change. In fact, things got worse, because now we had a forum to express and superficially dissipate the emotion around the ongoing abuse. It seemed to me that Lew's allowing me to put the episodes out in the open, which was not permitted before, made them go away from his point of view. Then he would focus on me for not getting over it, and from here the cycle continued – again and again.

*   *   *

In my desperation to seek assistance in "how do you let go of the pain" of being hit, struck, attacked, violated and abused, I arranged to have a "heart to heart" with Ingrid. Ingrid is Lew's sister who weathered the greatest amount of abuse from their mother, Cita. I invited her to come to my office on Michigan Avenue, hoping to talk and go out for lunch. She sat in one of the biofeedback chairs and I sat in the other. Ingrid was friendly, warm and enthusiastic about our getting together.

After some easy and light exchange, I pulled out my primary concern hoping to have a sisterly communion with her and possibly some guidance. I started by saying that I thought we had something in common and felt she may be able to help me see the light at the end of the tunnel. I said, "Over the years, I have come to learn of the history of abuse from your mother." I told her what had been happening to me and the children.

I pleaded with tears in my eyes, "Can you tell me how you get over being abused?" Ingrid turned to stone. The warm, loving human being became a frozen statue. There was no response. I merely wept and she watched. We went out to lunch and I recognized that Ingrid was not in a position to help me. I apologized for burdening her with my disclosure and left it at that.

*   *   *

Sometime shortly after we began our therapy with Mary Jo and Jeff, my father was diagnosed with cancer and significant heart disease. My Dad, Richard King, was a dear, loving, compassionate man in a rather quite and reserved fashion. From my first memories of him, I knew him as an incredibly strong, solid and stable person. He was about six feet tall, weighing a little over 200 pounds, and was handsome, generous and the kindest human being I've ever known. Dad had a passion for animals and so we always had one or many in our home. I was "Daddy's little girl." I can remember posing for him, making the sweetest curtsy, smiling ear to ear and knowing the ocean of love he had for me and my two older brothers, Bobby and Lou.

In conversations with my Mom and Dad, before his receiving the definitive diagnosis, I could feel that his health was failing. He would vacillate from being unconcerned and almost indifferent about his health, to faintly expressing and verbally sounding very compromised. I decided that I needed to be near them, so I set out to go to California where they were living at the time. I made arrangements for Lisa to remain at our house to care for and watch the children around the clock until I got home. I had given her full instructions and made sure that money was available for her to take care of all of the children's needs in my absence. It was not easy for me to leave at this juncture, given the difficulties in my little family with Lew and I, but I felt my father and mother truly needed me and that was where I needed to be.

I arrived at my parents home in San Marcos and we visited. My Dad was scheduled for a procedure to remove tissue for a biopsy the next day. We drove him to the hospital and he checked into a private room at the end of the hall. Mom and Dad were so sweet with one another on this evening. It was like old times, with the two of them making jokes and having fun laughing. I was enjoying them, while simultaneously feeling an internal tremble that wouldn't go away. The nurses did the routine preparations for surgery with Dad and then he got comfortable and ready for bed. Mother and I left, to return in the morning.

We arrived back at the hospital very early. My mother and I were in the prep area with Dad, waiting for him to be taken into the operating room. It seemed like several hours. Dad was pretty frisky. I recall his saying he wished he wasn't going in there, as he was in good health. I was a bit apprehensive also about what was ahead. I put my hand on Dad's chest just before they were to take him in for the procedure, and I had a knowing that something was there beyond what had been discussed. I didn't want to take my hand away. I leaned over and gave him a kiss and told him, "I love you and we're waiting for you outside."

Mother and I waited until after the procedure was complete. It seem like forever. Eventually, we bumped into one of the doctors working with Dad, and he told us that it looked like lung cancer. Dad's diagnosis was confirmed, while the primary cancer was never determined. Dad had a massive tumor in his chest the size of a baseball. After they closed him up, they told us that his heart condition was so severe that they did not think he would survive the radiation regimen that was recommended. He was basically thriving on collateral arteries, due to there being 90 percent blockage to his heart in the primary arteries. It was determined that Dad should first have bypass surgery. Dad was a real trooper after the surgery and healed rapidly. His spirit returned and I could see that he had a clear sense of hope for recovery. I returned to Chicago and we kept in constant touch on the phone over the weeks while he was healing. He began chemotherapy, and then it was time for the radiation. I returned to California to be there with Dad for the initial treatment. It was extremely hard for all of us.

My father's illness and the needs that arose in my family were too stressful to interrupt the therapy that Lew and I began with Mary Jo and Jeff. I wanted and needed the continuity of Mary Jo in my life, and was not in the mood for therapist shopping. It was really hard to come to grips with my father's failing health, his cancer and the possibility of losing him. There were many nights at home where I simply retreated into my bedroom to cry. I don't know if Lew or the children ever knew how difficult a period this was for me.

*   *   *

Over the course of the preceding year before Dad's diagnosis, he had spent numerous evenings on the phone talking business with me. He had been helping me with my financial projections and the development of a business that I was envisioning. We sent projections back and forth via fax. It was exhilarating. Then one day Dad phoned and with unwavering sureness he said, "Jeanne, it looks like a good plan to me, go for it." I was ecstatic with joy, receiving his support which complimented my passionate vision.

I selected the perfect location, in downtown Chicago on Wacker Drive, and built a lovely office from the ground up. I orchestrated every facet of the lease negotiations, office design, its construction, decorating and the purchase of furnishings and office equipment. It was both stressful and exhilarating; and without Dad's faith it may not have happened. I think, on some level, Dad wanted me to be self-sufficient, and I wanted to show us both that I could and would carry my own.

I recall pouring over blueprints, having such fun in the birthing of this new vision and Lew coming over to me, putting me down and bad mouthing my business venture. It became so uncomfortable that I decided to leave him out of every aspect of what I was doing just so I didn't have to hear him complain about my work. I learned to protect myself from his verbal harassment by not exposing myself to the darts he was trying to throw into my sail. I saw him as a "spirit breaker," because that is exactly what it felt like when I allowed it to happen.

                    *   *   *

Lew and I continued in therapy with Mary Jo and Jeff for almost a year. Our sessions seemed to center around weekly coping with current matters, along with some revisiting of the past. Once again, Lew disclosed the terror that he lived in his childhood with his mother's brutality. I could see his pain, just as I had felt it in the therapy with Dr. Kanter. I believe that Lew's honesty about his past kept me in the process, but this time without much faith. While we used our sessions to discuss the current incidents of abuse and its aftermath, the frequency of altercations increased.

As Marc learned to exercise his will, he became an eligible target for what Lew called "physical force" and what I termed "physical abuse." I believe my youngest child was exerting his will in a developmentally appropriate way, but his conduct was curtailed in a destructive and unhealthy fashion. Lew had slowly developed a habit with Marc of pulling his ear to elicit cooperation. Evening after evening, we made the rounds putting all three children to sleep. I frequently asked Lew to be with two of the children while I put one to bed, or sometimes to watch one while I put the other two to bed together.

On this particular evening in May of 1994, I was tending to David and Bradley and I heard Lew and Marc struggling in the other room. I rushed into the room and saw Lew trying to get Marc to cooperate to put on his pajamas. Lew had his fingers gripped tightly around Marc's little ear. He was pulling his ear, while Marc was crouched to the floor and Lew was moving into an upright position.

"I'm going to pull your ear until you follow it," Lew yelled.

Marc was in tears and I was stunned. I intervened and insisted that Lew let him go. I picked up Marc and we went into my bedroom. Marc's ear was fiery red and he was crying hysterically.

"Mommy it stings, it burns," Marc cried. "Daddy was going to pull my ear off."

He wept and we rocked. The next day he had bruises on both sides of his little ear.

Later, when I addressed this with Lew, he claimed that his actions were Marc's fault. He said had the child listened, he would not have had to pull his ear. What puzzled me was that Lew saw no other options other than resorting to physical force. I wanted him to elicit cooperation from Marc by motivating Marc from the inside; but, at that time, I was not articulate enough about what I was doing in my getting this from the children, much less how to share this with Lew. I became frustrated, and again we widened the gap in our different perspectives on child rearing. Over the months to follow, I became more vigilant in my supervisory role, trying to minimize flare-ups between Lew and the boys.

However, since there was one of me and three of them, it was not as easy to oversee all three simultaneously, as I was able to do when they were less mobile in their earlier years. In the following month, June of 1994, Lew and I were putting the boys to bed and again, while tending to the others, I heard an hysterical scream from a child. This time it was David, with Lew's ring marks on his little rear end. Lew smacked David so hard over getting dressed, that I

could see a black and blue mark forming. Davey cried and cried, and
we cuddled as he went off to sleep.

*   *   *

An agreement had been made in therapy that Lew and I were
only to discuss these matters during sessions, so I waited until our
next appointment with Mary Jo and Jeff to talk about what had
occurred. We talked about it with them for most of the session. Both
therapists told Lew there was "no justification for hitting children;"
it was "unacceptable conduct." Unfortunately the therapist's words
didn't stop the incidents from happening.

The following month, July 1994, David got it again, but this
time there were three finger prints from Lew's hand. On this night, I
held David as he was crying and said, "*Mommy is going to get
Daddy to stop this hitting, I promise.*" Later, I asked Lew to apologize to David for what had been done and his reply was, "It was an
accident," and it was "no big deal." I told him I thought it was a big
deal when you hit a child so hard that you leave a mark. He refused
to apologize, and we never managed to agree on the meaning of
leaving marks on children.

Within the same month, Bradley and Lew were having an
argument in which it was obvious that they were merely in a power
struggle. Lew was telling Brad to do something. Brad's unwillingness to follow the exact order in the exact fashion as it was
delivered, resulted in the two of them fighting. Bradley retreated to
the first floor and remained sitting on the second step at the bottom
of the stairs in the foyer, with his back leaning against the wall.
Their fighting escalated and Lew tore into Bradley in the cruelest
way.

Lew yelled in fury, "I'm going to give it to you so hard that I'm
going to put you in the hospital!!!" "I'm going to beat the hell out of
you," Lew shouted.

It was said so viciously and it was so scary that Bradley started shaking. I intervened, interrupting Lew and telling him that was out of line.

I sat on the stair next to Bradley and comforted him. As I held Bradley, shaking, I recalled how I had heard the same message from Lew. I was flooded with my own memories of his saying, "I'm going to break your back, and I'm going to break your neck." I remembered how hearing these words affected me and I thought to myself – here I am 41 years old and I am just beginning to realize the impact of what this was doing to me. I shivered, thinking of how this must be affecting my child.

I looked at Bradley and said, "I will not let anything like this happen." I promised him I would not allow his father hurt him.

I walked Bradley to my car and he sat in the passenger seat, and we drove off. I had no idea where we were going; I was just driving. I needed to get my child out of there. I recall looking at him as I was passing the Old Orchard exit on the expressway about 15 minutes from our home, and his little body was still shaking. He reclined his seat, and I held his hand and sang one of his old favorite comforting songs. I kept singing until he fell off to sleep.

Hours later we came home and Bradley retreated into his room. I talked with Lew about his interaction with Bradley. I told him I felt it was wrong to talk to a child like that. I explained that those threatening statements are very serious and have significant consequences to the child.

"I don't want you talking to Bradley like that," I insisted.

Lew said, "Bradley drove me to talk like that."

Lew's continued commitment to thwart off his accountability for his actions to the children created an air of self-righteousness on his part. I could see that our therapy had become another forum for rationalization and denial, merely pushing the responsibility of emotional and physical abuse onto whomever was the target or victim for the day. I lost the little faith I had in our intervention and no longer looked to it for remedy.

| Why Marital Therapy Is Ineffective Treatment |
| for Family Abuse |

Marital or couples therapy, based on a family systems perspective, is more likely to maintain the pathology of abuse in order to sustain the dynamic of the relationship. Violence, from the family systems orientation, is a relationship issue which is perceived as a symptom of a disturbed, dysfunctional or pathological relationship.

A basic premise of systems theory is that all parts of the system, including each family member, contribute to maintaining the homeostasis of the system. Homeostasis is the "tendency of a system to maintain a dynamic equilibrium and to undertake operations to restore that equilibrium whenever it is threatened" (Stordeur & Stille, 1989, citing Goldenberg & Goldenberg, 1985). The family system continually works to sustain its homeostasis, even when it is achieved through dysfunctional interaction. In this context all family members carry responsibility for the battering syndrome, and the battering behavior serves a functional role in maintaining the relationship dynamics within the family system.

Accordingly, the family system therapist moves to equalize the responsibility for the violence, and thereby implicitly or explicitly blames the victim for the batterer's abusive behavior. From this therapeutic orientation, "it becomes the victim's responsibility to change her behavior to stop the violence perpetrated against her" by her abuser. Treatment success is often defined as "keeping the relationship together, rather than stopping the abuse" (Stordeur & Stille, 1989, citing Adams, 1988; Brygger & Edelson, 1987). The treatment invariably results in the victim being assigned the responsibility for controlling her husband's feelings and behavior. Clinicians Stordeur and Stille view "this treatment modality as abusive to women, sexist in nature, not effective in stopping men's violence, and dangerous for battered women" (1989, p. 56).

R. Stordeur and R. Stille, *Ending Men's Violence Against Their Partners*, 1989.

CHAPTER 6

Welts Bring the Family Secret Out

Beatings and Belts

Welts and Police

Domestic Battery Arrest

Order of Protection: A Wake-up Call

Dual Denial

July 1994 was the month the final construction was going on in my new office. I did what was necessary to follow through on these plans as my Dad and I had set forth. Deep inside I felt this business would be important for the future of me and my children, as I knew of Lew's expressed commitment to shut me out of any financial support.

I moved into my new office in August 1994. On September 6th an incident occurred which was the straw that broke the camel's back. In retrospect, I see a clear pattern of escalation in Lew's abuse to me and the children while I was evidencing my independence, self-sufficiency and personal growth.

On this particular day, September 6, 1994, we were preparing to go to temple at Temple Jeremiah for the Jewish High Holy Days. Chicago was having another of its Indian Summers, in which the fall air was replaced by a pocket of warm days. I had selected clothing for David and Marc to wear to Temple as I routinely did for each of our outings. Bradley had reached the age where he was making choices in his selections for our family outings. The rule of thumb being that he choose something appropriate for the event.

I was in the master bedroom getting ready, and David and Marc were close to being fully dressed. I heard bickering back and forth between Bradley and Lew in the hallway outside of the children's bathroom. Their fight escalated into Lew screaming at Bradley to wear a long sleeve shirt and Bradley wanting to wear short sleeves because he did not want to be hot. Lew demanded compliance and Bradley insisted on having his way. They continued fighting, and Bradley rolled to the floor outside of the bathroom and had a temper tantrum on the floor in the hallway. He was kicking his feet, and in his fit Bradley kicked the wall. When he did this, he kicked a hole in the wall about two-and-a-half inches wide. I came rushing in, hearing the storm.

Initially, I was upset with Bradley, along with Lew, because of the hole in the wall; but at this point I was unaware of how their outburst had evolved. All I knew was that I had to get composure between the two of them quickly. Lew and I followed Bradley into his room; Lew's temper leading. In my effort to avert what appeared to be escalating fury, I told Lew that we should not allow Brad to go to Temple if he was unwilling to dress as Lew felt was appropriate for the day. We told Brad that he was not going to come with us and he would have to remain in time out until we returned, at which point we would deal with the hole in the wall.

Lew was so angered, with the intensity already in progress, he lost it. He went after Bradley, beating him, slapping him, hitting him with his hand on Bradley's rear end. Lew was holding Bradley down against the bed and kept slapping and slapping him, again and again. I was screaming at Lew to stop hitting him. Bradley was weeping and pleading with his father, begging him to stop, stop, stop. Lew couldn't get a hold of himself. I continued screaming and trying to get Lew off of Bradley.

"What are you doing...STOP...STOP," I pleaded, yelling and begging.

Lew continued hitting him with full force – beating him – smacking him over 14 times, harder and harder and harder. I called Lisa, who was downstairs at the other end of the house. Lew reached for a belt continuing to go after Bradley.

"You've lost it ... back off," I screamed even louder.

Lew positioned to use the belt, and I continued screaming to interrupt him.

"Lew, stop it, you've got to step away, you've got to back off. You're losing control," I hollered. I continued begging him to back off, saying, "You're out of control."

Eventually he stopped. It may have been when Lisa came up; I don't recall, as it was happening so fast.

Lew walked out of Brad's room and went into another room, giving me the impression that he had indeed backed off. I stayed with Brad in his room and laid next to him comforting him. He continued to cry and eventually settled down somewhat. I left his room to check on David and Marc and then went into my bedroom.

Within moments I heard screaming coming from Brad's room. I rushed back into the room and Lew was in there with the belt in his hand swinging the buckle end of the belt at Bradley. He had Brad's underpants down and braced against the bed. Bradley was struggling and Lew was brutally beating his thigh, hip and groan.

"Stop this ... You are out of line ... Leave him alone," I desperately yelled. Lew continued with the belt as I was screaming.

"You've got to stop ... you've got to stop," I pleaded; but he wouldn't stop.

Lew left a nine inch welt across Bradley's groan, with the buckle end of the belt. With this final hit, it looked as though Lew had climaxed and then he left the room.

Bradley laid on his bed crying, weeping; he couldn't get a hold of himself. I laid on his bed next to him and held him quietly. I don't know how long I remained there, but when I left his room, I felt sick inside. I felt that violation to Brad as though it were my own. I remembered two months before I had promised my child that I wouldn't let his father hurt him. I recalled the promised I had made to David that I would get Daddy to stop hitting us. I felt like I had betrayed my children and it made me more nauseous. I realized that I could not get Lew to stop abusing the children.

Lew retreated into the master bedroom. I went into the master bathroom and he followed me and sat on the edge of the bath tub along side of me. We talked and I told him that he crossed that line again, and this time he had gone way too far. I asked if he heard me trying to stop him and he acknowledged that he did. It appeared that he was compelled to follow through with his desire to beat Brad with the belt, irrespective of what I was saying. I told him that it was over for me and I couldn't take this anymore.

"I cannot let this go on," I said,

He leaned his head forward into his hands and started crying. In tears, he said, "I'm a monster."

"It feels like it," I replied.

He asked me to hold him, but I couldn't. Being near him made me sick and I distinctly recall hating the way he smelled. We just sat there and he promised never to lose control like that again. His words were shallow to me, as I had heard those words before, so I didn't believe him. There was no more hope for me. It was over.

*   *   *

I got up and went into Bradley's room to check on him. Lew followed me and we both crawled onto Brad's bed to rest and commune along side him. It was really uncomfortable and awkward for me to be laying on the bed with my wounded child and what I saw as a pathetic, confused man. The tension of the three of us in that moment grew. Bradley asked to be alone. Lew and I exited Brad's room and I encouraged Lew to leave the house. We had missed the Temple services and so I told him to go to his sister's house for the family gathering to follow. Lew left and I stayed home with Bradley.

Bradley fell asleep. He woke up within the hour and came into my room. We talked, I comforted him and he showed me his leg and groin. He had deep red welts covering half the length of his upper leg, nine inches long and almost four inches wide. The area was darkening and bluish, purple bruises were setting in. I couldn't stand the sight of what was before me. It was clear to me that things were getting worse, as Lew's violence advanced from hand to belt and from bruises to welts. I had this knowing that if something happened to my child, leaving him lamed, and I didn't act on the possibility of seeing it coming, I would never forgive myself.

I told Brad to put on some pants and a shirt. He did and I said, "Come with me we're going out." I knew I ought go to the police, but I hadn't yet told him. He and I drove to Northbrook Police and walked inside. My intention was to file a report and seek assistance from the police to help me get Lew to stop hitting us. I had no idea what was before me, all I knew is I had to approach the domestic violence in our home in a different way than had been done before.

Brad and I were taken into a small room in which we both told the story of what had occurred earlier that day. Brad pulled down his pants and showed the officer his welts.

The officer turned to me and said, "So, are you here to file a complaint, ma'am."

Not knowing the difference between a report and a complaint, I innocently said, "I'm here to ask for your help in getting my husband to stop hurting my children."

"Well, Miss if you're not going to file the complaint," the officer said, "then I will."

I thought about the import of what he was saying, and realized I needed to send a clear message to Lew that his abusing us was something I would no longer tolerate. So, I filed the complaint.

A domestic battery complaint was filed, and the social worker at the police station talked at length with Brad and me. She took information from Bradley about other incidents of violence in the home, between Lew and himself and between Lew and the other children. Brad and I got into the car, and Brad appeared emotionally lighter and I believed that I had done the right thing.

*   *   *

Shortly after Lew arrived home, the police came to the house to arrest him. Before this I hadn't really recognized the enormity of what was to come. Lew was casual but stunned as the officers walked into our home. They met Lew in the foyer and told him that he was under arrest for domestic battery. One of the officers placed handcuffs on Lew. I was standing on the stairs watching him and he had tears in his eyes. He looked at me and said, "I understand your frustration." For the first time since 1988, I felt he really heard me and my heart opened to him. The officers walked Lew outside and took him to the police station.

We were both informed that there was a 72 hour "no contact" Order placed on Lew by the Northbrook Police. However, he violated it by calling me that evening. He initially said he was calling to get his pager and he wanted me to bring it to him. We continued to talk for a very long time, in which there was significant tenderness and love exchanged. He promised me that he would work on his abuse problem and that it would "go away." He talked of going to see a psychiatrist for intensive therapy and doing what would be necessary to change. We ended the conversation with our making plans for me to drop the pager off at the hotel where he was staying during the "no contact period."

I went to the hotel to drop Lew's pager off and didn't expect to see him, but there he was standing at the front desk in the hotel. The affection from our last phone conversation was clearly gone. He was hostile and offensive to me, so I put his pager on the front desk and walked away.

The police social worker, Ms. Marie Rodregus-Hallisey, had scheduled an appointment for me to meet with her at the Skokie Court House in conjunction with the domestic battery charge from the weekend. She arranged to go before the Judge with me to seek an Order of Protection. It wasn't clear to me at the time what that meant, but she advised that it appeared to be something I needed.

We went before Judge Marcia Orr and the State's Attorney represented the matter of the domestic battery charge in the belt beating of Bradley. Judge Orr asked me numerous questions concerning our situation and the history of abuse in the family. Based on what spontaneously poured forth under oath, she insisted that the Emergency Order of Protection include keeping Lew away from the children, myself and our home for two weeks. I was extremely frightened and told her that I was not there to cause trouble; I only wanted Lew to change what he was doing to us in the home. I recall my exact words: "I'm not here to nail him (my husband)." But she saw what was wrong in our family and wanted to help. Judge Orr appeared astounded by our circumstances.

"Your husband needs a wake up call," she said. "Eight or ten years of violence problems has gone on too long now. "

I learned more from this woman on that day about abuse and abuse treatment than I had been exposed to up to this point. She elaborated on the fact that an abuser can not be cured in marital (couples) therapy, and I recognized, once again, why our therapy was not working. Judge Orr said:

"It has been my experience and I think the experience of just about everybody who was involved in these types of cases that these court couple therapists are not appropriate to resolve domestic violence issues and it then makes it, and I am trying to think of the word, it makes it possible for the perpetrator to still perceive this as a marital or couple's issue. Therefore, it gives the abuser a way of whether consciously or subconsciously avoiding and recognizing this as a problem because there is at least one other problem involved in therapy, what can be challenged or confronted and whose behavior might not be appropriate, and it looks like something has to be resolved by the two people working together, when it is not that. These violent problems are problems that can only be resolved by a person suffering the violence and by a person who was acting out sometimes it is because of alcohol or drug abuse problem, but the abuse of substance is a problem for the person doing and can only be addressed or corrected by that person and not by any other person like friends or family or anything else. But this is not to be done together with the abuser at the same time the issue has to be separate and discreet. Do you see what I am saying?" (Report of Proceedings, No. 94 MC 2004605, September 9, 1994, pgs. 14-15)

*   *   *

During the two weeks away from me and the children, Lew's family convinced him that he did not have a problem with abuse. He was even saying that Bradley had gotten off easy with the belt beating. Suddenly, he perceived himself as the victim in this situation and Bradley as deserving of the belt beating. I was shocked at his 180 degree turn around from the promises he had made before. Lew had been residing with his family, and after talking to them about our situation with the police, Lew said that he "could never trust me again." He expressed concern that, should he leave another mark on a child, and I call the police, it could damage his career, and this chance he was not going to take. Lew said, "Jeanne, There can be no future for us. It's over."

Lew's rage escalated and now he had postured me as the bad guy, because I was responsible for bringing the police in, and the Department of Children and Family Services were setting out to do an investigation of suspected child abuse. All of this, according to Lew, was my fault. I recognized that we were no further along than we had been before his arrest, so I sought out to meet with an attorney.

I made the appointment, but Lew's business attorney started romancing me before I got there. Lew's attorney was calling me and sending me letters urging me to drop the charges, pleading with me to let Lew come back home; telling me of his love for us, promising me that he would submit to a psychiatric intervention two times per week, on and on.

I met with an attorney and I told him about my situation. In sorting out my options, I explained that what was most important to me was that Lew no longer be abusive to the children.

"He will always be their father," I said. "I think it would be best for their relationship if he were not abusive to them."

The attorney said, "You will have a harder time getting him to change with an arrest charge hanging over his head." He pointed out, "With this (the criminal charge) you will be in a divorce."

I thought that it would be far more difficult to get Lew to change after a divorce was in progress, and so I wanted to do all that could be done now. Even though all the cards were in front of me – Lew was not changing – and I was positioned best at that point, I was still hanging on to wanting Lew to change and feeling it was my job to do all I could to assist in this.

In the days following I thought this over. Objectively, I did know that divorce was the most immediate and appropriate remedy to my family problems and the abuse I could no longer weather. However, my heart was numb and my inner strength was depleted. My Dad's condition had worsened, as he was developing severe complications from the radiation. Dad was dying and his days were limited. The real decision for me in that week was can I handle both divorce and death in a matter of months? In retrospect, I regret that I did not go back for a session with the police social worker, because I believe I would have gotten the courage I needed at that time. Instead, I bounced between attorneys and lost perspective.

"Batterers and battered women have similar difficulty recognizing and accepting when they are in trouble." (Walker, 1979, p 73.)

MISDEMEANOR COMPLAINT

Skokie, Illinois
Room B

(6/2/94) CCG 0655

IN THE CIRCUIT COURT OF COOK COUNTY, ILLINOIS

The People of State of Illinois
Plaintiff

v.

NO. .....'94MC2004605

Lewis S. Blumenthal
....
Defendant

Jeanne K. Blumenthal
.... complainant, now appears before
(Complainant's Name Printed or Typed)

The Circuit Court of Cook County and states that

Lewis S. Blumenthal, 1221 Thornapple Ln., Northbrook, Cook County, Illinois .... has, on or about
(defendant)   (address)

September 6, 1994 .... at 1221 Thornapple, Northbrook, Cook County, Illinois ....
(date)   (place of offense)

committed the offense of .... **DOMESTIC BATTERY** .... in that he/she
intentionally and without legal justification caused bodily harm to his son, Bradley
Blumenthal, age 10, by striking him on the left thigh with a belt. Offense occurred in the
Village of Northbrook, Cook County, Illinois.
....
....

In violation of .... 720 .... Illinois Compiled Statute .... 5 ...... /12-3.2(a)(1) ......
(Chapter)   (Act)   (Sub Section)

STATE OF ILLINOIS
COOK COUNTY   } ss.

....
(Complainant's Signature)
1221 Thornapple Lane
Northbrook, Illinois 708/498-6648
(Complainant's Address)   (Telephone No.)

Jeanne K. Blumenthal
....
(Complainant's Name Printed or Typed)

being first duly sworn, ... by her .... on oath, deposes and says that he/she read the foregoing
complaint by him/her subscribed and that the same is true.

....
(Complainant's Signature)

Subscribed and sworn to before me .... September 6, ...,19 94.

For Aurelia Pucinski by: Ofc. R. Adamick #119
....
(Judge or Clerk)

I have examined the above complaint and the person presenting the same and have heard evidence thereon, and am satisfied that there is
probable cause for filing same. Leave is given to file said complaint.

Summons issued,   Judge ....
or   Judge's No.
Warrant Issued,   Bail set at, ...
or
Bail set at ..... $2,000.00 I-Bond .... Judge ... Sullivan ....
NO CONTACT FOR 72 HOURS   Judge's No.

AURELIA PUCINSKI, CLERK OF THE CIRCUIT COURT OF COOK COUNTY

Domestic Battery: September 6, 1994

Deindividuated violence is a term coined by social psychologist, Phil Zimbardo, referring to "out-of-control" violence. A breakdown of restraints occurs within the batterer, resulting in his being caught in the grip of rage and violence, while being "unresponsive to cues from his victim." This violence is driven from within and the "physical action is even pleasurable" for the perpetrator (cited in Dutton, 1995, pg. 47). Police officers call this "seeing red."

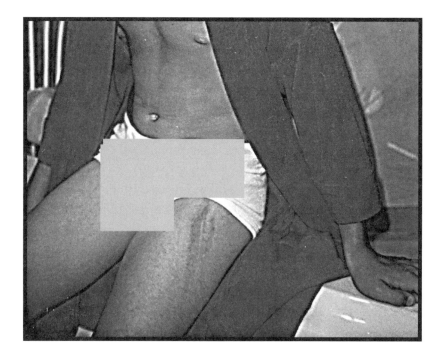

Marks of Domestic Battery:
Belt Welts and Bruises, September 1994

CHAPTER 7

Death Calls Before Divorce

Promises, Lies and Misrepresentations

Abuse Finding by Department of Children & Family Services

Therapist's Prognosis on Lew's Battering

A Miraculous Union

My Dad Dies and Lew Seeks to Stage Allies

U p to this point our family secret was a secret that remained in the family, hidden behind therapists' and doctors' doors. Now that the domestic violence in our home was being discussed in open criminal court and evaluated by public protective agencies, politics replaced blood and professional ethics to maintain the secrecy.

Over a hundred individuals were directly or indirectly involved in the politics of our proceedings. I have included the names of individuals who identified themselves in the court records and/or in media covering our story. Their names are public record along with every document contained in this manuscript. The documentation referred to herein, including all reports, pleadings and correspondence, is part of case number 94 MC 2004605, Circuit Court of Cook County Illinois, Municipal Department – Second Municipal District; and/or case number 95 D 6150, Circuit Court of Cook County Illinois, Domestic Relations Division.

My attorney and Lew's attorney made a deal that Lew would see a psychiatrist if I would drop the charges. The State's Attorney representing the criminal matter of the domestic battery toward Bradley met with me and Bradley. We told her the history and answered her questions. She said she would drop the charges against Lew if he would get proper help from a medical doctor regarding his physical abuse. This was to involve individual sessions with a psychiatrist two times per week. That was the understanding and that was the agreement.

The State's Attorney knew about the pending investigation by the Department of Children and Family Services (DCFS) and their involvement in our case. We talked about it in our preliminary meeting and it was available for her review in the police reports. What puzzled me was, in the next hour, when we went before the Judge to tell him what the agreement was concerning the criminal charges, the Judge specifically asked her if DCFS was involved in this case and she responded, "No." I knew that wasn't right and I nudged my attorney and he ignored it. In that moment, I did not trust that Lew would actually follow through with the treatment. Something seemed wrong; the States Attorney's misrepresentation of the matter of the DCFS involvement was a red flag that haunted me.

As we all stood before the Judge, I wanted to object to our dropping the criminal charges, but I was freighted that if I proceeded with the charges Lew might come back and hurt me in a most devastating way. I was scared and frozen, and started to delude myself with a fantasy that if I gave him this chance than maybe he would change and we could keep the family together. Then, I clearly remember reassuring myself by thinking the threat to Lew of going through this again might be enough of a deterrent to keep him from hurting us again. I was wrong. My fear and my wishful thinking allowed me to drop the criminal charges, which kept us locked in the abuse dynamic for five more years.

Following the Hearing, we bumped into Lew and his attorney in the hallway of the courthouse. His demeanor was cold and I knew my concerns in the courtroom were true. I could see that Lew had no intention of making good on his promise. Unfortunately, I did not know that I could have reinstated those criminal charges. In fact, one year later I learned that I could have done so up to six months after dropping the charges. In my innocence I used this time to nudge Lew to follow through and hope that he would, whereas he used this time to prepare for divorce.

Lew moved back into the house and we had endless conversations concerning the agreement and his promise to seek psychiatric help. These encounters dove-tailed into rounds of further abuse by Lew toward myself. His position became, "I do not have a problem with abuse. You are making a big deal out of nothing." He would then go on to say my persistence in his seeking help was an indication that I had some deep seated abuse issues from my past and I should be the one to see the psychiatrist. I recall one day his saying, "You're *acting* like a victim of abuse." And I thought to myself, you're right, I am.

Almost immediately after Lew moved back into our house the Department of Children and Family Services visited our home to investigate the matter of suspected child abuse prompted by the domestic battery charge. Today I recognize that the timing of events here did not follow proper procedure. DCFS is required to initiate a face-to-face visit with parties involved in the investigation within days after their being called, not weeks. However on September 21, 1994, representative Sandra La Grande came to our house to investigate the child abuse reported by the police in conjunction with the domestic battery charge of September 7, 1994.

Ms. La Grande was a young woman who played right into Lew's hand. We were sitting in our breakfast room. Lew began the interview by telling her that he was an obstetrician/gynecologist. Within five minutes he was giving her advise regarding her recent miscarriage, which she so candidly shared with us at the onset of the interview. It was apparent to me that Lew had manipulated the direction of the interview by involving Ms. La Grande in her current personal grief and then promising her some advice to prevent subsequent miscarriages. After establishing this "rapport," Lew told

Ms. La Grande that there is no abuse problem. He said it was a domestic matter; a possible divorce and he was the abused partner in our marriage. His evidence for this was the time the police were called to our house January 1993 when I put my arms out to prevent myself from going through the glass shower door. I was as stunned at his telling her this as I was when he called the police over the incident. But this time, I was angered knowing what a liar he was being with this woman and how I had been manipulated into allowing him to come back home.

Then, Lew took it even further and told Ms. La Grande that I was the parent who was abusive to the kids. I couldn't believe what I was hearing. She asked to interview the children and me. Brad talked to her and told her of the incident that led to our going to the police. In my interview with her, I described much of the abuse to both the children and to me by Lew over the last six years and showed her documentation with photos.

She brought Lew and I back together and, as she was gathering her papers to leave she said, "Sometimes it is okay to leave marks on kids." She added, "As a child I was hit by my father and I came out okay. " Her departing words with Lew were, "Maybe I'll call you in your office for the consult about my problem," (referring to her medical problems). It was clear to me that this woman came in like an investigator and left like a patient. When this occurred I thought Lew merely pulled one over on her but, in retrospect, she may have been prepped for this interview to go as it did.

For weeks following Ms. La Grande's meeting at our home, Lew went around saying that Brad "deserved" the belt beating and the Department of Children and Family Services "supported his hitting Bradley." Lew said that he did not need to see the psychiatrist because even the state protective agency supported his position. I was quite concerned with the way Lew was using this interview, which appeared far from objective, to get out of his promise for therapy. I called my attorney to inform him of what had transpired. He recommended writing a letter to DCFS to notify them of the way

Ms. La Grande conducted herself in this interview and of the possibility of there being a loss of objectivity in the investigation.

*   *   *

The Department of Children and Family Services did indeed determine that there had been child abuse by Lewis Blumenthal and gave an "indicated" finding of abuse, (Central Registration Number 598497A). Shortly after Lew learned about the DCFS abuse finding, he initiated an appeal. After months of re-evaluation by DCFS they informed me that the "indicated" finding was upheld, meaning it would not be discharged. In the meantime, Lew repeatedly informed parties including the Court that there was "never a finding by DCFS of abuse," yet I had obtained written notice of the "indicated" abuse finding and so had he.

Lew continued to deny his long history of physical abuse to me and the children and maintained his old abusive habits, which I started to see as reflexive actions to frustration and conflict. Just one week after I had dropped the criminal domestic battery charge, Marc, age 5 at the time, was in the kitchen with me and Lew. We were making breakfast and Marc wanted to flip the pancakes. He was standing on a stool leaning over the open fire, and I told him he was too young to flip the pancakes over an open fire. He got off the stool and started whining. I knew eventually he would quiet down and get over it. Lew was rather irritated with Marc's crying and insisted that he stop immediately. Lew's demanding that Marc stop seemed to add to Marc's distress and further crying. In Lew's frustration he grabbed Marc, lifted him up and ran him over to the fire holding his hand extended out toward the flame and shouted at Marc, "OK Marc, put your hands in the fire."

As Lew was moving Marc's hand into the fire, Marc became hysterical. He started screaming and broke out of Lew's grip and started running. Lew chased after him, jumped onto him and held him to the floor. Marc's crying continued, and Lew pulled his arms outward as he often did with me. I was shocked at what was happening and insisted that he get off of Marc. Marc was crying saying, "Daddy hurt me." Somehow Lew didn't see anything wrong with this "intervention" with Marc.

Within the same week, Lew was playing with David and Marc. It appeared that Marc did something that Lew didn't like. Instead of correcting Marc, Lew grabbed his torso and threw him to the floor head first. As I saw Marc flying across the room and crashing to the floor from several feet above, it occurred to me that Lew could have broken his neck or hurt his collar bone. Marc was crying for about 20 minutes and couldn't settle down. I laid down on the floor with Marc and made sure his head and neck were okay. He said he was hurting and continued to cry.

Hours later I told Lew that these actions needed to stop, before he seriously injures one of the children. He tore into me, telling me that something was wrong with me because I shouldn't be concerned about his hitting, restraining, throwing or using physical force on us. He told me how weird this was and that I should seek therapy for my intolerance to these actions. I could see that we were going nowhere, and so I stopped trying.

The next day I called Jeff Levy, one of the therapists who had been seeing us for abuse counseling. I wanted Jeff's direct impressions of what he observed in Lew. Jeff said:

"I see Lew as abusive." He added, "Lew has a problem with violence, and he uses what he is reacting to to justify his violence." Jeff further explained, "Lew comes from a family of violence where he witnessed a lot of domestic violence and physical abuse in his home."

I asked Jeff what he recommended, because I didn't observe Lew improving. I asked him two questions. First, I said, "Tell me if abuse, as you see in Lew, ever changes?"

There was a pause and he said, "The person has to want to change." He noted that Lew had once made the first step in that he had initially admitted that he had a problem with abuse. Where Lew was at this juncture was unclear to Jeff, but he made me realize that as long as one remains in denial, nothing is likely to change.

I then asked Jeff if he saw me and my children in danger. I felt his empathy toward my fear, and my question seemed to pose some awkwardness for him. He stated that he was uncomfortable responding to that question and merely acknowledged how difficult it must be for me. I recall hanging up the phone and crying. I felt there was no hope and did not know where to turn.

*   *   *

During the course of this month my father's status worsened. A call from my mother came and I knew I needed to get to California if I were to see my Dad again. He was in the hospital and there was significant concern as to whether he would make it. I arranged for Lisa to stay at the house around the clock until I returned. She was well aware of what was going on and promised me that she would take care of the children in my absence. She knew to stay with them at all times. I knew that Lew's outbursts would be curtailed by her presence, because when she was around he typically let her take care of matters. Lisa dealt with the children from the heart and was able to manage them quite effectively.

When I got to California my Mom and I drove to the hospital to see my Dad. As I walked in the door of his hospital room, Dad was sitting on the bed and tears rolled down his face. I had never before seen my father cry. I felt he knew he was dying. I don't know if my mother recognized how Dad was feeling because his expression was one of sheer pleasure to see me, along with his gentle tears. We visited and it was our last joyous time together.

As family was arriving, I retreated into one of the off rooms in the hospital to regain my strength. I recall sitting in this cold room in which there were two chairs and a desk with a telephone. I pulled one of the chairs up to a window and sat facing the outdoors, closed my eyes and slipped into one of the most profound and deepest meditations that I have ever had. During this period of sitting, I had a clear, sharp, intense and distinct feeling of a solid iron object in my chest. As I focused on it, within moments it expanded and I felt it as though it were coming out of my sternum with such impactful inertia busting from me. The intensity of this sensation alarmed me, and I eventually broke its hold and eased back into my everyday physical presence. I sat with what had occurred, resting to regain my composure. In the minutes that lingered, I thought to myself that I had experienced that sensation of when people literally assume the symptoms of those close to them. In my understanding of this moment, I thought how incredible that I may have been feeling the tumor that was interfering with my father's breath and taking his life.

Of course, I did not tell anyone of this experience. I held it as sacred and went on my way to join my family in the matters before us. In the days that followed, serious decisions were ahead. Dad had a pneumonitis caused by the radiation and his lungs were seriously impaired. He was placed on large doses of prednisone in hopes to decrease the inflammation and tumor growth in his lungs, and was relocated to the Intensive Cardiac Care Unit.

We had a family meeting between the Doctor and my mother, brothers and myself, in which we decided to place Dad on a respirator for a few days to see if the treatment would work. At the time we were all making the decision, the Doctor told us that this was a very difficult decision and was a personal matter for each of us. I thought the difficult part was placing him on the respirator, and at that time I didn't realize that there was much more to this decision.

Putting Dad on the respirator was extremely difficult for all of us. The Doctor came in and he held Dad's hand and told Dad that we were going to try this and asked if that was what he wanted. Dad said, "Yes." Then, there was a struggle initially to get it set up. As the nurses were prepping the area, I recall my mother and I in the room and Dad being agitated, and he called out: "Audree (my mother) turn out the lights." On some level I felt he was talking about the bigger lights, but couldn't grasp it all in the moment. We proceeded with the plan and Dad was successfully maintained on the respirator. My mother and I stayed at the hospital until the wee hours that evening, praying, hoping, comforting Dad and not knowing what was next.

I drove us home that evening from the hospital in San Diego to her house in San Marco. As I was driving, my mother was talking and suddenly something shifted in me and I felt like I was high, actually more than high. The highway opened up and I experienced it as wide as it was long. I had such a brilliant surge of expansive bliss pouring from me and expanding within me. I think I told mother something miraculous was happening, but I couldn't put words on it. It was absolutely one of those experiences that gives meaning to the meaning of life. During this drive, I was keenly aware of my desire for Dad to have some communion with God as I had known before he die. In retrospect, I recognize that he was probably having it in that moment, as I was, but I could not comprehend this at that time.

Mother and I arrived home and I was still radiating this incredible boundless feeling, and mother thought I was just over tired. We both went to bed and, as I laid on her guest bed, I remained conscious for what appeared to be the evening and witnessed my dreams. This experience was not foreign to me as it was something I had known on various retreats over the years. I simply honored it and saw it as an extension of what had occurred before. I believe that I actually fell asleep in the morning for a few hours, in some unconscious traditional sleep.

When I awakened, my mother and brother were trying to get us out of the house to get back to the hospital. My brother, Bobby, was quite upset with me for not waking up earlier. His coming over to the house interfered with his going directly to the hospital and he was angered at me, saying that my actions cheated him out of his having those last few hours with Dad. When we got to the hospital we were all rushing about and converging with the Doctor to determine what next.

The medication wasn't making a difference, and Dad's condition remained the same. The Doctor informed us that he was going to take Dad off the respirator that day, and told us this was the time to say good-bye to Dad. My mother and brothers appeared to be in agreement with this plan, but I kept thinking of my vague recollection of the original agreement. I said, "I thought we were going to give the medication a few days to see if it would work in bringing down the mass and, if it didn't work, then we would take Dad off the respirator." I was the only one hanging onto this plan, which became the beginning of our different perspectives on Dad's dying.

I asked my mother to bring in the Rabbi for a blessing and told her that I wanted to ask him for assistance in what was before us. An Orthodox Rabbi came to the hospital because we were not able to locate a Reformed Rabbi that was available in the moment. He talked with each of us; me, my father's sister and my mother. He said, "In the Jewish faith we do not remove someone from a respirator, as this is taking life." He explained that once you catch someone and interrupt the dying process, "in our faith we wait until some natural event occurs yielding death." His comments made perfect sense to me and were in total congruence with what I had experienced the night before. I recognized that if one had not met God in life, that dying was the occasion to do so, and natural death enabled this to happen.

So from my perspective, I was wanting Dad to have his final communion with God before we took his life. The rest of my family felt prolonging it was putting Dad in agony. I stood at Dad's bed with the Rabbi and asked, "Is he in pain?" The Rabbi told me that the family was in more pain than Dad. I knew he was right, but didn't know how to reconcile our differences. I, in no way, wanted to encourage my father's suffering and could see that my mother and brother had reached their end after going through his cancer treatments for a full year. They were angered at me saying I was listening to the preaching of an Orthodox Rabbi, and since we were Reformed Jews his message was not appropriate for our family. I saw the absurdity here and realized that we were not going to see eye to eye on this one. I realized what it meant when people say that different perspectives in individuals can make for difficulty when a family member dies. I knew what was going on between me and my family was temporary and would resolve itself over time.

We decided to follow the Doctor's recommendation and each had an opportunity to have private time with Dad before he was taken off the respirator. During my time, I told Dad how much I loved him, all he meant to me, that I would fulfill the projections we made together, and how I would see that his grandchildren grew up to be as sound, solid and caring as he. I promised that the children would always have an animal and that I would continue to talk to him as long as I was alive. I recall this as though it were yesterday. I was holding Dad's hand, but couldn't tell if the responses I was getting from him were his knowing that I was talking to him or random movements.

As he was taken off the respirator we all stood around his bed. It was quite painful watching him take his last breath. With the rift between me and my family over this, I gravitated to my sister-in-law, Ho Sun, Bobby's wife, for comfort after Dad took his last breath. In the days to come, I was numb.

I phoned Lew from the hospital and told him that Dad had died and asked him to please bring the children for the funeral. He said, "So, you pulled the plug." I fell into tears and don't remember anything further about our conversation. Within a few days Lew arrived with the children. It was so good to have us all together. At one point we were sitting on mother's white couch in their living room and the whole family was situated in a circle. Lew was making a blessing in Hebrew and it was quite touching. Little did I know he was setting the stage for his data collection and team building in preparation for a custody battle as we "sat shiva" over my father's death.

Lew spent the entire time during the days before and immediately following my Dad's funeral interviewing my family members, going out for walks with one or two of my relatives at a time. He was pitching them to side with him in helping him take my children away from me. Cleverly, Lew picked up on the rift between me and the family around taking Dad off the respirator as it was done, and used these bad feelings to launch his efforts to create an alliance with each of them to testify against me in an upcoming divorce that had not even been formally announced nor initiated.

The letters and phone calls between Lew and my family, during the month following my Dad's death, were disgraceful. Once my family realized what he was doing, they demanded that he stop calling them, but Lew refused to do so. He continued and enlisted them in petitions and subpoenas to assist in his severing me from my children. Finally, my brother put a stop to it by writing a letter and directing it to Lew and his legal team. My brother told Lew he saw him for what he was and knew of his abusing me and the children. He informed Lew that he was not going to let Lew use him to hurt me.

Immediately after our return back to Chicago, I was so turned off by Lew's manipulative use of this most sacred period of my Dad's days of remembrance that I couldn't interact with him. He made me sick. I avoided contact and went on my way, mourning my Dad's death, grieving my losses, re-uniting with my children and eventually setting out to fulfill the promises I had made to my Dad.

STATE OF ILLINOIS

JESS MCDONALD
DIRECTOR

DEPARTMENT OF
CHILDREN AND FAMILY SERVICES

406 EAST MONROE
SPRINGFIELD, ILLINOIS 62701-1498

INVESTIGATION OF SUSPECTED CHILD ABUSE OR NEGLECT--NON-INVOLVED SUBJECT
November 28, 1994

Jeanne Blumethal
1221 Thornapple
Northbrook, IL 60062

Dear Ms. Blumethal,

                              RE: SCR# - 0596497- A
                              Name - Blumenthal, Lewis

You were previously notified that this Department was investigating a report of
suspected child abuse or neglect in fulfillment of its responsibilities under
law.

After a thorough evaluation, we have determined the report to be "indicated."
This means that credible evidence of child abuse or neglect has been found.

Although the report has been indicated, you were not named as a person
responsible for the child abuse or neglect.

Information on this report will remain in a confidential file in the State Central Register of child abuse and neglect reports. Access to the register is
governed by State law. You may request a copy of the report; however, it will
not include the names of any persons who made the report or cooperated in the
investigation.

If you think that all or part of the report is inaccurate, you may request that
the report be amended or destroyed. The Department has an appeal process which
is used to consider such requests. A full explanation of the appeal process will
be sent when your request for an appeal is received. By law your request must
be made in writing within 60 days of the date of this letter.

A request for a copy of the report or a request for an appeal must be made by
writing to me at the above address. If you request an appeal of the "Indicated"
finding within the 60 day time frame, a copy of the report will be sent to you.
Please do not call for information as it cannot be released over the phone.

All requests for information should include:
- Your full name and address, including Zip Code
- The full name(s) of the child(ren) in the report
- The SCR case number which appears in the upper right-hand corner of this letter

If an attorney is making a request on your behalf, a notarized authorization
from you will also be necessary.

                              Sincerely,

                              Edward E. Cotton

                              Edward E. Cotton, Administrator
                              State Central Register

2B40

Abuse Finding by the Department of Children and Family Services

CHAPTER 8

Perpetrator as Legal Enemy

The Divorce Foundation

House Victim to Court Litigant

Another Emergency Order of Protection

Initially, I was raw in the weeks that followed Dad's death. Slowly, I regained my sense of me in the world as an adult embodying that in Dad which I cherished, and it expanded within me. I felt I could let Lew go, as I trusted in my own inner strength. My life no longer had to be around pleasing the un-pleasable, jumping through meaningless hoops, and reaching for carrots, never to be delivered. I longed a life of respect, without walking on eggshells and remaining open to a stream of continuous violations.

I spent the month of January repairing the disturbances Lew managed to create in my immediate family. I stopped asking Lew about his failed promise to go into therapy with the psychiatrist, because I knew he had no intention of going. At the earlier suggestion of counsel, I began keeping meticulous records of the ongoing altercations in our home. After several weeks of this, I could see a pattern of a jolting and numbing incident weekly and numerous minor hits, cracks, rug burns, ring marks, and abusive battering to the children by Lew several times per week. Divorce became imminent. I called everyone I knew who had knowledge of the divorce community of lawyers to get referrals and started interviewing seriously over the next month.

* * *

Before divorce proceedings were initiated, Lew and I attempted two last ditch efforts to salvage our marriage. At the time I thought they were last ditch efforts, but now as I look back I recognize that we were simply going through the motions of dealing with last minute reservations before our final actions to sever the marriage. During Spring break of 1995, we attempted a family vacation to see "if we could keep the family together." We went to Mexico, and it was a total disaster. Lew and I had conversations all seeming to result in bitter fighting, which escalated into some rather outrageous threats.

In one effort on April 6, 1995, we were sitting on the patio of our hotel room talking about our situation. Our conversation appeared to be going nowhere except into the spiraling bickering, fault finding and thwarting of accountability that characterized most of our "heart-to-heart" conversations during the marriage and all of them since Lew's domestic battery arrest. I recall expressing my frustration, saying, "Talking to you feels like hitting my head against a concrete wall." Lew was telling me that there was something wrong with me for being repulsed by seeing welts on my child and my feeling nauseous in the face of the other altercations to them and to me. He was angered by my going to the police and concerned about "what was going to happen to us" by virtue of my reaching out. Somehow the conversation moved to our openly saying, "Why don't we just get a divorce."

I could feel us both vacillating and, in a moment of compassion, I said: "I understand a major reason for your struggling with the decision to stay together, or not, maybe your concern about being with the children." I meant splitting our time with them, how much, when and the back and forth that this would involve. There was no threat, no meanness, nothing hostile about my demeanor or tone; all that came from me in this moment was the concern of one parent reflecting with another about the realities of breaking up a family and how we would share our time with the children. Lew's interpretation of my statement was far different from the way I had intended. His body lunged forward into fighting mode and an oral dart was released from him that literally changed my life.

"I'm going to BUTT FUCK YOU in this divorce," he said and then promised, "I'm going to DESTROY YOU as I take the kids from you." With hatred and vengeance he added, "We'll see who breaks first!!!!"

Hearing this left me shaking in a way similar to the impact of his other threats, which had penetrated into my very being. I couldn't listen any longer and got up and walked away. I recall ending the heated dialogue by saying, "I guess we can't talk about this." I told Lew there was nothing more for me to say. Being with him for the balance of the trip was like traveling with a stranger, mixed with moments of knowing I was clearly with an enemy. I did my thing and he did his, and when we came together the tension built. I could hardly wait to get home.

In the days after our return to Chicago, I tried to come to grips with his comments. I couldn't understand where he was coming from at that time. From my perspective, I assumed we would be breaking up the marriage, but I never anticipated that we would be fighting over the children. It had never even occurred to me as something that Lew would want, as I had been their primary caretaker over the years, and I didn't think Lew wanted the responsibility of or the commitment to the children. Further, given his well-documented history of abuse to the children and myself, I assumed that he'd have no standing for such a mission, to sever me, the protective parent, from our children. First of all, he was the abuser and, secondly, I was not unfit. So, in my mind I couldn't comprehend the cause or the potential of his threat.

I wrote it off as Lew being vicious and merely unrealistic. Both my family and attorneys assured me that *an abuser can't fight for custody, much less get it.* So I proceeded with confidence in my preparations for divorce. I met with two law firms and secured as much information about divorce and family law as I could assimilate at the time. There was so much to process and the emotions that came forward made this difficult. I assumed that Lew was doing his homework as well, because I observed a radical shift in his demeanor toward me and a subtle shift in the delivery of his verbal violence toward the children. His attorney may have told him not to hit the children.

The following exemplifies Lew's effort to restrain himself. On April 15, 1995, Lew and Brad were having one of their typical fights emerging out of a power struggle. Lew was sitting at his desk in his home office and Bradley was in his room working on an art project. Lew wanted Bradley before him at once.

"Come here," Lew called.

I assumed that Bradley did not leave what he was doing and yield to Lew's command, because Lew repeated firmly, sternly and with growing anger, "Come here, right here, right now." Bradley went over to his father, but did not stand in the place his father wanted him to stand.

"You don't respect me," said Lew.

"Because you don't respect me," Brad responded.

Lew's anger escalated into rage and he yelled, "I'm going to knock your head off!!!!" Screaming louder Lew said, "When you're old enough to defend yourself, I'm going to BEAT the hell out of you!!!"

I overheard them and rushed down the hall where I saw Bradley shaking. I took Bradley back into his room and once again promised, "Mommy is going to stop this." This time I added, "Trust it's coming." I continued comforting Bradley, and Lew left us alone.

Lew's adding "when you're old enough to defend yourself" in front of his threat suggested to me that he had been informed by one of the people looking into our lives that it was wrong to strike a child of weaker strength than he. However, I saw that Lew was no further along in the way he choose to reconcile his strength relative to the child's vulnerability, that being: give the threat of the violence to come. In my mind, Lew was still dealing with conflict through abuse, and I saw this as psychologically damaging to the children. What I didn't realize at this juncture was that abuse is a syndrome primarily about control. What I learned over the next four years is that domestic violence is not only about violence; violence is one of the manifestations, but rather this syndrome is more about control. In the chapters to come I will show how this understanding was revealed to me. It wasn't until I could fully grasp this that I could break the cycle of abuse.

*   *   *

Days before the sacred divorce petition, Lew and I had our last conversation, presumably to grab at whatever last thread remained just in case it was sufficient to hold the two of us together. We were sitting at our breakfast table outside of our kitchen, where many family discussions took place. There was some talk about whether we could make it together and what it would take for each of us to want to try to stay together. I told Lew that I needed him to follow through with the commitment that he made when I dropped the criminal charges. I reminded him of his promise for abuse treatment with the psychiatrist.

Lew somehow maneuvered the conversation away from his promise and, as usual, the focus shifted to me. He told me that he could only stay with me if I gave up meditation.

"Will you stop meditating?" He said, "Give it a try so I can see if I like you without your meditation."

His request seemed ridiculous to me. I felt that our problems stemmed from violence and I couldn't grasp how my routine taste of non-violence, which was private, innocent and discrete, could compromise any relationship. In fact, I clearly knew that the meditation was enriching me as a human being, making me a more patient, compassionate, loving, happy and vital person. Lew knew I had come to rely on the meditation. There's no doubt it provided me a sense of wholeness, which he longed to take from me. The solace of meditating served to offset being bombarded with Lew's ongoing abuse. In retrospect, I realize that it is what kept me solid in the face of adversity and pure in the midst of Lew's hatred and rage. There was no way I could give that up; I needed it to survive with Lew in my life.

I paused as I reflected on his request and looked into my hands and said nothing. Initially I thought I could tell him "yes," and keep the practice to myself even more than I had done before. But the integrity of me, as I had come to know it in meditation, gently opened up in all its dignity.

I looked at Lew and gently said, "No."

"Well, then that's it," he said.

He pushed himself away from the table, got up and walked out of the room. I felt my Dad's inner strength with me and simply sat there quietly, knowing all would be well regardless of the outcome.

I could feel Lew's internal preparations for divorce and saw his exterior maneuvering. It was very clear that this was where we were going. I just wasn't sure how we were going to get there. On some level, I feared carrying the burden of being the one to throw the towel in and still harbored some reservation about being in a divorce with an abuser. I privately mulled over my guilt and fear. Today, I recognize Lew had probably already taken care of his reservations about the divorce, and at that juncture he needed to share the responsibility. I believe his "proposal" in our last conversation enabled him to do as he wished without carrying all the responsibility for doing so.

On April 27, 1995 I was in my office at One East Wacker Drive. I had sent my secretary out to get us lunch and was taking care of some phone work. She and I had been quite busy working toward the development of my new business, the Chicago Center for the Treatment of Pain and Stress. We were going to take a break for lunch. From my back corner office, I heard someone pounding at the receptionist's window very loud. I knew that my secretary had the key and so it couldn't have been her.

Startled, I went to the front and heard a man calling, "Dr. King, I have something for you." I opened the door leading out into the patient waiting room, and the man said, "Are you Dr. King?" I answered, "Yes, I'm Dr. King." He told me he had some papers for me. My heart started pounding and I asked him to come into the office. We walked down the corridor together and he gave me Lew's Petition for Dissolution of Marriage. I was flooded with shock and exhilaration, simultaneously. When I recognized what this was, I welcomely said, "Oh, thank you." He looked at me with surprise. I could tell that I did not have the run of the mill reaction to receiving these kind of papers. It was as though Lew had done it for me. I was relieved. Now there was direction and no more sitting on the fence.

I called David Grund, an attorney, who I previously interviewed, to inform him of the delivery of the Petition. He arranged to see me that day. Mr. Grund had already been appraised of my marital situation and Lew's abuse to me and the children. He insisted that we obtain an Emergency Order of Protection. He asked me for no money, took me by the hand, assured me that he had personal knowledge about abuse and told me that he would protect me and the children. I felt his authenticity in his knowing about abuse and followed his lead.

We went to the Daily Center Court House in downtown Chicago, Cook County. He provided a synopsis of the salient incidents of domestic violence by Lew to me and the children, and immediately obtained an Emergency Order of Protection against Lew. No questions were asked, as it was quite obvious that we were in need of this protective order. Bradley, David, Marc and I were all listed as the protected parties, and Lew was removed from our home and restrained from contact until a further hearing. I was granted temporary custody of the three children and we were to reside in the marital residence.

The no contact portion of the Order did not stop Lew from being in contact with me and the children. I was reminded of the way he had ignored the first "no contact" requirement placed by the Northbrook Police. What was obvious was that Lew appeared to see himself as above the restrictions of this "authority."

As per my attorney's recommendation, I notified the children's school and the Northbrook Police of our Protective Order and changed the locks at our residence. However, when I went to pay the locksmith, I learned that I no longer had access to our visa, and suddenly I realized that moneys were being cut off.

After the locksmith left, I received a phone call from Mary Jo inquiring about our status. Evidently, Lew had informed her office of his being removed from our house. I told her that we began divorce proceedings and she said, "*Expect the system to fail you.*" Her words were deeply imprinted in my mind, though I did not grasp the meaning of what she said at the time. It hadn't even occurred to me to ask her what she meant. I felt her compassion and that seemed to satisfy me.

Continuing to go through the motions as per counsel, I went to my bank safety deposit box where I had stored photographs over the years of bruises on me and the children. He wanted me to secure all of the evidence that I could gather in preparation for our upcoming Evidentiary Hearing to keep our Order of Protection in place. I brought the box into one of the little rooms and closed the door. I sat down with my box on the table in front of me, and as I opened it and started pulling the photographs out, my stomach turned inside out and vomit came forward. I had not realized how long and how many photos I had accumulated. All of a sudden I felt a sense of a serious sickness both inside and around me.

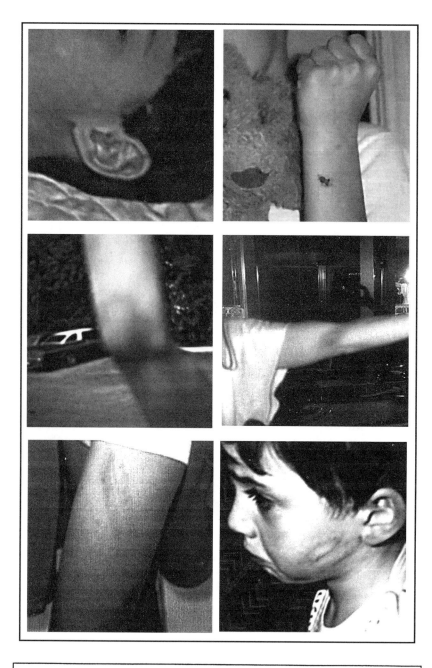

Marks of Family Abuse:
Bruises and Injuries to Mother and Children

CHAPTER 9

The Civil Finding of Abuse

The Evidentiary Hearing

Lew's Abuse Finding

Plenary Order of Protection

The Evidentiary Hearing opened the door for our family illness to be formally, socially and legally identified. This Hearing was the most cathartic experience in the history of my life with Lew. It was held as an emergency because of the fact that it concerned abuse, children and an Order of Protection. The Hearing began on Friday May 19, 1995 in the early afternoon and continued until completion through Sunday, May 21, 1995. Larry Starkoff, David Grund's partner, served as my counsel and Lew was represented by Joy Feinberg, a female lawyer specializing in custody. The children had an attorney assigned to them by the name of David Wessel. However, I do not recall Mr. Wessel participating in any line of questioning during this Hearing, other than to observe and, toward the end, negotiate Lew's visitation with the children via the Court.

The Hearing was conducted in the Daily Center in downtown Chicago in room 1905, Judge Timothy Evans' Courtroom. The 1905 courtroom is one of the largest courtrooms on the floor, with wood walls and high ceilings, giving a vast spacious yet warm feeling. Initially, I came to know this space as a place of justice for me and my children. Energetically, it was a place were I had come to know and express my greatest vulnerability and ultimately learn where my real invincibility truly resides.

The Hearing began with opening statements by counsel and then the securing of testimony from three witnesses brought in by my attorney: Maria Rodregus-Hallisey, the police social worker; Jerome Levin, my counsel on Lew's criminal charges; and Jeff Levy, one of the psychotherapists from our abuse counseling. Maria Rodregus-Hallisey's testimony revealed a clear understanding of Lew's abuse to me and the children by a third party. It was obvious that I had been reaching out to her, and even after police intervention the incidents continued. Her perception of the incidents from her interviews with me and Bradley validated the existence of domestic violence in our family.

Mr. Levin's testimony disclosed the basis of the "promised" agreement, which served as the conditions for my dropping the criminal charges of domestic battery against Lew. He stated Lew's proposed commitment to participate in individual psychotherapy for abuse with a psychiatrist two times per week. Mr. Levin's testimony substantiated Lew's recognition and admission of his abuse to us and the need for professional therapeutic intervention.

As these witnesses put forth testimony on the record, I felt I wasn't alone. It was as though my message was now being expressed by something beyond me, a force within others' witnessing my predicament. I was also aware that my message was being heard with interest and intrigue to hear more, as my attorney pulled forth testimony and the Judge listened. The ambient sensitivity budding in the courtroom was further enhanced for me as the court reporter looked over at me while the police social worker was speaking and gave me a gentle loving node with her head. I felt her saying with her body and gestures; we hear you and it will be okay.

The momentum began and, as is typical of court procedure, it was met with much resistance. Jeff Levy was called to the stand and more time was spent attempting to prevent this man's testimony from being placed on the record by Lew's counsel than one might ever expect in a case like this. My attorney's persistence enabled the truth of Jeff's perceptions concerning the danger to me and my children to be disclosed. Though inadvertently, it was quite obvious.

I was the next witness called to the stand. My heart was pounding as I was being sworn in before the court reporter and the Judge. I felt myself getting both excited about the prospect of speaking my truth and fearful of not knowing how to tell my story; and then there was the anxiety of merely talking and exposing my inner world to the strangers before me. I had not really been prepared for giving testimony and had never before sat in a witness chair in an open courtroom. I had no idea how this was going to proceed, and wondered how I was going to get the story out. It occurred to me that I hadn't even told Mr. Starkoff the story, and Mr. Grund wasn't with us in the courtroom. All I recall is Mr. Starkoff saying to me, "I'll ask the questions and you just give the Court your answers." A junior partner accompanying Mr. Starkoff said to me before I was called to testify, "You know your story; it's inside of you. Mr. Starkoff will ask the questions to draw it out."

Mr. Starkoff asked the questions and, indeed, he did draw out six hours of testimony from me on May 20, 1995 covering ten years of domestic violence by Lew to me and our children. He started most of the inquiry with questions like: "Calling your attention to..." Then he stated the date and asked if there was an altercation. In my responding, I told much of our story. I relived in full blown emotional color nearly thirty separate incidents of physical and psychological abuse to me and my children. I saw the places where these blows occurred, heard the words exchanged, smelled the odors associated with each episode, while my body was demonstrating how it was pushed, shoved, pulled, hit, dragged and battered. The tears flowed as I became that vulnerable woman blindly trapped in a family nightmare. The recount of my children's stories was as though I was telling my own; they were my own. I felt such pain as I enacted their smacks, cracks, belting, and the resulting impact to their bodies, their emotions and their innocent beings. There were pictures of bruises and marks on all of us, hospital records and police reports, providing a litany of irrefutable evidence.

At one point, I recall losing myself in reporting my child's words and I gazed off at the court reporter. She was crying as I was speaking and I was touched by the way my words and our experience was impacting her. There were a few occasions when I looked directly at Lew and saw him crying. At one point, he leaned forward in his chair and placed his head in his crossed arms on the table. I watched his body bobbing like a child weeping at his desk. Our family problem was no longer a secret.

Midway into my testimony the Court took a lunch break. All counsel congregated into a little room adjoining the courtroom. I was getting up from the witness stand and Lew was sitting where he had been during the proceedings, at a table alongside the parameter of the courtroom to my left. As I stepped down, clutching a wad of wet Kleenex in one hand and my purse under my other arm, I looked up at Lew and he was signaling me to come over to him. It was a tender gesture, like his old familiar come over here; kind of demanding, but wanting to deliver something affectionate. I knew this gesture very well and I really wanted to go to him. On some level, I thought maybe he had the "I'm sorry" that I had been wanting for the last 10 years. I wanted it so much and I feared getting it as well. I knew if he offered it, I could have easily fallen into tears and allowed him to touch my heart. I knew I was vulnerable after reliving that testimony and was concerned that I would get sucked back into loving him and then trapped into remaining his victim.

I took a deep breath and continued walking straight on until I exited the courtroom. Like a confused child, I retreated into the bathroom and started to cry and cry and cry. I just let it flow because I knew I could not stop what was coming forward. After some time passed, I looked at myself in the mirror and saw this beautiful and pathetic woman, dressed in a lovely off-white $300 designer suit. I was aware of my striking facial features and the makeup rolling down my cheeks. It occurred to me that I needed to pull myself together, so I cleaned my face, drank some water and assured myself I was leaving behind this nightmare of abuse.

*   *   *

My counsel, his junior associate and I left the courthouse and walked down the street to get some lunch. In my uneasiness, I asked my counsel, "Do you think the Judge heard me, and does he understand what's going on?" I asked this question even though I kind of knew the Judge did hear me, as I could tell by his responsiveness to me on the stand and the look in his eyes as I talked about the abuse; but, I needed more assurance and so I asked the attorneys.

They both replied with support and enthusiasm. They told me to keep going, and assured me that I was doing fine. I appreciated their support, but wasn't sure what to make of their enthusiasm. They said, "You were so authentic, Jeanne. You were even apologizing to Lew from the stand during your testimony." At the time I didn't quite get the impact of what they were saying, but it appeared that they were happy that my victimhood and battered mentality was reflected in the testimony.

It occurred to me that they were correct in their recollection of me apologizing to Lew from the stand. I told Lew "I'm sorry" when I revealed my efforts to reach out to my obstetrician (who was also Lew's colleague) to protect myself behind Lew's back. I lived those years muting out my personal potency in front of Lew to keep peace. Now, I recognize this was part of how I kept the abuse dynamic in tack. In my longing to keep abuse at bay, I enabled it.

*   *   *

At the end of my testimony toward late afternoon on Saturday, I was informed by my counsel that the following day would be one in which Lew's counsel would cross-examine me. I had no idea what that meant, and he assured me that I would do fine. I was emotion-ally drained upon my exit from the courtroom that day, and was taken back by a rather peculiar encounter I had with David Wessel, the man who called himself the children's attorney. He said nothing to me about any of my testimony and expressed no interest in any further information about the horrific impact of Lew's abuse on our children. I was surprised at his demeanor and his seemingly inappro-priate focus for the moment.

David Wessel is a man in his 40's, short and meek in appear-ance, with dark blond hair and a pot belly at the time. He seemed to be my height and, more often than not, had his fingers in his mouth, biting at his nails and cuticles. He stepped up to me as I was crying, consumed by the emotion that had come forward in my testimony, and in a peculiar panicky fashion he said, "We must arrange for the children's visitation with their father." I can't recall if supervised visitation or no contact was in place at this juncture. The comment in and of itself seemed appropriate, but what puzzled me was Mr. Wessel's timing and his indifference to all else that had transpired in the Hearing.

*   *   *

All parties, including attorneys, Lew and myself reconvened in court on Sunday, May 21, 1995. Instead of proceeding with further testimony, Lew's counsel elected not to cross-examine me and Lew put forward no defense to anything that was said the day before. This was interpreted by my counsel as a hands-up acknowledgment by Lew and his counsel of the fact that my testimony could not be refuted. I was told that it was a unanimous recognition of the abuse problem in our family. At one point I even overheard Lew's counsel speaking to him, telling him that he had a "serious problem" and needed to "get therapeutic help."

My attorneys met with me in the small room adjoining the courtroom and told me that Lew wanted to enter into an "agreement," granting an Order of Protection for me and the children and giving me temporary custody of the children. The children and I were given exclusive possession of the marital residence and the property was off limits for Lew. Lew was given supervised visitation two afternoons per week and alternating weekends. The visits were to commence once an appropriate supervisor was hired. There was also psychiatric intervention for Lew which was required as part of this Order. It was all set forth on paper and read into the record, and then the Judge gave his findings.

We stood before the Judge all in a row. Facing the Judge from left to right was: David Wessel, Lew Blumenthal, Joy Feinberg, Larry Starkoff and myself. The provisions of the agreement were articulated clearly and all parties were given an opportunity to ask questions and clarify their particular obligations and responsibilities. As this legal remedy was placed on the record, I felt my body open, relax and let go and was keenly alert and aware of the fact that everyone in the courtroom saw what had been going on in our family. With this acknowledgment and remedy, it felt like we were on our road to recovery.

After all the details of the agreement were spelled out, the Judge said, "Now, I'd like to make my Findings." He proceeded, giving his findings and said verbatim: "I find **prolonged and severe physical abuse to the wife and three minor children**." He went on to add details about "emotional abuse," "intimidation," "harassment" and "interference of personal liberties" by Lew to me, and expounded on the detrimental effects of Lew's actions on the children. The Judge looked at Lew and me and he said:

"The Petitioner (referring to me in this Hearing) has proven by a preponderance of evidence that the children were subjected to serious endangerment by the Respondent (Lew in this Hearing), and further that there was an adverse and detrimental impact on the children as a result of those actions. And to that end, it seems appropriate in this case that reasonable visitation be restricted and that supervised visitation be the order of the day." (Cited from Court Transcript, May 21, 1995, p. 8)

The Judge's language permeated every fiber of my being, and in that moment I felt the burden of my nightmare was being shouldered by something bigger than me. It was as though a debilitating weight was being lifted off of me. It was incredibly moving, so bittersweet, so comforting; and for the first time I felt certain that I was really heard.

My counsel and his junior associate escorted me out of the courtroom and the court reporter met us. She gave me a hug and I fell into tears. As she was hugging me, she confirmed that I was indeed heard. The attorney instructed her to get me the transcript of the Hearing of the Judge's abuse findings. He wanted me to have this portion of the transcript right away. She agreed to transcribe this part immediately and her phone number was given to me.

My attorneys and I proceeded out of the courtroom and Mr. Starkoff was exuberant about his observations when the abuse finding was provided by the Judge. He said, "I was watching Lew when the Judge was giving his finding, and Lew's mouth dropped open in shock." Mr. Starkoff said he believed that Lew and his counsel were under the impression that if Lew entered into an "agreed order" giving me our Order of Protection that it would go no further. They both believed that the Judge caught Lew by surprise.

Mr. Starkoff's junior partner expanded on the importance of the Judge giving Lew an abuse finding, in respect to our litigation. He said, "Now all we have to do is regroup and deal with the finances. *Custody is **not** an issue with this kind of abuse finding on the record.*" They both encouraged me to go home, take good care of myself and focus on a new and safe life for me and the children. I trusted my counsel, and for the first time I thought my children and I were safe. I was wrong.

IN THE CIRCUIT COURT OF COOK COUNTY

People ex rel. _____
_____ on behalf of
_____ self and/or behalf of

LEWIS B. BLUMENTHAL,
_____
Petitioner

-vs-

JEANNE KING BLUMENTHAL,
_____
Respondent

Case No. _____ 95 D 06150

☐ Independent Proceeding

☒ Other Civil Proceeding
(Specify) ___ Dissolution

☐ Criminal Proceeding

☐ Juvenile Proceeding

~~LEADS NO.~~ _____

PETITIONER Jeanne King Blumenthal	ADDRESS 1221 Thornapple	CITY Northbrook

☐ (Check if omitted pursuant to Statute)

RESPONDENT Lewis S. Blumenthal	ADDRESS 1221 Thornapple	CITY Northbrook

Birthdate 02/04/53	Sex M	Race White	Height 5'10"	Weight 150 lbs	Hair Brown Receding	Eyes Hazel	Social Security Number *(if known)* 3 2 4 4 0 2 0 6 0
(Required for LEADS)							

ORDER OF PROTECTION

4652   ☐ INTERIM   4652   ☒ PLENARY

ANY KNOWING VIOLATION OF ANY ORDER OF PROTECTION FORBIDDING PHYSICAL ABUSE, NEGLECT, EXPLOITATION, HARASSMENT, INTIMIDATION, INTERFERENCE WITH PERSONAL LIBERTY, WILLFUL DEPRIVATION, OR ENTERING OR REMAINING PRESENT AT SPECIFIED PLACES WHEN THE PROTECTED PERSON IS PRESENT OR GRANTING EXCLUSIVE POSSESSION OF THE RESIDENCE OR HOUSEHOLD, PROHIBITING ENTERING OR REMAINING AT THE HOUSEHOLD WHILE UNDER THE INFLUENCE OF ALCOHOL OR DRUGS AND SO CONSTITUTING A THREAT TO THE SAFETY AND WELL-BEING OF ANY PROTECTED PERSON, OR GRANTING A STAY AWAY ORDER, IS A CLASS A MISDEMEANOR. GRANT OF EXCLUSIVE POSSESSION OF THE RESIDENCE OR HOUSEHOLD SHALL CONSTITUTE NOTICE FORBIDDING TRESPASS TO LAND. ANY KNOWING VIOLATION OF ANY ORDER AWARDING LEGAL CUSTODY OR PHYSICAL CARE OF A CHILD, OR PROHIBITING REMOVAL OR CONCEALMENT OF A CHILD MAY BE A CLASS 4 FELONY. ANY WILLFUL VIOLATION OF ANY ORDER IS CONTEMPT OF COURT. ANY VIOLATION MAY RESULT IN FINE OR IMPRISONMENT. STALKING IS A FELONY.

(Definitions of prohibited conduct on reverse)

The following persons are protected by this Order: Jeanne King Blumenthal, Bradley Blumenthal, David Blumenthal and Marc Blumenthal

"The minor child/ren" referred to herein are: Bradley Blumenthal, David Blumenthal and MarcBlumenthal

Date, time and place for further hearing *(if Interim Order)*:

Date _____ Time _____ Courtroom/Calendar No. _____
Location _____

This Order was issued on:	This Order will be in effect until:
Date, May 22, 1995 Time, 10:00 a.m.	☐ Date _____ Time _____ ☐ vacated py court order ☒ Specified event: Termination of dissolution proceedings.

Order of Protection: May 22, 1995, page 1

BASED ON THE FINDINGS OF THIS COURT, ☒ WHICH WERE MADE ORALLY FOR TRANSCRIPTION, OR ☐ WHICH ARE SET OUT IN A SEPARATE INSTRUMENT FILED WITH THE COURT, AND WITH THE COURT HAVING JURISDICTION OF THE SUBJECT MATTER AND OVER ALL NECESSARY PARTIES, IT IS HEREBY ORDERED THAT:

☒☒ 1. With respect to all Protected Persons, Respondent is prohibited from committing the following:
☒ Physical abuse;   ☒ Harassment; ☒ Interference with personal liberty; ☒ Intimidation of a dependent;
☒ Willful deprivation; ☐ Neglect;   ☐ Exploitation; ☐ Stalking,

☒☐ 2. Petitioner is granted exclusive possession of the residence and Respondent shall not enter or remain in the household or premises located at:
1221 Thornapple, Northbrook, IL   Multiplex in
(This remedy does not affect title to property)   Deerfield

☒☒ 3. ☒ a. Respondent is ordered to stay away from Petitioner and other protected persons; and/or
Meadowbrook School, Northbrook, IL ,
☐ b. Respondent is prohibited from entering or remaining at
Sample Jeremiah, Tai-Kwon-Do, Northbrook, IL, 1 E. Wacker, Suite 3700 Chi. Ill
except for public service or special events of the children while any Protected Person is present; and/or

☐ c. Respondent is allowed access to the residence on (date) _____ at (time) _____ in the presence of
(name) _____ to remove items of clothing, personal adornments, medications used exclusively by the Respondent and other items, as follows: _____

☒ 4. Respondent is ordered to undergo counseling at To be determined with a psychiatrist
for a duration of _____

☐ 5. ☐ a. Petitioner is granted physical care and possession of the minor child/ren; and/or
☐ b. Respondent is ordered to:
☐ Return the minor child/ren _____ to the physical care of
_____ ; and/or
☐ Not remove the minor child/ren _____ from
the physical care of Petitioner or _____

☒ 6. Petitioner is granted temporary legal custody of the minor child/ren Bradley, David and Marc

☒ 7. ☐ a. Respondent is awarded visitation rights on the following dates and times or under the following conditions or parameters:
(No order shall merely refer to the term "reasonable visitation") Tues,Thurs,4p.m. & alt.
weekends from 6:00pm to Sundays 4:00pm, teleph contact daily with children
1 to 3 times maximum except for emergency,other calls over 3 to go thru attorney
for minor children
☒ b. Respondent's visitation is restricted as follows:
Suspended visitation only
SUPERVISED

☐ c. Respondent's visitation is denied.
(Petitioner may deny Respondent access to the minor child/ren if, when Respondent arrives for visitation, Respondent is under the influence of drugs or alcohol and constitutes a threat to the safety and well-being of Petitioner or Petitioner's minor child/ren or is behaving in a violent or abusive manner.)

☒ 8. Respondent is prohibited from removing the minor child/ren from Illinois or concealing them within Illinois.
☐ 9. Respondent is ordered to appear in Courtroom/Calendar _____ at _____
_____ on _____ at _____ AM/PM, with/without the minor child/ren.

☒ 10. Petitioner is granted exclusive possession of the following personal property and the Respondent is ordered to promptly make available to Petitioner said property that is in Respondent's possession or control, to wit:
1988 Mercedes Auto (300E), 1982 Corvette (stingray) household furniture,
furnishings and art work.
(This remedy does not affect title to property)

☒ 11. Respondent is prohibited from taking, encumbering, concealing, damaging or otherwise disposing of the following personal property:
1988 Mercedes Auto (300 E), 1982 (Stingray)household furniture, furnishings
and art work.
_____ , except as explicitly authorized by the Court.
☐ Further, Respondent is prohibited from improperly using the financial or other resources of an aged member of the family or household for the profit or advantage of Respondent or any other person.

☐ 12. Respondent is ordered to pay temporary support for ☐ Petitioner and/or ☐ the minor child/ren of the parties as follows:
$ _____ per _____ , starting _____ , payable ☐ through the Clerk of the Circuit Court,
or ☐ directly to Petitioner

☐ 13. Respondent is ordered to pay $ _____ as actual monetary compensation for loss(es) to _____
on or before _____
☐ Further, Respondent is ordered to pay court costs in the amount of $ _____ and attorney fees in the amount of $ _____
to _____ in connection with any action to obtain, modify, enforce, appeal or reopen any order of protection on or before _____

CASE NO. 95D 06150

Order of Protection: May 22, 1995, page 2

☑ 14. Respondent is prohibited from entering or remaining at the household or residence located at __**as previously indicated**__ _____ while under the influence of alcohol or drugs and so constituting a threat to the safety and well-being of any Protected Person.

☐ 15. Respondent is denied access to school and/or any other records of the minor child/ren and is prohibited from inspecting, obtaining, or attempting to inspect or obtain such records.

☐ 16. Respondent is ordered to pay $ _____ to the following shelter _____ on or before _____

☐ 17. Respondent is further ordered and/or enjoined as follows:

_____

☐ 18. The relief requested in paragraph(s) _____ of the petition is *(DENIED) (RESERVED)*, because:

_____

PLENARY ORDERS ONLY

This order shall remain in effect until

☑ 1. Two years following the date of entry of such Order, such expiration date being **May 22, 1997** _____, or such earlier date, as ordered by the Court, such expiration date being **termination of pending dissolution proceeding.**

☐ 2. Final judgment in conjoined proceeding is rendered.

☒ 3. This Order is modified or vacated (provided such Order is incorporated into the final judgment of another civil proceeding)

☐ 4. Termination of any voluntary or involuntary commitment, or until _____

☐ 5. Final disposition when a Bond Forfeiture Warrant has issued, or until _____ *(not to exceed 2 years)*

☐ 6. Expiration of any supervision, conditional discharge, probation, periodic imprisonment, parole, or supervised mandatory release, plus 2 years.

☐ 7. Expiration of a term of imprisonment set by this Court, plus 2 years.

NOTICE: Upon 2 days notice to Petitioner, or such shorter notice as the Court may prescribe, a Respondent subject to an Interim Order of Protection issued under the IDVA may appear and petition the Court to re-hear the original or amended Petition. Respondent's petition shall be verified and shall allege lack of notice and a meritorious defense.

Attorney (or Pro Se Petitioner) Name   **Grund and Starkopf**

Address   **111 East Wacker Drive, 28th Floor**

City   **Chicago**

Phone   **312/616-6600**

Attorney   **1308**

Service by Facsimile ☒ will be accepted ☐ will not be accepted

Facsimile Number   **312/616-6606**

ENTERED
CLERK OF THE CIRCUIT COURT
AURELIA PUCINSKI

Date _____

Judge   MAY 2 2 1995

JUDGE TIMOTHY C. EVANS - 1592   Judge's No.

DEPUTY CLERK _____

SERVED IN OPEN COURT

CASE NO. **950 D6150**

From private to public
From home to court
From fantasy to reality
With blind faith ....

PART TWO

Domestic Violence Transformed Into Litigation Abuse

CHAPTER 10

Pseudo-Protection

Rebuilding the Nest

The Reconciliation Offer

Abuse is About Control

Financial Control: Litigation Control

Counsel's Reality Shatters Mine

What first presented as justice and a long overdue remedy, eventually became a legal nightmare and a forum for further abuse to me and my children. The legal proceedings that followed did not insure the end of our being abused, but rather marked the beginning of a new way to abuse us. For the first half of the first year I was completely blind to this dynamic being set in motion in the legal arena. I expected, I trusted and I sought justice from this judicial process. I was naive and very busy with the children.

On the night I came home from the final day of the Evidentiary Hearing, May 21, 1995, I was so relieved and light. I took the children out for ice cream. Inside I was celebrating what I saw as a major shift for us, and what counsel called "an extraordinary remedy." Externally, the children and I were celebrating Mommy being back home after three long days of being away. We had such fun. Going out for ice cream had become our way of ushering in any new event, rewarding ourselves for work well done, or just an excuse for having a good time.

*   *   *

In the weeks and months to follow, my days vacillated between taking care of my little family directly in our home and indirectly through the courts. First my attention went to getting the children ready for the end of the school year and taking care of the necessary preparations for summer camp. I also enrolled the boys in Tae Kwon Do Martial Arts and made a routine of these classes. There was much support that came from this group and the children blossomed in the training.

During this time of adjustment, we bought two animals. One was purchased just before the Hearing and the other a few months after. Marc had a well established liking for cats since he was 18 months old. A week before his sixth birthday, he and I were discussing what we would get for his birthday, May 1995. I wanted him to bond with an animal during this adjustment period and recalled the promise I made to my Dad about having animals in our home. After our discussion, I said, "Let's go to the nearby pet store and take a look." We walked into More Pets in Northbrook, and immediately Marc and I fell in love with a five week old soft white Himalayan Blue Point kitten. When the store manager put this little kitty in my hands, Marc and I melted. We walked away to think about it, and six hours later she was Marc's little "Kitty."

Dexter, our Golden Retriever, came into the family in a similar fashion as a birthday present for David and Bradley. Dexter was ten weeks old when the boys and I purchased him. I watched him go after David's shoe strings and was reminded of the famous Norman Rockwell photograph of the child with the dog. David quickly bonded to our new Golden Retriever, who looked a lot like the stuffed doggie David had been sleeping with since birth. The boys named our new puppy Dexter, and we enthusiastically house trained him and played with him for hours. It was quite clear to me that our new animals helped the boys cope with the changes in our family and the ups and downs of divorce.

*   *   *

During these initial weeks of adjustment, I received a call from David Grund, my attorney, to come to his office for a meeting. On the phone, he told me that we would be planning to arrange for obtaining money for child support, maintenance and legal fees for the proceedings. However when I arrived, Mr. Grund's personal office was filled with several attorneys from his firm, sitting around a table in his office. I was asked to come in and join them. The meeting began with one of his female associates addressing me.

"Lew's counsel has been in contact with our office and they want to know if you would be willing to reconcile with Lew and drop all matters related to the Evidentiary Hearing," she said.

I looked at the woman and then at David Grund and I said, "I need the Order of Protection and I don't think I can sleep with Lew until he completes the promised treatment."

I was flooded with visions of my dropping the criminal charges and knew if I did this again, I would be right back where I was before. I was not going to set myself up for Lew telling me there is no abuse problem and it is all in my head. I knew I couldn't go back to that. Just the thought of it made me sick.

"I can't be near him," I said to the female attorney. "I can't stand the way he smells." I explained that Lew had hurt me so much that his odor bothered me. They all looked at one another and then said we should proceed as we have set forth.

One of the attorneys left the room, and the others remained to inform me of what was ahead. I was told that there was an order for a custody evaluation, called a 604(b) evaluation. This made no sense to me, as I was under the impression that a custody evaluator would be consulted for the purpose of matters related to Lew's supervised visitation, not the determination of custody. I told David Grund that I believed Lew's desire to fight me for custody had nothing to do with his wanting the children, but rather had more to do with money.

Mr. Grund looked at me and said clearly, definitively and firmly, *"No, it's not about money; it is about **control**."*

He said it like he knew this as fact, with more certainly than he had words to articulate. I didn't quite get it at the time. While I was beginning to appreciate the connection between control and abuse, I did not understand the connection between control and litigation, much less abuse and litigation. Boy, was I naive. I had assumed that the court was omnipotently powerful and there to protect us – or at least do what was right, just and fair. I carried this belief as a way of protecting myself. I was projecting onto the court an expectation of "right" and "power." It is only today that I recognize how I empowered the court in the same way I empowered Lew. I had none and they had it all.

The more Mr. Grund spoke, the more I realized that he did know exactly what he was talking about, and even knew how it would play out and what the implications were to him and his law firm. David Grund is an attractive man, about 5' 10'', handsome facial features, average weight, and well put together. He shared with me that he was abused by his father as a child and he was quite familiar with what drives abusers. He expressed a grave concern that he would be working very hard on my case for very long hours, with Lew fighting on every issue. He said:

> "Your husband is going to fight this case like it is a six million dollar case, even though he will only have two million dollars to do it. Then, we'll get to court for the final judgment with two million dollars in legal fees and the Judge will say, 'Counsel, Why did you let these people spend so much money on this matter? – I'm cutting your fees in half."

Mr. Grund was quite candid with me in going on to tell me that he did not want to make such an investment of his time and legal resources, knowing that he would not be compensated for it. Intuitively, I knew he was right and, in the moment, I felt compassion for his predicament. But the idealist in me never thought his interests would supersede protecting me and my children. I thought, since I was the client and he initially showed compassion for my circumstances, that he would find a way to bring closure to the case, keeping the protection set in place for me and the children. I had assumed that attorneys follow the ethics guidelines concerning client's interest over their own. As a psychologist of numerous lawyers over the years, I knew of this "professional obligation." As a victim, I had become helplessly attached to him, hoping he would be instrumental in protecting us.

I was being awfully wishful and totally wrong. Mr. Grund realistically couldn't afford to carry my case, and I could not digest the full reality of that at the time. He had no ethical cause to bail out and no legal grounds to do so. Thus, what proceeded was a tactful way of his making his exit. I did not recognize this as it was happening.

*   *   *

Mr. Grund told me that we must turn our attention to the finances. He said that it was essential that I put together an income and expense affidavit and prepare a financial statement for the Court. He said that we would be doing this in order to secure legal fees for his firm as well as child support and maintenance for me. Following his direction to the "tee," I went home and put all of my check entries over the last year in my computer and compiled every expense that was needed for me to sustain the children in the lifestyle to which they were accustomed, as well as every fixed expense necessary to keep us in the marital residence. I remember spending the entire Memorial Day weekend doing this and keeping myself going by motivating myself with the thought that he would stick with us if he was going to get paid and I would be able to secure what the children and I needed because it was available from our marital resources. I kept saying to myself, "The money is here; my job is to show the Court our standard of living, and counsel will show the Court Lew's earnings."

Mr. Grund assured me that, since Lew's last reported net income was $450,000, we would be able to get what was necessary to keep the children in the house and his fees would come out of the marital estate. He said, "We'll get it from Lew." His confidence in our "getting the money from Lew" seemed reasonable. It was the only means to support us and the litigation.

Our family had been supported by Lew's income over the full course of our marriage. My professional practice, though it had earning potential, did not yet yield income, because my commitment for it to do so had only begun. Lew and I had a traditional family structure in which he was the primary "provider," and we were committed to my being with our children during their younger years. At the time, my annual income was less than our monthly fixed household expenses. All parties involved in our case knew of the gross disparity in our incomes. I was earning less that $10,000 from my business, which was two percent of Lew's income from his successful medical practice. The size of the estate was no secret either, and it was obviously sufficient to cover the cost of our litigation.

The problem, of course, was that Lew controlled his business income, our bank accounts and other investments, stocks and our pension. Lew controlled our financial resources – practically every cent – used to run our home, our family, our lives; and the Court never took that control away from Lew. They allowed him to maintain control over our estate which gave him the mechanism to continue to abuse us. I later learned from John Lietzau, a domestic violence expert, how this financial posturing enabled the main-tenance of the abuse cycle. Mr. Lietzau's contribution to my understanding will be detailed in Chapters to come.

On June 15, 1995 I went to court as scheduled for our Hearing on child support, maintenance and legal fees. I brought all of the information and documentation that I was told to compile. Lew and his counsel did not show up for the court Hearing. I was told that the Court was going to "order" that Lew pay the mortgage, taxes, insurance and $2900 per month for child support and maintenance. Ten thousand dollars from the estate was to go to David Grund's firm to cover his retainer fees. Instead of taking this offer, Larry Starkoff blew up and David Grund refused to accept this financial arrangement.

I told Mr. Grund that I could barely pay for food, and had no idea how we were going to pay our $5400 mortgage. I had become quite desperate, and was shocked that he did not take this money. A $10,000 retainer is what most lawyers would take for a divorce and custody case with an estate the size of ours. But, as Mr. Grund had made very clear, I don't think he really wanted to be "financially" retained, though he had already filed the appropriate papers legally committing him to represent me. This would have locked him into endlessly working for nothing, at least until he could create another scenario to exit.

He insisted that he wanted to hold out for more, and demanded having a trial. He said to me dispassionately, "You will have to beg, borrow or steal!!" I told him I did not know how to beg, could not get a loan and would not steal. We remained at an impasse. At some point in our conversation, he told me I should accept the support offer of $2900 and the money for the mortgage and not pay the mortgage. I could see this would set me up for the children losing their home, and I didn't think this was in their best interest to do this at the time. I was happy to take the offer as it was originally suggested, but my counsel wasn't satisfied with it. We were left with nothing except worries and unpaid bills, and I could see my counsel was not facilitating a remedy to our financial dilemma.

In desperation, I borrowed $20,000 from my mother to carry the children and I through until we got to trial, in hopes that Mr. Grund would follow through with his promised rigorous efforts to secure funding for the children, myself and his fees. My innocent faith in him was partly that I wanted and needed to believe in someone. What I hadn't come to grips with, at that time, was that Mr. Grund was not the person for me to place my trust in.

Prior to the scheduled Hearing for our support and legal fees, Mr. Grund informed me that he had reviewed my full financial disclosure and noted that I had a little over $15,000 in my business. He demanded that I give this entire amount to him "or else he would withdraw" as my counsel. He insisted that I empty my business *before and instead of* looking to our million dollar plus estate. I told Mr. Grund that this money was to pay off the construction costs of my office built-out to my landlord. I explained that if I didn't honor this commitment I would be in default on my new ten year lease agreement, and this would destroy my immediate future earning potential. I said that I was not in a position to "belly-up" on my business, as I needed to be able to rely on it for our future.

Mr. Grund knew that I could not count on Lew for anything and that I needed to become self-sufficient. Yet, his understanding of my predicament didn't enter into our negotiations.

He insisted, "I want to present you to the Court as a helpless victim."

"We already accomplished the victim part," I replied, "and now helpless is not what I need, psychologically."

I explained that the only way I could get through this was to empower myself, not make me more dependent on Lew. He watched my unwillingness to yield to his demand and became more frustrated with me.

With firmness and clarity in his voice he said, "You will never be controlled by another man again."

I didn't know what to make of his comment, but recognized that he saw something in me which I hadn't truly appreciated at the time. His parting words were, "You have seven days to think about it."

So, for seven days I thought about it and I realized that it would be absurd for me to throw out the entire investment that I had made over the last year on the construction of my new office, thus losing my lease and leaving me with no place for my practice and new business. His offer did not feel as tough it served me and so I refused. Seven days later, I received three notices from Mr. Grund's office to withdraw from my case. It was apparent to me that he wanted out. I recognized that it was not a good business decision for him to remain as my counsel in our case.

I called a friend, who was an attorney well-connected in the legal community, to vent my frustrations. He consoled me and told me that Mr. Grund's actions were typical of him. He recognized that Mr. Grund was a good litigator but said, "When Grund wants his money, he wants it and there's no seeing beyond it." He advised that I go to a law firm with good standing in the courts and work with someone that has a good relationship with Lew's counsel. A recommendation was given and I felt hopeful, once again.

Power and Control Wheel

The **Power and Control Wheel** illustrates various tactics used to establish and maintain power and control. Physical and sexual violence occupy the rim of the wheel, depicted to show it as the most extreme method for maintaining abusive power over another. The inner segments of the wheel display numerous abusive strategies used as coercive methods to establish control. Typically, one or more violent incidents are accompanied by a variety of the coercive strategies to establish a pattern of intimidation and control in the relationship.

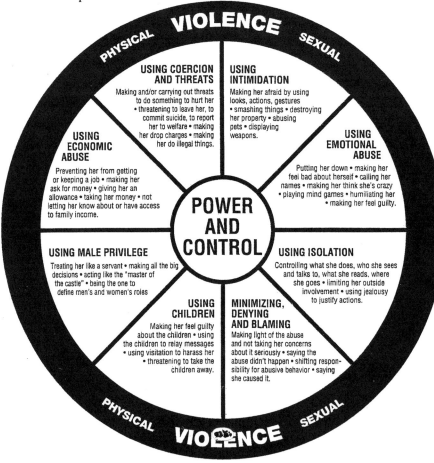

The Power and Control Wheel of the Domestic Abuse Intervention Project
Reproduced with permission by Minnesota Program Development, Inc.

CHAPTER 11

Permitted Abuse

Meeting Mr. Hopkins

The Stop Gap and Starve-Out

The Second Production

Air-Brushed Transcripts

Gasoline Kerosene Socks

D avid Hopkins from Shiller, DuCanto and Flick came to me with the highest of all recommendations. I was told he was from one of the most prestigious divorce law firms in the country and that he was a "peacemaker." The notion of working with a peacemaker was what was important to me. I was looking to bring closure to our marriage – not inflame matters in litigation.

July 1995, I met with Mr. Hopkins. He was quite professional and ever so warm. David Hopkins appeared to be in his late 50's, about 5' 11" and weighing over 200 pounds, most of which was around his middle. He was a very kindly looking gentleman, dressed in suspenders and a distinguished tie. The classic exterior of the "distinguished attorney" look was offset by his personal demeanor and his office, covered with piles of paper, like the professors in my college days, and pictures of hunting dogs on the walls.

In our first meeting, he told me that he was instrumental in writing the "Domestic Violence Act" and, with this experience, he was quite familiar with the issues in my case and the laws that would help me and my children. There was no question that Mr. Hopkins was superb in rhetoric and probably could have written any of the legal statues. However, this did not mean that he really understood domestic violence, nor would he be willing to act as a crusader for me and my children, at least not in domestic relations court.

He promised to bring closure to our divorce as efficiently as possible and assured me that *"no abuser can obtain custody of the children."* He provided me with the Domestic Violence Act, which he presented to me like he was showing off his own art. He pointed out that the laws don't provide for such and consoled me by saying, "Anybody can fight for anything, but that doesn't mean they will get it." He said we'd probably end up with some kind of a "pseudo-parenting agreement" just to appease Lew, and the children would continue to live with me. Not caring much about legal formality around the word "custody," I just wanted to be done with the marriage and know that the children and I were safe. I didn't care what we called it, I only wanted security and closure.

Immediately after I retained him, he reviewed the record and noted that my previous counsel had not filed a Response to Lew's initial Petition for Dissolution, nor had he prepared a Response to the same. He explained the importance of our doing this, saying that anything in the court record that is not responded to in a certain time period is considered uncontested or true (that is, not opposed or refuted by the other side). Within a matter of weeks he did what was necessary to file the proper paper work concerning these pleadings.

In Mr. Hopkins' swift manner, he then plunged forward to assist me in getting a court order for child support and maintenance and legal fees for the balance of the proceedings. I was impressed by his eagerness to dive in and take care of business. He was very much aware of my need for a support order from the Court, because he saw moneys withheld. I informed him that I had no idea how we were going to make ends meet month-to-month. He jokingly referred to Lew's strategy as the "starve-out" campaign. In fact during the first week of August, Mr. Hopkins had to rush into court for a "Stop

Gap" Order to get money so I could purchase items necessary to start the school year.

His bringing the starve-out to the Court did not stop Lew's campaign. For ten months the tension would start building for me around the third week of each month, as my mortgage had to be paid by the fifth of the month. During this period I became incredibly creative in finding ways to do more with little. As much as I hated worrying about how the bills would get paid, I truly felt blessed that the boys and I learned how to enjoy time without spending. It seemed to bring us together and into more creative and resourceful play.

While the adjustments that the children and I made were good and my ability to see and feel the silver lining was valuable, I hadn't realized until years later that this month-to-month money game was part of how Lew kept me in the abuse cycle. There were many times when I would call Lew to inform him that I had no money to pay the mortgage or pay for utilities. His standard response was, "I don't have to give you any money; there's no court order in."

*   *   *

On August 22, 1995, I was finishing up in my office, putting patient materials away from the day, and a fax came through from Mr. Hopkins. It was a court-ordered "Request for Production" Notice, detailing documentation that was being requested by Lew's financial attorney, Ira Feldman. There were over 25 separate entries on the list and it specified the securing of **All** my records, including every check, every statement and much more, dating back several years. The most amazing part of this request was that the production of documents was expected to be delivered by 12:00 noon the next day.

I called Mr. Hopkins immediately and told him that it would be virtually impossible for me to gather all of this by tomorrow. His response was that I should try my hardest to get as much of it as possible, because if I didn't have it all, this would give Ira Feldman cause not to cooperate in our securing a court order for child support and maintenance from the Court. I told him that I would do my best to pull the paper work together, but there was no way I could have it copied before it was to be delivered, as it would take every available hour just to gather it. He told me not to worry and promised that his office would copy all of my documents before sending them out to Ira Feldman's office. He assured me that the copying would be done while I was at his office tomorrow, and reiterated the importance of my having the information to his office on time.

At first I was angered that I hadn't been given more notice to comply with this production of documents. I left my office and went for a walk to cool down, and came back and meditated. This, as usual, renewed me. Something came over me that said, "give it your best, you need the money." I spent the night at my office gathering every document on that list that I could get my hands on. I came home in the middle of the night around 2:00 AM and continued compiling bank statements, credit card information and the balance of the information on the list. This became an all-night affair. I had collected more information than I could carry and needed a roller to haul three boxes of documentation downtown.

I arrived in his office in casual attire, looking like I had a "nighter," because I did. Ms. Warning, a junior associate from his firm, sat down with me and went over every document contained in my production and we made an inventory. I retained a copy of this for my records. The time was passing rapidly and Mr. Hopkins had not made arrangements for my documents to be copied, though he kept promising to do so. I informed Ms. Warning of Mr. Hopkins' commitment to have my originals copied before they were sent out, and informed her that I intended to wait for this to be done before my leaving. I expressed my concern about my originals, removed from my office, and told her that I could not leave without them.

Ms. Warning exited the room and came back saying Lew's Production was being delivered to their office within the hour. With an air of urgency she told me that my documentation had to be sent to Mr. Feldman's office within the hour in order for us to be in compliance with the Court Order. I insisted that my documents be copied and she told me that I had no choice in this matter. She said, "If we do something that is not in compliance with the Court Order, it will give them an out and cause for possible trouble." I wouldn't budge with Ms. Warning, so she called Mr. Hopkins in to talk with me.

Mr. Hopkins came into the office where we were working and promised me that he and I would retrieve all of my documents tomorrow at the scheduled deposition. He said that if I did not get these documents to opposing counsel, they could claim not to be ready for tomorrow's deposition. He forcefully said this could lead to incomplete discovery and would be used as cause to delay our Hearing on support, indefinitely. Having reached a point of total exhaustion, I yielded to this allowing Mr. Hopkins to use my originals. I felt like I was between a rock and a hard place, as I could not feed my children with these documents, and I may not be able to feed them unless I gave them up.

The deposition proceeded as scheduled and the discovery was indeed complete. But still there was no court order for child support and maintenance for the next six months. So my counsel's urgency and my compliance did not appear to insure an expeditious court order, giving financial security to me and the children. Delays seemed to be the rule, not the exception and had nothing to do with me, my actions or our document production.

Forty per cent of my documents were never returned to us by Ira Feldman and the sixty per cent that came back were shuffled and looked like scrambled eggs. I was beside myself with anger and tears. Mr. Hopkins attempted to console me by telling me if I ever need any of the bank records that were released, I could easily obtain these directly from the bank. What he said seemed reasonable but I was still upset, having been accustomed to keeping organized records, and now the last four years of all my financial records were incomplete and in total disarray.

As the days worn on, I got over it, thinking things could be worse. I recall telling myself that at least the boys and I are healthy and now we are on our way to getting the funds that I need to keep our utilities turned on. What I didn't know at this time was that the stage had been set for what eventually became a nightmare of an "Abuse of the Discovery Process" and another legal strategy to harass me. Because I could no longer produce all original documents, I was repeatedly taunted with the possibility of a "default judgment" over future incomplete discovery of documents I no longer possessed. A default judgment is a judgment given without the defendant being heard in his or her own defense. In the Court's threatening me with this possibility, I was basically being told that Lew would be granted all he had requested, without my having a hearing. And of course, he had requested to take custody of our children.

*   *   *

On August 29, 1995 I received the transcripts of the Evidentiary Hearing of May 19-21, 1995. I had been expecting to receive this the first week in June, yet with my tug of war over money with David Grund, it never happened. I was relieved to have it, even though it was almost three months late. But then when I read the transcript of the final proceeding covering the Judge's abuse finding, I knew that the transcript had been changed. The Judge's actual "abuse finding" was stated by Judge Timothy Evans on May 21, 1995 after our agreement was entered at the close of the Hearing. However, in the transcript it had been placed in the first few pages as though it was given first, before the agreement was spelled out in the record. As I read on, I saw that the actual and exact wording of the abuse finding had been changed as well.

Now it read: "physical abuse, harassment and interference with personal liberties to wife ... and intimidation to minor children." But the "adverse and detrimental impact" of "serious endangerment" to the children resulting in the court remedy of "supervised visitation" was there and so were nearly 200 pages of text containing my complete detailed testimony of numerous physical altercations between Lew and the three children. Even I knew that my children's bruises, the belt welts, Bradley's dislocated and casted arm, David's rug burns, Marc's black and blue marks from his ears being pulled, the police reports, Lew's domestic battery arrest, the photographs and the testimony of the witnesses was far more than "intimidation." **It was physical abuse**. It was exactly as the Judge found it to be on May 21, 1995 **"prolonged and severe physical abuse to the wife and three minor children."** These words had been imprinted in my mind on that day and also typed in my journal, verbatim, on the evening of May 21, 1995.

I brought this to the attention of my counsel, Mr. Hopkins. Initially, he was taken back and then he looked over the transcript and calmly and confidently said to me not to worry, because even if the transcript was tampered with, they did a "sloppy job." He pointed out that they left all the incriminating evidence in and the reference to the severe endangerment, and its detrimental and adverse effects was by law "an abuse finding" that would hold to all the same legal protection according to the Domestic Violence Act. During this dialogue between me and counsel, once again, he ran to get the Domestic Violence Act, showing me the legal definition of abuse and the laws protecting victims.

While I was certainly consoled by our conversation, I was quite concerned about the implication of the transcript having been altered. It meant to me that Lew was trying to bury the evidence of his abuse to the children. I assumed that he was doing so to posture himself for a custody dispute and/or to protect his public image and save face in the community. The former possibility disturbed me.

I called my attorney friend, George Collins, who had directed me to Mr. Hopkins to discuss this further. Over the years, I had developed a significant trust in this man. He was a seasoned lawyer in his sixties. Mr. Collins acted as an attorney for attorneys, so I knew he was familiar with all possible tactics in the practice of law. He said, "Yes, the transcript may have been 'air-brushed'," and added, "It does sometimes happen." I told him that I wanted to do something about this to hold those accountable to this unethical practice and to insure the future protection of my children. He said that if Mr. Hopkins thought the evidence in the record stood on its own, I should let it go. He explained it would not be worth fighting a transcript fraud battle in the midst of the war I was already in. He explained to me that I was in "a system" and I needed to stay focused to get to the end, so that my children and I could go on with our lives.

*   *   *

My trust remained with Mr. Hopkins, but I questioned the way that he passively accepted the continued abuse to me and my children even though on the surface he expressed surprise. One afternoon I called him from my office to tell him that Bradley and I had discovered gasoline kerosene soaked socks in my car. He was shocked hearing the story, but nothing was done to inform the courts, other than what I attempted, which accomplished nothing except giving me a greater feeling of vulnerability and impotence.

Bradley and I were running errands one afternoon and as we pulled into the garage I said, "Lets each reach for an object and help clean the car." Bradley lifted up a rolled soaked sock positioned near his feet in the front passenger's seat. He said, "What is this?" We took it upstairs and I opened it carefully over the bathroom sink. Black oil filled the sink and the smell of kerosene permeated the bathroom. I asked Neil, Lisa's son, to come over and look at it, because I thought he could identify the pungent odor and black oil in the sink. He walked in the bathroom and said, "It is gasoline and possibly some kerosene."

Immediately, I called the police to inform them of this. I showed them what we discovered and told them that I had an Order of Protection and that there was a history of domestic violence toward me and my children. I explained that I had never personally come into contact with gasoline, as I typically had my car filed by an attendant and had no idea how this got into my car. I did recall, as I was telling the officer the sequence of events, that I had parked my car the day before in a parking lot that Lew and I both used years ago and that he continues to use today.

The officer looked at the sink containing the sock saturated with black fluid. I could tell that he recognized what was going on here, and he took a report and offered to take the soaked sock to his lab to investigate its contents. He lifted it out of the sink and placed it in a plastic bag and gave me the phone number of a person to contact to obtain the results of the laboratory investigation.

Weeks later, I was informed that there was "nothing" found in the sock. When this news came, Lisa and I agreed that the black substance was not a figment of our imagination. I realized that there was some reason for this feedback, but didn't know what it was. At some future point, I hired a detective and he offered to go to the police investigative service to determine what had transpired and to obtain the sock. He felt it was important that we secure this evidence. He was informed that the laboratory study on the sock was not done, because "it was considered a civil matter." This was my first encounter with law enforcement's enabling of the domestic violence in our family through passive consent.

CHAPTER 12

Psychologicals Tell All

Psychologicals Tell the Inside Story

David's Alleged Facial Tic

Professional Practice Harassment

M r. Hopkins often referred to Lew's divorce strategy as "two-pronged." On the one hand, there was the "starve-out" campaign in which his attorneys were steadfast in preventing me from accessing financial resources for myself, the children or any legal representation that did not support Lew's agenda. The second campaign was the effort by his attorneys to present Lew as the "reformed abuser" and the superior human being, thus implying the better parent. Now, in order to claim that Lew was a superior person, they had to find some psychological flaw with me; so we were court ordered to each have psychological evaluations.

The evaluations were conducted by the Counseling Connection, a rather benign sounding therapy service in Lake Bluff, Illinois. Its innocent and innocuous name evokes trust. At least for me it did, for approximately one month. The greatest lesson in my encounter with Counseling Connection was that "you can't tell a business by its name." It was revealed to me that this little counseling service was one of the most well-connected "counseling/judicial" outfits in the state. This I learned three years later. What was exposed and how it was disclosed will be explained in this book at the point at which I discovered it myself. Suffice it to say for now that I walked in with full faith, trust and total innocence.

There were approximately six separate initial meetings as part of this evaluation and numerous standard psychological tests administered to Lew and myself during the Summer and Fall of 1995. Psychological testing is a cornerstone for the determination of an individual's mental and psychological health, and traditionally carries rather significant weight in forensic evaluations and court matters.

The testing was conducted by a professional psychologist by the name of Paul Kredow, Psy.D. Dr. Kredow was a man in his 40's, average height and build, dressed conservatively yet professionally, in a sport jacket and comfortable shoes. He presented with the typical casual suburban psychologist look. He was extremely compassion, articulate, perceptive, and clearly the most ethical person I encountered in my dealings with Counseling Connection.

Dr. Kredow did a thorough evaluation of me and Lew and administered a full battery of standardized psychological tests to both of us. Included in this testing battery was the MMPI, known as the Minnesota Multiphasic Personality Inventory. It consists of over 500 questions and is the most rigorous, reliable and valid testing instrument for the disclosure and assessment of psychopathology. There is more research on this one instrument than any other of its kind in the field of psychological measurement.

I recall the day of the administration of my MMPI quite vividly. It was a Saturday, shortly after my September 20, 1995 meeting with Dr. Kredow. The testing took place at their Lake Bluff office. I was escorted into the testing room where I sat alone for several hours taking the psychological tests, inventories and assessments.

It was my first time to see the MMPI, even though it is a popular psychological test and I am a clinical psychologist. The instructions were to read the questions and choose your initial and natural gut response from the multiple choice answers. It was rather simple, but extremely lengthy and tedious. I saw this as part of what needed to be done and merely followed the routine, trusting my psychological health and still believing that my children and I would be safe in the long run.

Upon my completion of the tests, I was asked to wait in the main business office area of their suite. Sitting there holding my testing response packet, the copying machine caught my eye. Having lost some of my faith in actual and factual data remaining intact, I wanted to secure a copy of my test answers. So I asked the secretary if I could use their copier. She said that would be fine, and so I copied my testing answer sheets. I don't think she realized what I was copying, but at this juncture I figured why not, better to be safe than sorry.

In the months that followed, the actual testing results were kept out of the Court Record and were not made know to us until January of 1996. I was aware that opposing counsel was not happy with what they obtained or with what they did not obtain from the psychological testing, interpretive analysis and the outcome of Dr. Kredow's evaluation of Lew and myself.

Before these profiles were presented to the Court and to the litigants, there was much fuss in the courtroom around the expressed concern by opposing counsel that my psychological results were not valid because I was a psychologist. They refused to hear that I had absolutely no familiarity or expertise in psychological testing. My specialty, since receiving my doctorate at Northwestern University in 1979, was mind/body medicine. There was never a need for me to conduct psychological tests of this nature, nor was I interested in this field of study or professional inquiry.

Once the actual interpretive report of the psychological tests were made available to all of us, I realized why there was a strong effort to try to negate the validity of my testing results. Lew's legal team appeared eager to shield Lew's psychological profile and invalidate mine. I now recognize that the effort to shift the attention to invalidating my profile mirrors the same dynamic of Lew's shifting the focus onto me as being the cause of his abuse to me.

Lew's counsel and legal team remained in denial around what was revealed in Lew's profile and found non-existent fault in mine.

Lew's psychological profile revealed the following personality characteristics, obtained from the MMPI-II:

"The profile was deemed to be valid. The scores suggest that he was cooperative enough during the evaluation. He does have some tendency to present an overly positive self-image and to minimize personal faults. Lewis Blumenthal has a profile suggestive of someone who is somewhat immature and impulsive. He tends to be generally oriented toward pleasure seeking and self-gratification. He may occasionally show bad judgment, and tends to be somewhat self-centered, pleasure-oriented, narcissistic and manipulative." "He views himself as confident in social situations and tends to be forceful in expressing his views. Individuals with this profile pattern tend to be rather likable, personable and may make a good first impression. However his relationships tend to be superficial and he may have some difficulty with close relationships at this time. He is outgoing and sociable with a strong need to be around others." (He) "may seek attention from others, especially to gain social recognition. Overall the profile indicates difficulties with control of impulse and relationship problems."(Kredow, October 23, 1995, p.5)

Emotional findings on Lew's psychological profile were obtained in part by the Thematic Apperception Test, Incomplete Sentences, and projective drawings. These findings included:

"Dr. Blumenthal presents as a very confident individual." "The projective evaluation indicated that at the time Lewis Blumenthal was under significant stress and he was a rather well-defended person. His stories tended to indicate the use of denial as a major defense."... (and) indicated he "appeared to have difficulty with conflict in relationships and not being able to judge the needs of others in a relationship. Although the relationship with Jeanne King appears to be over, there appears to still be some wish on his part for reunification and reconciliation."

Dr. Kredow concluded the interpretive report of Lew's psychological evaluation stating, "The above finding suggest that Lewis has difficulty with impulsivity and relationships."

My suspicion at this juncture is that Lew's profile so obviously revealed that of a classic abuser, it had to be kept off the record. In *A Psychiatric Study of Parents Who Abuse Infants and Small Children*, Drs. Steele and Pollock state:

"Child abusers have been described as 'immature,' 'impulsive ridden,' 'dependent,' 'sado-masochistic,' 'egocentric,' 'narcissistic,' and 'demanding.'" (Helfer and Kempe (Eds), 1997, p. 95)

The interpretive report of my psychological evaluation showed the following personality findings, obtained from the MMPI-II:

"This was considered to be a valid MMPI-II Clinical profile. The scores suggest that she was cooperative enough during the evaluation to provide useful clinical scale information." "The scale was found to be within normal limits for all measured subscales. There appears to be no sex-role conflict and a range of interests includes, but is not limited to, homemaking and cultural activities. Personally, she is an outgoing and gregarious person, with a strong need to be around others and enjoying interpersonal attention. Dr. King usually tries to project a positive outlook about her life and typically enters new social relationships with an open and accepting attitude." "No indication of depression, anxiety, or overt hostility was noted on this evaluation. Hence there is no evidence of an affective disorder. Simultaneously, there is no evidence suggestive of a psychotic disorder. Since the MMPI clinical profile is within normal limits, no clinical diagnosis is provided." (Kredow, October 23, 1995, p. 3)

Emotional findings derived from the Proverbs Projective Test and the commutative composite of the psychological evaluation revealed that:

"Jeanne King answered in a way to indicate that she had more than adequate abstract thought versus concrete thinking. No evidence of affective or psychotic dimensions was found on this evaluation. Her most unpleasant experience has been her neck injury allegedly perpetrated by her husband, and observing him verbally and physically abuse their children." (She) "had remorse over the breakup of her marriage and the turn toward abusiveness which it had taken. She had concerns about the effect upon her children and their happiness."

In the concluding discussion of my psychological evaluation, Dr. Kredow noted, "Overall, she is a normally functioning individual with no specific personality problems."

In reviewing the two psychological profiles today, I have discovered that there was a Clinical Impression Category listed in my interpretive report. It specified the following: Axis I: "None" and Axis II: "None." The "axis" designation is the format for providing a psychiatric diagnosis. In Lew's interpretive report, the section for Clinical Impression Category containing the axis designation was *omitted* from of the report. How or why this was done, I do not know. But I am aware that the production of an interpretive report without clinical impressions specifying an axis designation is highly atypical. It is quite likely that a diagnosis emerged out of the profile specifying a pathology that needed to be kept off the record.

My curiosity as to why this important part of the report was left out has led me to review its contents further. In doing so, I am aware that there was mention of there being "no clinical diagnosis" stated twice, in the "Personality" section and in the "Discussion" section of my report. Yet, in Lew's report there is no mention anywhere in the entire report of there being "no clinical diagnosis" and there is no disclosure of any specific diagnosis, either. Since the primary function for administering the MMPI is for the detection of psychopathology and the production of a clinical diagnosis, this omission in the interpretive report of Lew's evaluation is highly suspect of a tampered report. Either you have a diagnosis or you have "no diagnosis."

*　　*　　*

Days before the results of our psychological testing were presented to the Court, a swift shift occurred in which there was an effort toward unwarranted psychiatrics for the children. We were in court, on January 12, 1996 on the matter of finances, child support and legal fees. Toward the end of the court proceeding, the children's attorney and Lew's attorney unexpectantly spread a rumor claiming my second child had a psychiatric disorder. It appeared that there was a need to place the focus of "psychiatric disturbance" onto the children. I was unaware of the motivation for this as it was happening. In retrospect, it was the natural direction to take, given the two psychological profiles of Lew and myself.

David Wessel, the man who called himself the children's attorney, rushed over to my counsel, Mr. Hopkins. He handed my counsel a Petition concerning my son as though it was an absolute utter emergency and without acknowledging that I, the custodial parent, was sitting there.

"The second child has a facial tic and we must get him into to see Dr. Rosenfeld immediately," Mr. Wessel said, in a huff, to my counsel.

Mr. Hopkins acknowledged the alleged urgency without any questions asked. He didn't even turn to me, though I was sitting right next to him, and inquire, "Does your child have a facial tic?" I would think since I lived with my son and took care of him that I would know this, wouldn't you? Instead, my counsel joined the fury with opposing counsel to present to the Court that indeed, David, my second child, required an immediate psychiatric evaluation by a psychiatrist of Lew's choosing for this alleged emergency condition.

I sat steaming inside, knowing that my child had no evidence of a psychiatric disorder. David was an excellent student, socially well-adjusted, and exhibited fine character and integrity. He also had demonstrated inner strength in the face of adversity. He was in perfect health. I knew my child did not deserve to be treated for a condition he did not have.

My counsel and I walked out of the courtroom together, and I told him that my child does not have a facial tic. Further, I said, "It is psychologically detrimental to a child to send him to treatment for a condition that does not exist." I added that doing so sets in motion the development of the alleged psychological handicap, symptom or some other related condition. I insisted that we not allow this violation to my innocent child. I pleaded that he put himself in my position and consider if he would do the same to his child. Mr. Hopkins looked directly at me and there was a clear connection between us in that moment. He said:

"If you are certain that David does not have a facial tic, secure signed Affidavits from people who come into contact with him on a regular basis, who can attest to this." He advised, "Go to his teacher, go to the school principle, go to the baby-sitter, go to all of them and do it immediately."

So, I went home that afternoon and told Lisa, my baby-sitter and housekeeper, what had transpired in court. She said, "Dr. King, David doesn't have a facial tic." Lisa had been a school teacher for 20 years prior to her employment with me. I knew that she would know a facial tic on a child if she saw it. She was very happy to provide an Affidavit on the matter.

Then the next day, I went to Meadowbrook Elementary School and met with David's teachers and the school principle. I asked point blank, "Would you know a facial tic if you saw it?" Then I asked, "Have you observed a facial tic in my child?" Both of David's teachers said, "David does not have a facial tic," and acknowledged that they would know if he did. They agreed to provide me with an Affidavit testifying to their observations concerning David not having a facial tic.

Securing these documents was quite an ordeal, as I had to get the consent of both the School Principal and the Superintendent of the School District in order to do so. However, they were quite cooperative as they too were concerned about my child's interests. Within a matter of days, I had secured three Affidavits clearly stating that David did not have a facial tic. I submitted these to my counsel and he prepared a counter Petition, attaching these Affidavits, for the Court's review. Subsequently, the issue of David's alleged facial tic faded into the background, and the immediate necessity of a psychiatric intervention disappeared. I was relieved and this action rekindled my faith in my counsel.

Soon after this trust was felt, I became disenchanted once again in light of my counsel's passivity around further violations to me. It is only today that I see why he acted as he did and how my expectations of him to stop the abuse to me only reinforced my being victimized.

*   *   *

Almost immediately after the divorce proceedings began, there was a dramatic change in my experience of myself in my work. I became more authentic, more clear, more present and more dynamic. My work was coming through me magically and having the most uplifting effect on me and transformational effect on my patients. There was an exponential leap in my abilities, my functioning and effectiveness as a psychologist and meditation instructor. Within in a matter of months my calendar started to fill, and by the first half year in my new office, I had doubled my patient load and fulfilled the financial projections that my Dad and I speculated. It was quite satisfying.

These projections for the first six months involved my bringing in enough income to cover the additional overhead of the new office and business operations. Step two in our projections was to begin offering classes in which I was teaching the Biofeedback and Stress Reduction Program in small groups. I had filled, designed, managed, and completed two of these ten-week programs in six months, and the feedback from the patients was outstanding. Business was booming, and I was the radiant proud doctor of the new Chicago Center for the Treatment of Pain and Stress.

Then, out of the blue, my secretary and I started noticing that several of the new patient initial sessions that she was scheduling were "no show" appointments. My secretary served as a receptionist and initial phone contact person, freeing me up for more direct patient time and creative development of treatment programs and business promotion. However with the "no shows" on my calendar, I decided to intercept all new prospective patients and make the initial appointment myself.

I did this to see if it would reduce the number of "no shows" on the initial appointments. The incidence of this was far beyond what I had ever encountered in the lifetime of my career as a practicing psychologist. Typically, if a new patient needs to cancel their first appointment, they call to cancel and I generally reschedule their appointment within the week or sometime soon after. Patients interested in treatment rarely make an appointment and not show up without calling. Over the last 14 years of professional practice, I may have had this happen three times. But over a nine month period during the litigation, beginning around the Fall of 1995, I had over 30 of these "no show" appointments. In one month 50 percent of my potential income hours were filled with these "no show" appointments.

My intercepting the calls did not decrease the "no show" appointments, until I limited taking patients to referral sources that I was accustomed to working with over the years. When I recognized how disruptive this was to the growing momentum of my practice, I told Mr. Hopkins what was happening and asked for his assistance in protecting me from this violation to my business. He advised that I hire a detective to investigate the connection between these callers.

With the help of caller ID and the telephone company's internal phone tracing service, we were able to see that many of the calls came from Lew's sister's business and various phones at Michael Reese Hospital. Even without this evidence, I had known the source of this harassment to my practice. I assumed it was coming from Lew and or his family. But Mr. Hopkins convinced me that, without actual factual proof of the source of these calls, he could not present this to the Court. Then, after I obtained confirmation of my suspicions, he remained unwilling to bring this violation by Lew before the Court.

The harassment continued, and subsequently became threats of sexual assault by some of the "new prospective patients." The details of these callers' comments and threats were so disgraceful that it is hard for me to reiterate what was said. Over the course of my professional career, I had never been subjected to sexual terrorism. My patient population primarily had been limited to chronic medical conditions of fast-paced professionals – not sexual deviants.

This type of intrusion to a psychological practice was too atypical for my patient population. With a highly provocative and intimidating caller, I inquired how my name was obtained. I was told

I was selected from the phone book because of my specialty as a sex therapist. This was utterly ridiculous, given that my yellow page advertising stated my expertise with headaches, high blood pressure and stress-related stomach disorders.

I called the detective and asked that he directly contact the last caller by going out to the individual's home, because I could not take it any longer. When he arrived at this person's door, the individual started "stuttering" in response to the detective's inquiry concerning a call placed to Dr. King.

Additionally, an investigator placed "rouse" calls to every one of the "no show" new patients, asking questions about seeking psychological services. Within four business days, the calls went from over 30 in nine months to none during the next four months. It was clear that these callers had more in common than a call from my detective agency. As one writer investigating my case wrote:

> "After 30 phony callers were tracked down and questioned, the barrage of no-shows evaporated, indicating that they shared something in common: a person with the motivation to destroy Dr. King's source of income."

I strongly believe that Lew was working on his earlier promise: *"I'll show you what it is like to have nothing. You won't get a dime from me and will not earn a dime."* Even though my office was listed as a place covered under my Order of Protection, the phone harassment and numerous other suspicious visits to the actual physical location were never brought to the Court's attention.

My expectation that my counsel "fix" this violation to me by bringing it before the Court and the frustration I felt by his not doing so kept me believing that I was helpless. From a mental, emotional, and psychological perspective, this supported my being a victim. Maintaining this mental image of myself proved to keep me in the abuse dynamic.

I now realize that Mr. Hopkins was not in a position to bring these violations to the Court's attention. Doing so would have interfered with assisting in fulfilling Lew's counsel's agenda. Due to the economics and politics of the case, my counsel couldn't act as my legal representative unless he was assisting in supporting opposing counsel's campaign. This became clearly evidenced by his actions in the months to follow.

Psychology of the Abusive Personality

Adult Abusive Personality

Fragile, Weak Sense of Self
Inability to Trust
Delusional Jealously
Mood Cycles
Overly Demanding and Critical
Angry or Ambivalent Attachment
Inability to Articulate Intimacy Needs

————

Control and Domination Keep the Fragile Sense of Self Intact
Denial and Projection are Primary Defense Mechanisms

↑   ↑   ↑

Learned Trauma Reaction

Emotional Volatility and Rage
to Cope with Being Victimized

↑   ↑   ↑

Parental Foundation of the Abusive Personality

Global Attacks on Selfhood
Humiliation, Embarrassment and Shame
Conditional Love
Random Punishment
Insecure Attachment to One's Mother
Direct Experience of Abuse in Home

Text adapted from D. Dutton, *The Batterer: A Psychological Profile*, 1995.

CHAPTER 13

Agreed Orders Get It Done

Financial Agreed Order

Gradually Lifting the Supervision

Physical Endangerment to Marc

Falling out with Mr. Hopkins

M r. Hopkins projected an image of being the kind of person that gets done what he wants done. I truly believed that he wanted to bring an expeditious closure to my case, as that is what he expressed to me. However, the closure that he was working toward and the closure that I wanted were not the same.

During the late Fall of 1995, we had numerous discussions about strategies for bringing an end to the case. He presented Lew's counsels' proposal to first litigate the finances, and then in a separate trial litigate custody.

After considering the pros and cons of doing this, I told him that I could not litigate finances before custody. I expressed my concern, that if I am given my part of the marital estate, Lew and his counsel would keep the proceedings going until my resources were depleted and then proceed to a custody trial without me having any means for supporting the litigation. I knew that Lew could out-spend me in court. It was clear to everyone that, with his estimated current $500,000 income, he could continue financing his counsel long after my bucket was empty, and I did not have the means to replenish my resources. So that option was out of the question for me.

Mr. Hopkins saw my predicament, but from his perspective "cutting up the pie," as he put it, was the next natural step because he needed to get paid. So we had to find a way to appease both of us. At the time, I did not recognize that our agendas were incompatible. His desire was to access the pie, while I wanted to preserve it. Nonetheless, he expressed empathy for my predicament to first resolve custody and then finances. Since I already had temporary custody but no temporary support order, working on interim finances was the next step, with a long term strategy for the final trial.

Accordingly, we set out to get a Court Order for Child Support and Maintenance and for Legal Fees. He petitioned the Court for the continuation of the Hearing, and we began the necessary preparations. He explained to me that there was a new law in Illinois called "Leveling of the Playing Field," which allowed both parties in a divorce case to have equal access to the marital estate to fund litigation. Mr. Hopkins was so enthusiastic in his telling me how this particular statue would serve us well. He shared his confidence that the Judge would rule in his favor because both the Judge, Joy Feinberg (opposing counsel) and himself were all part of a recent committee meeting in which they were all in favor of this new law. He said it would be politically incorrect if the Judge did not honor his supporting this law now.

Mr. Hopkins wanted to know how much I thought Lew had already spent on his counsel, so that he could ask for the same for himself, as per the Leveling of the Playing Field Law. It was my belief, at the time, that Lew had spent about $75,000. Mr. Hopkins substantiated this from the information he obtained and subsequently said, "I think we should ask for $100,000 for your interim legal fees, which will level the playing field and give me $25,000 more for the litigation." I was under the impression, from input by many other lawyers, that this figure would cover both the upcoming hearing on finances and the final trial.

Previously, there had been some discussion about accessing our $800,000 pension to cover his legal fees, because accessing Lew's income had been like walking into a brick wall. So, Mr. Hopkins set forth to investigate how this would be executed and drafted a Pleading asking for this to be done. He petitioned the Court, requesting $100,000 from our pension to pay his fees. Additionally, he asked for monthly support commensurate with our household bills and the children's expenses over the last year. He showed how this maintenance and support could be financed from Lew's medical practice income.

Another discovery of all financials had to be done to update the last financial discovery prior our going before the Court on our Petition. I submitted to my counsel a copied set of my current records since last August. Mr. Hopkins and I met for me to read and sign the Pleading he was going to put before the Court. Mr. Hopkins told me that it would be very costly to go into court and have a full Hearing on finances. He said that doing so would cost the estate nearly $70,000 and would be extremely time consuming. He recommended that a more expeditious way of bringing closure to the financial issues to hold us over during the divorce proceedings was to enter into an Agreed Order for Child Support and Maintenance, plus Legal Fees.

An "agreed order" is an agreement between parties which does not require a hearing or adjudication by a judge. On the surface, agreed orders give the appearance of a peaceful expeditious divorce proceeding. However, in the years that followed, our agreed orders proved to be the foundation for my "sinking ship."

Mr. Hopkins presented this proposed method of bringing closure to the immediate financial issues based on the "conservation principle" and moving the case forward expeditiously. The most salient selling point of his proposal to me was his saying this Agreed Order would encompass a "time table" that would lock in a definitive "end" to the litigation. This was to be done by designating a specific final trial date for the custody trial that would commence immediately after the custody report was issued by Dr. Norman Chapman, the court-appointed custody evaluator.

The timetable was to unfold in the following sequence: the custody evaluator would submit his report by July 1996; the custody trial would then take place during December 1996. Mr. Hopkins estimated that it would take a few weeks, and by the end of January 1997 a final custody determination would be adjudicated.

Immediately after final custody was determined, the proceedings for the ultimate distribution of finances would take place. Mr. Hopkins said both he and opposing counsel wanted to have this done through arbitration rather than through the regular divorce courts. He explained that arbitration was a more expedient way to bring closure to the matter, because the trial would proceed without interruptions. He even promised that he would have input in selecting an arbitrator who would be completely impartial to the case, which would serve us well. With all of this in place, it was promised that the divorce would be concluded by Spring of 1997.

The most attractive and compelling aspect of his proposal to me was that it put a clear and definitive timeline in place and an end date to the litigation. Further, it postured the determination of final custody before the distribution of finances. These two points were the most important to me, as I wanted to see the light at the end of the tunnel and I needed to know that I would have the financial means still intact to get us there. It was for this reason that I proceeded with his concept of the Agreed Order. The Order was drafted, encompassing the above time and dateline with the sequence of events as we discussed.

We could not arrive at an agreement to cover the fixed household expenses of the marital residence where the children and I were living, nor could we agree on the amount to cover the children's living expenses. In order to avoid going to court and having a Hearing on this, it was decided to use a Home Equity line of credit during the limited interim. Mr. Hopkins said that, in the "final judgment," Lew would pay the second mortgage of $40,000 off and my home mortgage would be as it had been in the past. The amount taken was precisely commensurate with the timeline established in order to provide the finances necessary to get us to the projected end of the divorce, Spring 1997.

*   *   *

Concurrently as this Order was being negotiated and refined, we were dealing with numerous issues around Lew's supervised visitation. Mr. Hopkins told me that Lew was going to petition the Court to lift his supervision so he could have unsupervised visits with the children. He shared his personal belief that Lew's counsel's position would be that there had been no altercations between Lew and the children during the supervised visitation since its beginning in April 1995. However, Mr. Hopkins expressed he thought that this indicated the supervision was working, not that it should be lifted. He and I both appeared to agree that it would be reasonable for Lew to *evidence* rehabilitation before lifting the supervision, not just control in front of the supervisor.

In preparation for an upcoming Hearing on the matter of lifting Lew's supervision, Mr. Hopkins suggested that I gather all the factual evidence of Lew's denial about and around his having a problem with abuse. He stated to me that he was aware this was the first step toward showing signs of rehabilitation. I learned through numerous sources that this indeed was true, and Lew was far from accomplishing this point in the process of recovery. Lew was in complete denial about his abuse to me and the children.

As per Mr. Hopkins' direction, I compiled a lengthy list of numerous examples evidencing Lew's denial of his abuse to us. Most of the examples I gave were Lew's expressed comments directly to me or to other relevant parties during the litigation. For example, on September 27, 1995, Lew and I had an appointment with a staff social worker at the Counseling Connection as part of our psychological evaluation. Following the appointment, we were sitting outside on a bench near the parking lot. Lew and I were having a discussion about why we were spending so much on the divorce. In an absolute huff, Lew said:

"This (meaning the litigation) is all your doing because of the criminal charges and the supervised visitation." He added in an angry tone, "All that abuse stuff is in your head."

What struck me as most peculiar was his failure to assume responsibility for the incidents which he refused to defend in court, and his unwillingness to see any personal accountability for these consequences, even though he entered into an agreement for supervised visitation. From Lew's perspective, he was the victim and I had become the villain.

I then supplemented the list of statements, including the above comment, showing denial of the abuse problem with examples of further incidents of abuse to both me and the children. I submitted over three pages of information, and none of this was brought to the Court's attention by my attorney.

Instead, before our Hearing on this matter, Mr. Hopkins approached me saying that we should enter into an Agreed Order incorporating a proposal of gradually moving from supervised visitation to monitoring with a psychiatrist. I was taken aback by the change in Mr. Hopkins' positioning with respect to our presenting Lew's lack of rehabilitation to the Court. I told him that I would not enter into an Agreed Order, because I did not agree with what was being proposed by Lew and his legal team.

Mr. Hopkins' reply was, "The Judge is going to order it any way." I said, "Fine, let him." I wanted this Hearing because I wanted the facts out in the open and wanted the Judge to take responsibility for this decision. I could not and would not condone unsupervised visitation without there being rehabilitation.

Mr. Hopkins said that I would appear as though *I* was interfering with Lew's effort to have a relationship with the children and this would negatively effect the Judge's opinion of me in our upcoming custody litigation. I felt like Mr. Hopkins had been talking out of two sides of his mouth and I didn't know which to believe. Holding to the need for rehabilitation seemed most appropriate, and the permissive posture appeared to encompass more of the politics of custody litigation, none of which were familiar to me.

My counsel and I went back and forth on this, and my concerns about the children's immediate safety took precedent for me. Mr. Hopkins then promised me that, in the event of any signs of abuse communicated by the children or through the monitor, he would immediately go into court and reinstate the supervision. He pointed out that the monitor's job was to "detect any indications of trends toward physical abuse and prevent any occurrences of violence experienced by the children during visitation with their father," as specified in Dr. Chapman's "Protocol for Monitoring of Visitation," submitted January 10, 1996. He assured me that I would have equal access to the monitoring psychiatrist and would know what was going on between Lew and the boys.

I reminded myself of my conversation with the attorney who recommended Mr. Hopkins to me in which he told me that I was "caught in a system" and just needed to work with my counsel to get to the end. I felt that I needed to trust his vision of the bigger picture to get the desired end we were seeking, which was closure for the family and long term safety for my children. I also believed that he would take care of any immediate trouble if it presented itself, so I went along. The Agreed Order of gradually stepping down Lew's supervised visitation over a four month period and instituting the monitoring psychiatrist visits was drafted and entered into the Court Record on January 29, 1996. And this was done in conjunction with and while our Order of Protection – *protecting* Bradley, David, Marc and me – remained in effect.

*   *   *

At this juncture, the details of the Agreed Order concerning finances were still being negotiated. In a meeting with my counsel to refine the terms of the agreement, he mentioned that we could take $100,000 from our pension for his fees, but the tax penalty would be $65,000 for doing so. I told him that I thought it was wasteful to incur that excessive expense to the estate, particularly in light of Lew's current earnings. I informed him that the only way I could proceed with this arrangement via Agreed Order, would be if it stipulated that Lew's portion of the estate be charged this tax penalty.

Mr. Hopkins told me the only way the Agreed Order could be drafted was to make the tax consequence "unallocated," to be determined at the final trial. I did not like this uncertainty, but he assured me that he could prove there were other options for paying his fees, which Lew was controlling and using all along for his benefit. He predicted that his evidencing this to the Court would result in Lew most likely being charged the tax penalty.

However, when the Agreed Order was given to me to read, initially there was mention that the tax penalty was to be split between Lew and myself. I reminded Mr. Hopkins of my position on this matter and he replied, *"If you don't sign this Agreed Order, I will withdraw from the case."* I had no words for the empty feeling I experienced inside. I was nine months without a court order for support, and could no longer take the uncertainty of how I would make ends meet. I had used all of the money that my mother loaned me to cover us in the interim.

Again, being backed up against the wall, I consented to proceed with the Agreed Order out of my vulnerability and later realized, out of my ignorance and innocence. Our discussions of entering this order clearly suggested that **all** the financial matters, including my children's support and his fees, would be taken care of in **one** Order. The expectation of this certainly did influence my decision-making at that time. In the final analysis, two separate Agreed Orders were entered into the Court Record March and April 1996, and they were not contingent upon one another. Further, the tax penalty according to the final Order or Lew's interpretation of the Order, was placed on me. I was only made aware of this months later.

*   *   *

Up until this point, I was cooperating with the concept of Agreed Orders to avoid litigation, conflict, legal costs and delayed time for me and my children to go on with our lives. However, the next Agreed Order that was entered made me realize that the concept of our Agreed Orders was not serving me, but rather assisting Lew and his legal campaign.

June 13, 1996, my counsel, in cooperation with opposing counsel, drafted an Order that called for the children's religious affiliation, including past and present dues and building funds, to come out of a Home Equity line of credit against the equity in our marital residence. The mere idea of paying a religious congregation's building fund by taking from the very foundation of one's own place of residence was absolutely absurd to me. I had always known my charitable contributions to the synagogue and financial obligations like contributing to the maintenance of the building used for our prayer to come from one's "extra" finances, not from the basics, much less the foundation of one's own home. This being done both before and instead of looking to Lew's half-a-million dollar net income ($1,600,000 gross) from his successful medical practice made this even more outrageous to me.

The whole proposal made me see the absurdity of the Home Equity loan "agreements," but I was so desperate its full impact did not register at that time. The people at the Temple were willing to delay this payment until we settled the case, which we all trusted would occur within six months. I believe they were in agreement with extending this courtesy because, in the Jewish faith, charitable donations to one's source of spiritual inspiration are to come from

10 percent of one's income, not unravel the very core of one's foundation.

*   *   *

The final straw that broke my faith in Mr. Hopkins occurred over the next few months. I was in my office finishing up for the day, and the children were on visitation with their father. This was seven weeks after Lew's weekday supervision was lifted. It was Thursday July 11, 1996 around 7:55 PM. I got a phone call from Marc, crying hysterically. He was quite upset as he told me that his father hurt him again.

"Dad's doing it again," Marc cried. "He's going to kill me. I hate him."

I asked, "What happened, Marci?"

"Dad threw me to the ground and I fell on my arm," he said, sobbing. "He is the worst father in the world."

I know the difference between a child crying because he is being punished or not getting his way, versus a child truly terrorized, hurting and in trouble. My little boy was authentically traumatized and scared. I just listened, and he continued to tell me more.

Marc said that his Dad wanted him to pick up some cones from the ground after playing soccer. Marc felt he had done his share and believed the rest of the cones were for David.

"Dad was forcing me to pick them up," Marc said, "and he picked me up real high, carried me inside, and threw me down to the floor."

As Marc was telling me this story, he was continuing to cry, telling me that his arm was hurting. Lew heard Marc on the phone and demanded that he get off the phone. We were disconnected. They came home late from the visitation.

The next day, I learned more about the abuse dynamic than I had ever been able to digest before. While I had repeatedly experienced and witnessed the dynamic, I saw through more objective eyes than were available to me in the past.

Marc now said, "It was an accident."

I was stunned at his changed perspective and I inquired, "Did your Dad apologize?"

"No," Marc said, "I apologized to him for not picking up the cones."

I felt Marc's discomfort and awkwardness in the way he relayed this to me. He was harboring an internal contradiction, apparently causing conflict.

He said, "Dad told me it didn't hurt; but, Mom, it did." Marc was also told that he was not to talk about the incident with the monitoring psychiatrist at their next visit because "it would get to the Court."

What concerned me most about this incident was that it was quite clear that Marc knew that something was done to him that was wrong, and then was led to believe that it was an accident which was his fault. I told my counsel about this and expressed my concern around my children growing up being hit, hurt, or injured; and made to believe that they have to assume responsibility for it or cover up for their father.

It was clear to Mr. Hopkins that Lew was relaxing back into his old tactics that led to his visitations being supervised and the abuse finding originally established. While this incident did not result in an injury or actual physical mark, we saw it as similar to the pattern of altercations in the past, suggesting a lack of rehabilitation. Mr. Hopkins told me that we would petition the Court to reinstate the supervision full time.

Three weeks went by, and he did nothing. When I asked him to follow up on this he told me he was working on the "QDRO" (Qualified Domestic Relations Order) arrangement to access the $165,000 from the pension and he would tend to it after that was complete. That was not acceptable to me, so I filed a complaint with the Department of Children and Family Services so that someone would intervene in what was happening to my child.

When the DCFS worker came out to the house, I overheard Marc tell her, "It was an *accident on purpose*...he was angry." I could see my child wanting to be honest, but he was scared of the ramifications to his dad and from his dad. The DCFS worker, upon leaving our home, told me, "Lew should have a "hands-off policy" in his disciple with the children, given the history of abuse." She said that, in light of the history, she was most likely going to consider it an "indicated" finding of abuse. Her report was withheld from me and the Court. I later learned that the story of the events of her investigation were altered after Lew's legal team intervened.

*   *   *

By mid-September, Mr. Hopkins had completed his mission in obtaining the disbursement from the pension. A package was delivered to me containing a $190,000 check for me to sign, releasing $100,000 to Mr. Hopkins' law firm, $15,000 to me and $75,000 for federal and state taxes. Along with the check was a Petition from opposing counsel requesting another $100,000 for Lew's legal funding. At this juncture, Lew had already spent $75,000 and had taken an additional $50,000 as part of the Agreed Order.

Lew's counsel was using my signing the check, releasing the funds from the pension, as the establishment of a precedent for their right to receive $100,000 from this portion of our estate. I informed Mr. Hopkins that we arrived at this agreement in order to "level the playing field," not as a measure "to open the gates." I asked my counsel to request that opposing counsel withdraw their Petition before I sign the check. I told him that I did not want releasing these funds to be used as a vehicle to continue what I believed to be a wasteful dissipation of assets. Over $300,000 had already been spent on legal funding, and I recognized that we were headed into an estate plunder by our counsel.

Mr. Hopkins refused to ask opposing counsel to withdraw their Petition, and so I told him that I wanted to think it over and would call him in the morning. Before our conversation, I obtained a second opinion concerning opposing counsel's Petition and recognized it was not in my family's interest. I assured Mr. Hopkins that the check was secure in a safe and would not be endorsed. The next morning Lew's attorney informed the Court that I was "stealing" the check. Before I was able to get back to my counsel in the morning, I had learned that he went behind my back and had the funds directly wired to him. The next day, he filed a Motion to Withdraw as my counsel with the Court.

It became very clear to me that Mr. Hopkins and I did not have the same goal in mind with respect to bringing my family to closure in the most expeditious and cost-effective manner. My belief was that the estate was for the children's benefit and their college education. I do not think Mr. Hopkins shared this belief.

I recognized that he probably could not ask opposing to withdraw their Petition because of the likelihood of their already having worked out an agreement to assist one another in the further plundering of the estate. It also occurred to me that Mr. Hopkins' unwillingness to petition the Court to reinstate Lew's supervised visitation before he received his $100,000 could have compromised Mr. Hopkins obtaining it, because of the internal commitments between counsel. While I understand that people operate from their own interest, I was quite disenchanted and felt betrayed.

Accepting submission and yielding to the will of one's husband (or attorney) – no matter what – may provide for the type of relationship some people desire. It is the patriarchal perspective in which both parties believe "all she has to do is agree." However, when abusive control is the driving dynamic a wife (or client) "can never 'give him his way' enough because he will change his way to tighten the grip of control." (parenthetical added, Miller, 1995, p. 197)

CHAPTER 14

Betrayal, Betrayal, Betrayal

Passing Time with Mr. Rosenfeld

The Missing Computer Tapes

Lee Knohl Discloses Court Practices

Legislators Look In

Dr. Norman Chapman

Being Pro Se

Now I had tried the "barracuda" type attorney and the "peace maker" style of counsel and neither worked for me, so I pulled back to regroup before picking my next attorney. As is typical of me, I resorted to my local book store and library and consumed as much on the subject of divorce and abuse as I could digest. I recognized that I needed to know more about what I was dealing with before I took my next step.

What struck me in my reading was that I started to see a parallel in the dynamic of the litigation and that of the family violence I had experienced in our home. It occurred to me that I needed an attorney who truly understood the abuse syndrome. I wanted someone who would align with our cause and fight to carry me and my children out of this dynamic. While this did appear to be the appropriate means to my goal, it proved to orient my family in the wrong direction – that being further into the abuse dynamic.

Initially I met with a female attorney whose partner had written a book about abuse. After our first session, I was informed that she was over scheduled and would not be able to take my case. My sense of it was that she did not want to be in court with Joy Feinberg. I believe that the type of domestic violence case to which her firm was more accustomed merely involved getting the battered spouse a protective order and keeping safe distance between litigants as they divorce.

My case was postured as a continuation of the domestic violence in the courtroom. Instead of Lew's fists, he was now using our money to control me. This can be quite time consuming and non-compensating for an attorney on the victim side of the litigation. I understood her situation, and so I continued my search. I consulted with a trusted divorce attorney to get his opinion and some direction on lawyers that could be appropriate and available for my case.

The man was quite taken by my story and reinforced the direction I was moving toward in selecting my next attorney. He said, "I would never take a case with an abuser, as it would be an abusive headache for me." He added, "I don't deal with those kind of people." Then, he directed me to an attorney whom he believed to be an excellent litigator. He said, "Your husband is going to fight this no matter what you do, so you will need someone who can fight in court."

I was led to Mr. Rosenfeld. Mr. Rosenfeld was a warm hearted man who projected strength and commitment to doing what was right. I paid him $10,000 that had been given to me for my mainte-nance, hoping he would get me to the end. I lived on very little during the interim and taught myself how to juggle our expenses on credit cards.

Six months after I retained Mr. Rosenfeld, I learned that he still had not obtained my file from my previous counsel. I became disenchanted and I recognized that our case was stagnating. The proceedings focused primarily on how the estate was going to pay

David Grund's fees, an obligation typically dealt with during or after the final judgment.

Further, my meetings with Mr. Rosenfeld seemed as unproductive to the proceedings as was the litigation around paying my former attorney. In our last meeting I inquired, "What is your strategy for moving the case to closure and settling the final custody and finances." His response was a directive that I should get a boyfriend, because the comforting from a romantic relationship would benefit me during this period.

Mr. Rosenfeld may have been an excellent litigator but, once taking on my case, he appeared to give up the battle. In retrospect, I recognize that Mr. Rosenfeld knew more about what was ahead of me than I could see, and I don't believe he had the heart to contribute to it. At the time, it led me to question the politics inherent in my case. However, being as naive as I was, I didn't know what questions to ask, much less how to find the answers. Mr. Rosenfeld and I parted.

*   *   *

Before awakening to my stagnation with Mr. Rosenfeld, I was met with an unexpected and peculiar violation that appeared to be related to the litigation. My secretary, Pat Rybarski, approached me asking for a raise. I told her I was not in a position to give it to her. She had another job lined up with more pay, so I wished her well and encouraged her to take it. She was in need of an income beyond my means. Under normal circumstances, I may have negotiated with her and given her a raise at that time because she had been with me for almost a year. However, I had slowed down in my practice because of the demands of the litigation and the needs of my children, and therefore no longer required as much secretarial support.

Her last day of employment was January 14, 1997. On this day I asked her to show me where all of the matters were that I had delegated to her. The backing up of my computer was one of these responsibilities. During this time she was in possession of one of our back-up tapes to the computer and was directed to return it to the office during the previous week. When I inventoried the office for various items, I noted that it had not been returned. I told her to deliver it the same day, before picking up her belongings and final paycheck.

She claimed to have misplaced it, and said she was too upset to look for it. The dialogue between us was most peculiar and I knew something was up. I continued calling her, insisting that she locate this computer tape. She had been directed as my employee to hold it for safe keeping while I was away for the Christmas holidays. We agreed to keep the office backup on her premises because of the harassment to me and my home by Lew over the last year. We were both aware of the importance of this tape. I delegated her as the person to maintain this off-site backup, specifically for its security during the period of my absence *only*. I kept the tape at all other times.

I told her that if the back-up tape was not returned to my office within 24 hours, I would have to file a report with the police, because of the confidential information held on the tape. The tape was not returned and numerous other computer tapes had been removed from my office, without my knowledge.

I notified the Chicago police and a report was filed. An investigator went out to her home to attempt to retrieve the tape. Pat did not answer the door. Later that evening, she claimed that the tape had been left in a shopping bag on the day she purchased her Christmas tree – December 23, 1996 – and was subsequently thrown out with the garbage. The officer taking the report said, "Her rendition of the events was garbage." It was obvious to both of us that an item of this importance, with which she was entrusted and assigned to maintain as part of her fiduciary responsibilities to the practice, would not be carelessly left in a shopping bag.

Since there was no way for me to retrieve the tape and no way for me to prove that she had it, I had to file a Permanent Injunctive Order prohibiting the dissemination of any contents on the tape. A criminal attorney proceeded with this action on my behalf. It was a necessary step in protecting my practice. On our day in court, Pat was a different woman. She was not the gentle sweet lady I had come to rely on, but rather she stood in court with an attorney from Lew Blumenthal's divorce lawyer's law firm. In Chicago where there are many hundreds of law firms, this was a highly unlikely coincidence.

*   *   *

Shortly after I recovered from the incident of my secretary's betrayal, a friend recommended that I read *Divorced From Justice: How Women and Children Are Abused by Divorce Lawyers and Judges*. I inhaled this book in a matter of days, and was stunned to see myself and my predicament in black and white. I recognized that the things that my attorneys were doing with me were done to women all over the country. Sadly, I was informed that the tactics in my case were the very same strategies used to leave women childless, homeless and bankrupt. I learned that 70 percent of men fighting for custody get it, and in most cases, abusive men fight for custody. My worst nightmare was looking like a reality. What everyone said couldn't be done was happening to battered women and children coast to coast.

The same woman, who had recommended that I read this book, suggested that I speak to Lee Khnol from a citizens' court advocacy group to evaluate my case and to determine if it was in the same category as the litigation injustices outlined in the book. I compiled my file immediately and met with Mr. Knohl. Mr. Knohl is a man in his late 40's, about 5' 11", with a medium build. He was devoted to assisting victims of litigation abuse and those who had fallen through the cracks of the system. After a thorough review of my case from the Court Record, the documented evidence and a full briefing of various events in my proceedings, Mr. Knohl was convinced without a shadow of a doubt that I was being "railroaded" in my divorce. At the time I did not know what this word meant, but over the years that followed I became intimately familiar with the concept. The balance of this judicial story will describe court railroading better than I can define it.

Mr. Knohl and his assistant taught me several things about divorce court proceedings, unethical strategies and unlawful tactics. They were astounded by the fact that hundreds of thousands of dollars had been spent with nothing actually litigated in the case. They were also shocked that the majority of the legal fees incurred were spent trying to secure legal fees for litigation or prevent me from obtaining financial support.

They used the term "estate plunder," and noted that this was quite typical of the divorce industry. They forewarned me that, "what often happens is the estate is emptied by counsel, and then and only then does counsel encourage closure." They recognized that a problem for me in this scenario was Lew's ability to kept the attorneys fed, making closure "unpredictable."

They pointed out that **all** of the decisions in the case came about from "agreed orders" and explained the grave implications of this for me. I had learned that an agreed order is an agreement between parties, which does not require a judge's input or consideration. But, this meant that the Court was not formally apprised of the details leading up to these agreements. The relevant issues remained off the Court Record and the Court did not assume responsibility for any of the contents of the agreement. They pointed out that the parties (Lew and I) can agree on anything, even the most absurd arrangement and the Judge is not held liable for any resulting injustice, because it did not evolve out of his formal court ruling. They laughed at how Judge Evans was "hiding behind the Agreed Orders," and helped me see the implications of this in my case. For example, they pointed out that entering into an Agreed Order for Support and the Agreed Order for Legal Fees allowed counsel to continue to leave my husband's near $500,000 income off the Court Record.

Unfortunately, Lew's income remained out of the Court Record for several more years and this posturing interfered with my utilizing our family money. The way this played out was as follows. Each request for access to the marital estate for anything, from child support to expert witness fees to legal fees, necessitated the demand for another production. Since my records were never returned from the first production in August 1995, I could never satisfy the discovery requirement. My inability to produce what I no longer possessed became Lew's excuse not to disclose his complete financial records to the Court. This impasse before the Court became the Judge's cause for not making any determinations about the distribution of funds from our estate. As I write this today, it occurs to me that the attorneys actually took control over our estate. It was now their estate, and Lew maintained the ability to open and close the pocketbook according to his needs and wishes.

The implication of the Agreed Order, with respect to lifting Lew's supervised visitation, was that his ongoing abuse to me and the children also remained off the record. Consequently, the Judge was not apprised of the full situation, or at least not publicly informed. Mr. Knohl recognized that since the Judge was *aware* of the details of the case from the May 1995 Evidentiary Hearing in which he gave Dr. Lewis Blumenthal an abuse finding, he was *blindly* allowing judicial absurdities in his courtroom.

*   *   *

After Mr. Knohl and his assistant had reflected on the proceedings and legal posturing, they examined the background information concerning the abuse to me and the children again. They were repulsed by the photographs, showing bruises on me and my boys, particularly in the context of the way the court appeared to be poised for the continuation of abuse to me and my children.

Mr. Khnol wanted to contact the legislators in the state of Illinois to inform them of the abuse that was being enabled in the Domestic Relations Division of Cook County Court. He put together a packet of information describing the salient points in our case and sent it to every Senator and Representative in Springfield, Illinois.

This outreach led to my having numerous conversations with Illinois legislators. The general consensus among the legislators I consulted was that my case was, as they called it, **"An Abuse Promotion Supported By A Feeding Frenzy."** These exact words were stated by far too many individuals looking in at our case. A legal representative from my local senator's office gave me support and the following advice to manage my dilemma. He said:

"Protect the Court Record by keeping the record straight (that is, with your side of the facts disclosed) and get your case to the media, immediately."

His words remained with me, and I did my best to follow the recommendations. It was an excellent suggestion, because it empowered me and slowed down our falling through the cracks of the judicial system. However, the better I got at doing this, the more abuse I received. As I put the facts favorable to my case in our Court Record and provided evidence correcting Lew's false allegations, counsel found more creative ways to continue the "legal domestic abuse" to me and my children. Protecting myself and my children in this manner, left me merely fighting with a bigger bully. This cyclic warfare did not arrest the abuse cycle; it became exponentially more dangerous.

Mr. Knohl felt a true compassion for the devastating consequences of our circumstances to my children. He elected to circulate our story to various abuse agencies throughout the state and to many nationwide abuse organizations. The blessings that came from this outreach led me to numerous sympathetic ears. Several of these people served as confidants and assistants to me during my plight.

Unfortunately, many who truly understood my irrational and tragic predicament were not in a position to impact the proceedings. As I brought them forward, the attorneys spent much time keeping their voices muffled and, of course, preventing their input from leaking into the Court Record.

*   *   *

My discussions with Mr. Knohl helped me clarify my uneasiness around Dr. Norman Chapman, the court-appointed custody evaluator. Dr. Chapman was selected to conduct the 604 (b) custody evaluation through his psychological service, the Counseling Connection. He is a rather small framed man, roughly 5'8", weighing about 140 pounds, with blond hair and in his mid 40's. From the exterior he appeared rather benign, but as I learned, some exteriors can mislead.

In our first session during the July 1996 initial evaluation, I recall being quite surprised that he had little or no interest in looking at the photographs of bruises which evidenced some of the incidents of abuse to me and the children. I felt as though he was put off that I was wasting his time with this sharing. At first, I didn't know what to make of this.

At some point in our initial discussion, I expressed my surprise that Lew would or could posture for a custody dispute. I told him that I believed it was wrong to place abused children in a contemptuous and stressful situation, as is typical of a custody trial. I even said, "My children have suffered enough pain," and pleaded, "the time has come for them to heal." I asked why is it that the Court would allow them to be placed in a custody battle, after it acknowledged the detrimental and adverse impact of their father's long history of abuse to them. It made no sense to me, and I told him I was puzzled. He said, "Well, a custody battle is not as bad as cancer." His response was too peculiar for me to process at the time.

What distressed Mr. Knohl about Dr. Chapman was that he withheld his custody recommendations for over a year-and-a-half; an evaluation which should have taken only months. Mr. Knohl saw the holding out of this evaluation, particularly after all the meetings had been completed, as the key to enabling the protracted litigation. He spent hours reviewing Dr. Chapman's preliminary report and his deposition taken by counsel in January, 1996. It was obvious to Mr. Knohl that Dr. Chapman recognized Lew's abuse problem. Dr. Chapman made recommendations for a psychiatrist to serve as a "monitor" for signs of abuse and violence to the children during visits with their father. Yet, Dr. Chapman aided in the continued detriment to the children by prolonging closure and entertaining the idea of placing them right back in the hands of their abuser.

The lack of professional ethics was blinding here and quite disturbing to all of us. Mr. Knohl sent the package prepared for the legislators to the President of Forest Hospital, where Dr. Chapman served as a psychiatrist. He also sent a letter to the Department of Professional Regulations, informing them of Dr. Chapman's actions.

*   *   *

The backfire in the court over this effort to reach out and correct a social wrong-doing and professional injustice to children was extraordinary. I was Pro Se at the time, meaning that I was without counsel and therefore representing myself. I had been drafting my own pleadings with the assistance of individuals who were quite knowledgeable about family law, filing them with the Court, and doing my best to keep up with responding to opposing counsel's pleadings and false allegations.

In the course of this particular week, after news spread concerning Mr. Knohl's disclosures, I received five separate Pleadings and was required to attend four separate Hearings all within five working days. It was physically impossible for me to keep up with the legal paper chase and court appearances, much less represent myself to the Court without any familiarity about court procedure. But, I did my best to hold my own.

In this same week, at the request of opposing counsel, the Court ordered that I attend another session with Dr. Chapman and the monitoring psychiatrist. They alleged that it was necessary, because Mr. Knohl's involvement in our case and the outreach implied that I had "delusional thinking about the system."

Now, the most absurd part of this effort to rush me to the doctor for a visit was that it was required that I go there at the same time I was suppose to be in court for one of these four Hearings. Subsequently, I was severely penalized for not being able to represent myself Pro Se in the courtroom in downtown Chicago and visit with the doctor 45 minutes away in the suburbs, simultaneously. This was the second time that my position in the court was compromised by my inability to be in two places at one time.

I recognized that there was no way that I could keep up the pace. There was no time for meals, no time to sleep, no time for anything other than the court chase. I lost ten pounds during this period, bringing my weight below 110 pounds.

It seemed absurd that I was fighting this in court by myself for four months, while Lew was represented in court by two law firms and not in court himself, so I decided to find another attorney. I didn't know this at the time, but this is probably what the Court wanted me to do. While having the attorney helped me regroup, rebuild and give the children the attention they needed, it provided a way for my case to fall back into being manipulated to Lew's liking and his legal team's agenda.

OFFICE OF THE SENATE PRESIDENT
ILLINOIS SENATE

JAMES "PATE" PHILIP
SENATE PRESIDENT
AND
MAJORITY LEADER

March 20, 1997

327 STATE CAPITOL
SPRINGFIELD, ILLINOIS 62706
217/782-8194

Ms. Denise Kane
Inspector General
Department of Children and Family Services
406 E. Monroe St. - Floor 1
Springfield, IL 62701

Dear Denise:

Attached is information I have received from Lee E. Knohl regarding Michael Reese Doctor Lewis Blumenthal who has repeatedly physically abused his children. And, if I read this right, he has been given custody of his children after his divorce. Also attached are photos taken of these children who have suffered the abuse.

Could you look into this?

Sincerely,

James "Pate" Philip
Senate President

JPP/ob

Attachments

cc: Lee E. Knohl

Senator James "Pate" Philip's Response to Mr. Knohl's Outreach

Senator Philip was the first person to respond to Mr. Knohl's information packet. While it was not clear to our Senate President whether the children were placed in Lewis' custody, it was clear that making this placement warranted investigation. I was not contacted by DCFS in response to this letter, though I was the appropriate contact person – the custodial parent – and my phone numbers were in their files. Further, there was no response by DCFS to my efforts to communicate with them concerning this letter.

CHAPTER 15

The Lawyers Know
the Inside Story

My Interviews with Lawyers

Steve Stern Comes Aboard

Chapman's Fishing Expedition

Children Flourishing: Brad's Party and Hospital Threat

In my search for appropriate counsel to represent me, I brought my story to twelve potentially eligible attorneys. Why so many? Because, with each interview, the reality of the fabric molding my predicament unfolded and tightened, sending me from one attorney to the next. A pattern emerged from this interviewing that confirmed my hunches concerning the underlying politics governing my case and my position within the system.

With every single one of these attorneys, the initial interview was one of surprise by and commitment from the attorneys. I was repeatedly told the following:

- "Your husband has no standing to fight you for custody; and if he does proceed with custody litigation, he can't get it with an abuse finding,"

- "Illinois law provides for your litigation to be funded by the marital estate, and the dictates of these disbursements should

be a function of your needs as put forth by your attorney, not
a function of your husband's whims."

- "Your previous counsel has not done the proper things to
  access the resources you are entitled to receive."

In one particular meeting with Karen Shields, a lawyer who was
a former judge, I learned the most about my predicament. Upon first
hearing about my situation she said, "*Something is wrong here.*" The
look on this woman's face was one of being as puzzled as I. It was
ever so obvious to me that, indeed, something was wrong. She told
me that she wanted to make some phone calls to inquire as to what
was happening in my case and get the perspective of the court-
appointed *children's attorney.* I consented for her to speak with him.

She told me that she would get back to me in a couple of days,
but I did not hear from her. I called her office and was informed that
it would be best for me to meet with her partner and work with him.
I was willing to do this because I had learned through other sources
that he had excellent standing in the court, superior presence and
communication skills; and, further, was as fair and honest as the day
is long.

He met with me that week and he was quite cordial, warm and
articulate. There was authentic interest and eye contact, until we got
to the true business of my case. His head fell into the paper work and
didn't come up to even acknowledge that I was in the room for the
entire time that I talked about my predicament. Continuing to keep
his eyes glued to his pad upon which he was taking notes as I spoke,
he made me an offer. He said, "We'll take your case for $50,000
retainer, up front."

The fact that he said this, knowing that I could not access any
funding from the estate on my own and had more debt than I could
manage, was amazing. But even more telling was his inability to
look me square in the eye as he spoke. I remember feeling his
discomfort in that moment and thinking to myself, he is an honest

person struggling with his words, but his body is speaking his truth. I recognized that he couldn't look me in the eye, because he couldn't give me an authentic offer. He was making an offer he knew I wouldn't bite. I believe he did this because he wanted no part of my predicament. It was politically detrimental to his office and the stature of his firm, with judges in partnership, to be a party to this case.

*   *   *

The pattern that emerged from the stream of interviews in my search for counsel was this. Initially they jumped in, saying this was wrong and they could help or fix it because the laws were on my side. Then, after dialoguing with opposing counsel or David Wessel, who called himself the children's attorney, it was no longer possible to bring forward these same laws before the Court, or else the lawyer became too busy to do so. Or, as in the case described above, an offer was made that I could only refuse.

I saw the counsel falling into two groups. There were the ones who really didn't want to be involved in the messy matter, either because it would hurt them or they didn't want to be a party to directly hurt me. These attorneys quickly and unexpectedly got busy or gave me offers beyond my reach.

Then there were those who came back to me after talking with other counsel in the case, eager to jump into my case, but singing a new song. Somehow the winds of "justice" got blown out of their sail. I was given excuses and double talk about the laws which had been straight-forward in our first meeting and were now spoken of as not intended to be put before the Court. These attorneys provided me with many of the strategies and tactics already played out in my case, which were promises to help me yet only kept me spinning. Since I didn't want to walk down the frustrating roads that I had known from former counsel, I elected not to engage their services.

*   *   *

I felt my impasse and was ready to give up, but the phone calls kept coming in from Lee Knohl's outreach to abuse agencies, and more options were made available to me. Lee called me with the phone number of a lady who identified herself as head of a domestic violence organization that had been honored by our governor. I called her and she explained how she, too, had been a victim of abuse and truly empathized with my situation. She offered the name of the attorney who represented her and proudly said, "He took care of my case and drove my husband out of town." I wasn't sure why she was so happy about this result, but valued the fact that her counsel brought her to closure and she remained with her children. That's all that mattered to me so I called the attorney, Steven Stern.

Steven Stern is about 6 feet tall, dark, and has a solid, heavy physique. His hair was dark brown and he had a mustache which gave him the "hardened fighter" look, but more like the type I'd meet on the street, not in court. His rugged appearance and solid presence gave me a mixed impression of him. I thought he could handle the fight, but wasn't sure he could manage the politics. His personal warmth and human compassion toward me is what won me over.

Mr. Stern required a $10,000 retainer up front to take my case. I was broke and resorted to a credit card with a $10,000 credit limit, which I had recently obtained and was holding for an emergency. I thought his rescuing me and my children from this endless war was our emergency, so I gave him a check for the entire line of credit. That day he took my file and went through the pressing and salient issues with me.

We spent many hours on the phone over the weekend exchanging information; me giving him facts and events, and he educating me about the law. In this one weekend we generated three excellent Pleadings, which were Responses to frivolous and misleading allegations that opposing counsel had previously put before the Court. I was relieved that someone was finally cleaning up our Court Record on my behalf. Then Mr. Stern drafted and filed a Pleading asking the Court to dismiss Dr. Chapman, based on the numerous facts showing his apparent bias and unethical conduct evidenced over the years.

This beginning with Mr. Stern enhanced my faith in his commitment to our cause and ability to represent me in court. That faith in many ways saved me, as it allowed me to regroup, rebuild and restore my physical strength.

*   *   *

While Steve was working hard to clarify many old misrepresentations in the court and attempting to keep further assaults by opposing counsel at bay, Lew's legal team put forth greater ingenuity and creativity in their legal attacks. Their first effort centered around ushering me into a court-ordered visit with Dr. Chapman. This visit was Lew's attorney's follow-up effort to "get Jeanne to the doctor" after Mr. Knohl's outreach to legislators and Dr. Chapman's superiors.

The session was a legal psychiatric ploy to corner me into a diagnosis in the "paranoid" category. Dr. Chapman wasn't interested in the alleged cause for bringing me into his office, that being how are the children or even how was I as a parent, but rather it was to label me as having "delusional thinking about the system" to substantiate the allegations in Lew's counsel's Pleadings. Dr. Chapman was interested in and only in: Lee Knohl's actions, what information was circulated and to whom; my trust in DCFS in their handling the investigation of the incident in which Lew threw Marc to the ground in July 1996; my faith in David Wessel as representing the children's interests; and how I felt about my attorneys and their representation of me. It was obviously not a clinical follow-up custody evaluation. It was a desperate attempt at what Dr. Kaufman, my own psychiatrist, called a "fishing expedition," and it failed. I knew I didn't need this appointment and so did my psychiatrist. Dr.

Kaufman helped me see how these legal psychiatric ploys were created.

Practically 85 percent of my time with Dr. Chapman during this session centered around two lines of inquiry, serving as his bait. The first being my trust in the Department of Children and Family Services (DCFS) as a protective agency and the second having to do with my faith in David Wessel. When Dr. Chapman was not getting the answers that he was fishing for, he continued throwing the same question out poised 10 to 15 different ways. At one point, I was stunned with his persistence, so I made a record of his questions and my answers to the same questions, being asked over and over again.

The following is an excerpt from this meeting on April 30, 1997:

Dr. Chapman: "What do you think it means that the DCFS file was gone?"

Jeanne: "I don't know what it means."

Dr. Chapman: "Why do you think Lew's attorney called DCFS?"

Jeanne: "I don't know why. I suppose he was calling as Lew's attorney."

Dr. Chapman: "Why did you link these two statements together (Lew's attorney calling DCFS and then the file was gone)?"

Jeanne: "I was only telling you the sequence of events, as I discovered them and as they were told to me."

Dr. Chapman: "Do you think that it is unusual that Lew's attorney called DCFS?"

Jeanne: "I don't know if it is unusual or not. My attorney called DCFS, so I guess it's something that is done."

Dr. Chapman: "Well what do you think happened to the DCFS record?"

Jeanne: "I don't know what happened to it."

Dr. Chapman: "What do you imagine happened to it?"

Jeanne: "I told you, I don't know what happened to it."

Dr. Chapman: "Well, can you imagine what happened to it?"

Jeanne: "How can I know what happened to the records."

Then the same question was asked again and again. Eventually, Dr. Chapman started moving about in his chair and became agitated. He said, "You're not cooperating," and added, "This is frustrating." It was frustrating and I could feel his frustration, yet he continued on.

Dr. Chapman: "You implied that Lew's attorney's call had something to do with the whole record being gone."

Jeanne: "I'd didn't mean the original abuse finding." "Dr. Chapman, this last DCFS investigation was several months ago; I'm only giving you the events as they were brought to my attention."

Dr. Chapman: "Oh yes, it is now April, lets go on." "Why do you think David Wessel was upset with your reporting the incident to DCFS?"

Jeanne: "I don't know."

Dr. Chapman: "Well did you ask him?"

Jeanne: "No, I didn't ask him."

Dr. Chapman: "Why not?"

Jeanne: "It didn't occur to me to ask him."

Dr. Chapman: "Wouldn't you want to know this?"

Jeanne: "Yes, but I wasn't aware of his reaction for quite some time."

Dr. Chapman: "But wouldn't you want to know this; he is your children's attorney, isn't he?"

Jeanne: "I said I didn't learn of his reaction until several months later, sometime in November."

Dr. Chapman then asked if I thought David Wessel was representing my children's interests, posing the question in numerous ways, over and over and over again.

Dr. Chapman: "What is the role of the children's attorney?"

Jeanne: "To represent the children."

Dr. Chapman: "How does he do this?"

Jeanne: He represents to the court the various issues like camp, vacations, temple, visitation... day to day things concerning the children."

Dr. Chapman: "What is he doing to do this?"

Jeanne: "I have not observed."

Dr. Chapman: Do you think David Wessel is here to represent the children?"

Jeanne: pause

Dr. Chapman: "Do you think he is representing the best interest of the children?"

Dr. Chapman: "Well, he is representing your children's interests?"

Jeanne: "I did not know I was here to discuss David Wessel."

Dr. Chapman: "What is your attorney's duty and role?"

Dr. Chapman was eagerly pursuing me confiding my perception of my counsel and David Wessel with him, and I realized the inappropriateness of this line of inquiry. I recognized he wanted me to reveal my sense of me and my children being re-victimized by the legal process, and saw how that type of candor with this man would backfire even more.

*   *   *

I informed my counsel of what had transpired in the interview, and it was obvious to me that he was in agreement with my perceptions of this being an unethical "fishing expedition" and not an impartial authentic clinical custody evaluation. Mr. Stern brought our Petition to Disqualify Dr. Chapman to the Court and added a number of points showing his failure to comply with custody evaluation protocol and the Court Orders for completion of his report, as well as Dr. Chapman's lying to the Court about his not having knowledge of Lee Knohl's circulated packet.

At this point, Mr. Stern gave the appearance of being committed to our cause. I recall watching him in court in our first few months together. He stood before the Judge with his legs parted, arms behind his back and his torso held in a Martial Arts pose. When he spoke, his position was firm, convincing and sincere. In time, I realized that this was not enough, because the Court ignored him. His Pleadings lingered, unresolved and the Judge managed to avoid ruling on that which he presented.

One day, I recall walking out of court with him, and he said to me, "The problem with this Judge is that he doesn't make any decisions." Mr. Stern added, "He just can't make a decision." I realized that Steve knew what he was up against, and when his $10,000 retainer ran out his court posture changed. It was hard for me to admit the shift I was observing in Mr. Stern, because I didn't know where I would turn if he couldn't help us. I decided not to judge him harshly and, instead, to give it time.

*   *   *

The children were doing very well. Steve's coming aboard after my four months of being Pro Se made it possible for me to give my sons what they needed and wanted. They were each flourishing, and I was delighted that I was available to be with them without the burden of my having to study law books and write pleadings. In retrospect, I believe I was probably holding onto the time I had with my children, more than I was counting on Steve.

Our lives were busy with the usual care, from new shoes to clean teeth. I took them to their regular doctor, dentist, hair cut appointments, and we made each outing an enjoyable trip. All other excursions were pure fun. These involved school activities, educational trips, movies, bowling, game houses, go-carting, swimming, neighborhood parks, amusement parks, outings with friends and much play with our animals. At home we made fires, read, did school projects, visited, cooked together, watched movies, played basketball, went biking and found numerous creative avenues for growth and play.

School was approaching the year's end, and we were busy bringing closure to their academic work and preparing for 1997 summer activities. Marc, age 7 at the time, was completing 2nd grade with excellent marks and outstanding accomplishments in math. David, age 9 at the time, was completing 3rd grade, also with excellent marks and superior comments by his teachers. They were consistently praised by their teachers for being cooperative, responsible, hard working students. Bradley, age 12 at the time, was completing 7th grade. During this particular period, he was evidencing such progress that the school principle awarded him with a special certificate acknowledging his success. I was pleased that all three children were doing well academically in school. Their social development was also progressing quite well. They were maintaining good relationships with friends and neighbors in our community.

*   *   *

Brad and I were planning a birthday party to celebrate his 13th birthday, August 16th. We decided to schedule it at the end of the school year in order to include his school friends. All the arrangements were made and his classmates and friends were invited. I appreciated the sweet way in which Marc and David were also enjoying our preparations for this special event.

The day before our celebration, I was in court on numerous matters which rolled over into what was to be a Hearing on all "pending issues" This essentially meant, anything of the everything that still remained unresolved. I was met with two surprises that convinced me that David Wessel was not aligned with my children's best interest.

All parties, including Lew, myself, Lew's counsel, my counsel and David Wessel were sitting around a table in the courtroom. There was no judge. For some reason, Judge Evans was not available on this particular day. We proceeded with discussions that had the appearance of pooling opinions and collaboration. I was open to this kind of interaction.

As the discussion unfolded, David Wessel and Lew's counsel proposed a 30 day in-patient psychiatric hospitalization for Bradley. This proposal came out of the blue for me and I was very shocked. From my perspective, such an intervention was inappropriate, unwarranted and clearly not in my child's interest. I informed them that involuntary hospitalization was psychiatricly inappropriate unless the patient was in danger to himself or others. I was very clear and firm about the medical and mental health criteria for in-patient psychiatric hospitalization. My counsel, Steve, appeared open to and appreciative of my input, but David Wessel and Lew's counsel looked at me like I had thrown a brick wall in front of their plan. Unfortunately, my input was not sufficient to halt their efforts; it only delayed it for the day.

Our dialogue continued, and next David Wessel and Lew's counsel were trying to talk me into canceling Bradley's party 24 hours before nearly 20 guests were to arrive. They were suggesting that, since Brad didn't have the phone numbers of all of his guests from school, I should drive around Northbrook Friday night and go to each person's house to give notice of the cancellation. Their rationale for canceling the party was that Lew allegedly had placed Brad in a "time out" from social events, due to his acting out in Lew's car two weeks ago. This was so absurd to me, particularly in light of the fact that I hadn't been informed of this punishment. Bradley wasn't even aware of it, as he had been partaking in social activities with Lew during this two week period.

What was clear to me was that this appeared to be another opportunity to intervene and prohibit the children from having a fun activity orchestrated by me in my home. This had been the pattern over the years during the proceeding. Lew maintained the monopoly on giving gifts, taking the children on vacations, going to family social outings and being the entertaining parent. I decided not to interrupt this special event, taking it away from Bradley, because I knew the social embarrassment it would cause him and the unnecessary personal disappointment he would feel. I elected not to cancel the party given the circumstances, and of course there were further legal consequences for my holding my own.

RICHARD KAUFMAN, M.D.
1775 WALTERS AVE.
NORTHBROOK, IL 60062

TELEPHONE: (708) 272-4472

April 29, 1997

To Those Concerned

Jeanne King, Ph D., has consulted with me regularly since January 17, 1996 to better understand, serve and protect the needs of her children during her divorce. She has been concerned about the effects of loss, loyalty conflicts, confusion and unpredictability upon the children's development.

I see Doctor King as a solid, compassionate, sensitive and moral parent. During this difficult time she has maintained decorum and balance, has valued the integrity and welfare of her children above her own interests and has demonstrated a high level of competent parental skills.

Sincerely,

Richard Kaufman

Dr. Richard Kaufman's Observations of Jeanne

CHAPTER 16

Legal Psychiatric Ploys

Fighting the Hospitalization Threat

Order for Another 100 K in Legal Fees

Dr. Freedman's Exit

The Bar Mitzvah Ploy

Dr. Heinrich and the Restraining Order

The next day the children and I had a very successful party for Bradley, and he was most appreciative. They were extremely helpful in cleaning up our recreation room and Brad glowed in the aftermath of his celebration.

Once the dishes were done, I dove into my reference books on in-patient psychiatric hospitalization, because I knew what was around the corner. I read everything I could get my hands on, and secured the statue on Mental Health Law for involuntary hospitalization of adolescents. The laws were in Brad's favor, and I was relieved. I discovered the following:

A) Children 12 years and over are to be informed of an intent to hospitalize.

B) It is their right to object to hospitalization.

C) The party proposing the hospitalization is obligated to inform the custodial parent of their intent.

D) There is a responsibility to exhaust "least restrictive
   alternatives" first.

Given that the laws were on Brad's side, I believed I could
prevent Lew's attorney and David Wessel's expressed desire to
hospitalize Brad if I could get this law before the Judge. Things
moved rapidly, and Mr. Wessel managed to get a Petition in the
court, allegedly supported by a document that he obtained from the
monitoring psychiatrist, to substantiate the need for hospitalization. I
thought it was rather clever the way they had woven in the criteria
for hospitalization that I talked about in our prior gathering. But, I
was livid that Mr. Wessel's proposal was in violation of Mental
Health Law. It violated Bradley's right to "object" to such an intervention, as well as the hospitalizing party's obligation to "exhaust
least restrictive" measures first.

I informed my counsel of this, and he advised that I immediately secure a psychiatric evaluation of Bradley. He and I were both
aware of the fact that the recommendation to hospitalize was made
in the absence of sufficient contact with the child. Dr. Freedman, the
monitoring psychiatrist, had only seem Bradley for two or three 15
minute visits over the last three months. Dr. Freedman had given
Bradley permission to miss his visits, because Bradley had been
taking caddy lessons from our neighborhood country club golf
instructor in preparation for summer employment.

Nonetheless the "instrument" that was used as a vehicle for this
hospitalization was placed in the Court Record and it was "sealed,"
which meant it couldn't be viewed by other individuals. I recognized
that this was to protect the psychiatrist and David Wessel, and
thought that it could limit my ability to secure the second opinion.
My counsel advised that I secure the second opinion anyway, and
assured me that the "instrument" would not be essential to our
obtaining an outside psychiatric evaluation.

I was directed to a highly respected child psychiatrist by the
name of Dr. Marvin Schwartz. Dr. Schwartz was also educated and

licensed in the practice of law. He was clearly a blessing for me and my child. Dr. Schwartz met with Bradley and determined that he was not in need of an in-patient hospitalization. I remember the day of his evaluation with Brad. Bradley had given a presentation on Einstein in school the day before, and it was so obvious that he was a child thriving – not a child ready for a psychiatric hospitalization.

Dr. Schwartz informed Bradley of the laws pertaining to involuntary hospitalization of a child his age and assisted him in composing a letter to all parties, articulating his objections to the hospitalization. I entered this letter into the Court Record and told my counsel that I insisted that this matter be brought to Mental Health Court, because the determination of a hospitalization for Bradley was beyond the jurisdiction of the Judge in Domestic Relations Court.

Two days later, the issue of Bradley's hospitalization disappeared from our proceedings. My counsel informed me that they backed off, and I felt relieved that I had assisted my child in preventing an unwarranted intervention. I knew in my heart that to place a healthy child in a psychiatric hospital involuntarily for 30 days would be extremely detrimental to the child's immediate and long-range well being.

*   *   *

The issue of a mental health intervention for Bradley evaporated from the front line concerns of the Court, and the focus shifted to the deliberation of how we were going to pay counsel. Months had passed since Steve spent his retainer in legal fees, and now I owed him another ten to twenty thousand dollars. He had reached a point where he needed to be compensated for his work.

In addition, months before this, I had run out of the supplemental money that had been allotted for child support and maintenance from the Home Equity line of credit, because the divorce was suppose to have ended Spring 1997. Given that we were both in need of money from the estate, Steve petitioned the Court for funding for himself and for me and the children. I did all the necessary discovery production of my current financial records. As usual Lew's counsel spent more in legal and court fees to keep us from getting any money than we were requiring and asking for ourselves.

The negotiations and legal back and forth in court was tedious, and was only costing Steve more in time and expense. I believe that Steve reached a point where his getting paid took precedent over all other matters. On July 2, 1997, Steve entered into an Order giving him $50,000 and $50,000 to Ira Feldman, Lew's financial attorney. I was both shocked and outraged that my counsel managed to secure money to cover both his metered time as well as prospective fees, before and instead of any funding for me and my children. This was particularly bothersome to me, given that all parties had previously acknowledged the necessity of this additional support to maintain my household overhead and the economic needs of the children. I thought, how could he get for himself that which had not been previously part of the court-ordered expense for the litigation and not get the funding for us that was previously agreed as necessary?

Seeing this order on paper gave me memories of my exchanges with Mr. Hopkins, and I realized that Mr. Grund's predictions concerning the withholding of funding provided a clear dilemma and conflict of interest for any attorney representing me. I waited and hoped that Steve would continue to pursue support for the children and myself. But this never happened, so I utilized credit cards to make up the difference we were deficient each month and tightened our belts further, once again.

*   *   *

While Steve was negotiating finances in court, there were some changes occurring in the arrangement with Dr. Freedman, the monitoring psychiatrist. In the visits that followed the effort to hospitalize Brad, I noted that Dr. Freedman was pulling back. On numerous occasions, he expressed his frustration in being a party to the case. He told me that he saw Mr. Wessel talking out of two sides of his mouth; saying he wanted to encourage the Blumenthal family to settle the case so the children could heal, while he was also posturing for the continuation of litigation and an upcoming custody dispute. Mr. Wessel had become the monitoring psychiatrist's primary communication link to our case. The monitor's court-designated schedule for communication with Dr. Chapman was neglected by Dr. Chapman's failure to return the monitor's calls.

In July of 1997, the monitoring psychiatrist gave notice that he would no longer serve the function of monitoring and surveillance of abuse in our family. My sense was that he recognized he had been manipulated by Mr. Wessel to provide a report which lacked in the ethics that were fundamental to the way this man practiced psychiatry. I believe he wanted no part of what he saw as an unethical manipulation of family dynamics at the expense of children's well-being and his own professional integrity. On the day he told me it would be our last visit and that he would no longer be seeing Lew and the children, I recall saying, "I understand how it must be for you and I believe this is your integrity speaking." I told him I respected his choice and we parted.

Even though I recognized that Dr. Freedman was probably placed in a convoluted unethical situation, the hospital legal psychiatric ploy remained with me for months. I was concerned about the fact the that Lew and Mr. Wessel would even consider compromising a child in order to carry out their agenda. It was suggested to me that this was done as a result of Dr. Chapman's failed "fishing exposition" with me last Spring. The way it was explained was, since they were not successful in placing a psychiatric label on me, they redirected their efforts to accomplish the same end by placing a label on my child. This had been the same strategy used January 1996 in the alleged emergency to get David into psychiatric treatment for a condition he didn't have, the fictitious "facial tic." I was told this tactic was typical in legal psychiatric ploys to wrestle custody; first prove the mom is nuts and if that doesn't work, prove that the kids are becoming nuts while in her custody. I consoled myself, knowing I was mentally stable and so were my children. But, that didn't stop the ploys.

*   *   *

It appeared that if Lew and his legal team couldn't directly walk Bradley into a mental hospital, they were committed to compromising him psychologically until the child became a candidate for a psychiatric setting. The years that followed were replete with actions that directly damaged my children's emotional health. It made me sick, watching the destructive mission of the children's father and their own attorney. Ultimately, it wore me out trying to prevent and offset what I believed were perverted efforts to wrestle custody.

The most prolonged and pathetic psychological ploy directed at Bradley was the effort to convince him that I, his mother, didn't love him enough to be involved in the events surrounding his Bar Mitzvah. But the fact is I was "walled out" of the planning and participation in his Bar Mitzvah, while he was coaxed into believing that I was not interested in this most important milestone in his life.

An Agreed Order was entered in June of 1996, by my counsel of record, David Hopkins, that allowed for the payment of the children's' affiliation in Temple Jeremiah. This Order directed Lew as responsible for the payment of the Bar Mitzvah and I was to pay him a percentage of the meal cost per guest for my family and friends. This payment was to be given after the Bar Mitzvah, which was scheduled for October 18, 1997, or at least after the affirmed guest response list was determined.

However, on July 3, 1997, I received a letter from Lew's sister, Marlene Mann, stating that Lew would not release invitations for my guests until I paid him $3000 up front. The problem with this arrangement was that it was not in compliance with the Court Order, and Lew knew from numerous Pleadings submitted to the Court that I was living on credit cards and did not have the funds.

Lew and his sisters repeatedly told Bradley, "If your mother loved you and cared enough about this special occasion, she would find a way to get the money." My poor son felt burdened to help me figure out how I would get the money. One night while I was putting the children to bed, I sat on the side of Brad's bed giving him a head message and back rub. This was something we did often, especially when he was feeling stressed. On that particular evening, as I was massaging his shoulders he said, "Mom you could sell your ring, so you and Grandma Audree (his maternal grandmother) and my cousins can come to my Bar Mitzvah." I felt his pain and his desperation in wanting me to find the funds so his maternal family and I could attend his Bar Mitzvah. I reassured him that I was doing everything I could, and that the Court had made provisions for me to secure reservations for my family.

The emotional manipulation surrounding his Bar Mitzvah party with respect to my love for my child was a source of tremendous conflict and upheaval for Bradley. In August he developed psycho-somatic symptoms of both daily headaches and stomach disturbance. I continued to assure my child that my love for him had nothing to do with the invitations, whether given to me or not; but from his perspective, my impotence in this matter was connected to my commitment to him. It took many hours of talking and working together to show him otherwise.

As the weeks approached the Bar Mitzvah of October 18, 1997, I started getting nervous myself because I could see that Lew was not going to budge on this one. Finally, in a discussion with Steve Stern, I broke down into tears pleading for his help so my family and I could attend my son's Bar Mitzvah. On September 29, 1997, three weeks before the Bar Mitzvah, Steve secured a Court Order that required Lew to release six invitations in order for my immediate family to attend and participate in Bradley's Bar Mitzvah.

Shortly after this was accomplished, Bradley and I were in a meeting with the Rabbi in preparation for the Bar Mitzvah. The Rabbi said to me, "I understand that you do not want to make an 'aliyah' (blessing) during the ceremony." I looked at him in shock, because I had never expressed that, and Brad and I had both been counting on me being part of the ceremony. The Rabbi noted my surprised look, and said that Brad's father told him I wasn't interested in doing this. I corrected the misinformation and told him how honored and happy I would be to make an aliyah for Bradley in his Bar Mitzvah. A part was given to me.

Later that evening, Bradley called his father on the phone and said, "Why did you tell the Rabbi that Mom didn't want to make an aliyah for me in my Bar Mitzvah." Lew told Bradley that the Rabbi was lying and that he never said this. I was listening as Bradley spoke, and he said, "The Rabbi doesn't lie, Dad." The two of them started bickering and it escalated into a huge fight with Bradley hanging up the phone on Lew.

From this point on, I believe that Bradley saw through the emotional manipulations surrounding his Bar Mitzvah and the psychological abuse by his father to him with respect to it. Bradley's behavior expressed his resentment about the numerous months of emotional turmoil evolving out of false, conflicting and bothersome information by Lew's family. Brad's actions spoke his truth. He repeatedly refused to go on visitation with his Dad for the next six months. There were endless afternoons of Lew coming to the house to pick up the children for their scheduled visitation in which Bradley and Lew would negotiate and fight on the threshold of our front door over Bradley's partaking in the visitations.

*   *   *

I observed the effect of the Bar Mitzvah ploy along with many other efforts in "middling." Lew used each and every issue that came up as an occasion to polarize Bradley, ad nauseam. Bradley's inner strength was weakening, and he was expressing this vulnerability through aggression with people and matters that didn't support his wishes, and in general defiance with authority. I could see that he was losing trust in himself and those around him, and he was modeling what he knew best as a means for dealing with conflict; that being, exercise control at all cost. I felt that if Bradley didn't have an intervention at this juncture that these patterns would stabilize and cause grave problems in his adult life. I saw it as my responsibility, as the custodial parent and as his mother, to get him appropriate help.

In my search, I spoke with half-a-dozen respected psychiatrists and psychologists throughout the Chicago area. Ultimately, I was led to Larry Heinrich, Ph.D., a specialist in the area of adolescence and behavioral issues around abuse. Dr. Larry Heinrich was a published, knowledgeable and seasoned psychologist recommended by our local police department social worker who had known our family over the years.

I made an appointment for Bradley to see Dr. Heinrich, after learning about his expertise with adolescent boys and his experience with issues pertaining to divorce and domestic violence. Bradley and Dr. Heinrich developed an immediate rapport. Dr. Heinrich engaged Bradley in establishing his own commitment to treatment. On the way home from their first session, Bradley said, "Mom, you find the best doctors." I felt hopeful that Brad was establishing trust with a neutral professional where he could develop a relationship in which he would heal and grow.

Bradley carried Dr. Heinrich's telephone number in his wallet and kept his own diary of their appointments. I brought Bradley to his weekly sessions with Dr. Heinrich, and during the course of their first month together, I observed a dramatic change in Bradley. Instead of striking when he was angry, he went outside and played basketball, or would retreat to his room and listen to music. Sometimes he played the piano or called a friend. I noticed he was developing healthy and productive ways of dealing with anger and conflict. The activities he resorted to dissipated his distress and allowed him to regroup, upon which he brought clarity and sensitivity to his circumstances.

David and Marc said, "Bradley is much nicer now that he sees Dr. Heinrich." The kids knew that the Doctor was helping Bradley and Lisa, too, was very much aware of his positive attitude, his cooperation and his overall improvement. In school, he was embracing his studies, and his grades reflected his efforts. After a few months of the therapy, Bradley got two A's on quizzes, joined the soccer team in school and fixed his room up like his own immaculate sanctuary. My child was developing self-respect and personal honoring. I was relieved and happy to see Bradley healing and moving in a healthier direction.

As their therapy progressed, Bradley utilized sessions to deal with past abuse perpetrated upon him by his Dad as well as the immediate psychological strain evolving out of the emotional manipulations around his Bar Mitzvah. He was growing and he was benefiting. He knew it, and so did I.

Then one day, out of the blue, I received a Temporary Restraining Order prohibiting Bradley from receiving therapy with Dr. Heinrich. This Order evolved out of an Emergency Hearing by virtue of a Petition submitted to the Court by Lew's counsel. The Hearing took place without my being informed that it was even to occur.

I was perplexed by Lew's action, outraged by David Wessel's inaction and my counsel's compliance. What disturbed me most was that, nearly four months ago, Lew and David Wessel were attempting an unwarranted and inappropriate psychiatric intervention for Bradley, and then now they were taking away a necessary and appropriate treatment from which he was benefiting. Mr. Wessel participated in this action without consulting Bradley or myself as to the efficacy and value of Brad's therapy. I would expect anyone alleging to represent a 13 year old to ask his client about his commitment to his therapy, his relationship with his therapist and as to whether any benefit was being derived, before abruptly cutting off his therapy.

I was truly livid by my counsel Steve Stern's proceeding with this Hearing without me, and then failing to inform the Court of his knowledge of Bradley's need for the treatment and the benefits Bradley was deriving from this therapist. I was appalled, and my faith in Steve was shattered because I had previously communicated all of this to him a number of times.

*   *   *

Bradley had developed a significant alliance with Dr. Heinrich, and when he was informed that he could no longer see him, Bradley lost faith in adults. He said, "I'll never trust an adult again." He could not comprehend why this was being done. His father told him it was done "because the Judge thought it was best." Brad saw the absurdity in that and his actions reflected his lack of respect for authority.

I informed all adult parties in the proceeding in writing that I believed the Restraining Order against Bradley's therapy with Dr. Heinrich was contra-therapeutic. I listed all the changes in my child that I was observing since the abrupt termination of his treatment. There was no response to any of my correspondence. Bradley's misconduct escalated and the school noted his acting out. He began to treat school like a playground in which he lost all interest in his studies and failed to obey the requests of his teachers. My cries for help became more desperate, but still I was not heard.

IN THE CIRCUIT COURT OF COOK,
COUNTY DEPARTMENT-DOMESTIC RELATIONS DIVISION

IN RE: THE MARRIAGE OF   )
)
LEWIS BLUMENTHAL   )
)   95 D 6150
        Petitioner,   )   Calendar 01
)   Judge Evans
)
    v.   )
)
)
JEANNE KING-BLUMENTHAL   )

        Respondent.

                    ORDER

    This matter coming upon the Court's calendar by agreement of
the parties, the Court having been fully advised in the premises,
it is hereby ordered:

    1. That petitioner, Lewis Blumenthal shall provide to

respondent, Jeanne King-Blumenthal, six (6) invitations for

Bradley Blumenthal's upcoming, Bar Mitzvah reception.

    2. That the cost for the aforesaid invitations, and those

invitees who attend shall be assessed against respondent, Jeanne

King-Blumenthal's share of the marital estate at the conclusion of

these proceedings.

    3. Lewis shall supply Jeanne with the aforesaid invitations

within seven (7) days.

                                    E N T E R E D
                          ENTER: CLERK OF THE CIRCUIT COURT.
                                    AURELIA PUCINSKI

                          JUDGE EVANS   SEP 2 9 1997

                             JUDGE
STEVEN E. STERN
STERN & DEVITT, LTD.   FUTY CLERK
150 N. WACKER DRIVE
CHICAGO, IL 60606
312-726-4400
ATTORNEY ID # 15721

Court Order for Bar Mitzvah Invitations: September 29, 1997

CHAPTER 17

Legal Domestic Abuse

Shelter Says, "Go Underground"

Reporting Dr. Chapman to Authorities

David Wessel and Dr. Chapman's Recommendations

Domestic Violence Representative's Suggestions

A Child Advocate Steps In

October 1997 was truly a month of passage for me and my children. Bradley experienced the traditional rites of passage inherent in the Jewish tradition of a young boy crossing the threshold to adulthood. He was a beaming star and his ceremony was a true success. However, on the other side of this passage, Bradley spun off into the conflicted realities and inconsistencies of our judicial system, acted out 13 year old style. David and Marc came to know Bradley as a different person, one they feared.

My passage was more of an awakening. In my effort to secure protection for my children, I awakened to the fact that our security and justice may not be found in the domestic relations courtroom. Prompted by my recent close contact with the Temple, I decided to follow through on a recommendation given to me by our Rabbi years ago. I bit the bullet and went to a domestic violence shelter. There was no more denying that my children and I were being battered; it had merely shifted into court-sanctioned domestic violence and abuse of the legal process. I was as blind and innocent in my efforts to offset these crimes, as I was in my dealing with the bruises in our home. I knew it was wrong, but I didn't know how to stop it.

I met a lovely woman who was the head counselor of the shelter, and learned more in this afternoon than I was ready to digest or could psychologically process. She greeted me at the locked front door. Welcoming my entry, she explained that the locked door was for the protection of the victims, and pointed out the importance of the confidentiality of the shelter's location.

She walked me into her consulting office and I let my hair down, telling her the whole story. Several hours passed. She reviewed my documentation, listened to me carefully, heard our predicament, felt our entrapment and then made a recommendation that was beyond my comprehension. This suggestion was given to me in confidence and a name was passed on for me to pursue the details. Her awkwardness in giving this option to me almost paralleled my difficulty in comprehending it.

"You need resources beyond what we have to offer here." she said. "I'm going to give you the name of someone who assists people in going underground."

I wasn't sure what all of this meant, and then I recognized the gravity of my circumstances from her next comment. She said, "In my 15 years of doing this work, I have never come across a situation of abuse that has gone to this extreme."

I felt her compassion and sensed her impasse. She gave me a hug and a beautiful sweet smelling flower that was sitting on her desk. It was a gift someone had given to her. She said, "I want you to have this." The tears were welling up in me. I did all I could to contain my vulnerable emotion. I left her office, walked to my car, but could not drive. It took me quite some time to process what had transpired that afternoon.

*   *   *

When I got home I was numb. I walked into my bedroom and picked up a book that Dr. Heinrich had given me after his last visit with Brad, *Bad Things Happen to Good People*. While I knew I needed to face my circumstances, I still wouldn't let myself read this book, nor could I make the phone call for going underground.

Eventually I made the call, but I did not prevail in making the connection. I called the shelter, and I was referred to a woman with only a first name and a pager. After many attempts, I did not receive a call back and eventually weakened in my efforts to follow through. I became distracted by the immediate distress around us. My oldest child was so compromised by the proceedings that I didn't have the heart to make his life more unstable by uprooting him. I held onto the belief that there was more I could try to do in Chicago first to help me and my children.

I called Evelyn Delmar, a child advocate from an organization named "HEAR MY VOICE: Protecting Our Nation's Children." Evelyn was the local representative of this national organization. She was also the director of another local organization called "Children Remembered." Evelyn had been a source of support for me and had always taken the position of what was best for the children. I told her that I was close to giving up, as I believed that I had exhausted my resources. I was praying that she would bring other avenues to the table for me to pursue.

Evelyn is a kind and compassionate woman in her late 40's, quite articulate, resourceful, and was always willing to help us. Since working with me over the last six months, she had repeatedly expressed her despair over Dr. Chapman's delayed report. Both Evelyn and Lee Knohl clearly saw how this report being withheld had become the excuse for the protracted litigation. I recall her saying:

"The Court is allowing Lew to suspend the lives of you and your children in litigation, and this is keeping you and the boys bound to your abuser."

I recognized that her observations were correct. With this perspective, I thought that the course of action was to direct my energy toward insisting that Dr. Chapman produce his report so closure could be established for our family. I recalled a conversation that I had six months earlier in which I pleaded with David Wessel to assist in getting Dr. Chapman to produce his final report. I remember telling Mr. Wessel my concern about the prolonged time period and how this was impacting the children. In this conversation, I tried to appeal to Mr. Wessel's social work background, knowing that he had once served as a social worker.

I said, "The continuation of these proceedings and the uncertainly it generates for the children is impeding their healing and interfering with moving our lives forward." I expressed how unsettling it was for the children to be repeatedly led to believe, by Lew, that their home life and residency was "temporary."

"The children need closure and the freedom to rebuild, please help," I pleaded.

Mr. Wessel responded, "Jeanne, it takes longer when there is this much money in the estate."

The connection between the financial value of our estate and a doctor's evaluation report made no sense to me. I recall knowing this comment reeked with corruption. There had been four Court Orders since July 1996 for Dr. Chapman to produce his report. As we approached each date, there was no report and no sanctions by the Court to encourage subsequent cooperation from Dr. Chapman.

I decided to reach out to the Department of Professional Regulations, the organization responsible for the licensing of professionals, including psychiatrists. I drafted a letter to the Director, Ms. Nikki Zollar, informing her that Dr. Chapman had spent two-and-a-half years of my children's young lives without providing his custody recommendation to the Court. I explained that this had become counsels' excuse for meritless protracted litigation that was psychologically damaging my oldest child. My intention was to inform her of the lack of ethics in Dr. Chapman's professional conduct. My hope was that she might intervene.

I informed my counsel, Steve Stern, of my intent to reach out to the Department of Professional Regulations. I told him I could no longer subject my children to destructive litigation which was prolonged by Dr. Chapman's delayed report. He said, "Do what you feel you need to do." He clearly understood my frustration. But, I doubt he knew our pain. I suspect he informed David Wessel and/or Lew's counsel of my plan to report Dr. Chapman to his professional authorities, because within days the legal backfire began.

*   *   *

Two business days after my letter to Ms. Zollar was sent out, I received an Emergency Motion for Transfer of Temporary Physical Possession of the Minor Children from David Wessel. This Pleading consisted of 47 allegations, none of which were true. Even more astounding was the fact that 90 percent of these false statements and frivolous accusations had been the subject of seven prior Petitions by Lew's attorney, Joy Feinberg, attempting to transfer custody. Further, Lew's counsel had already invested hundreds of thousands of dollars putting this false information before the Court in order to misrepresent the status of our circumstances. However, neither David Wessel nor Joy Feinberg were able to provide any factual basis for the false statements. Besides which, I had already, through my counsel's court Responses, given evidence showing the accusations were completely false.

This Pleading was a "blind ax." It remained before the Court without being heard or ruled upon for over a year-and-a-half. I was later told it couldn't be heard legitimately because it was already proven false. Further, and even more disturbing, was the fact that this Pleading legally could not be submitted before the Court by David Wessel, serving as the "children's attorney." The responsibility of the children's attorney is to *advise* the court concerning the children's residence and custody; not *petition* the court to transfer the children. This very instrument was an unlawful maneuver by David Wessel to assist Joy Feinberg in the wrestling of custody.

*   *   *

Later, we learned the purpose of this Pleading was not really for the court directly, but rather to serve as a vehicle and skeleton for the custody evaluator to make recommendations concerning custody. The Pleading was never heard in the court, it only served as a resource of false information to give Dr. Chapman some specifics upon which to make his custody recommendations. On the next day, Dr. Chapman submitted his report recommending sole custody to Lewis Blumenthal on the basis of 20 points, mirroring David Wessel's Emergency Motion to transfer the children to Lew. Nineteen of the 20 points were completely false.

It was clear that Dr. Chapman, using David Wessel's misrepresentations to the Court, quickly delivered his recommendations the day after his authorities learned of the delay of his report. The Doctor's report, like Mr. Wessel's Pleading, was without truth and without substance. Further, the matters alleged failed to fulfill the standard legal criteria for transferring custody.

The following exemplifies the type of complaints against me which served as the grounds for the custody recommendations in Dr. Chapman's October 7, 1997 report:

"Permitting Bradley to cut Saturday detention."

This was a detention canceled by the school Principal, because Bradley had already served it. The message to cancel this detention was personally left on my voice mail by the Principal and was retained for my counsel. The false allegation had already been rebutted with this information in an earlier Pleading by my counsel. Dr. Chapman was making his recommendations for the custody of my children based on heresy information that he failed to corrobo-rate with all the relevant parties. He never consulted with the school, nor did he ask me about this alleged missed detention, even though I was the residential and custodial parent.

The majority of points set forth by Dr. Chapman had as much merit as the school detention allegation. Other assertions by Dr. Chapman which were the basis of his recommendations to transfer custody to Lew were the Doctor accusing me of the following:

"Denying/minimizing the children's needs for psycho-therapeutic support" and "Avoiding the children's needs for psychotherapeutic support."

The most outrageous part of this assertion was that it was not me interfering with the children's therapeutic process; this was done by the actions of the Court at the request of the children's father. Moreover, I had sent numerous letters to Dr. Chapman expressing my concern for my children's welfare and pleading for an inter-vention for Bradley. Dr. Chapman did not respond by phone or mail to any of this correspondence. I can only assume that the above accusations were based on my efforts to shield my children from David Wessel and Lew Blumenthal's legal psychiatric ploys.

Then there was the assertion of "failure to protect," which was preposterous in light of our proceedings. Dr. Chapman writes:

"Neglect of a child's safety, failing to report to DCFS an incident in which she stated she believed the child had been physically abused by the paternal grandmother, despite having taken photographs of this abuse."

Dr. Chapman had been notified by me that I reported this incident to Judge Evans and showed the Court the pictures of the abuse to Marc. I informed Dr. Chapman that I reported the abuse in this way to the civil authorities, rather than with the Department of

Children and Family Services, because DCFS failed to assist my children after David Wessel and Lew's counsel intervened in their last investigation of abuse to Marc by the children's father. Most outrageous, however, is that Dr. Chapman would put forth this alleged "neglect to protect from abuse" as cause to place the children with the side of their family responsible for abusing them.

*   *   *

It was becoming more evident that I was not going to be dealt with in an impartial manner by the court agents, David Wessel and Dr. Chapman. I decided to reach out to government agencies familiar with domestic violence, hoping that they could assist in the politics of my case. I sought out city officials who had a vested interest in helping victims of abuse. I called the Mayor's office and was led to Ms. Leslie Landis, the Director of the Task Force for the Prevention of Domestic Violence. We had a lengthy conversation and she was extremely sympathetic and informative.

She said, **"Your whole proceeding is a violation of your Order of Protection."** Ms. Landis explained the Order of Protection for the children and myself, and Lew's "abuse finding," gave me custody and made him ineligible for custody. She pointed out, "His effort to transfer custody through these proceedings at this juncture is **harassment**."

She encouraged me to review the Illinois Domestic Violence Act. In doing so, I recognized that she was correct. An Order of Protection results in the petitioning parent being awarded legal temporary custody of the children, as occurred in our case. Further, the Illinois Domestic Violence Act specifies a "custody presumption" once an Order of Protection is issued. Accordingly the law states:

"If a court finds, after a hearing, that respondent has committed abuse (as defined in Section 103) of a minor child, there shall be a rebuttable presumption that *awarding physical care* (or) *temporary legal custody* to respondent would **not** be in the minor child's best interest." (Illinois Domestic Violence Act of 1986, Order of Protection Remedies, 60/214-5 and 6 combined, emphasis added)

Given this custody presumption, there was no legal basis for Lew's court plight to obtain custody. Moreover, his effort to do so violated the our Order of Protection, because the action in itself is defined as "harassment" according to the Illinois Domestic Violence Act.

"*Harassment* means knowing conduct which is not necessary to accomplish a purpose that is reasonable under the circumstances; would cause a reasonable person emotional distress; and does cause emotional distress to the petitioner..."

"The following types of conduct shall be presumed to cause emotional distress: ...improperly concealing a minor child from petitioner, repeatedly threatening to improperly remove a minor child of petitioner's from the jurisdiction or from the physical care of petitioner.." (60/103 Definitions 7)

The ongoing effort to transfer custody and threat of removing children from the custodial protective parent is clearly harassment – another form of abuse. As the Illinois Domestic Violence Act states, "Abuse means physical abuse, harassment, intimidation of a dependent, interference with personal liberty or willful deprivation..." Our Order of Protection specified that Lew was to be restrained from the following forms of abuse: Physical Abuse, Harassment, Interference with Personal Liberty and Intimidation of a Dependent; but, this did not insure that the Court would enforce this prohibition. To the contrary, the Court and its agents aided Lew in violating our Order of Protection.

*   *   *

Ms. Landis made several recommendations. First, she elaborated on the importance of holding my counsel accountable for his actions. I was encouraged to put everything in writing, which fortunately I had already been doing. Ms. Landis suggested I insist that my counsel petition the Domestic Relations Court to shift the determination of transferring custody and physical residence of the children into Juvenile Court immediately. She advised that I inform my counsel that the basis for this Petition would be as follows:

A) The Court is positioning to place abused children back in the hands of the parent with the well-documented history of abuse, a parent that continues, to date, to place the children's physical safety at risk.

B) The Court intends to do this transfer on frivolous and unfounded cause, and we all know this.

C) Bradley's physical safety and emotional life will be severely compromised when he responds to the unwanted situation.

Secondly, Ms. Landis encouraged me to ask my counsel to be my mouthpiece and submit before the Domestic Relations Court the following additional Petitions:

1) *Rule to Show Cause*: because this whole proceeding is "harassment." She said that everyone of the Pleadings put forth before the Court by David Wessel and Joy Feinberg, which we know to be unfounded, is "harassment," especially

given their unwillingness to withdraw those that they admittedly knew to be untrue.

2) *Violation of the Order of Protection*: because both Lew's and David Wessel's effort to force Brad to do what he has clearly expressed that he does not want to is "harassment to the child."

Ms. Landis was extremely generous with her time and very insightful concerning the needs of my children with respect to the judicial process. After I submitted the above recommendations in a letter to my counsel, Steve Stern, his attitude toward me became bitter. He said, "Ms. Landis doesn't know what she is talking about, because she isn't a divorce attorney." I knew this was a statement of anger and defensiveness, not one of truth. In retrospect, I believe what Steve meant was that Ms. Landis was not playing with the same set of political cards as the counsel in divorce court. Ms. Landis was trying to posture me on the *offensive*; but Steve knew we were "suppose to" remain on the *defensive*.

Steve was unwilling to put any of Ms. Landis' recommendations before the Court on behalf of me and my children. In the months to follow, the ocean between he and I widened on all matters related to my sons. I felt he was not able to represent me with the interest of my children in mind. It was later pointed out to me that his limitations were primarily a function of the politics between attorneys and the Court, and of Steve's ranking relative to opposing counsel.

*   *   *

While Steve may have wanted to help us at first, his hands were tied. He was clearly controlled by Joy Feinberg. In my efforts to cope with this impasse, I called Evelyn and was directed to John Lietzau. John was recommended to me because of his expertise in domestic violence, family therapy and divorce court matters. John called himself a child advocate, clearly aligned with the interests of children.

John is a man in his 40's, about 6 feet tall, attractive, very level-headed, and is a kind and good-natured human being. He was extremely knowledgeable about abuse and the abuse dynamic. He started accompanying me in court to serve as my support and as a witness to the proceedings. It became evident to John that the domestic violence in our family had merely transformed itself into the court forum.

Following a court hearing, John asked me, "Do you want an advocate for you and your children in court?" His question caught me by surprise. That was all I wanted, but had come to believe that it was politically impossible for me to have this type of representation. John believed Steve was not acting as my advocate on matters related to my children, and strongly urged me to meet with a man by the name of Jeff Leving.

I hesitated because Mr. Leving had earned a reputation in the Chicago divorce community as a father's advocate. My belief was that there were enough father advocates in my proceedings and I didn't need or want another. John explained that this reputation was misleading, but rather Mr. Leving aligns with children's rights as a priority. He said that the reputation grew out of the fact that men's rights with respect to children are more often denied in divorce matters.

My resistance continued, and finally John accompanied me to see Mr. Leving. "There will be no commitment," John said, "See for yourself, and if you believe he aligns with the children, we can go further."

After Mr. Leving heard my story in the first meeting he said, **"David Wessel and Dr. Chapman are screwing you!"** He was intense, angered, emphatic and clear.

I felt that he wanted to help us address the unethical foul play of these two men as our first primary focus. We believed this would bring the legal domestic abuse up and out of our proceedings, and I thought this would clear the path for justice for me and my children. We committed to work together with this goal first in mind.

During the meeting Mr. Leving pointed out, "If Mr. Wessel is doing this in your case, he is probably doing it in others." Mr. Leving was disgusted by Mr. Wessel's conduct. He acknowledged that posturing to place abused children right back in the hands of their abuser is wrong. He convinced me that he was coming from a place of pure intention to protect my children and bring their best interest before the Court. He said, "If I didn't care about the children here, I would not want to step on Mr. Wessel's toes, because he could benefit me in representing men in other cases."

*   *   *

Earlier in the proceedings, I had asked a detective referred to me by Steve Stern to investigate the observations, noted in my discussions with Mr. Leving, concerning the unethical conduct of David Wessel. I had known of two other cases in which Mr. Wessel worked in collaboration with Joy Feinberg or Dr. Chapman to throw custody to the highest bidder. I gave the investigator $2500 to search the court records for all cases over the last five years in which any combination of these individuals led to custody being delivered to the litigant controlling the financial estate. There were numerous leads I gave the investigator to pursue to assist in his disclosing the workings of this triangle of individuals. It is not surprising that the investigator took my money and refused to get back to me.

John and I were both comforted by the fact that Mr. Leving gave us the impression of wanting to direct his energy toward what we believed would make the biggest difference in the proceedings. So, we set forth to work as a team. John's role was to serve as support to me and as a witness during court proceedings for the benefit of Mr. Leving and myself. Mr. Leving planned to come aboard in my case for matters related to the custody of the children, while Mr. Stern remained as my counsel representing our financial interests.

Illinois Domestic Violence Act of 1986*

"'Domestic violence' means abuse," which is defined as "physical abuse, harassment, intimidation of a dependent, interference with personal liberty or willful deprivation..." (60/103. Definitions, p. 83)

The "Illinois Domestic Violence Act of 1986" is to be applied to promote "its underlying purposes" which include:

- "Recognize domestic violence as a serious crime against the individual and society which produces family disharmony in thousands of Illinois families, promotes a pattern of escalating violence which frequently culminates in intra-family homicide, and creates an emotional atmosphere that is not conducive to healthy childhood development."

- "Recognize that the legal system has ineffectively dealt with family violence in the past, allowing abusers to escape effective prosecution or financial liability, and has not adequately acknowledged the criminal nature of domestic violence; that, although many laws have changed, in practice there is still widespread failure to appropriately protect and assist victims."

- "Support the efforts of victims of domestic violence to avoid further abuse by promptly entering and diligently enforcing court orders which prohibit abuse and, when necessary, reduce the abuser's access to the victim and address any related issues of child custody and economic support, so that victims are not trapped in abusive situations by fear of retaliation, loss of a child, financial dependence, or loss of accessible housing or services." (60/102. Purposes, p. 83)

*Excerpt from Illinois Domestic Violence Act of 1986, Article I, General Provisions

FAMILY INTERVENTIONS: Psychotherapy and Mediation

John Lietzau, L. C. P. C.

55 E. Washington, Suite 1419
Chicago, Il. 60602-2109
U.S.A.

Phone 312-551-1440
Fax 312-551-1419
e mail: jkllietzau

April 22, 1998

To Whom It May Concern:

I am a licensed psychotherapist specializing in family therapy and domestic violence issues. Since September, 1997, I have attended a vast majority of the court litigation as a non-testifying expert and advisor for Dr. Jeanne King's divorce .

In my opinion, the dynamics of the domestic violence syndrome have continued. The only difference is that the brutal physical fighting has shifted from the home to the courtroom and is still going on.

One of the symptoms of domestic violence is manipulation of funds. I am Not an attorney but I do see three attorneys show up for the opposition at many hearings so that the "Levelling Of The Playing Field" clause appears not to have been enforced. How can one side be able to maintain a 3 or 4-1 ratio of spending on this case without any progress in the six months I've attended hearings?

Now there is a movement to exclude me from the courtroom. Why would there be an effort to do so now after I have stated over and over I am a Non-testifying expert?

Throughout the proceedings Dr. King has shown exemplary courage, fortitude and psychological stamina unparalled in my 25 years as a mental health professional. Please help this case from turning into a tragedy.

[signature] , LCPC

John Lietzau, LCPC

Mr. John Lietzau's Observation of the Court Proceedings

CHAPTER 18

Heart Is Not Enough

Mr. Leving Comes Aboard

ARDC Complaint Against David Wessel

DPR Complaints Against Mr. Wessel and Dr. Chapman

Escalating Abuse

Third Generation Domestic Violence

More Discovery and the Leving Fall Out

W e soon learned that having counsel with the right intentions was not enough. Lew's attorneys spent almost as much time and money preventing Mr. Leving from coming into my case as I spent finding counsel eager to align with the best interests of my children. It was obvious to all of us that Joy Feinberg and David Wessel did not want Mr. Leving as my counsel. The more they resisted his entry, the more Mr. Leving wanted to participate. Eventually, the reality of the withheld dollars to fund legal representation for me defined his limitations, and our dreams and hopes were shattered.

Our six month relationship clearly commenced in faith around a higher purpose and with more integrity than had been exhibited in the court proceeding to date. In our first few meetings in October, 1997, Mr. Leving took such pride in walking me over to a framed letter from Mother Theresa, hanging on a wall in his office. The cherished correspondence from Mother Theresa was a statement of her acknowledging and honoring Mr. Leving for his contribution to humanity through his efforts in supporting children's rights.

This same commitment to children's rights dominated our first few months together. Immediately after his initial court appearance on my behalf, he picked up the phone and called Corboy and Demetrio, a prominent personal injury law firm in Chicago, and requested that I meet with the head partner, Mr. Philip Corboy, Senior. After Mr. Leving witnessed the events in our case, he believed that I had a TORT Action against Lew on behalf of my children for his long history of abuse to them. A TORT Action is a type of personal injury lawsuit. Mr. Leving also suspected that we had a legal malpractice law suit against David Wessel for his unethical conduct and damages to my children during our proceedings.

John and I felt a breath of fresh air with this opening, and we pulled together all relevant and important information to bring to the meeting with Mr. Corboy. We sat with Mr. Philip Corboy, Senior and talked with him for hours. He was ever so delightful, articulate, sensitive and human. In our presence he read a full report that was the basis of a complaint I prepared against Mr. Wessel. In this report I detailed numerous infractions by Mr. Wessel, which directly compromised my children and violated my rights as the custodial parent during the course of the last two-and-half years.

It was clear that David Wessel was not representing my children's interest, but rather acted as co-counsel for Lew's attorney, and as a direct hired gun for Lew. The pattern that emerged, as documented throughout this manuscript, included the following:

1) Failure to honor the children's needs, if they wanted or needed something contrary to what their father wanted. Unfortunately this was done in all facets of the children's lives, including: psychotherapy, religious ceremonies, camp, vacation, time with their maternal family, and financial

support for the children's food, shelter, utilities, and ortho-dontic care when it was withheld or denied.

2) Failure to factor in my judgment in the important issues for my children, and to notify me regarding things in which Mr. Wessel attempted to involve my children. Yet, I was the residential and custodial parent. This was the case in every decision for every event and activity in my children lives. I frequently learned about decisions and plans that were "parental decisions" made by David Wessel, *through* my children.

After reading this report, detailing over a dozen examples of professional misconduct and unethical practice, Mr. Corboy looked up at John and me and said, "If this man did half of this, I would report him to the ARDC."

The ARDC stands for the Attorney Regulation and Disciplinary Committee. We were told that filing this report would be our first step in taking the appropriate action. From Mr. Corboy's office, John walked me directly to the ARDC office, and we filed the complaint against David Wessel.

I recall feeling some hesitancy, saying to John, "Shouldn't we wait until after Mr. Leving is paid." I pointed out that I realized filing the report would have repercussions, and I did not want to do anything that would compromise Mr. Leving's representing me. John believed that immediate follow-through on Mr. Corboy's suggestions was essential to our future relationship with him. He felt that the legal malpractice and potential TORT was the most critical part in turning things around, and he had personal faith in Mr. Leving sticking with us even before being paid. John had both a personal and professional relationship with Mr. Leving. I trusted John's belief in the commitment between himself and Mr. Leving. In retrospect, I probably would have served myself better had I trusted in my own inner voice.

*   *   *

Once the cat was out of the bag, we needed to move quickly in our addressing Mr. Wessel's misconduct. We were directed to proceed through the necessary steps in preparation for filing a malpractice TORT action against David Wessel. Mr. Leving decided he wanted this lawsuit to be handled through the office of George Collins, a reputable attorney with significant experience in legal malpractice. I was comfortable with this because I was familiar with Mr. Collins. We spent considerable time on the logistics involved in proceeding with this law suit, but before action was taken David Wessel learned of our intentions.

In the interim the Attorney Regulation and Disciplinary Committee responded to our complaint. They informed us that since a divorce matter was pending in which David Wessel was acting as a court-appointed attorney, they would not be able to proceed with an investigation of the matters brought to their attention. A letter was sent to me which basically dismissed the complaint and recommended that I pursue the issues of unethical conduct at the close of my divorce proceedings. It appeared that Mr. Wessel was shielded from scrutiny by his court-appointed status.

This news slowed down our efforts with the malpractice law suit against Mr. Wessel, because it brought to light potential problems due to the politics inherent in the divorce case. We were forced to evaluate the impact of what could be perceived as an attack on the divorce court. It was suggested that if David Wessel was asked to withdraw from the case because of a pending malpractice lawsuit, the Court could merely substitute another appointee to serve as the "children's attorney," acting in the same manner as Mr. Wessel in order to protect the Court.

At that juncture it seemed best to deal with one legal war at a time. John and I believed that it was also possible Mr. Leving would have suffered political consequences by being party to a lawsuit against a court agent in divorce court. We were told there were other ways to address Mr. Wessel's infractions toward my children while the divorce case was in progress.

In the meantime, Mr. Leving had encouraged John and I to pursue our formal complaints with both Mr. Wessel and Dr. Chapman through he Department of Professional Regulations. At the time, we had been under the impression that Mr. Wessel was a licensed social worker and we knew that Dr. Chapman was a licensed psychiatrist. Since the Department of Professional Regulations oversees both of these professionals, we directed our efforts here.

We were informed that Mr. Wessel's social work license had expired years before, even though John claimed to have seen his certificate currently displayed in Mr. Wessel's office. Initially, the representative from the Department of Professional Regulations was disturbed by this false representation to the public. He expressed a desired to have this taken up in another legal action between his legal department and David Wessel. I was not informed of the outcome of the Department of Professional Regulation's proposed intervention.

Concerning Dr. Chapman, we received a letter acknowledging our complaint, but no follow-up investigation or sanctions toward the Doctor occurred. It was suggested that Dr. Chapman was immune from public scrutiny because he, too, was a court-appointed agent. John and I started to recognize that the organizations designed to protect the consumer by overseeing the conduct of these health care professionals were limited by virtue of their involvement in the court.

*   *   *

While we recognized our limitations in shifting the dynamics in the court proceedings, it became more apparent that some change had to take place because the impact of abuse to the children began to escalate. Much of the children's upset appeared to stem from their reaction to the ongoing emotional and physical abuse by Lew and his family. However the more they cried, the less they were heard. Ultimately, my efforts to speak on their behalf resulted in a legal muffler placed upon me. We came to understand the term "court-sanctioned domestic violence."

Bradley was the most direct in his dealing with his feelings. He continued to refuse regular visitation with his father from October 1997 through mid-winter of 1998. Each week his resistance grew and, over time, he showed an increased ability to speak up for himself. Bradley reached a point of merely saying to Lew, "I'm not coming." Their 45 minute negotiations in the doorway, which had previously been plagued with Lew's threats to Bradley, were replaced with Bradley calling his father on the phone, informing him of his not partaking in the visitation and subsequently not being home upon Lew's arrival.

In my effort to better understand my son's actions, I learned that he was avoiding the visitations with his father because he was angry and hurt about much of the misrepresentations around his Bar Mitzvah. He explained that it angered him to hear Lew and his sisters "bad mouth" me and lie to him. I could see the obvious conflict being created in Bradley, and over the months witnessed it magnify to the point that he could no longer take being polarized. I recognized his need to not be used by his father as a weapon in Lew's war against me. The emotional manipulations and psychological abuse merely compounded the physical violence that simmered.

I was receiving calls almost every other time the children were on visitation with their father, in which David and Marc begged me to pick them up and bring them home. I responded to the calls that were cries for escape by driving over to Lew's house, picking up a child and bringing him to our home. The stories of continued abuse that I was learning about were quite disturbing, and convinced me that the dynamic of bullying, battering and physical abuse remained alive and active in Lew's residence. There was shoving, kicking, painful restraints, arms tied, limbs yanked and braced, children

thrown to the floor and against the wall, locked in closets, tormenting among siblings, hard objects thrown at one another, knives used,
all of which showed me that violence abounded.

*   *   *

In my effort to speak up for my children, and in my hope for
assistance in protecting them with a judicial remedy, I was routinely
penalized in court. I frequently informed the Court of what was
occurring in Lew's home. However, before and instead of assisting
my children, opposing counsel flooded the Court Record with
Pleadings alleging that I was interfering with Lew's visitation and
his efforts to "discipline" the children. Lew's counsel used this as
grounds for another rush to transfer both custody and physical
residence of the children to Lew. While it appeared absurd to me; it
was quite real. My time, energy and resources were spent being
punished through further irrational litigation for trying to protect my
children.

In my effort to keep court peace, I assumed the role of mediator
between Lew and the boys. I tried to encourage each of them to work
out any and all personal difficulties with their Dad, and secure his
consent before coming home. This then created significant polarization in me. On the one hand, I wanted to respond to their reaching
out to me in the moment and, on the other, I wanted to protect their
long-range residence and custody with me. They had made it very
clear to me that they wanted to continue living with me and visit
their Dad as they desired. I, too, felt this was best for them. So, we
established clear ground rules for my picking them up from a
visitation. This would only occur if they were physically harmed or
perceived immediate danger. If they were unhappy, I would come if
their father consented to allowing them to come home.

Then I reached a point in knowing if I picked them up
following a physical altercation with their Dad, my intervention
would create such painful repercussions in court that I became

paralyzed with respect to picking them up when they called. The first weekend in November 1997, David called 17 times begging, crying and pleading to come home. We spent about two hours on the phone over the course of the day, with me encouraging him to talk to his Dad and try to work out their differences.

In his last call on this day, he told me of a fight that he and his Dad just had, in which Lew grabbed his legs and dragged him on the floor down the hall, causing rug burns on his back. David said, "Mom, it really stings." Lew yanked the phone away from David and would not allow him further access to me. I spent the rest of weekend trying to cope with the internal conflict that this posed for me, knowing my child's pain and being aware of my having been rendered legally impotent.

*   *   *

My contact with the children during Lew's visitation then became the subject of further court pleadings and legal harassment to me. Eventually, I grew tired of Lew's using my presence or availability to the children as cause to penalize me. It both exhausted and angered me. I was also no longer willing to be held responsible for the children's unwillingness to have their visitation with their father, so I tried other ways of handling this.

On November 26, 1997, Bradley expressed a desire not to go on the weekend sleep-over visitation with his Dad. He had missed four consecutive overnight visitations during the last two months. In order to insure that the outcome of Lew and Brad's negotiations not be placed on me by Lew or the Court, I elected to leave the house and run errands shortly before Lew was to arrive to pick up the children. Lisa was at our home and quite willing to see the children off for their weekend visit with their Dad.

However, I went to my car and Brad followed me into the garage pleading to come with me. I told him that I was only going to the post office and he needed to be home for his Dad's arrival. He continued begging me to allow him to come with me, and I told him that if he was with me and not home when his father arrived that it would cause problems in the bigger picture. I encouraged him to work out the weekend plans with his Dad. Brad knew I was coming back and intended to be home for the weekend. Our agreement was he could stay home with me if it was okay with his Dad.

I arrived home within the hour to an awakening of the severity of my oldest son's internal conflict and the reality of the "inter-generational transmission of violence." In the driveway was my bike, totally and completely destroyed. I asked Lisa to tell me what happened.

"After you left," she said, "Bradley took a knife and cut the seat of your bike, let the air out of the tires, took a piece of stick and hit the bike repeatedly until it was of no use." She said she tried to talk him out of doing it, but he wouldn't listen.

She added, "He was swearing at me and telling me if I come near or touch him he is going to stab me with the knife." Lisa told me that she feared that if she approached Bradley that he may have stabbed her or, in his agitated violent state, may have gone after David with the knife. She said she continued talking to Bradley and, eventually, he threw the knife at the garage door and she was able to grab it.

Shortly after, Lew picked up David and Marc. Bradley refused to go on the visitation. Lisa said that Bradley was angry that I left him at home because he didn't want to go on the visitation and this is why he destroyed my bike. Later Bradley told me that he wanted me to tell his father that he did not want to go. I suspect that he no longer wanted the consequences of telling this to his Dad himself.

Brad continued fighting with Lisa for hours after I returned home. Bradley verbally assaulted Lisa, then threw objects at her. First, it was ice cream, and when corrected by Lisa, Brad grabbed some shoes and roller blades and hit her, punched her and kicked her. Bradley's anger escalated into a rampage in which he could not get a hold of himself. He threatened to "fight" Lisa and, as she was holding his hand off of her, Brad said he was going to call the cops; and he did.

The police came to the house and took a report, but their intervention did not bring a halt to Brad's violence. When the police left our home, Brad started throwing garbage cans filled with hangers down the stairs at the front door where the police exited, and then at Lisa and me. He was completely out of control, running through the house, destroying property, breaking glass, shattering a telescope, ruining David's roller blades by filling them with paint lacquer, and more. He was totally out of control. It was frightening.

It was obvious that my child had become both the perpetrator and the victim. This conduct continued, in one form or another, over the next six months. Lisa and I were aware that Bradley's budding violence re-emerged shortly after his therapy with Dr. Heinrich had been taken away from him. I pleaded with my counsel, with David Wessel and with Lew to allow me to get Bradley some help. They had obtained a Restraining Order, preventing me from bringing my children to a mental health care professional. It felt like I was watching an infection grow and I was not allowed to give my child the remedy he so desperately needed. My maternal instincts and parental rights to care for my child had been denied, and we all suffered.

One evening in the same month, Brad was cruelly terrorizing David. Bradley made a demand upon David. David refused to comply with Brad's request and all hell broke lose. Bradley cornered David in the kitchen and intimidated him until he was crying, shaking with terror. David continued to refuse to acquiesce to Bradley's wishes, and the taunting escalated into his slapping David on the face, just as Bradley had been slapped by Lew in the past.

I insisted that Brad back off of David, and he directed his hostility and rage to me. Bradley was punished for this conduct, but failed to recognize why his actions were wrong. From his perspective, David deserved this assault because of David's failure to comply with Brad's wishes.

*   *   *

The third generation of the family violence syndrome was undeniable. Since I was not allowed to get Brad professional help, I spent considerable time in what we called "heart-to heart" talks. We discussed personal rights, respecting others' preferences and physical boundaries. There were times I felt he recognized the impact of his conduct on others, and moments where his vulnerability expressed itself in desiring new ways of dealing with anger and frustration. We drew upon the insights Brad had obtained from his sessions with Dr. Heinrich. Clear consequences were established and strict punishments were imposed for any violence in our home.

Lisa assisted me in carrying out the interventions necessary to correct and curtail Brad's violence. However, the children were not living by the same guidelines when visiting their father's home. It became obvious that professional treatment was necessary for Bradley. Eventually, his behavior brought him a therapeutic remedy he needed, by the demand of the school district. He was diagnosed with a behavioral problem, which was quite disruptive to the learning environment. He showed little respect for authority and was unable to assume any personal accountability for his actions. Most everything was everyone else's fault, including his behavior and the consequences for misbehavior. His emotional turmoil and acting out in school necessitated a transfer to a therapeutic day school in January, 1998.

In many ways this intervention was a blessing in disguise. It provided individual and group therapy for Bradley and the opportunity for him to benefit from an ongoing therapeutic community. He reinvested himself in his studies, and some of the outward acting-out was curtailed. What remained was the tendency toward violence when things were not going his way, a refusal to assume personal accountability for his actions, and an unrelenting need to be in control, particularly in relation to his younger brothers.

*   *   *

While I was tending to the changing needs of my children, Mr. Leving was aggressively attempting for five months to secure money from the marital estate to represent our interests. His firm assisted in my doing another financial production and fact finding discovery of information through depositions of Lew and Dr. Chapman.

During this time, I noted a shift in Mr. Leving that appeared to arise out of his struggle to secure legal fees to fund our litigation. The change I sensed was most apparent when we all gathered for Dr. Chapman's deposition. This deposition was conducted in Mr. Leving's office. I watched Mr. Leving in his office corridor smoking a pipe. Not once did he come into the deposition to ask Dr. Chapman any questions. I requested that he participate in the deposition, but he refused any eye contact with me or any direct contact with John and myself concerning my case.

John and I recognized that Mr. Leving's commitment to our original cause posed some problems for him. After Mr. Leving had metered nearly $50,000 in fees, he refused further dealings on my behalf. Mr. Leving informed John and I that he could no longer carry my case without compensation. Opposing counsel had exhausted Mr. Leving's initial charity effort with frivolous legal back and forth and their steadfast resistance to prevent his accessing legal funding to represent me. He reached a point in which he was even unwilling to proceed with a court hearing on his fees.

We were not able to determine his motive for giving up his fight for our legal funding. It was suggested that he could not or would not expend the time or resources for a hearing without being paid; or his motives may have been more political than economic. There may have been political professional consequences to him for posturing the Court to rule on the distribution of finances to fund litigation for the interest of me and my children, or to proceed in opposition to the positioning of the Court by its court-appointed agents in collaboration with opposing counsel.

We parted when he informed us that opposing counsel was not willing to enter into an agreed order to release the fees necessary for him to fund a trial or pay our expert witnesses, and therefore he could not serve as my counsel. Mr. Leving was asking for $100,000 for legal fees, but they only agreed to give him $60,000, so he withdrew from the case.

Even though Mr. Leving could not represent me, he success-fully evidenced to the Court the continuation of abuse to me and my children by Lew, and consequently obtained an extension of our Order of Protection. I believe this effort demonstrated his knowing our truth and his good heart, despite his inability to protect us in the long run. In retrospect, I recognize that his securing the extension of our Order of Protection re-confirmed the absurdity of the Court's allowing Lew to seek custody, in light of the Illinois custody pre-sumption law.

The Damaged Bike

Intergenerational Transmission of Violence

Children raised in violent homes suffer extreme trauma from the abuse directed toward them and from their witnessing of abuse and violence. This exposure to family violence is associated with a high incidence of aggression, excessive anger, poor impulse control, low tolerance for frustration, low self-esteem, and feelings of helplessness and powerlessness.

In *When Violence Begins at Home*, Dr. Wilson describes the lessons that children learn from exposure to violence.

> "They learn how to keep family secrets. They learn how to get what they want through aggression and manipulation. They learn that people who love you hurt you. They learn that violence, albeit painful, is an acceptable part of life."
> (1997, p. 31)

The author points out the effects of family violence on boys. Boys learn that violence is an appropriate and acceptable way of resolving conflict. "Boys from violent homes are frequently described as being disruptive, acting aggressively toward objects and people, and throwing severe temper tantrums" (Wilson, 1997 citing Wolf, Wilson and Jaffe, 1986).

Dr. Wilson further notes the impact of family violence on these boys as they grow into teenagers. "Some teenagers begin to act out their anger and frustration in ways that result in delinquencies and the intervention of the juvenile justice system. Some teenage boys handle their frustrations by exhibiting the behavior that has been most clearly modeled for them, that is, by battering their mother or siblings" (1997, p. 35).

K. J. Wilson, *When Violence Begins at Home*, 1997.

CHAPTER 19

Domestic Violence: Family to Court

Regrouping after Leving

Too Rich To Be Poor and Too Poor To Be Rich

Court as Lew's Club for Control

To Stay or Flee

Dr. Galatzer-Levy's Recommendations

I t was time for reflection, regrouping and redirection. The end of our relationship with Mr. Leving left both John and I faced with loss and betrayal. For me, it was another attorney saying something that sounded great at first; but in the long run was politically or economically unfeasible. I was used to this, but was becoming exhausted in the process.

For John, our parting with Mr. Leving represented a betrayal of a personal friend and a shift in professional services he extended to Mr. Leving's clients. John was a very religious man and believed in a higher good in people and a higher order in all things. It was hard for him to come to grips with Mr. Leving's failure to follow through in our plight for the children's rights.

John believed that Mr. Leving's backing off when he was not offered the amount he requested, and then his failure to bring his Petition before the Judge, stemmed from opposing counsel's in-

volvement with the Judge. We had been made aware of Joy Feinberg's law firm's generous contribution to Judge Evans' campaign,
and his being elevated to the position of Presiding Judge of Domestic Relations in the first year of our proceedings.

Mr. Leving made his political priorities very clear to John prior
to his withdrawal from my case. Opposing counsel had insisted upon
deposing John, the same as had been done with Lee Knohl when he
came to our aid. However, Mr. Leving refused to provide John with
legal representation for his deposition. Mr. Leving provided two
attorneys from his office for this deposition, but neither of them
appeared on John's behalf. What struck John as most peculiar and
bothersome was that Mr. Leving had resources to provide his
associate attorney with support and/or a witness for this deposition,
but refused to offer John the assistance of any legal representation.
This demonstrated Mr. Leving's interest in protecting his law firm
over John, which John saw as a betrayal to himself.

The most disturbing part of Mr. Leving's withdrawal, for me,
was that prior to his exit, he was instrumental in severing my
relationship with Mr. Stern. He insisted on our doing this, because
he believed that Mr. Stern was responsible for interfering with his
accessing the marital estate for legal fees. Mr. Leving had convinced
both John and I that Steve Stern was controlled by Lew's attorneys.
He said, "I can't help you with Steve in my way." Then he dictated a
letter, as though from me, directing Mr. Stern's withdrawal. My
administering this notice to withdraw became Mr. Leving's condition for continuing to work as my attorney.

*   *   *

So now, I was once again without counsel, and with this came
the memories of how I was blasted with litigation to the point of
almost making me sick. I couldn't go back to that; it was far too
overwhelming. I was being "railroaded" in this process over the
years, and had been "fried-alive" in that courtroom representing

myself for the months I was without counsel within the last year. There was no way I would return to being Pro Se.

I had remained in contact with Dr. Schwartz ever since he had been helpful in protecting Bradley from the unwarranted psychiatric intervention. His insight and integrity won my trust, and I had arranged through Steve Stern for Dr. Schwartz to serve as my expert witness in the litigation. An Agreed Order was entered months before, allowing him to serve in this capacity. However, opposing counsel was adamant about not permitting Dr. Schwartz to assist me and my children as our expert witness.

Nonetheless, we had spent many hours preparing for him to proceed as our expert witness. These preparations involved numerous discussions around the accessing of funding for professional services and negotiating the loop holes that opposing counsel continued to place before the Court to prevent his participation in the case. Over the course of our relationship, Dr. Schwartz repeatedly recommended that I contact the State's Attorney concerning our case. He believed that we required counsel not tied to the politics of the Domestic Relations Court. I now realize that Dr. Schwartz saw the court agents barring me of my support and he probably knew I was being re-victimized by the divorce court.

Before seeking another domestic relations attorney, I followed Dr. Schwartz's advice and arranged to meet with the State's Attorney. This proved to be a rude awakening, not too much different than my consultations with the shelters and abuse agencies. After hearing our whole story, the State's Attorney claimed she could not assist us because our case was a "private matter" which was already being dealt with in Domestic Relations Court.

An individual from the State's Attorney's office spent further time with me, and her words both shocked and puzzled me. She said, "*The damage is **done**.*" She told me the matter has gotten "out-of-hand" in this case and acknowledged never seeing a case "mangled" as much as this one.

In an effort to console me, the State Attorney's office referred me to the city and state agencies dedicated to the protection of battered women and children. I spoke to many of these individuals. Everyone of these parties extended a sympathetic ear and an understanding of my predicament, but none were in a position to take my case. Each person and every organization refused involvement in the case because of the size of the estate. I was told, "We only provide legal services to the indigent." I soon learned that I was *too rich to be poor*, and *too poor to be rich*. From here, I fell through the cracks of the system.

The state organizations explained to me that they were unable to give legal aid to a case like mine because, as one attorney said, "Joy Feinberg will keep us in court endlessly, depleting all of our legal resources." It was explained that they were budgeted by the state to service many small matters, but did not have the legal resources to make a large investment in one major case.

*   *   *

I was then referred to private attorneys who specialized in domestic violence. I first consulted with an attorney who provided private legal services to victims referred by our local abuse agency. This woman was extremely compassionate. She heard our whole story and was quite familiar with the dynamics in our case. She noted that the domestic violence syndrome in the family was merely being played out in the litigation.

She explained to me how the legal forum supports the abuse dynamic of the perpetrator and victim. With this understanding, she claimed I needed counsel that had an appreciation of an abusive relationship and the commitment to interrupt and prevent the continuation of the dynamics through the courts. I recognized that she knew the Court was enabling the very dysfunction that it originally set out to arrest. She noted that the legal effort required for my case was not a standard attorney's investment. She said, "This type of litigation is not a typical case; it is a *career*."

My rounds with these individuals brought to light what I had learned earlier in my discussions with the personal injury attorneys. The head counsel of one of Chicago's largest personal injury law firms said, "The system is not your enemy, rather **your husband is using the system as a new weapon to abuse you**."

After watching the proceedings for six months and being my court witness, John similarly noted, "the dynamics of the domestic violence syndrome have continued. The only difference is that the brutal physical fighting has shifted from the home to the courtroom and is still going on." It was clear to most everyone we consulted that the domestic violence syndrome continued and I was still being battered. Other advocates said, "The only difference was Lew was now using our family money and the system rather than his fists or the threat of a gun to abuse us."

I realized that the more people I talked to, the more obvious it was that I could no longer deny I was between an rock and a hard place. My seeking remedy for our being abused through the courts kept me and my family in the battering cycle. It took me years to fully grasp the implications of the fact that litigation is inherently an *adversarial dynamic in which two parties fight for control*. I recognized that remaining an adversary to Lew, merely fueled his determination to continue fighting for control. I discovered the more I struggled against abuse through the court, the more I became entrapped. I saw no way out. At one point it felt like I was in a car moving forward rapidly and was unable to grab a hold of the steering wheel. It was clear a crash was imminent. Now, I had to figure out how to exit before being destroyed in the collision.

*   *   *

I revisited the idea of just leaving, but didn't have the strength or resources to carry it off. I was exhausted, emotionally depleted, and without the financial means to support me and my children indefinitely. I knew I could use my professional skills wherever I resided, but did not know how I would manage a practice if my name was hidden, as I thought this would interfere with my licensing for professional services.

The more I wanted to leave, the more I flooded my vision with excuses to stay. I prayed and hoped the court, the judicial process, the "system" would yield justice for me and my children. I started doing the same kind of unrealistic wishful thinking with respect to the attorneys and the Judge that I had done with Lew for ten years.

I kept saying to myself: "Oh this attorney couldn't put the laws favoring our case before the Judge because it would compromise his political standing among his peers." I'd then forgive him, move on and hope another would come along, willing to put themselves out for the "higher good" of abuse prevention and children's rights. It took a long time for me to recognize that I was the only one directly involved in our court process with this in mind. There were many who shared this belief and commitment, but they were either not allowed to participate or were extracted from the proceedings, one by one, with legal threats and harassment.

Fear also colored my vision when I was told that, if I left with my children, Lew would find me and I would receive a jail sentence for kidnapping. I recognized that I would be no good for my children under these circumstances and needed to keep the larger picture of their lives in view. It wasn't until one year later that I learned this advice was skewed by the bias of counsel associated with my case and the Domestic Relations Court.

*   *   *

In April, 1998 Dr. Galatzer-Levy was introduced into our case. At first I thought he was going to be the savior I longed for to shift the dynamic and, potentially, avoid the crash. He could have been this to me and my children, but he wasn't willing to play the role.

Instead, it better served the attorneys to use him as a "carrot." This strategy kept me reaching for our justice in the system, with him dangling hope before me for one more year.

Dr. Galatzer-Levy is a psychiatrist with considerable experience as a court "expert witness" and custody evaluator. He was selected by Mr. Leving (my counsel of record at the time) to serve the role of our expert witness to offset the biased and false report of Dr. Chapman. The reason Mr. Leving encouraged our engaging Dr. Galatzer-Levy was because, "When this Doctor sees abuse against women and children, he turns red." It was explained to me that he had no tolerance for such conduct. Further, I was told that he was highly respected in the court community and had extensive experience in providing testimony. I confirmed his being above board in my professional community, and learned he was honest. I was assured that he would not lie in a custody report or give false testimony to the Court. It didn't occur to me, at the time, that he would – or could – acknowledge our truth and sit on it.

At first, I was very hesitant in deviating from my commitment to work with Dr. Schwartz. I had already seen his pure intentions and commitment to the best interest of my child. He had a reputation of being a "maverick" in the system. I knew this could serve us well, and also thought that we would benefit from his dual licensing as both lawyer and psychiatrist. He knew the law and he knew psychiatry. He was the right man for us, but posed too much threat for opposing counsel. Accordingly, they found cause to prevent his entry into the case, even after an Agreed Order was entered into the Court Record to allow him to serve as my expert witness.

Before I had sorted out which doctor would best serve the interests of me and my children, Lew's counsel began their trail of Pleadings, suggesting to the Court that I was now "holding up" the custody evaluation of my own expert witness. This assertion was ludicrous, and merely served to engage Dr. Galatzer-Levy's services quickly, binding us to the doctor I had not completely committed myself to and thereby away from the doctor that threatened opposing counsel.

A contract was submitted to me by this doctor, requiring my signature to engage his services. Once I got over the hump, recognizing that he was the only one of the two candidates that my counsel was willing to hire as our expert witness, I faced the logistics of how we would proceed. Dr. Galatzer-Levy specified in his contract that payment of his services was to be delivered prior to his issuing his formal written report and giving court testimony.

Given this requirement, I informed my counsel that we must first secure the funding for the doctor's full service, including evaluation, report and court testimony before we engage his services. I said, "If he is honest and sees the abuse in our family, we will never see his report, because Lew will prevent payment and the money will not be forth coming." Instead of addressing my concerns of securing funding for Dr. Galatzer-Levy, my counsel jumped in with opposing counsel saying, "If you don't sign the doctor's contract, you will give the Court the appearance that you have something to hide." He said to me, "Just go see the doctor with the children and we will work out the finances later."

*   *   *

Going against my inner wisdom, I bought into the "avoiding havoc and false impressions with the court" scenario and I signed the contract. The children and I each saw the doctor. It was both the best and the worst move I had made. Dr. Galatzer-Levy was everything everyone said he would be. He was a source of support for me, but his presence in the case served to elicit my staying with an endless destructive war.

He had the typical downtown Chicago, Michigan Avenue, child psychiatrist look. He is in his 50's, about 5'8" and 180 pounds. His demeanor was gentle, soft, conservative, kind and very sensitive. His clinical interview was appropriate for a clinical custody evaluation.

His observations of the abuse dynamic in the family were right on target.

After meeting with all of us, Dr. Galatzer-Levy said, "Lew is still abusing you, now only through the courts." He observed and reported to me, "One day Lew is going to give it to Bradley." Dr. Galatzer-Levy predicted that Lew would haul off and smack Bradley, hurting him; that is if Bradley doesn't give it to Lew first. He recognized the budding abuse profile and apparent conduct disorder in Bradley. He perceived Bradley as being a threat to David and Marc, and recognized that Lew was blind to this, because abuse was Lew's norm. He saw Lew as endorsing violence in his home, and thereby enabling the continuation of the family abuse syndrome.

Dr. Galatzer-Levy informed me, "You are the children's psychological parent." He described psychological testing and picture drawings that he had administered to the children in my absence which confirmed their alliance with me and dependence on me. His recommendation was that David and Marc continue to live with me.

Dr. Galatzer-Levy suggested that the guidelines for a visitation schedule with their father be clearly defined so as to prevent fighting and abusive manipulation around visitation. He specified that Lew and I need definitive boundaries to keep our contact at a minimum. With respect to Bradley, Dr. Galatzer-Levy recommended a residential therapeutic school to remove him from being involved in further conflict imposed by a custody dispute, and to address his emotional disturbance around violence and personal responsibility.

The lawyers, collaboratively and with the passive consent of the Judge, spent one full year and nearly $100,000 to keep this vital information off the Court Record and out of the divorce proceedings. The promise of bringing Dr. Galatzer-Levy's report and testimony to benefit me and my children was used as a "carrot" to keep me "contained" in the court saga that proceeded over the next year.

Why Abused Women Stay In An Abuse Dynamic

Conscious and Unconscious Denial
Denial of being a battered woman
Internalized denial of the real altercations and/or injustices
Shame and embarrassment around being a victim of abuse

Emotional and Cognitive Trance
Fear of retaliation and further assault
Learned helplessness; perceived impotence
Brainwashing by the perpetrator/s
Wishful thinking and hope for change

Living in Abuser's Business
Shouldering responsibility for the altercations
Being responsible for changing perpetrator's behavior
Assuming the role of family peacemaker and/or legal repair person

Psycho-Social Entrapment
Addictive love and judicial faith
Mixing love, pity and promises
An unrealistic resolution of victim's cognitive dissidence
Traumatic bonding and an identification with the aggressor

Fulfilling Roles and Norms
Guilt and/or ethics concerning women's role as caretaker
Religious beliefs regarding marriage, family and divorce
Traditional ideas about loyalty, commitment and sexist roles

Lack of Resources
Physically handicapped by injuries
Physical and emotional depletion
Lack of economic and social resources

Complied from: D. Dutton, *The Batterer: A Psychological Profile*, 1995; J. King, *Domestic Violence Transformed into Litigation Abuse*, 1998; G. NiCarthy, *The Ones Who Got Away: Women Who Left Abusive Partners*, 1987; M. Weldon, *I Closed My Eyes: Revelations of a Battered Woman*, 1999.

CHAPTER 20

Third Generation
Domestic Violence

Domestic Violence Enablers

The Cycle of Violence

Supporting Battering Development

Intervention for Bradley's Violence

No Vision; No Potential for Correction

Days before the period elapsed in which I was to find counsel, I
met Nancy Murphy. Ms. Murphy claimed to be a domestic
violence specialist in family law. She told me that her practice was
predominately victims of abuse. In our initial meeting, I explained
my case and she clearly saw the operative dynamics both in the
relationship and in court. Her promise to me was that she would
address the abuse cycle and protect me and my children. She knew
that Dr. Galatzer-Levy was in place to serve as our expert witness
and that my goal was to remain with my children, keep us in our
community and prevent further family or judicial abuse.

I literally put two credit cards together to total a $1500 retainer
fee to engage her services. I was like a child who had just found a
lollipop. I felt such promise and hope in holding her business card,
which read: "Specializing in Domestic Violence."

Ms. Murphy was in her 40's, heavyset, with blond hair and quite unpolished looking. I wondered how she was going to pull off what no one else could do. She was trying to impress me with "Judge Evans loves me," and how he hugged her for her birthday at a social gathering. She wanted me to know that whenever she "goes before Judge Evans, he is reminded that domestic violence is central to the case." Of course, I realized that she was just trying to make me comfortable. I don't think she really knew what she was getting herself into, until she was in and it was too late to pull out legally or gracefully.

Within the first month of our being together she appeared before the Court and was able to secure a $28,000 loan against Lew's' life insurance policy; $18,000 of which was for her and her co-counsel, Mike Skoubis, and $10,000 of which was for Joy Feinberg. On this same day, Ms. Murphy obtained permission from the Court to engage Mike Skoubis to assist her in the management of my case. Ms. Murphy wanted Mr. Skoubis to handle all financial matters, while she took care of domestic violence and child custody issues. She insisted upon working with Mr. Skoubis because she claimed that the finances in this case were far too complicated for her to negotiate.

However, the finances were actually pretty straight forward, because Lew's income was traceable through his medical practice. We had already spent over $900,000 in legal fees, and all counsel was well aware of what remained in the estate. There was roughly $400,000 in the pension and $200,000 equity in the marital residence. We did not require sophisticated mathematics or financial expertise to split up the estate. In fact most of the work had been done. Steve Stern had already invested $5,000 in a financial expert's analysis of Lew's business and our other assets. We only needed to have the expert's report generated and submitted to the Court.

I don't think it was the finances. It was the politics, possibly driven by the finances, that Nancy Murphy couldn't handle on her own. I believe she had experience with domestic violence, but had never seen legal domestic abuse to this degree. It's more likely that her only way of survival, once stepping into the case was to bring in counsel to play "good guy, bad guy" and assist in the political maneuvering necessary to carry off the campaign already set in motion. Ms. Murphy did not present our case to the Court. She served to keep me "contained" and **prevent** our case from being entered into the Court Record. The only forward movement while she served as my counsel consisted of her playing into the hands of opposing counsel.

Trial dates were set, commencing September 28, 1998, to tend to all pending matters, including dissolution of marriage, custody, orders of protection, visitation and finances. It was not clear to me why Ms. Murphy was enabling the continuation of what transpired before her coming into the case, until I saw clearly what she was doing.

Mr. Leving had already obtained an extension of our Order of Protection on January 28, 1998. This was done by evidencing to the Court the continuation of ongoing physical and emotional abuse by Lew to our three children and to myself. By the Court's own ruling, it was acknowledged that domestic violence was still central to the case and Lew's rehabilitation had not been demonstrated, after nearly three years of therapy during the course of our proceedings.

In my mind, the mere enabling of a custody dispute at this juncture was morally and ethically wrong, and could only be a legal maneuver to allow for the continuation of the legal domestic abuse. The Court had re-established that Lew was an abuser and now admitted that he was not a "rehabilitated" abuser, so allowing him the liberty to prove otherwise could only be in the service of perpetuating the family abuse syndrome.

I had numerous communications with Ms. Murphy in which I explicitly articulated:

"To place an abused and compromised child through a custody dispute is like taking a truck that just hit a child and allowing the truck to back up and roll over the child again."

I wrote letter upon letter saying this and documenting how these proceedings were destroying my children. I pointed out how her posturing was enabling the same judicial violence to my family. Instead of addressing the content of my letters, Ms. Murphy was most disturbed that I was writing these letters. She did not want me to document what was going on and said, "Your letters could cause trouble for me." Then, she demanded that I stop writing her.

*   *   *

I had been writing letters to all of my counsel of record over the course of the proceedings. At first, it was for the purpose of communication only. Then, after the attorney from my state legislator's office told me to "document the proceedings and keep the record straight," I became very conscientious about writing on almost every legal action and reaction.

This letter writing served two purposes. First, it documented all matters between myself and all parties in the case and provided a wealth of information that I placed in the Court Record to keep the record straight. Second, it served as personal therapy for me. Some legal transgression or further abuse would occur, and I made a habit of putting it in writing. It was clarifying, cathartic and had an ongoing healing effect for me. In retrospect, had I not been writing, I may not have been able to keep up the demands of the cruel and frivolous litigation for four years.

From May 1998 to September 1998, Ms. Murphy and Mr. Skoubis sat on my case and, bit by bit, undid every positive legal protective measure accomplished by my prior counsel. It was progressing faster than I could keep up with, and during a period in which my attention was fully absorbed in the needs of my children and our deteriorating economic foundation. My days were spent juggling bills and dodging creditors, while addressing the increasing negative effects that the litigation and Lew's emotional polarization was having on our children.

In the first two years of these proceeding, Bradley was the primary target for his father's manipulation, polarization and psychological abuse; but as the years progressed new and more serious threats developed for David and Marc. It was no secret that Bradley had adopted tendencies toward violence which endangered all of us.

The litigation pattern had clearly supported and nurtured the domestic violence syndrome already existing in Lew, but now it was contributing to the establishment of the syndrome in Bradley. After four years of watching Lew respond to disclosure of the family violence in the courts with manipulation, deception and denial of personal accountability in order to maintain control, Bradley adopted the same behaviors and defense mechanisms. Unfortunately, this made Bradley's predisposition toward aggression more resistant to the therapeutic intervention provided by his new school.

The child advocates, abuse specialists and I saw the psychological, social and judicial factors contributing to Bradley's inheritance of the abuse syndrome and a third generation of domestic violence in the Blumenthal family. I began to understand the "intergenerational transmission of violence theory," as conceptualized by Harvey Wallace in *Family Violence: Legal, Medical and Social Perspectives*, and the "cycle of violence theory" working in my own family.

I learned that there are three phases in the "cycle of violence," a term coined by Lenore E. Walker, in *The Battered Woman*. They are the Tension Building Phase, the Explosive or Acute Battering Phase and the Calm, Loving, Respite Phase. I grew to be able to identify this cycle in our marriage, in the litigation pattern, and in repeated encounters in Lew's home as well as between Bradley and his brothers. The phases are distinct and cyclic, described as follows:

"Tension Building Phase"
On-going and progressively escalating incidents of psycho-logical, emotional and physical battering occur. Perpetrator experiences heightened averse arousal and uses battering to rebuild and fortify a fragile sense of self. Victim attempts to appease batterer through compliance or avoidance, while feeling "as if walking on egg shells." This is the longest phase, and it can be maintained for weeks, months or years.

"The Acute Battering Incident"
An uncontrollable release of tension and rage, culminating in a brutal altercation, characterize the acute battering phase. It is distinguished from the prior phase by the degree of disassociation, destruction and injury which climax the cycle. The acute attack is immediately followed with initial shock and disbelief around the severity and seriousness of the altercation by both the perpetrator and the victim.

"Kindness Contrite Loving Phase"
The calm after the explosion characterizes the third phase of the battering cycle. During this time, there is much denial and/or atonement, promises for reform, and a variety of efforts to manipulate and appease the victim in order for the abuser to re-engage control. The victim clings to this phase hoping it will overshadow the other phases of the cycle; instead, it reinstates the dynamic and the cycle ensues. (See Appendix B for more elaboration on the **Cycle of Violence**.)

*   *   *

The cycle of family violence became clearest for me to under-stand when I was an outsider looking in. My children's vignettes, though subtle, showed the live and active dynamics of the abuse cycle. Marc recalls the following story.

Marc and his brothers were roller-blading with their father during a visitation. Brad pushed Marc while they were roller-blading, and Marc fell to the ground. Marc said that he was crying. Instead of tending to Marc, Lew became upset and pushed Brad very hard while he was on his roller-blades and yelled, "See what it is like!!" As Lew pushed Brad to the ground, Brad fell down crashing into the concrete and onto Marc causing a bruise on Marc's leg. In Marc's recount of this story, he added with puzzlement, "After Dad pushed Brad, Brad was really hurt; but then Dad became very nice to Brad." Marc said, "It was **weird** how he became *nice* to Brad right *after* he was so mean and angry at him." Marc continued, saying, "Dad asked Brad, 'Could you show me how to do some tricks on the roller-blades?' and the two of them went on roller-blading."

Later that evening, when Lew returned the boys from their visitation, Bradley tore into Marc, violently hitting him with a firm cushioned bat. I demanded that Bradley stop, protected Marc and sent Bradley to his room. This was the beginning of another opportunity for legal maneuvering and polarization of Bradley, and the creation of conflict around his being violent and having to assume personal accountability for his actions. On that night, Bradley escaped the punishment by riding his bike to his father's house, after which Mr. Wessel and Lew supported Brad's avoidance of his punishment. Numerous Pleadings followed, alleging that I was responsible for "tormenting" Bradley. In this one evening Bradley visited the cycle from both sides, practiced his mechanism of denial and was rewarded for doing so.

* * *

As might be expected, Bradley's tendency toward violence only grew. It appeared to evolve out of not getting his own way, not being in control of surrounding circumstances or jealously of others. Bradley's increasing aggression, terrorizing behavior, bullying and violent outbursts led to Lew petitioning the Court for an Order of

Protection against Bradley, protecting David and Marc. The cat was out of the bag, and all parties recognized that Bradley truly needed an intervention for his battering behavior.

However, Lew and his legal team refused to assist or allow me to secure specialized help for Bradley; nor would they consider protecting David and Marc by having Bradley reside with Lew. Instead, Lew insisted that the only remedy for Bradley being a threat to David and Marc was that all three boys reside in Lew's home, without professional treatment for Bradley. The absurdity of this was too glaring and, of course, nothing came of Lew's Petition. In fact Bradley, just continued to abuse David and Marc, and this became even more excessive in Lew's home. It appeared that there was greater acceptance of the violence, as it was the normal backdrop of their environment.

In my home, Lisa and I placed clear surveillance over the children when they were together in order to reduce the incidents of sibling abuse. Whenever Bradley attempted to hit, shove, kick, slap or restrain David or Marc, we intervened. More often than not, we were successful in preventing it; but there were occasions in which Bradley went out of his way to wait until the adult left the room and then proceeded to batter his brothers. He was always punished for this conduct.

While Brad's aggressive acts were somewhat reduced in our home, the violent battering toward his brothers continued, particularly after visits with their father. David and Marc informed us that the hitting, shoving, kicking, punching and verbal abuse was allowed in their father's home. The children disclosed that sometimes it was so severe, it frightened Lew's baby-sitter and resulted in the baby-sitter becoming emotionally paralyzed rather than providing a correction.

I imagine that the inconsistency in the expectations in my home and Lew's home led to confusion and, on some occasions, became the root for further hostility. Brad vacillated between denial around abusing his brothers and entitlement to do so. When he expressed his right to batter and it was challenged, he shifted his violence onto us. There were times that Bradley attempted to assault Marc, and when Lisa or I intervened, we became the target for Brad's fury. June 7, 1998 was the straw that broke the camel's back for Lisa. She had made a personal commitment to herself that she was no longer willing to intercept Brad's physical abuse.

On this evening, Bradley came home, demanding to get some money. He took two dollars from the house, left and returned, insisting on needing a larger sum of money. He demanded that David buy some CD's from him so he could obtain the funds he so desperately wanted. David did not want to give his treasured savings to Bradley, but Bradley refused to respect David's wishes. Lisa and I pleaded with Bradley to back off, but his fury escalated into violence. He threw a jar at Marc, tossed a lamp which crashed at the door entrance where I stood, and continued to torment David. Lisa called the police and they came to the house, taking another juvenile report on domestic violence in our home.

The police's presence was still not sufficient to interrupt Brad's aggression. Bradley spoke to the officer with hostility, demanding that he leave our home. Then Bradley lunged forward threatening to go after Marc, attempting to scare him, terrorizing Marc as though he was going to hit him while the officer was sitting in our family room with Bradley for the purpose of containing him. The officer saw Bradley out of control, unwilling to submit to authority and potentially dangerous. The police officers insisted upon removing Bradley from the home and bringing him to Highland Park Hospital for the evening via a Petition for Involuntary Hospitalization.

The next day, I was called to sign papers releasing Bradley out of the police's custody while the hospital completed their evaluation. I was informed that if I didn't authorize the hospital's evaluation as the custodial parent, they would have to surrender custody of Bradley over to the Department of Children and Family Services. Knowing that Bradley needed this evaluation and recognizing that I did not want DCFS to claim custodial rights to my child, I signed the papers releasing the police custody and allowing the hospital to complete their evaluation. As would be expected, Bradley was extremely angry. It was numbing for me. Even though my love for him was present and led me through that afternoon, we could not connect. It was understandable, yet quite painful.

*   *   *

I consulted with Dr. Galatzer-Levy, and he supported the police's efforts and urged me to insist that Bradley have this intervention. However, Mr. Wessel and Lew managed to interrupt the evaluation and removed Bradley from the hospital before the doctor completed his study of Bradley's status with the proposed treatment options. Both Mr. Wessel and Lew told Brad, "Your mother is to blame for your being placed in the hospital, and you do not need to be here." Once again, my child requires an intervention and it was taken away from him. Then he was deceived into believing that his mother is the villain. The thought of this jockeying potential help for my son, and the emotional manipulation around the appropriateness of his conduct in order to support Lew's legal agenda to abusively control us, was utterly sickening to me.

Lew managed to get Bradley out of the hospital on the promise to the attending doctor that he would engage Bradley in the hospital's "day program" treatment. Instead, Lew parked Bradley at his sister's home for several days and, initially, forbid my having contact with him.

It was unbelievable the way Mr. Wessel and Lew managed to pull this off. Hours before Bradley was released from the hospital, I received a phone call from Ms. Murphy's office informing me that Mr. Wessel had filed a Petition to Transfer Physical Possession of Bradley to Lew. I was told not to come to court. Shocked by this maneuvering, I called Ms. Murphy and insisted on knowing what was being done. I canceled my morning patients and rushed to meet my counsel.

However, instead of meeting with Ms. Murphy alone, all counsel were present and eager to draft another Agreed Order. I was told that Brad was ready to be released from the hospital and we simply needed to determine where to place him. We discussed the importance of protecting David and Marc from Bradley, as we all acknowledged that it was best to separate them. I insisted upon having David and Marc remain with me, and counsel proposed that Bradley stay with Lew. I informed all parties that I did not think this would provide the remedy to Bradley that he so desperately needed.

I informed them that I did not want to agree to an arrangement which could suggest to the Court that I saw Lew as a "reformed" abuser or fit parent to assume physical possession of Bradley. I directed my counsel to draft wording that expressed my "strong reservations" about this transfer of Bradley's "physical possession" and the contingency that involved Lew engaging Bradley in treatment. Additionally, this transfer was for Bradley's *residence only*, while I maintained custody of him, and was "without prejudice to a full Hearing," implying that I was **not** waiving my right to a Hearing to determine Brad's final residence and custody. While I was not in full support of this arrangement, I saw it as a temporary measure that could insure Bradley's therapy and also maintain protection for David and Marc in the interim.

Lew had no intention of securing the recommended treatment for Bradley. From his point of view, Bradley's residence with him was "the treatment." In a phone conversation with Lew, I learned that he was angry about Bradley being hospitalized and projected denial around Bradley's abusive pattern.

He said, "Hospitalizing Bradley for throwing a jar of Vaseline is an inappropriate consequence for such a minor act."

I said, "The police recognized the pattern of behavior and witnessed Brad out of control, and this is why they proceeded with the intervention."

"That is ridiculous, because no one was hurt," Lew replied. "There was no just cause for such an action, as was done by the police years ago to me."

I recognized that Lew still did not realize on September 7, 1994, the police and I were responding to Lew's pattern of violent behavior, in addition to the nine inch belt welts Lew inflicted on Bradley that day. Lew's likening the intervention for Bradley's behavior with his own police arrest for striking Bradley showed me that Lew remained in denial about the abuse syndrome in our family. He did not see the bigger picture; he denied there being a pattern of abuse.

Knowing this merely reinforced my recognition that Lew was not a "rehabilitated" abuser; and he was blind to Brad's developing abusive tendencies. Lew didn't see it in himself and he couldn't see it in Bradley; or he was not willing to admit it. It was frightening to realize that Brad's condition was now more likely going to be enabled, not remedied.

Lew demanded knowing why Lisa called the police on June 7, 1998. He was angry and there was an air of suspicious paranoia, implying that this intervention was plotted. It took quite some time for me to grasp the contradiction in Lew's resentment of the police intervention with Bradley at a time of obvious need, when exactly one year ago Lew and Mr. Wessel were attempting to place Brad in an in-patient psychiatric hospital for 30 days, at a time when Lew was aware of Bradley's academic and social progress at school. I suspect that Lew was projecting the "plotting" maneuver onto me and Lisa.

*   *   *

Later, I asked Lisa why she called the police. She said, "I saw Brad was not going to stop until he got the money or one of the children were hurt." She told me she was tired of intervening and getting hit by Bradley. She said, "I can't take it anymore." Lisa pointed out that if we continued to act as Brad's control, by being the "house-police," Bradley would never develop internal control. We both recognized that Bradley needed intervention beyond supervision.

I told Lisa about my conversation with Lew, and she was quite surprised. She informed me that she was aware that Bradley was acting the same with Lew as he was with us. She reminded me of how frequently Lew was dropping Bradley off during their visitations when Bradley became abusive to his brothers or disrespectful to Lew. She said, "Dr. Lew knows Bradley is hurting his brothers and he is frustrated with it, too."

There were also a number of occasions in which there was an altercation between Bradley and his brothers in front of both Lew and Lisa when Lew picked up and dropped off the children at our home. Some of these incidents became the subject of Lew's Pleadings in which he attempted to allege that Lisa was deficient in her care-taking because these incidents happened in her presence. Yet it was interesting that Lew claimed no involvement in, responsibility for, or contribution to Bradley's aggressions, though he was there watching the same incidents without intervening; and, in fact, was the role model for Brad's abusive behavior.

"Dodge and his associates examined the effect of the cycle of violence on development of aggressive tendencies in children. ... They found that children who had been physically abused were more aggressive toward other children than those who had not been abused." (cited in Wallace, 1996, p. 19)

Sibling Abuse

Physical abuse by siblings includes "striking, kicking, punching, and the use of instruments such as sticks, appliances, and other items as weapons."(Wallace, 1996, p.102)

Emotional abuse of siblings includes "name-calling, ridicule, degradation, exacerbating a fear, destroying personal possessions, and torture or destruction of a pet." (Wallace, 1996. p. 102 citing Wieche)

Serial Abuse of siblings "occurs when the perpetrator who is a member of the family first abuses one child and then abuses another sibling." (Wallace, 1996, p. 105)

H. Wallace, *Family Violence: Legal, Medical and Social Perspectives,* 1996.

CHAPTER 21

Gross Legal Malpractice

The Aftermath of Brad's Transfer

Summer Vacations and Denied Phone Contact

Ongoing Battering to the Blumenthal Victims

Dr. Galatzer-Levy: The Dangling Carrot

The Un-Filed Petitions

Eventually, Bradley was moved to Lew's house to reside. His mental anguish, emotional turmoil and behavioral acting out continued. I witnessed the patterns of abuse and the profile of an adolescent batterer stabilize. Bradley became more clever in his manipulations, more convincing in his lying, more brutal in his assaults, and even more charming leading up to and following an altercation.

From the exterior he projected having it together, unless he wasn't in the midst of an episode as victim or perpetrator. Internally I saw, felt and knew his pain. I came to recognize that his striking out, and the maneuvering leading up to this, grew out of his vulnerability, not his power. I prayed that he would come to know authentic internal invincibility, and made the most out of whatever contact Lew allowed us to have. Unfortunately, it grew less and less.

My counsel, Ms. Murphy, refused to assist me in obtaining a visitation schedule and so the times I actually got to see Bradley were hit and miss. After Brad and I worked through the issues and resentments around his hospitalization in mother-son-family therapy sessions at his school, his heart re-opened and he eagerly tried to make our visits happen. We planned date after date to get together. We did enjoy several afternoons together, but more often than not, when I arrived to pick him up, Lew had seen to it that Brad was not at home.

It was quite painful for me to be denied contact with my son. These interruptions in our visitation were frustrating even for Marc; as we would drive over to retrieve Bradley, only to sit in front of an empty house. Bradley's frustration also grew and I came to understand his anger and hatred toward his Dad for keeping us apart. Brad knew exactly what was going on and so did I, but we both remained impotent in changing the physical distance that Lew was placing between us. Lew appeared to enjoy his success in arranging our failed visits and used this as the subject of further court Pleadings, alleging that I was "unwilling to see Bradley after he moved to Lew's house."

The absurdity of these allegations helped me understand the root meaning of the word "attorney." Attorney was derived from the Old French prefix *a*, meaning "to" and the verb *torner*, meaning "turn." The literal translation is "turn to;" however, "to turn" – that is *twist and turn* – is what was being done here and throughout the four year, million dollar plus proceeding.

*   *   *

As the weeks past after Bradley moved out of our house, I noticed a clear and distinct change in David. David progressed from being defensive, timid and withdrawn to becoming alive, vital, outgoing and self-assured. The absence of Bradley contributed to my understanding the impact that Brad's battering was having on David. When David was around Bradley, he was awkward and lacked confidence. But with Bradley gone, David blossomed into a shinning exuberant star.

I witnessed him share the nuances of his day, with pride and pleasure, extending himself and exposing who his was, how he felt and the richness of his growing mind. Whereas when Brad lived with us, David disappeared at the dinner table as though he was invisible. And when he spoke up to express himself he was blasted, berated, belittled, discounted and undermined by Bradley until he recoiled into silence, broke into tears, or engaged in battle with Brad. I believe that, on some level, David associated his own personal glory with pain when in Brad's presence. David and I both noticed the change in him, and we took pride in further nurturing his growing self-expression and self-respect.

David and Marc completed a very successful school year. David made all A's. He had always been an excellent student, disciplined with his homework, proud of his accomplishments, and now he shared his success more openly. I could see he was as proud as I in his progress. It was clear that he had internalized self-directed study habits, such as those which had been the root to my own academic success.

Marc was awarded for his excellence in Mathematics and Art. His math ability was outstanding, and he was demonstrating fifth grade math skills in third grade. He was accepted into an advanced math program at school. Marc and I took such pride in this accomplishment. My mathematician was also an excellent and honored artist. One of his art projects was framed and displayed in his elementary school for years, and another won a district award for its excellence.

David, Marc and I celebrated their academic accomplishments over the summer. They were each given money and gifts for their good grades and success in the school year. We spent the summer enjoying many outings at the local water park, in which there were three swimming pools. The children did extremely well on the high diving board and thoroughly loved the slide pool.

Our home was a neighborhood hub for the boys' friends. We entertained, had sleep-overs, parties, played sports and games, took pride in training Dexter and enjoyed cuddling Kitty. David and Marc also participated in a summer camp program for team sports, crafts and numerous enrichment activities.

*   *   *

A summer vacation had been a tradition in our family since the children were infants. Lew maintained this tradition with the boys and worked very hard to prevent the children from enjoying the same with me. Dates for our respective vacation travel with the children were submitted to the Court months before each trip. The summer of 1998, Lew and his counsel approved my taking the children on our vacation one day before the end of the designated vacation period. I recall thinking how nice that the children's father finally gave consent for us to go on vacation together, but how unfortunate it was that he failed to suggest how I might turn the clock back in order to make this possible.

At the time, I interpreted Lew's actions as an effort to prevent the children and I from having a life together. It was typical of him to want to monopolize the "having fun" and "enjoyment" time with the children, while I was assigned to all the work, maintenance and daily care-taking, from doctors to hair cuts to shoes. In retrospect, I imagine that he may have interfered with this trip as well as many others, out of his fear that I may flee with the boys or because of his jealously over our strong bond. I'll never know his motivation, whether from jealously, possessiveness, vulnerability, or all.

I noticed that the more Lew prevented our little fun outings and vacations, the more effort we put forward to sneak them in privately. David, Marc and I made an exciting adventure out of our one night vacation. We packed our car, drove to Pleasant, Indiana and stayed at the Fairfield Inn. The boys and I indulged in one fun activity after another, until it was time to go home. It was definitely a highlight of our summer.

The children and I grew accustomed to being denied extended vacations together, but found it very difficult to accept not being able to contact one another while on their trips with Lew. Years before, Lew and his sisters prevented the children from calling me while on their annual August vacation in Sannibel, Florida. I was both stunned and crushed the first time I witnessed this.

It was the Summer of 1996, and a full week passed before I was able to talk to the boys. They were informed by Lew and his sister, Marlene, that calling their mother was too expensive. They were prohibited from calling me direct, as they were told it would cost one dollar per minute.

Knowing that their trip cost thousands of dollars made their inability to make a long distance call to me even more hurtful to both me and the children. When I finally reached Bradley on the phone and asked how he felt about not being able to contact me, I learned that the interference of his phoning me created such emotional distress that he had withdrawn and retreated into silence. He said:

"Marlene grabbed the phone from me when I was trying to call you....They were yelling at me for calling you....I left the room and went silent for a half-an-hour."

I could feel my children's pain over this cruel maneuver. To avoid this interference in the future, I purchased pre-paid phone cards for each child and taught the boys how to use them. These cards, along with photos of Mom and their pets, were taken on subsequent trips and the children became adept in using the phone cards. We cherished our minutes together. I recall Marc using his card and, as I was speaking with his brothers, I overheard his concern, saying, "You're using up my minutes." I was happy that they at least had these minutes to be in contact with me.

*   *   *

In many ways, separating the boys proved to be beneficial in interrupting the ongoing cycle of daily battering. However, months after Bradley moved, the children were besieged with a new form of psychological abuse. Lew eagerly tried to re-program the children's memories of our history of violence. This confused and angered them.

Lew told David, "I never hit you...The things your mother has said are a lies...She is a liar...It never happened." In telling me about this effort to change his memories of abuse, David said, "Mom, he did hit us, I saw him." David recalled Lew punching me, belting Brad, causing rug burns on himself, and much more. David said, "Dad is trying to change my thinking about what happened." David was perplexed when his father explained that the hand mark on Bradley's face was "a bruise caused by Bradley falling." David had lived the history that Lew was denying; he knew his Dad was lying.

There were numerous efforts to alter Marc's memories of events. At one point, Lew said to Marc, "You don't remember me hitting you, do you?" Marc told me that he responded to his Dad, "Yes, I do remember." Marc said, "Dad wanted me to tell him I didn't remember, but Mom I do." The attempts to alter the children's memories of their past eroded their trust in their father and faith in his word.

What confused the children even more was Lew's effort to dilute, minimize and deny the current altercations that were continuing to take place in Lew's home between him and the children, as well as Brad's battering of David and Marc. David and Marc knew the hitting, shoving, kicking, throwing and the physical and emotional terrorizing was wrong; but, for the most part, they were helpless in their ability to stop it.

Marc became Brad's scapegoat for routine battering and David was now the recipient of major blows, only. I believe this shift occurred because David knew the contrast of not being hit and bullied by Brad in my home and came to enjoy being out of the line of fire. David developed the ability to dodge Brad. In staying out of his way, Marc rose to the plate and now became their main household victim.

The benefit for David in his new strategy to cope was that his daily life on the outside appeared more stable. But when it was his turn for being brutalized, it was so bad for him that on numerous occasions he called out, "I can't take this anymore. I want to die." One day when Lew had come to the house for the children, David was being tormented, kicked, shoved to the wall and beaten up by Bradley. David called out, pleading for someone to kill him, to escape the anguish of being abused. I believe that David was reaching a limit as he was getting the impact of the cycle of violence on two levels. One as a victim, and two as a witness to the ongoing violence in Lew's home.

Marc returned home to me in tears almost every other visit at their Dad's house. He repeatedly reported being hit, physically hurt or terrorized by Brad during the course of the visitation. It was so bad for him that he started to become depressed. During this time, Bradley and Lew campaigned their efforts to convince Marc and David that they were next to live with Dad. So, often when Marc wasn't being hit in the moment, he was tormented by his brother telling him he was going to have to live in an environment in which he would be bullied and battered daily. For Marc there was no way out of the family abuse. It became progressively more pathetic for my innocent, vulnerable youngest child.

*   *   *

When Brad would come to our home to visit, it was obvious to Lisa and I that Brad had not changed. It appeared that he believed he was even more entitled now to take advantage of his younger brothers; and abusing them was part of it. Lisa noted, "Bradley is constantly trying to control; ordering, manipulating, bullying, tormenting and beating up David and Marc." She recalls one afternoon in June, when Bradley came over and wanted some money and had insisted on using David's roller-blades. David did not want Brad to take his roller-blades. Bradley refused to take "no" for answer. He tore into David, battering him and terrorizing him, threatening to "beat the shit out of him," until David started crying and shaking. There were many occasions over the summer in 1998 that Bradley lost control of himself while punching, kicking and beating up David and Marc. Lisa and I were truly concerned for the safety of David and Marc.

Recognizing that separating the children did not change the family violence, I reached out to Dr. Galatzer-Levy. He told me that he was aware of Brad's behavior toward his brothers and had anticipated that it would continue without intervention. Dr. Galatzer-Levy was not surprised that Lew had not provided the hospital's recommended treatment for Brad, because he expected Lew not to see Brad's behavior as problematic or abusive. We spoke at length about how to get his report into the Court Record to insure the safety of David and Marc and to facilitate getting Brad an intervention that would address his aggressive conduct and the risk he posed to his younger brothers.

Dr. Galatzer-Levy was very generous with his time and attention on the phone with me. Unfortunately, he and I were unable to secure the funds that he required to generate his report and/or give testimony in court of his observations, impressions and recommendations. He encouraged me to work more aggressively through my counsel to get his fees. At this juncture he had already used the $6,000 provided to retain his services, in evaluating the members of our family and reviewing much of the documentation. He was now asking for an additional $16,000 to generate a written report of his findings and testify as my expert custody witness in court.

My efforts to seek assistance through my counsel ultimately revealed who their real client was in our case. Nancy Murphy and Mike Skoubis spent over three months telling me that they were unable to get funding for Dr. Galatzer-Levy's report. Their efforts to secure this money first entailed a new full discovery of financial records organized by Mr. Skoubis. Somehow in this discovery, Lew was not required to produce his tax returns documenting his income and Mr. Skoubis claimed that Mr. Leving, his predecessor, failed to give him my financial records that Mr. Leving's office and I spent months and thousands of dollars putting together.

The outcome of the discovery was that counsel could not find $16,000 available to finance my expert witness. So I asked Mr. Skoubis in writing how is it that we are positioning to undertake a $400,000 trial when we can not figure out how we can obtain $16,000. I wondered if Lew had intended to mortgage himself to this litigation for the next ten years. Then, I was informed that Lew's financial expert evaluated the estate at $1,600,000, and therefore we certainly could afford the proposed $400,000 litigation.

*   *   *

All evidence showed that Lew was still generating nearly a half-a-million dollars profit from his successful medical practice. He had been negotiating a merger with one of the renown obstetrician gynecologists in Chicago, and had already taken in an additional junior partner. So now instead of a two or three doctor practice, he headed a four plus doctor practice. We could never get the exact number from Lew, much less how many deliveries per month he was doing. We did learn that he was providing medical services at Northwestern Memorial Hospital in addition to his former position at Michael Reese Hospital, but when he started this was also a "secret."

I, on the other hand, had no income from my business as I had, basically, closed my practice to tend to the needs of my children and keep up with the demands of the litigation. After reaching a point of canceling as many appointments as I was able to keep for random and emergency court dates, I decided it would serve us all best to wait until I was out of court to resume my professional responsibilities. I didn't feel it was right taking a patient that I was not available to service.

At this point in the proceedings, I managed our household overhead and the children's expenses on credit cards. Lew had taken it upon himself to withhold portions and sometimes all of our support over the last four months. Four Petitions, Rules to Show Cause for Failed Support, were put before the Court, but the Judge refused to rule on any of these. Therefore, there was no remedy for me and the children, and no court sanctions to Lew for this financial withhold program he had imposed.

It is only today that I understand why counsel and the Court allowed this to occur. I am certain Lew and his legal team did not want me to have resources to fund Dr. Galatzer-Levy. At the time, I felt so victimized by the starve-out campaign that all I could see was Lew's $20,000 plus support arrears, my near $100,000 debt, two impotent counsel, and one court unwilling to remedy our predicament. It is no surprise that these moneys were withheld at the time I needed them most.

I insisted that my counsel petition the Court for the release of the funds to pay my expert witness as per the "leveling of the playing field laws." I reminded them that this is a case in which the children's safety is at risk. I expressed my belief that we deserved to have the input from my expert witness to assist in protecting David and Marc's current residence in which they were safe and thriving with me, and to address the issue of abuse in Lew's home. The United States Constitution does provide for my having this. My counsel metered $60,000 in legal fees charged to me to look for this $16,000, and wrote four Pleadings, none of which they submitted to the Court.

*   *   *

In my frustration, I went to the Court Clerk's Office and reviewed the Court Record. I figured if the Petitions that they were sending me were not ruled upon, there must be some reason. It turned out that the reason the Judge did not rule on the Petitions to disburse funds for my expert witness is because these Pleadings were never filed with the Court, and therefore were not formally placed before the Judge.

I submitted another letter to my lawyers, Nancy and Mike, on September 14, 1998, telling them I was aware that the Pleadings were not filed. I informed my counsel that it appeared they did *not* want to the get money for Dr. Galatzer-Levy, because they were not "formally" asking for it. I pointed out that what we don't ask for, we can only expect not to receive.

I realized that my counsel's not filing the Petitions to fund Dr. Galatzer-Levy contributed to the Judge's failure to follow the law which provides for payment of my expert witness from the marital estate. I could see how my counsel's conduct enabled the injustice to me and my children. I was informed that my attorneys were in violation of their fiduciary responsibilities to me, according to Illinois Law's dictating the professional ethics and obligations of lawyers to their clients. The next day, on September 15, 1998, all four Petitions, previously used to placate me, were filed with the Court.

September 16, 1998 was pay back time for my investigation of the Court Record and effort to hold my counsel accountable for their assisting in keeping my expert witness' report from coming forward to benefit me and my children. It has taken a full year for me to comprehend the relationship between the sequence of events and the ongoing cycle of legal domestic abuse to me and my children. In reviewing this today, I recognize why the next episode occurred. It appears that counsel never intended to assist in bringing my expert witness report out and formally into the proceedings. However, now that I had disclosed how this was being done behind my back, a new way had to be created to do the same, only this time involving me and an open court record.

CHAPTER 22

Quick Protected Exit

False Pretense Order Barring My Expert Witnesses

Sham Hearing for Murphy and Skoubis' Exit

Domestic Violence Transformed into Litigation Abuse

Falling Through the Cracks of System

Al Toback Sees the "Battered Woman"

It became clear to me that trying to hold an abuser, who was in denial, accountable for his/her actions creates further abuse, only to a higher degree. This had been my experience in the marriage. Now it had become the practice of my attorneys.

On September 16, 1998, we were in court allegedly – once again – attempting to get funding for Dr. Galatzer-Levy. Lew's counsel insisted that I take the children back to see Dr. Chapman for another evaluation. I told Ms. Murphy that I would not agree to do this, because I had a Motion to Disqualify Dr. Chapman before the Court and a compliant filed with the Department of Professional Regulations. Agreeing to bring my children to see him would nullify my objections to Dr. Chapman's actions and his custody recommendations. It was no secret that my prior counsel and I were aware of the unethical conduct of Dr. Chapman. Dr. Chapman was clearly serving as Lew's hired gun in the custody litigation.

Ms. Murphy told me that the Judge was going to "order" that I do this anyway and my compliance with this Order would assist in

our getting funds for Dr. Galatzer-Levy. Following the court proceeding, a Court Order was co-drafted by Ms. Murphy and Lew's
attorney, Joy Feinberg. Prior to my leaving the courtroom, Ms.
Feinberg said, "Jeanne should read this Order to insure that she is of
sound mind." I was initially put off by this insulting comment. I
wanted to proceed in exiting the courtroom, but out of deference to
Ms. Murphy, I remained to read the Court's Order.

There were numerous points in the Order that compromised the
securing of my expert custody witness' report. It established a time
frame on the production of his report that we all knew was
unrealistic. Further, it made the inclusion of my expert witness'
testimony in the scheduled upcoming custody trial contingent upon
my seeing Dr. Chapman again, by myself and with my children. I
told my counsel that I had strong objections to these points drafted in
the Order and asked that she bring up my objections with the Court.
She responded, "If you don't sign the Order, I am going to withdraw
from the case." In my frustration and out of my vulnerability and
desperation to hang on to counsel, I signed the Order to acknowledge that I had read it, as requested; not to suggest I was in
agreement.

During the next week, Ms. Murphy faxed me a copy of the
September 16, 1998 Court Order. Next to my name in Lew's
attorney's hand writing was the word "AGREED." Attached to the
Order was a letter from Ms. Murphy's office identifying it as an
Agreed Order. I realized that this alleged "Agreed Order" was
obtained under false pretense and under duress.

On September 23, 1998, I requested in writing that my counsel
take the proper legal steps to vacate the portions of the Order that I
was not in agreement with; those which I had pointed out in court. I
explained that these portions of the order nullified my position with
respect to Dr. Chapman and further prevented our submitting the
favorable evidence of Dr. Galatzer-Levy. I reminded her that the
Order was obtained under false pretense and duress. We both knew
that she was in violation of her professional responsibility to me by

assisting in securing this Order. I now recognize that an attorney
who is back-stabbing you cannot go into court on your behalf and
admit it. It's probably not much different than Lew's unwillingness
to admit to the police that he abuses us.

The next day, on September 24, 1998, Nancy Murphy meet me
in court handing me her Motion to Withdraw from the case. She was
flustered and said:

> "I am concerned about my professional liability. I have no
> choice. I need to protect my license." She added, "You did
> not do your part in getting me the witness list and I cannot
> be ready for trial next week."

I was holding my witness list, which she and I personally
reviewed together many times over the last two months. It consisted
of 144 individuals who had direct and or indirect contact with the
domestic violence in our family and many who knew me as my
children's Mom and their primary caretaker. I am certain she was
embarrassed about using the witness list as her excuse, because I had
it with me and gave her an additional copy as she was telling me this
story. On this copy it stated, "Submitted July 24, 1998."

We both knew of her malpractice concerning the *un*-filed
Petitions and the false pretense Order, which probably had more to
do with her need for a quick exit. Or, it may have been that posturing
me without counsel days before trial was part of the legal plan, to
wrestle custody from me. Nonetheless, she did not have legal
grounds to terminate our relationship at this juncture. These grounds
needed to be created, and it appeared that counsel had further
damage to do.

                    *   *   *

Mr. Bruce Richman, Lew's financial expert was asked to give
testimony on the value of our pension. He said, "There is only $500

remaining in the pension to use." I couldn't believe what I was hearing, as the last review months before showed nearly $400,000. Then I was asked to take the stand. Ira Feldman, Lew's financial attorney, asked me questions about my current practice, the liquidation of my pension and credit card expenditures used to sustain me and my children.

Following my testimony, Mr. Skoubis completed the work of burying my case by "co-authoring" with Ms. Feinberg another Court Order. Ms Feinberg, while she was Lew's designated custody attorney, managed to appear in court for most of the financial matters as well. This particular Order granted me two business days, one of which was a special religious holiday, to submit my financial expert witness' report to the Court. But my financial expert witness also had not been paid in full, and at this juncture claimed not to have Lew's complete current production.

In a matter of one week, Ms. Murphy and Mr. Skoubis managed to position my case, barring both my expert custody and expert finance witnesses from providing testimony in our upcoming trial. This prevented my presentation to the Court of all the favorable expert evidence that could have and should have been submitted to protect me and my children. These actions by my counsel convinced me that it was not in my interest to go to trial with Nancy Murphy and Mike Skoubis representing me. No matter how strong one's case might be, if counsel is preventing its presentation to the judge, rulings will be made as though it doesn't exist. It was clear that I was better off without the legal muffler that my counsel placed upon me.

However, my past experience also made it quite convincing that I could not go to trial alone. Yet, I knew that obtaining substitute counsel at this juncture would be next to impossible. I felt like I was between a rock and a hard place, again, with no place to turn. After much thought and soul searching, I decided not to eagerly resist letting my counsel go and to trust that whatever came next had to be better than where I stood with them.

I drafted and filed a Pleading, entitled Objections to Amended Emergency Motion to Withdraw, to keep the Court Record straight. This Pleading was a recount of numerous litigation infractions to me and my case to date. It showed how the withholding of marital resources to fund legal support to benefit me had been the method of Lew's control and the means the Trial Court utilized to bury the central issue of abuse in the case. It evidenced my being kept from having legal representation unless I allowed my counsel to work against me. It showed how my current counsel had postured me to go to trial without legal representation or expert witnesses, which obviously placed me at a substantial disadvantage and seriously prejudiced my case. This Pleading clearly explained how Ms. Murphy and Mr. Skoubis' actions and inactions blatantly sabotaged my legal rights to protect me and my children. In closing the Pleading, I requested assistance in directing Lew and I to negotiate a settlement through mediation.

*   *   *

On September 28, 1998, the day originally designated as the commencement of our trial, all parties met in court for the purpose of my counsel's emergency Motion to Withdraw. Ms. Murphy appeared before the Court with another Amended Emergency Motion to Withdraw, requesting that she and Mr. Skoubis both withdraw as my counsel. Judge Evans informed all parties that he could not hear this Motion or review my Pleading because it posed some ethical issues and a conflict of interest for him. In my innocence, I hoped that some truths were going to come forward. I was wrong.

My counsel was giving the appearance to the Court that they intended to expose unethical conduct of mine, which would prejudice me. The false excuse to go before another judge served to preserve Judge Evans' "appearance" of impartiality and thereby his involvement in the case. Opposing counsel needed this Judge in order to bring the closure to the case that we were headed toward. This positioning got Judge Evans off the hook, so he would not formally be apprised of the information contained in my Objections to Ms. Murphy's Withdrawal, nor would he be postured to have to rule on leaving me without counsel at the threshold of trial.

Judge Evans referred the Hearing on my counsels' withdrawal and my objections to Judge Lisa Murphy. John Lietzau accompanied me to Judge Lisa Murphy's Courtroom, but he was not allowed to observe this Hearing. All non-participating parties and witnesses were asked to leave the "open" courtroom. Ms. Murphy and Mr. Skoubis presented to Judge Murphy that they needed to withdraw because I was not planning to follow the Court Order of September 16, 1998. Yet I never told her that, I only ask for help in correcting the portions of the Order that damaged my case. Then they presented their recently fabricated ethical problem which they claimed to have with me. They said the testimony I gave yesterday, in which I was unable to recall the exact date I cashed my $4,000 IRA, differed from my more precise recollection I disclosed to them of the date I liquidated my pension. This was my unethical conduct, for which they could not compromise their license representing me.

I was sickened by the staged sequence of events and my own counsel's lying and misrepresentations to this Judge. I realized that they were desperate to withdraw from the case and recognized that it was a blessing that they were no longer going to represent me. I proceeded to inform the Court of all the infractions to me over the course of the litigation, particularly the recent acts of malpractice by Ms. Murphy and Mr. Skoubis. Without using the word "malprac-tice," I clearly described the un-filed Petitions for Dr. Galatzer-Levy's funding that had been dangled before me over the last four months, as well as the Order barring my expert witnesses which had been obtained under false pretense and duress.

The Judge gave Ms. Murphy and Mr. Skoubis permission to withdraw on the basis of the obvious loss of trust and inability to have further communications. The Judge left the bench and exited the courtroom. John came back into the courtroom and we talked about what had transpired. Overhearing our conversation, Ms. Murphy and Mr. Wessel insisted on writing in the Order that the Court "seal" the testimony and transcript of this Hearing. John and I objected, but they ordered to seal it anyway. We recognized that this maneuver was to protect the court agents that were a party to this sham Hearing.

John and I were both appalled by counsels' actions. We were in shock that my attorneys had been working to bury my case for over four months and then had left me on the threshold of trial with no legal representation and with legal logistic tape over the mouths of my expert witnesses. Then, they had the nerve to exit my case, alleging that I was unethical. This reminded me of Lew's effort to establish that he is the victim and I am the villain or the batterer after and while he abuses me.

I had reached my limit in which I could no longer take the manipulation, misrepresentations, blatant lying and failure to find justice in the courtroom. I walked back to my office and went to the bathroom. I noticed I was bleeding from the rectum! This symptom was incredibly symbolic, as I have never had any gastrointestinal or bowel complications in my life. It felt like I was getting what Lew had promised years before – to *"butt fuck (me) in our divorce."*

Adding insult to injury, one hour later I received a page from Nancy Murphy calling me from Judge Evans' Courtroom. It was 2:30, and she was telling my answering service, "It is an emergency that you immediately go to court as they are proceeding on a Motion." I wondered how can Ms. Murphy proceed on anything, given that she has withdrawn as my counsel and I am not there. Judge Lisa Murphy had granted me 21 days, which is customary, to obtain substitute counsel. Knowing that they can't legally proceed without me, I ignored Ms. Murphy's page and went home to relax, recover and reunite with my children.

*   *   *

Around 9:00 in the evening, Dr. Galatzer-Levy called my home. I communicated the days events and my disenchantment around counsel setting it up so he wouldn't get paid. He was aware that I had been to court attempting to secure his fees dozens of times over the last six months.

A light went off in me and I said, "So you have been the carrot in this."

He paused for several very long and uncomfortable minutes. Dr. Galatzer-Levy said he believed that my not securing his funding had more to do with, as he said, "Your counsel had been incompetent in getting the job done."

He recommended that I consult with Al Toback, an attorney who he had worked with on some very difficult high profile cases. He tried to encourage me to stay with it, because "all it takes is one good attorney and a competent favorable witness" to offset Dr. Chapman's biased report and the actions of David Wessel. As we ended the conversation, Dr. Galatzer-Levy suggested that I read the book, *Whores of the Court: The Fraud of Psychiatric Testimony and the Rape of American Justice*, by Dr. Margaret Hagen.

I couldn't read, nor could I write any more about legal psychiatric rape. I had to find another way to move my life forward. Speaking became my new method. Weeks before, I had been lamenting with Jay Stein, a media specialist with whom I had been involved professionally for quite some time. He recommended that I put my whole story on film.

Jay directed me to a gentleman with expertise in making documentary videos. This man sat down and listened to me tell my story. After hearing me for 30 continuous minutes, he said, "We must get you on film." We produced a four hour tape of my entire story. It was cathartic and healing for me. Reviewing my movie created for me some objectivity and clarity with respect to my predicament. We edited the four hours of film down to a 45-minute video, capturing the salient points and entitled it *Domestic Violence Transformed into Litigation Abuse*.

I obtained several hundred copies of this film and sent it to every legislator in the state of Illinois who had an expressed investment in child abuse, domestic violence and civil rights issues. The tape was also circulated to numerous abuse agencies in the country and several federal organizations committed to the protection of children and prevention of domestic violence. My support team, who consisted of John Lietzau and Evelyn Delmar, assisted me in the distribution of this tape.

We received files of response letters, most of which expressed deep concern, sympathy and direction to our local Department of Children and Family Services or some agency other than themselves. After chasing from one group to another, the common response to our out-reach revealed an impasse due to the bifurcation of government. We were informed that the legislative lawmakers and the law enforcement court agents operate in two separate arenas, and cannot intervene in the actions of one another. Consequently, no one outside of the Court could help us.

*   *   *

It appeared that the people who seemed to understand my predicament kept sending me back to the Court, which I came to know as the "lion's den." Surrendering to the reality that I had to find a way to negotiate my closure through the Court, I pursued every legal lead made available to me.

I first met with Mr. Alan Toback. He called Dr. Galatzer-Levy in front of me and during this conversation he said, "We'll let the older boy go, and save the little ones, so they live with their Mom."

After their conversation, Mr. Toback said to me, "Dr. Galatzer-Levy is substantiating all that you are saying." He added, "There is a **real injustice** here!"

His requirement to represent me was that I obtain nearly $75,000 funding for legal fees and for my expert witnesses by petitioning the Court, acting as my own counsel. Initially I tried this strategy with his assistance, and immediately there was much resistance.

After consulting with opposing counsel, Mr. Toback said, "The deck is stacked against you. "You realize you are a *battered woman,* don't you?"

In that moment, I wasn't quite sure what to make of his observation, because all along I had rejected the stigma associated with the concept of a "battered woman." In writing this manuscript, I have since understood the concept battered woman, a term coined by Lenore Walker in *The Battered Woman.* Mr. Toback was correct, though I didn't realize it at the time. A battered woman, according to Dr. Walker, is:

"a woman who is repeatedly subjected to any forceful physical or psychological behavior by a man in order to coerce her to do something he wants her to do without any concern for her rights." (1979, pg. xv)

During my conversation with Mr. Toback, he asked if I intended to go underground with David and Marc. He appeared to be aware of my informing Nancy Murphy of the recommendations given to me by the domestic violence shelter. I suspect this was relayed to him through Dr. Galatzer-Levy. I told Mr. Toback that I had not made plans to runaway and go underground with the children, but rather hoped we could be protected by the Court. In response, he forewarned me with a story of a woman doctor who fled with her abused children. He said, "The mother is now in jail." In closing he added, "Taking on this case at this point is very difficult." He revealed, "Everyone says I'm crazy to come into this case." I appreciated his honesty. It was a wake up call.

Later, I recognized that Mr. Toback's insistence on my securing his fees from the marital estate before he filed an appearance on my behalf showed his disbelief in the likelihood of getting these funds. I knew that if six seasoned attorneys over three years couldn't obtain proper funding to represent my interests, I would not be able to either. I had had my fill of my prior Petitions being ignored by the Court and my pro se appearances used as opportunities to railroad me into the ground. I could not go back to this abuse and its strain again, so I backed off from the effort. In the interim, as I was deciding what to do, Mr. Toback said, "The Judge may make you go to trial without Dr. Galatzer-Levy." Knowing that the law provided for me to have an expert witness, counsel's shift became self-evident.

Therefore, I directed my attention to potential legal representation that worked from the heart, without an economic interest or political tie to the court. This lead me to every law clinic in the city of Chicago at the major universities and local law schools. I was hoping to find a professor to take my case as an educational experience or as an opportunity to be a hero in what was looking like an impossible situation. This was wishful thinking, and only sent me back to the public resources of "pro-bono" counsel. From here I learned, once again, I was "too rich to be poor and too poor to be rich." I knew I was falling through the cracks of the system; and the cruel, relentless process was destroying me.

Reaching forward proved to lead me nowhere other than into a more debilitating sense of grave hopelessness. So, I decided to reach back into the past and draw from whatever could be salvaged from those who had opened their hearts to me. Doing this may have been what killed me or saved me, depending on how you look at it.

Similarities in the Battering Histories of Battered Women

1) Initial surprise of battering potential, masked by a "layer of gentleness," before the onset of an acute battering incident

2) Unpredictability of acute battering incidents, as the time and severity of acute battering incidents were controlled by batterers

3) Overwhelming jealousy of batterer toward all facets of their victim's lives, including: children, family, friends, jobs and hobbies

4) Unusual kinds of bizarre sexual behavior, expected or demanded by batterers in their relationships with their victims

5) Lucid recall of the details of acute battering incidents, including each spoken word and every blow delivered in the violent incidents

6) Participated in the denial and concealment of battering incidents, and denied batterer's responsibility for abusive episodes

7) Trend toward alcohol (or substance) abuse by batterer

8) Battered with extreme psychological abuse, ongoing verbal harassment, criticism, brainwashing and losing-power struggles

9) Batterer sincerely and dispassionately threatens to harm family members or close friends of the battered woman

10) Repeatedly frightened with terrorizing descriptions by batterer of his plans to torture or destroy his victim, often with a weapon

11) Omnipotence is projected by batterer, and victim believes he can do things others can't do; but she also knows he is fragile

12) Battered women have an awareness of a death potential and the knowledge of their perpetrator's capacity for murder

Cited from L. Walker, *The Battered Woman*, 1979.

CHAPTER 23

Victims Cry Out

$40,000 Liquidated from Our Pension

Marc's Acting-Out and Suicidal Thoughts

October 19, 1998: Re-victimizing the Victims

Reaching Out to Judge Orr and Back to Mr. Stern

Another Violation of Our Order of Protection

October 1998 was a month of truths. Lew evidenced his truth, Marc spoke his truth and Mommy reached out on behalf of Hers. I believe everyone in the family felt the tension of this litigation. Something had to shift.

Lew withheld our court-ordered support again this month, and the Court was unwilling to do anything about this violation of the Order. Instead, Lew engaged in a wasteful and cruel action, supported by the Court. He liquidated $40,000 from our pension which, according to his own expert weeks ago, only had $500 to utilize. It was clear that the money was available, as long as it was not used on my legal support by someone who was professionally obligated to disclose the domestic abuse by Lew to me and the children. It cost Lew nearly $20,000 in taxes and penalties to liquidate these funds.

David Wessel was given his share from the balance, and $5,000 was given to a psychiatrist from Lew's hospital to evaluate all three children. Our marital funds could be used to pre-pay a psychiatrist of Lew's choosing, but not to pay Dr. Galatzer-Levy, the psychiatrist who already evaluated our family and was sitting on diagnostic therapeutic information. This was a true display of Lew's manipulative control of our financial resources, used to further his campaign and bury the needs of me and our children.

As we approached the second week of October, the strain of the economic tension started building. With no income this month, things became extremely tenuous. I was receiving foreclosure notices on our home and was having to cut back considerably on our everyday expenditures. It appeared indefinite as to how long we would remain in this starve-out mode. It was clear that Lew and his legal team did not want me to have an extra dime for anything.

On the evening of Wednesday, October 14th, David, Marc and I were selecting photo packages for their school pictures. The packages are ordered before the pictures are taken. I chose a standard package, because of my limited resources. Marc wanted a more elaborate package. I explained to Marc that this was what we could afford, and should he like the pictures, I would purchase the additional set next month. I was not going to write a check beyond what our account could cover. Marc had a temper tantrum and called his father to see if he would finance the larger package now. This led to an exacerbation of Marc's temper tantrum.

The next day Marc went to school with a chip on his shoulder. He dove into a verbal confrontation with his teacher, literally assaulting her with his words. He alleged to be angry and upset that she had informed me of an assignment which was incomplete. He tore into her for what he identified as "lying" to his Mom. The encounter escalated and Marc became even more disrespectful, leading to his being removed from the classroom.

Marc was taken to the social worker Maria McCabe, and they talked. Ms. McCabe asked Marc what was going on with his parents divorce, and this opened the door for Marc to express his feelings about the divorce continuing for so long and the threat of living with his older brother. Marc said that he would rather die than have to live with his Dad and Brad. Marc stated that if he has to live where he is hurt all the time, he might as well kill himself. Ms. McCabe probed further and asked how he would do this. Marc said he would use a knife and put it in his heart.

The intensity of Marc's emotion must have been so significant that it moved Ms. McCabe. She first called me and then Lew to report Marc's distress and his statements.

"I could see the fear in his eyes," Ms. McCabe said to me. "He is afraid of his brother."

She expressed her concern over Marc being confused about his father trying to push him into living in a situation that caused him so much pain. Ms. McCabe said, "Jeanne, this is making Marc question his Dad's love for him, and I find this quite disturbing." She told me that Marc wanted her to tell his Dad this, because he did not know how to say it. She wanted me to know about Marc's turmoil, his despair and talk of killing himself if forced to live with his Dad and Brad. She said she saw Marc as severely distressed, but not actually suicidal.

I informed her of what was going on in the litigation, and we concluded the conversation with the agreement that she would provide counseling for Marc at school. We both felt this would serve Marc best, because she already had a rapport with Marc. Over the years she had worked with him in Rainbows, a support group for children going through divorce or other losses. Ms. McCabe believed she could help Marc express his feelings and maintain emotional balance.

*   *   *

The stress of the litigation and the impact of the threat of having to live with Lew and Brad was used as the means to wrestle Marc right out of his safe protective home with me to be placed in the environment that caused his suicidal thoughts. It was remarkable how Lew and his legal team used this child's innocent outreach to bring closure to Lew's campaign to "get rid of Mommy." Here is how this incredible deliverance occurred.

On October 19, 1998, I was in court with all counsel, Lew's attorneys and Mr. Wessel. As was more common than not, Lew was not present as he had two law firms to represent his efforts. I was without counsel and had two Pleadings before the Court, submitted to all parties on October 15, 1998. One Pleading was a Motion to Vacate the Orders obtained by my prior counsel barring my expert witnesses, and the other was an Emergency Motion for Extension of Time and Continuance which requested an extension of time before our upcoming trial. My Pleadings disclosed the actions of my former attorney, which postured me so that I was not able to have an impartial trial. I explained its contents to the Judge.

Ms. Feinberg attempted to suggest that my request of the Court for a continuance was a "delay tactic." I explained to the Court that I had wanted to bring closure to these proceedings for years, but I believed it would be reasonable to ask that we proceed on equal footing and I not be expected to go to trial without representation against Lew's two seasoned law firms. I was investigating securing counsel out of state though I did not mention this in court. I recognized that it would serve me best to have counsel, whose practice was not dependent on his involvement in Cook County Court or the Chicago divorce network of lawyers. Lew's attorneys wanted the record to reflect that I was without counsel because of some flaw in myself which prevented me from maintaining a relationship with an attorney.

I articulated the sequence of events leading me from one attorney to the next. I was clear and respectful while I voiced the disturbing aspects of my plight to the Judge. I made it very clear that the litigation process prevented me from having legal representation supporting my interests in court. I showed how my counsel was not able to remain on the case unless they were playing into the hands of opposing counsel, because of the manipulation of funding from the estate. I showed how this left me with legal representation only so long as I was willing to work against myself. I illustrated that on each occasion in which I confronted this, my counsel withdrew. The pattern was clear; everyone saw it, yet the Judge ignored it and Lew's counsel distracted, distorted and denied it. The Judge's handling of this day re-opened a very disturbing question, *Is the Judge in on it?*

To overshadow my request of the Court, Lew's attorney, Ms. Feinberg, submitted an Emergency Petition to Transfer Temporary Custody of Marc and David based on Marc's so-called "suicide threat." I was not given the standard court procedural time to read this Pleading, much less time to provide a written Response to the Court. The Pleading alleged an Emergency which there was no evidence to support other than the word of Lew's counsel, twisting Marc's exchange with his social worker into a "suicide attempt." In the face of this gross misrepresentation of my young child's distress, I was not granted my Motion for Continuance and, instead, a pretrial Hearing commenced immediately.

*   *   *

I saw the train coming and I wasn't sure what to do next. My first impulse was to call out to someone who clearly knew of the domestic violence syndrome in our family and hope that I would get heard. I thought Judge Orr from the Skokie Criminal Court was just that person. On October 25, 1998, I sent her a letter reminding her that she had granted me and my children an Order of Protection against my husband in September 1994, because she recognized our danger and felt Lew needed a "wake up call." I told her that my children and I were now "falling through the cracks" of the judicial system in divorce court and I was running out of legal resources and strategies to assist us. I informed her that the process was compromising my children and the Court appeared to be posturing to place them in the hands of their abuser with no real or true cause. In closing, I pleaded for her help to "break the cycle of abuse, from family to court." Along with this letter, I sent my video, *Domestic Violence Transformed into Litigation Abuse*, and some written documentation.

I never heard back from her. I was later informed that judges' alliance to one another was not much different than attorneys' commitment to one another. It was suggested to me that she may have sent my tape to Judge Evans, and now with the actions of the court agents exposed, the Court would dig in further to protect itself. This is exactly what happened. I do not know if this was a coincidence or a true continuation of the abuse cycle. I also recall the day I mailed this tape; I was ambivalent and uncertain of possible consequences of this action. All I knew in the moment was I needed to reach out, speaking our truth because my children and I could take no more. I longed for justice and closure.

The imminent railroading rapidly progressed, and I needed counsel in place to represent me in court. I was not granted the time to seek assistance out of state and didn't think I could learn enough about trial proceedings to carry myself through the final trial pro se. The absurdity of the Court's consideration of Lew's attorneys' unfounded misrepresentations and distortions of the facts and its unwillingness to consider three years of litigation abuse to me, made me realize that standing in court alone would leave me "lame duck." I needed someone who could serve as a pillar that I could stand behind and survive, as we approached the end.

I went back to Steve Stern in tears explaining the status of our case. He was compassionate and clearly committed to keeping David and Marc with me. I knew from my last dealings with him that he didn't have the same standing in court as did Lew's attorneys, but he knew the case and I needed legal assistance quickly. While I knew Steve would be limited by the politics of the case, I didn't think he was vicious enough to hurt me, nor deviously clever enough to pull off Lew's campaign to destroy me. It was a selection of salvation to just get to the end and protect me before the crash.

Steve came aboard as my counsel and he performed exactly as would be expected, given the history. Initially, he eagerly worked on my behalf, submitting Pleadings supporting my position to vacate the Orders that interfered with our having a fair and impartial trial. He alleged to put forth an effort to secure Dr. Galatzer-Levy's report and he filed additional Pleadings to disqualify Dr. Chapman. I lived one day at a time, not knowing what tomorrow would bring. Each day more truths came forward.

Lew's attorneys intended to present Lew to the Court as a "rehabilitated abuser." In order to do this, they needed to dissolve the Order of Protection against Lew, protecting Bradley, David, Marc and me. So a Pleading was submitted in an effort to dissolve my Order of Protection, but there was no evidence substantiating Lew's alleged rehabilitation and the filing of this Pleading failed to follow court protocol. Lew's counsel merely issued a stale Pleading of January 28, 1998, which had been submitted to the Court prior to the Court's determination to extend our Order of Protection through January 28, 2000. Before all of this could be corrected, Lew's truth revealed itself.

*   *   *

On October 27, Marc, Brad and Lew were involved in an altercation that occurred at Lew's home during their visitation and continued before my front door as Lew was dropping off the children. It began with Marc wanting to bring his bike home to my house where he resided. Lew and Brad refused to allow Marc to take his bike with him. Their fight escalated, and Lew grabbed Marc by his clothing at the neck with one hand and with the other hand lifted him up in the air by his pants and threw him into the car. Having been thrown into the back seat, Marc hit his face and neck on the seat buckle and started crying and kicking his legs. Lew grabbed his legs and shoved them into the car and slammed the door.

Upon reaching my home, Lew instructed Brad to pull Marc out of the car. Marc was thrown to the ground and kicked a number of times in the driveway, while Lew sat in the car. Finally, Lew drove away and Marc picked himself up. Marc was emotionally distraught. Lew drove back to our house to pick up Brad. Marc approached Lew's car and grabbed the door handle of the passenger side of the car. In Lew's frustration and anger, he drove his car through the driveway and down the road with Marc hanging onto the door handle outside of the car. Lisa was standing in front of the house and witnessed Marc hanging onto Lew's moving vehicle. She was concerned for Marc's safety as he could have easily been crushed under the wheels of Lew's car.

I took Marc to the police and we filed a report on the incident. The police officer was appalled by the incident and the surrounding circumstances of the family history and the litigation. He sat down with Marc and informed him of his rights to be protected, not injured or put at risk for physical harm. The officer, who was also a former attorney, suggested that I seek remedy in the court. He claimed that the action was a violation of our Order of Protection and recommended that I attempt to have Lew's supervision reinstated through my counsel.

"If the Court doesn't grant this," he said, "you shouldn't allow the children to go on visitation."

The officer was firm and clear in his demeanor; I felt like someone threw another rock between my eyes. It was a wake up call for both me and Marc.

Our Order of Protection prohibited Lew from committing acts or conduct of "physical abuse" to the minor children. Physical abuse, according to the Illinois Domestic Violence Act of 1986, includes:

"knowing or reckless use of physical force, confinement or restraint; ...or knowing or reckless conduct which creates an immediate risk of physical harm." (60/103 Definitions 14-i, iii)

It was obvious to me that my child had been placed at risk of physical harm and that Lew was not acting in Marc's interest, but rather resorted to the use of reckless conduct and physical force to deal with conflict. In my mind there were other ways to remove an upset child from a car other than driving away and continuing down the road with the child hanging on. I visualized Marc under Lew's car and I, too, was frightened.

Marc and I both took much from this encounter. I rekindled my commitment to hold my own in what I believed to be true in the court, and Marc started his own self-preservation routine when battered in Lew's home. The firmer I was in court, the more my efforts were used against me. The more Marc exerted his will to reach out for help or exert his own initiative in protecting himself, the more his efforts were used to compromise him further. We were trapped in a cycle of battering. Our question was how to find a way out.

Dear David W.

Since I did not get to talk to you a few days ago this is what I wanted to tell you I want to live with my mom becase if I live my dad It will get hit evry day of my life soplease tell t
this to the court
court

from Marc blumenthal

Marc Blumenthal
9\13\98

DEAR, DAVID WESSEL
I WANT TO LIVE WITH MY MOM
BECAUSE I FEEL ALOT SAFER
WITH MY MOM. I ALSO WANT
TO LIVE WITH MY MOM BECAUSE
THERE IS NO HITTING GOING ON
WITH MY MOM. BUT THERE IS
AT MY DAD'S HOUSE. PLEASE
SHARE THIS LETTER WITH THE
COURT.

David Blumenthal
9 - 13 - 98

Marc and David's Letters to Mr. Wessel

Reckless Father; Careless Court

Dr. Chapman's Perjury

The Erroneous Order of November 10, 1998

Denial and Discount of Recklessness

Transferring Brad's Custody *Without* a Hearing

My Appeal to the Appellate Court

The Swiss Army Knife: Daddy's Gift

The King Family Cruise

As the Blumenthals showed the family truths in October, the court agents evidenced their truths in the months to follow. On November 2, 1998, Dr. Chapman, the court-appointed custody evaluator, provided oral testimony by telephone to the Court in the Judge's chambers. His comments were used to support the requests of Joy Feinberg to give me supervised visitation and transfer the children out of my custody, because of the "stress of the litigation" as evidenced by Marc's reaching out to Ms. McCabe.

Dr. Chapman was subsequently brought into court for further cross examination and questioning by the attorneys. My counsel, Steve Stern, brought out several facts evidencing Dr. Chapman's bias and lack of impartiality. He showed that Dr. Chapman's actions did not support the belief that Marc's emotional status was an "emergency." To the contrary, in an evaluation with Marc on October 30, 1998, Dr. Chapman failed to address Marc's comments or thoughts of hurting himself. Marc was eager to tell Dr. Chapman about his distress around being battered in Lew's' home. As Marc was speaking of getting hit on visitation at his Dad's house, Dr. Chapman interrupted him and said, "I retract that question." and stopped Marc from saying anything further about the ongoing abuse.

Mr. Stern exposed how Dr. Chapman failed to comply with the court's legal requirement to supply his recommendations in the form of a written report. Instead, Dr. Chapman submitted transcribed letters from Dr. Freedman, the monitor, dating back from December 6, 1996 to July 23, 1997. However, Dr. Freedman's letters were stale and, furthermore, were "non-admissible." A prior Court Order prevented Dr. Freedman from giving testimony directly to the Court; thus the submission of his letters denied me "due process." Technically any testimony entered into evidence can be questioned by both sides. But one can not ask questions to letters. So Mr. Stern pointed out that our rights for due process were denied by his inability to cross examine the Freedman letters. It was also common knowledge that Mr. Wessel was Dr. Freedman's primary contact.

Mr. Stern also showed how Dr. Chapman's oral recommendations supporting Ms. Feinberg's request were entirely predicated upon stale and unfounded information obtained October 1997, predominantly from David Wessel and Lew Blumenthal. My counsel exposed that the heresy input was not investigated and corroborated by the Doctor with the relevant parties in the children's lives. There was also evidence that Dr. Chapman failed to consult with the domestic violence expert in his own office, yet he was well aware that abuse was a central theme in the case.

Mr. Stern was doing great on my behalf and even got better when he caught Dr. Chapman in a lie and aggressively confronted this perjury on the stand. Dr. Chapman was exhibiting his truth, and it became apparent in open court. He provided a long explanation of how Dr. Kredow did not make a favorable report on myself because my MMPI test was "uninterpretable." Mr. Stern placed Dr. Kredow's interpretive report of my favorable MMPI results in front of Dr. Chapman. The report stated it was a "valid clinical profile"; not a testing found to be *un*interpretable. Dr. Chapman turned pale and his body became awkward and strained. He said, "Well now, there is a conflict here between what I am remembering and what the report itself states." The entire courtroom became as quiet as a church, and Steve capitalized on the moment.

It was obvious that the court-appointed custody evaluator was lying, and now his lack of impartiality was evident to all. Mr. Stern was thrilled in believing he now had sufficient grounds to disqualify Dr. Chapman. He was probably right, and this could have been done from a technical and legal perspective, particularly in light of the other numerous flaws in Dr. Chapman's report.

I was ecstatic, and John Lietzau was quite impressed with Mr. Stern's effectiveness. Cautiously, John said, "Let's see what the Court does with what was disclosed today." The next day in court, Steve went from being a bold, competent and aggressive interrogator to becoming a limp court agent, appearing fearful to further dissect Dr. Chapman's inconsistencies and dismantle the Doctor's credibility. John was sitting with me in court and noted, "Steve looks like they got to him last night. He has sold you out." We were both aware of the dramatic shift in Mr. Stern.

I recognized that Mr. Stern was not going to be able to campaign for me and my children, no matter what he believed was right, proper, just or in the interest of my boys. This appeared to become secondary to Mr. Stern's need to protect his own professional alliances and the interest of the Court. I think he had no other choice. The politics governing the case appeared to interrupt the legal competence Mr. Stern displayed the day before. Instead, Steve took steps to assist in covering up yesterday's disclosures. From here, Mr. Stern appeared to have been assigned the job of holding my hand as we went down.

The day culminated in the creation of a Court Order which looked like it came out of someone else's proceedings. The Order was based on incorrect information about both parties' discovery. Specifically, it stated that Lew had complied with discovery, which my counsel was not in possession of, and that I had not complied with discovery; yet I had confirmation letters and opposing counsel's open court acknowledgment of my having done so. The Order also contained language saying that Lew's Petition to Dissolve our Order of Protection was to be heard at our next court date. But there was no valid Petition to dissolve our Order of Protection before the Court. It was suggested that this Order was obtained to provide an acceptable technical legal means to transfer the custody without having to rely on the court's custody evaluator.

I asked Steve to file a Pleading to vacate this erroneous Order because of the false information contained in it, and the fact that the incorrect statements concerning financial disclosure opened me up for a Default Judgment. He agreed to do so, but never did. Two weeks later, I gave up waiting and drafted the Motion myself. I presented it to Mr. Stern. He said he would file it with the Court, but wanted his office to put it on his "stationery." This never happened. Eventually, I filed the Pleading myself.

*   *   *

Steve straddled the fence in his effort to support me without making too many waves with the Court. He filed another Motion to Disqualify Dr. Chapman and a Petition to Strike Dr. Chapman's recent testimony. At first, I was appreciative of this action, but soon recognized that it was a futile effort because our objections to Dr. Chapman were not heard by the Court before and were not likely to be heard at this juncture. I could see his efforts were to appease me, but I don't know if it was to keep me contained or if his concern was sincere.

There were many moments in which he appeared outraged by the actions of opposing counsel and the posturing of the Court. When his anger and my sadness blended in the same conversation, he encouraged me to do whatever I could to assist myself. We talked about contacting legislators, media and investigative reporters. I recognized that much of what I needed at this point, he could not do for me. It was time for me to do whatever it took to get heard inside the Court as well as outside, in the court of public opinion. The Video, *Domestic Violence Transformed into Litigation* Abuse, was distributed to various TV stations and newspapers throughout Chicago. Up-dated facts about the proceedings were sent to key legislators who had taken an interest in the case. Steve supported this outreach until local media responded with concern regarding our plight.

Before the wave of public concern came forward, I asked Steve to file the Pleading recommended by the police officer concerning Lew's Violation of our Order of Protection. Initially, he did not want to introduce this incident into the Court Record. I could see the conflict it posed for him politically. So I drafted the Pleading and filed it myself. I explained to him that I needed to protect my children and I would take action where he was limited due any conflicting alliances he had in representing me. This way he could save face with his colleagues and the Court. This was acceptable to him, and he joined me in presenting the Violation of the Order of Protection and the evidence of Lew driving his automobile with Marc hanging onto the outside.

On November 16, 1998, shortly after this Pleading was filed, Lew provided testimony in open court denying that he drove his car with Marc hanging onto the outside of it. On the next day, my counsel brought Lisa in to provide testimony of exactly what she witnessed. She informed the Court of her seeing Lew driving his car with Marc hanging on the exterior of the car by the door handle. It was apparent that Lew's counsel and Mr. Wessel were quite upset with Mr. Stern's bringing this evidence before the Judge. They attempted to suggest that Lew was "unaware" that Marc was hanging onto the car as he was driving.

Subsequently, I could see the dichotomy and a shift in my counsel. I felt his own personal confusion and conflict evolving out of the contradiction that he lived. Now Mr. Stern wanted me to believe that the incident was completely Marc's fault. While it is true that Marc was responsible for hanging onto the moving vehicle, Marc was not responsible for Lew driving the car down the road. The attorneys claimed that Lew had *no* control in his decision to drive his car, in a state of anger, with an upset child holding onto the outside of it. I couldn't reconcile this with myself, because I knew I would have found some way to remove my child off the car before driving it. I could see how counsel acted as an extension of Lew. They were merely shifting the burden of responsibility away from Lew either into the air or onto the child; anywhere but with Lew.

The Court refused to rule on our Petition concerning Lew's violation of the Order of Protection. Mr. Stern continued to ride the fence with me. On the one hand, he encouraged our public outreach, yet he assisted the collaborative effort in court to undermine my defending myself by protecting the Court Record. On November 25, 1998, Mr. Stern appeared in court without my knowledge, and in collaboration with opposing counsel and the Court, my Order of Protection was **modified**. This Modified Order of Protection transferred the temporary legal custody of Bradley to Lew, while maintaining temporary legal custody of David and Marc with me. This Order was secured behind my back and the transfer of Brad's temporary custody was done *without* a Hearing. I was outraged by this action.

It was suggested to me that this was a legal strategy to circumvent the Court's having to rule on Lew's violation of our Order of Protection. Modifying our Order of Protection made our former Order of Protection obsolete, and thereby the violation legally became a mute issue. Technically, however, the trial court's transfer of the temporary custody of Bradley was improper because my custody of Bradley hinged on a Plenary Order of Protection, which evolved out of the Domestic Violence Act. The only time such an Order can be altered before its expiration is in the event of there being sufficient evidence of danger to the child brought before the Court *in a formal Hearing.*

I realized that Steve was as impotent in protecting me as I was feeling, but for different reasons. So, I followed his first advice to pursue whatever outreach I could to protect me and my children. It was obvious that the Modified Order of Protection prejudiced me before trial and made David and Marc more vulnerable, as well as further interfering with my parental involvement with Bradley. On December 3, 1998, I appealed this Modification of my Order of Protection and the transfer of temporary custody of Bradley with the Appellate Court.

Dating back to the time I was representing myself, I had been working with a gentleman who called himself Mike. He knew how the system worked, was proficient in writing pleadings and he did excellent legal research. Mike taught me more about law during the course of my proceedings than I may have learned in graduate level study. While I never developed enough skill to take on two seasoned law firms in court, I managed to produce superb pleadings. These pleadings were extremely polished and so convincing that counsels' discomfort in reviewing them became a comic relief for witnesses in the courtroom.

However, when we ventured into the Appellate Court, I was beyond my abilities and my resources. Now I was battling the same attorneys in two courts and it became overwhelming for me. A Docket Statement was produced for the Appellate Court, outlining the themes and judicial irregularities in my case. It showed the whole story and made it sickenly obvious that we were getting railroaded in the Trial Court.

*   *   *

The way an appeal works in the context of an ongoing trial court proceeding is that, once a specific judicial decision is turned over to the appellate court, the issue is taken out of the discretion of the trial court and remains under the jurisdiction of the appellate court until the appeal is complete. One can make such an appeal on the issue of custody before a final judgment; and this is what was done. Filing my Notice of Appeal removed the issue of custody from the jurisdiction of the Trial Court. Needless to say, all the attorneys were extremely angry with this action.

Their resentment was expressed in new trial court Pleadings faulting me for "wrestling the custody decision from the trial court." Instead of dealing with the actual grounds and merits of my Appeal, Lew's counsel created an issue out of my effort to stand up to the injustice to me and my children. This caused the level of combat in the trial court to rise to another level; one in which there was less care taken in trying to follow the law.

Weeks before I initiated the Appeal, and for some time there after, the Trial Court displayed the same Dr. Jekyll/Mr. Hyde personality split that I had come to know in Lew. On varying days, and sometimes within the same day, I was told by my counsel, "The Judge is going to remove you from your home and a supervisor is going to be placed in your home." Then, instead, on the same day, a 60-day continuance to prepare for trial was granted and $7,500 was allotted for Dr. Galatzer-Levy and the balance of $8,500 for the Doctor's fees were proposed to be obtained from a lien on the marital residence.

However, with every promise, there was no follow through, instead there was a shift in the opposite direction. None of our pleadings were ruled upon, no money was forthcoming for my expert witness nor for the $20,000 plus support arrears. Besides, none of my witnesses were allowed to give testimony after Lisa's disclosures, and a pre-trial Hearing proceeded to transfer the custody of David and Marc away from me.

The Hearing predominately focused upon a regurgitation of the three years of unfounded and meritless pleadings of Lew's counsel and Mr. Wessel to jockey and transfer custody. The issues and cause for this emergency transfer of David and Marc were false and frivolous allegations, none of which pertained to a current emergency. For example:

1) I interfered with Brad's therapy because I had him involved in treatment with Dr. Heinrich in 1997.
2) I allowed Bradley to visit his maternal uncle and cousins for a long weekend in February 1997 even though we obtained his Dad's consent.
3) I interfered with David seeing a psychiatrist for a facial tic (that he did not have) in January 1996.
4) I did not follow a Court Order to take Marc to see Dr. Garber, Lew's pre-paid psychiatrist, on the day that I brought Marc to his pediatrician for a physical condition.
5) I failed to see Dr. Freedman, the monitor, Spring 1997 when the Doctor was on vacation, and also on a day I was in court defending one of opposing counsel's unfounded pleadings.
6) The children had limited contact with my mother since her move to Indiana.

What amazed me was how we were spending tens of thousands of dollars a day supporting five attorneys and court time reviewing the last three years of unfounded allegations which, even if true, failed to meet the criteria for such a transfer, much less the grounds for a current emergency. I was informed that the effort to transfer David and Marc's custody was a pre-trial tactic to better position Lew for the upcoming trial. Either that, or it was possibly the only way to accomplish transferring custody as a temporary maneuver, since there was no grounds for a transfer of custody in the Final Judgment.

* * *

During the course of this alleged Emergency Hearing based on Marc's statements of suicide, Lew gave Marc a Swiss Army Knife for Chanukah. The timing of this gift evidenced the absurdity of the so called Emergency Hearing. Here is a father with two law firms fighting in court to remove the child from Mommy's custody because he is allegedly suicidal, and this same father gives the child a Swiss Army Knife to play with as a holiday gift.

On December 18, 1998 I brought the Swiss Army Knife to court and my counsel put me on the stand to present this weapon-toy into evidence. Steve walked me through an explicit show and tell demonstration of the Swiss Army Knife, consisting of knives, picks, scissors and more. My counsel held it in front Judge Evans and placed it before him. I was struck by the Judge's unwillingness to look at it. I found this quite telling of a conflict for him, which I then became more compelled to understand.

Legislators, media and investigative reporters started responding with concern to my out-reach. In a conversation with one of our state representatives, it was suggested that I obtain the Judge's Statement of Economic Interest. The legislator was convinced that Judge Evans was involved in what seemed to interfere with the enforcement of law and the protection of my children. He believed the case was "fixed" and the Court was merely finding a way to deliver without posing an insurmountable political conflict for the Judge. He offered to assist me in obtaining this information about Judge Evans.

In the meantime, we were approaching the 1998-1999 Winter Break and the celebration of the holidays. My family was planning a King family reunion on a Caribbean Disney cruise, specifically for the grandchildren. My mother has six grandchildren and she wanted to treat us all for this wonderful vacation for the holidays. Fortunately, they were going on the week that was already designated as my week with the children for Winter Break, according to a previous court-ordered two year holiday schedule, entirely selected by Lew and his counsel.

However, since there had been much fuss in court concerning Brad's three day trip to Indiana almost two years ago, I thought it would be best to clear my going with Steve and the Court first. So I informed Steve of the trip. He was happy for me that we had this opportunity, but was ineffective in getting cooperation from Lew's counsel to allow us to go. Their expressed problem with our going was that the boat's arrival and our connecting flight to Chicago was hours after Lew's week with the children was to begin.

Over the years, when Lew had a family gathering that spilled over into my designated time with the children, I was expected and required to be flexible with the schedule to allow the children to be with their paternal family. This happened on numerous occasions, resulting in my swapping days or adjusting hours of my time with children. The expectation of the children being with their maternal family did not exist; instead. it was discouraged vehemently by Lew, Ms. Feinberg and Mr. Wessel.

*   *   *

Day after day, Lew repeatedly told the children that he could not allow them to go on the King family cruise because we would be getting home too late. I tried every way possible to negotiate the four to six hours, by giving him an extra day and more, but nothing satisfied Lew. He refused to be flexible over these hours, even though his out-of-town vacation with the children to go to his girlfriend's mother's house in Colorado did not start until a full day or two later. Lew said, "What if there was a snow storm and our flight was one day late. This would interfere with our flight on the next day." So, my brother called Lew and promised to drive the children to Colorado to insure that they not miss any of their vacation with their father. This did not satisfy Lew, either.

It became apparent to my family that Lew was determined not to allow the children the opportunity for this outing with the King family. The more Lew resisted, the more the children pestered him to go. They had numerous conversations on the phone in which Marc and David pleaded with Lew, but their Dad kept telling them they could not go. In Marc's frustration he said to his Dad, "You never let us go with Mom's family." The next day in court, Lew's attorney alleged Marc spoke with Lew on the speaker phone from my house and someone said that his Dad was "ruining Marc's life by not agreeing to the trip."

I certainly did not say this, and I didn't recall that Marc made this statement; but if he did, I would not be surprised. More alarming was that Lew's counsel and Mr. Wessel used the comment to further the argument to transfer custody of David and Marc because they claimed that "Mommy was talking about the divorce in front of the children." With this, I recognized that the proceedings were progressing from the absurd to the ridiculous.

Lew and Mr. Wessel had spent nearly three years engaging the children in numerous parental decisions, usually before and often instead of communicating with me. Then, after they succeeded in looping the boys in, they used them to plead with me over whatever Lew wanted. In the context of these years of Lew's and Mr. Wessel's polarizing the children, the allegation and the way it was then used was outrageous to me.

To gain even more legal positioning from this allegation, my mother was subpoenaed to Chicago from Indiana to appear in court the day before her flight for this family cruise. They were requiring her to testify in court to determine whether she was a suitable person to serve as my supervisor. The Court was posturing to offer that I *agree* to supervised visitation as a requirement to go on this trip.

My counsel approached me asking if I would sign an Agreed Order giving me supervised visitation so I could "enjoy" my vacation. Recognizing that I would be walking myself into supervised visitation indefinitely, I elected not to take the offer. It was also not feasible for me at the time to even consider going as it would have meant my packing all of us and finding care for our animals in order to leave for a 6:00 AM flight, only 12 hours from my getting the Court's consent.

Then, in a phone conversation the children were informed by my mother that she also would not be able to make the trip because she "had to be in court." This comment served as grounds for Lew's counsel to ask the Court to require my mother to have supervised visitation with her grandchildren, because now she, too, "talked about the divorce with the children."

I realized that the actions of mother, my children and myself had little to do with securing the best interest of my children or protecting us from further abuse. David, Marc and I remained in Chicago for our Winter Break, and I encouraged my Mom to go on her vacation. As was customary for the kids and I, we made a treat of each day together with special outings and celebration. I realized that the time had come to make each day with the boys a vacation, because I didn't know how many more days we had left.

IN THE CIRCUIT COURT OF COOK COUNTY, ILLINOIS

People ex rel ....
.... on behalf of
.... self and/or behalf of

Lewis Blumenthal
Petitioner

-vs-

Jeanne Blumenthal
Respondent

Case No. **95 D 6150**

☐ Independent Proceeding (Filed)
☐ Other Civil Proceeding of the Circuit
(Specify) Aurelia Pucinski
☐ Criminal Proceeding NOV 25 1998
☐ Juvenile Proceeding

LEADS NO. _____

Judge Timothy C. Evans #1592

PETITIONER	ADDRESS	CITY/ZIP
Jeanne King Blumenthal	**1221 Thornapple** ☐ (check if omitted pursuant to Statute)	**Northbrook**

RESPONDENT	ADDRESS	CITY/ZIP
Lewis Blumenthal	**690 Chestnut**	**Glencoe IL 6002**

Birthdate	Sex	Race	Height	Weight	Hair	Eyes	Social Security Number (if known)
2-4-53 (Required for LEADS)	**M**	**W**	**5'10**	**160 lb**	**Black**	**Hazel**	**324-02-0060**

MODIFIED

ORDER OF PROTECTION

4552 ☐ INTERIM   4652 ☒ PLENARY

ANY KNOWING VIOLATION OF ANY ORDER OF PROTECTION FORBIDDING PHYSICAL ABUSE, NEGLECT, EXPLOITATION, HARASSMENT, INTIMIDATION, INTERFERENCE WITH PERSONAL LIBERTY, WILLFUL DEPRIVATION, OR ENTERING OR REMAINING PRESENT AT SPECIFIED PLACES WHEN THE PROTECTED PERSON IS PRESENT OR GRANTING EXCLUSIVE POSSESSION OF THE RESIDENCE OR HOUSEHOLD, PROHIBITING ENTERING OR REMAINING AT THE HOUSEHOLD WHILE UNDER THE INFLUENCE OF ALCOHOL OR DRUGS AND SO CONSTITUTING A THREAT TO THE SAFETY AND WELL-BEING OF ANY PROTECTED PERSON, OR GRANTING A STAY AWAY ORDER, IS A CLASS A MISDEMEANOR. GRANT OF EXCLUSIVE POSSESSION OF THE RESIDENCE OR HOUSEHOLD SHALL CONSTITUTE NOTICE FORBIDDING TRESPASS TO LAND. ANY KNOWING VIOLATION OF ANY ORDER AWARDING LEGAL CUSTODY OR PHYSICAL CARE OF A CHILD, OR PROHIBITING REMOVAL OR CONCEALMENT OF A CHILD MAY BE A CLASS 4 FELONY. ANY WILLFUL VIOLATION OF ANY ORDER IS CONTEMPT OF COURT. ANY VIOLATION MAY RESULT IN FINE OR IMPRISONMENT. STALKING IS A FELONY.

(Definitions of prohibited conduct on reverse)

The following persons are protected by this Order: **JEANNE, BRAD, DAVID, MARC**

"The minor child/ren" referred to herein are: **Brad, DAVID & MARC BLUMENTHAL**

Date _____ Time _____ Courtroom/Calendar No. _____
Location _____

This Order will be in effect until:
Date **Nov 25 1998**   Time **12:30 p.m.**
☐ Date _____ Time _____
☐ Vacated by court order.
☒ Specified event: **Termination of current proceedings**

AURELIA PUCINSKI, CLERK OF THE CIRCUIT COURT

Modified Order of Protection: November 25, 1998, page 1

☒ 1   With respect to all Protected Persons, **Respondent** is prohibited from committing the following:
- ☒ Physical abuse.   ☒ Harassment.   ☒ Interference with personal liberty.   ☒ Intimidation of a dependent
- ☐ Willful deprivation.   ☐ Neglect.   ☐ Exploitation. ☐ Stalking

☒ 2   Petitioner is granted exclusive possession of the residence and Respondent shall not enter or remain in the household or premises located at

1221 Thornapple, Northbrook IL

(This remedy does not affect title to property.)

☒ 3   ☒ a Respondent is ordered to stay away from Petitioner ~~and other protected persons; and/or~~
- ☐ b Respondent is prohibited from entering or remaining at _____ while any Protected Person is present; and/or
- ☐ c Respondent is allowed access to the residence on (date) _____ at (time) _____ in the presence of (name) _____ to remove items of clothing, personal adornments, medications used exclusively by the Respondent and other items, as follows: _____

☐ 4   Respondent is ordered to undergo counseling : _____
for a duration of _____

☐ 5   ☐ a Petitioner is granted physical care and possession of the minor child/ren, and/or
- ☐ b Respondent is ordered to:
  - ☐ Return the minor child/ren _____ to the physical care of _____; and/or
  - ☐ Not remove the minor child/ren _____ from the physical care of Petitioner or _____

☒ 6   Petitioner is granted temporary legal custody of the minor child/ren _MARC & DAVID_
Lewis Blumenthal is granted temporary custody of Bradley

☒ 7   ☐ a Respondent is awarded visitation rights on the following dates and times or under the following conditions/or parameters:
(No order shall merely refer to the term "reasonable visitation.")
See Holiday Visitation Order dated 9-15-97 and weekly-
Tues & Thurs 4pm to 8pm; Alternate weekends, Fridays at 6pm thru Sundays at
- ☐ b Respondent's visitation is restricted as follows: _7pm; daily telephone contact with children_

☐ c Respondent's visitation is denied.
(Petitioner may deny Respondent access to the minor child/ren if, when Respondent arrives for visitation, Respondent is under the influence of drugs or alcohol and constitutes a threat to the safety and well-being of Petitioner or Petitioner's minor child/ren or is behaving in a violent or abusive manner.)

☐ 8.   Respondent is prohibited from removing the minor child/ren from Illinois or concealing them within Illinois

☐ 9.   Respondent is ordered to appear in Courtroom/Calendar _____ at _____ on _____ at _____ AM/PM, with/without the minor child/ren.

☐ 10.   Petitioner is granted exclusive possession of the following personal property and the Respondent is ordered to promptly make available to Petitioner said property that is in Respondent's possession or control, to wit: _____

(This remedy does not affect title to property.)

☐ 11.   Respondent is prohibited from taking, encumbering, concealing, damaging or otherwise disposing of the following personal property _____, except as explicitly authorized by the Court
☐ Further, Respondent is prohibited from improperly using the financial or other resources of an aged member of the family or household for the point or advantage of Respondent or any other person.

☐ 12.   Respondent is ordered to pay temporary support for ☐ Petitioner and/or ☐ the minor child/ren of the parties as follows:
$_____ per _____, starting _____, payable ☐ through the Clerk of the Circuit Court, or ☐ directly to Petitioner.

☐ 13   Respondent is ordered to pay $_____ as actual monetary compensation for loss(es) to _____ on or before _____
☐ Further, Respondent is ordered to pay court costs in the amount of $_____ and attorney fees in the amount of $_____ to _____ in connection with any action to obtain, modify, enforce, appeal or reopen any order of protection, on or before _____

AURELIA PUCINSKI, CLERK OF THE CIRCUIT COURT

CASE NO _95 D 6150_

Modified Order of Protection: November 25, 1998, page 2

☒ 14 Respondent is prohibited from entering or remaining at the household or residence located at **1221 Thornapple Northbrook, IL** _____ while under the influence of alcohol or drugs and so constituting a threat to the safety and well-being of any Protected Person.

☐ 14.5 Respondent is ordered to surrender all firearms to the local law enforcement agency, i.e. the police department. If the Respondent is a law enforcement officer, those firearms shall be surrendered to the Respondent's employer. All surrendered firearms shall remain confiscated for a period not to exceed two years to police agency_____

☐ 15. Respondent is denied access to school and/or any other records of the minor child/ren and is prohibited from inspecting, obtaining, or attempting to inspect or obtain such records.

☐ 16 Respondent is ordered to pay $ _____ to the following shelter _____ on or before _____

☐ 17 Respondent is further ordered and/or enjoined as follows: _____

☐ 18 The relief requested in paragraph(s) _____ of the petition is (DENIED) (RESERVED) because _____

PLENARY ORDERS ONLY

This order shall remain in effect until

☒ 1 Two years following the date of entry of such Order, such expiration date being **1-29-▓ O1** or such earlier date, as ordered by the Court, such expiration date being **termination pending dissolution proceeding**

☐ 2 Final judgment in conjoined proceeding is rendered.

☒ 3. This Order is modified or vacated (provided such Order is incorporated into the final judgment of another civil proceeding).

☐ 4 Termination of any voluntary or involuntary commitment, or until _____ *(may not exceed 1 year.)*

☐ 5 Final disposition when a Bond Forfeiture Warrant has issued, or until _____ *(may not exceed 2 years.)*

☐ 6 Expiration of any supervision, conditional discharge, probation, periodic imprisonment, parole, or supervised mandatory release, plus 2 years.

☐ 7 Expiration of a term of imprisonment set by this Court, plus 2 years.

NOTICE: Upon 2 days notice to Petitioner, or such shorter notice as the Court may prescribe, a Respondent subject to an Interim Order of Protection issued under the IDVA may appear and petition the Court to re-hear the original or amended Petition. Respondent's petition shall be verified and shall allege lack of notice and a meritorious defense.

ENTERED:

Date _____

Judge _____   Judge's No. **7L**

Attorney (or Pro Se Petitioner) Name **Feinberg & Barry**
Attorney for Lewis Blumenthal
Address **3 First National Suite 2715**
City/Zip **Chicago IL 60602**
Phone **312-444-1050**
Attorney # **138464**

CASE NO. **95 P 6150**

Modified Order of Protection: November 25, 1998, page 3

"Once an appeal has been duly filed in the appellate court by filing a notice of appeal, the **trial court is restrained** from entering ANY ORDER which would change or modify the judgment or its SCOPE, and from entering ANY ORDER which would have the effect of INTERFERING with the review of the judgment. Cite of: *Dunn v. Dunn, 71 Ill. App. 3rd 649, 28 Ill. Dec. 154, 390 N.E. 2d 136 (1st Dist. 1979).*"
(legal research assistant)

CHAPTER 25

Bench Blind To The Law

Kid's In-camera

Unlawful Ruling to Transfer Custody to Third Party

Judge's Conflict of Interest

Petition for Substitution of Judge Evans for Cause

The Transfer and Its Aftermath

Lew's "Legal" Effort to Push Mommy Further Away

The Court confirmed that neither my actions, nor those of my children or my Mom really mattered. I was in the same battering cycle with the Court that I had been in with Lew. The dynamic was not going to stop by my defending myself, holding the court agents accountable for their actions, nor by any attempt to fight back. The Court's intentions were already established and secured. My resisting their agenda only inflamed the process.

Shortly after the Winter Break, David, Marc and I were walking out of a movie together on Martin Luther King Day. Unfortunately, I had my cell phone and a call came through. It was around 8:00 PM and Mr. Stern's assistant insisted I bring the children to court the next day. Before Winter Break, I had been consoled by being told the Judge would not make a ruling to transfer the children without speaking to them in what is called an "in-camera" session. Since all parties knew the boys wanted to remain with me, it was suggested that their in-camera would take place in the distant future; if at all. But for some reason, Mr. Stern's assistant demanded that it take place tomorrow.

I explained that I would not be able to bring the boys tomorrow because my older son, Brad, had a legal matter that I wanted to attend. He informed me that Lew would be handling Brad's legal matter. As it turns out, Lew handled Brad's legal problem very much like he handled his own, through some manipulation of the system. Lew was successful in thwarting off Brad's responsibility and personal accountability around the matter. On the exterior it gave the appearance of "working" to make the problem go away. However authentic ownership did not occur and the problem persisted.

In retrospect, the timing of the "in camera," when Brad could not be there served on many levels. It insured no interruption of Lew's handling of Brad's court matter by my being present, thereby removing it as an issue impacting Lew's custody campaign. Secondly, it prevented Brad from exercising his right to speak to the Judge and have his voice heard. Brad wanted this all along because he wanted to inform Judge Evans of his desire to have contact with me. However, Lew and his attorney had much invested in a false story that I did *not* want to have contact with my son, to whom I was denied access for almost a half of a year. Brad's presence would have compromised Lew's story. Also, Brad's participation in an in-camera would have brought to light the obvious battering dynamic between Brad and his brothers. This, too, needed to be shielded from the Court by Lew and the lawyers.

Instead of seeing the full picture or recognizing that the anger I felt over being given such short notice was reasonable, I allowed myself to get swept up in the court "fear-provoking" strategy. I was told that if I didn't show up with David and Marc, the Judge would believe that I did not want to cooperate with the children's in-camera session.

Knowing that I wanted my children to have this opportunity to speak their truth and that I had nothing to hide by not allowing this, I fell right into the apparent legal "lip-service in-camera." In my effort to jump through this hoop, I put David and Marc to bed and in the morning I brought them downtown to court for their opportunity to speak with the Judge and the attorneys. I was not allowed access to this, nor was I allowed to have my court reporter in chambers to secure a record. The Judge sealed the transcript of my children's testimony and claimed this was customary. I have since been told it is not. Further, I have been informed that being denied access to a record of the in-camera was another violation of my due process rights.

David and Marc presented like two clean cut, well-behaved, bright and sweet young boys. The Judge escorted the children out from their session and said, "Mrs. Blumenthal, you have two fine young boys." He added they are "bright and well-mannered." My counsel on the side confirmed the Judge's observations. He said, "Don't tell anyone I'm telling you this, but they were great. They were well-behaved, expressive and nothing was said that could hurt you." He acknowledged it was obvious that "the children are thriving in your custody."

David and Marc informed the Judge that they wanted to continue living with me in our home and maintain the same visitation schedule with their father. They said that they felt safer with me and did not want to live with their father and Bradley. When asked what would you want changed to make your life better, they said, "All I want is for the divorce to be over."

We all came to realize that it didn't matter how great my kids were, what they wanted or how well they were doing in my home. The proceeding was not about the best interest of the children, it had become more about each party covering for himself and protecting one another. The Court had no intention to factor in anything my children said, because everything they said was ignored or dismissed as being "coached." The in-camera appeared to satisfy the Court's requirement to have one.

In open court Mr. Wessel admitted to knowing that the children preferred to remain with me and that they expressed feeling safer with me. However, he informed the Judge that the children's desires and comments to the Court were "coached." The amazing part of his allegation was that I was given no time to have coached my children. I put them to bed, and the next morning we were off to court.

My boys knew what they wanted, and had been informing Mr. Wessel of their desire to live with me for over a year. Yet, each time they expressed their wishes, either on the phone or in a meeting, Mr. Wessel ignored and dismissed them, and failed to report their requests to the Court. Then in response to the children's candor with the Judge, Mr. Wessel asserted that the children's wishes were their Mom's desires, not their own.

To support this position, Lew's attorney alleged that David and Marc's expressed concern about being battered in Lew's home was *"Jeanne projecting her internal experience onto the children."* However, Lisa, my baby-sitter, and Dennis, Lew's baby-sitter, had witnessed both David and Marc being tormented, harassed, bullied, manipulated and intimidated almost daily by Bradley and/or Lew.

I wondered how this "projection" could occur in my absence, given that the battering and its initial impact often happened when I was away from our home involved in court matters; or it happened at Lew's home where I was not present to observe them. I knew that striking a child with a stick; throwing a child against the wall; pulling them by the ear; repeatedly kicking, shoving and punching a vulnerable distressed child; threatening to "beat the shit out of them" and saying "I'm going to fucking kill you" evoked fear in and of itself.

The abuse and battering, which David and Marc experienced, was real and everyone who was a party to the litigation was aware of it. Lew and his counsel would not have pursued an Order of Protection protecting David and Marc from Bradley's aggression if the children's fear and perceived risk was planted in their head by me. It appeared that the threat to the younger children was only real so long as it furthered Lew's campaign to "get rid of Mommy."

*   *   *

On January 20, 1999, all parties appeared in court and each attorney provided their statements summarizing the evidence supporting their position on the immediate change of "temporary custody" of David and Marc. Mr. Wessel and Lew's attorney, Ms. Feinberg, reiterated all their unfounded allegations set forth in the last two month "pre-trial" Hearing, Dr. Chapman's non-factual and unsubstantiated assertions and distortions, as well as the "projection" misrepresentation concerning the children's fear. My counsel, Mr. Stern, showed how the proposed transfer of custody was a litigation ploy to jockey for custody in the final trial. He provided an abundance of evidence against Dr. Chapman and details illustrating Lew's continued denial of his abuse of the children. Media was present in the courtroom, and Judge Evans did not make a ruling.

On January 21, 1999, all parties were called to court again. The media representative did not appear to witness the proceedings. The Judge made the first ruling of substance in the case since his ruling of May 21, 1995. First, he granted our motion for continuance, ostensibly to give us time to prepare for trial. Secondly, he denied our motion to disqualify Dr. Chapman. Thirdly, he granted Lew's motion for the "modification of temporary custody" of David and Marc, based on Dr. Chapman's recommendations.

Hence, Judge Evans ruled to remove David and Marc from my custody because:

"Dr. King appears to be under stress, perhaps regarding this litigation, and appears to be unable to keep herself from communicating that stress and anxiety to her children. Dr. King appears to have engaged the children as allies and in some instances, it appears that Dr. King has coached the children." (Report of Proceedings January 21, 1999, p. 8)

Temporary custody was not awarded to Lew. The reason for not granting temporary custody of David and Marc to Lew was because of his failure to overcome the rebuttable presumption set forth in the Domestic Violence Act concerning someone who has been found to have abused children. Citing the Law, 750 ILCS 60-214, Judge Evans stated:

"If a court finds after a hearing that a Respondent has committed abuse of a minor child, there shall be a rebuttable presumption that awarding temporary legal custody to the Respondent would not be in the child's best interest."

Accordingly, the Judge said, "I don't believe at this time it would be appropriate for Dr. Lewis Blumenthal to be the temporary custodian of the children either." Judge Evans asserted, "While Lew is attempting to deal with his problem of being unable to discipline the children without abuse..," he did not believe that Lew had evidenced the rehabilitation required to warrant his being eligible to be the custodial parent. (Report of Proceedings, January 21, 1999, p. 9)

Temporary legal custody of David and Marc was awarded to Marlene Mann, Lew's sister, and the children were to be transferred on February 1, 1999 to her River Forest home, nearly 40 minutes by car from the children's current home and school. An objective independent supervisor was to be present when David and Marc were with Lew and Bradley, and also when the boys were visiting me. Lew was to pay 80 percent of the costs and I was to be responsible for the remaining 20 percent.

Mr. Stern and I were shocked by this ruling and went back to his office to regroup. We were both aware that third party custody to a non-parent was an unlawful ruling. Custody cannot be given to a non-parent who is not a party to the case; and, further, the legal criteria for transferring custody was not met. Additionally, the ruling to restrict my visitation with supervision prejudiced my parental rights without there being lawful cause for doing so. I was given restricted visitation, a remedy for endangerment, in the absence of there being an abuse finding toward myself.

*   *   *

As Steve and I were discussing the ruling, he called Ms. Feinberg to inform her of his knowledge that the ruling was not in compliance with the law. He told me that Ms. Feinberg claimed Lew was unhappy with the ruling because he did not want to pay for the supervisors. Steve and I discussed some options, but he was most discouraging. He suggested to me that the Judge took the boys away because he was *angry* at me for attracting media attention.

Apparently, the Judge was bitter over a New York investigative reporter calling the court and media coming to the courthouse with cameras. My counsel suggested that the outreach was backfiring by inflaming the Judge. While it was true that reporters had been snooping in on the case since the first of November, I was surprised that Mr. Stern no longer supported the outreach. I realized that the exposure posed further conflict for him. It appeared that the threat of public scrutiny led to the Court's desire for immediate closure.

In the meantime, Mr. Wessel and Lew had been in communication with David and Marc concerning the transfer of their residence to Marlene Mann. Upon my return home, Marc asked if they were going to have to live with Marlene. We were sitting on the landing of the second floor in our home. David and Lisa joined us upstairs and we talked about the possibility of this upcoming change. When David realized that it was in fact real, he flipped out. He was standing, and his legs buckled and his body crashed to the floor.

I rushed over to make sure that David was not hurt by his fall to the ground. He was crying and crying, and then yelling of how he told the Judge he wanted to stay with me at our home. Marc broke into tears, and I held him as he sobbed. Marc cried from his core. He was pathetically distraught. We held each other and then he went to get his kitty. We all curled up in tears. I knew this ruling supported Lew's litigation campaign and was not in the interest of my children.

*   *   *

While it was true that I had been inundated with litigation and the pleadings were piling up in my room beyond control, my boys were happy under my care at our home. In my effort to reconcile our being torn apart, I started telling myself that my children shouldn't have to witness their mother being brutalized and taunted by the proceedings. I likened it to the impact on them of seeing Lew beat me up. I knew that was not good, and this couldn't be healthy either. Lew's attorneys and Mr. Wessel had flooded me with more pleadings than were humanly possible to manage. The legal paper work had been coming so fast that I didn't have time to put away one pile before another would arrive. From October 1998 on, it grew to where there were no empty surfaces in my room. My bedroom looked like a legal nightmare that wouldn't go away.

After I put the children to bed that evening, I opened my mail and received the Judge's Statement of Economic Interest, obtained by my state representative. It showed that Judge Timothy Evans' wife, Dr. Selma Evans', was currently affiliated with Humana Health Care HMO, in either of the following: an officer, director or salaried employee. My body quivered as I read this document. It was apparent that presiding over the Blumenthal divorce posed a conflict of interest for Judge Evans, because of Lewis Blumenthal's relationship with a source of the Judge's family income. Lew also served as a physician at Humana Health Care HMO.

Humana Health Care HMO is a doctor owned facility, which at the time was called Advocate Health Center. This business establishment had a financial affiliation and professional connection with Michael Reese Hospital, a doctor owned corporation, where Lew Blumenthal served as an attending physician for over 15 years. I recognized that Judge Evans could not be objective in our case, and I believed I understood why.

I presented this document to numerous individuals, including attorneys, legislators and city officials. My suspicions were supported; a financial conflict of interest was clear to each person reviewing the matter. In consulting with specialists on judge disqualification, it was recommended that I submit this information to the Court and request a Substitution of Judges for Cause.

I wanted to believe that the Judge erred in his ruling, and by presenting the obvious we may have a chance at getting the ruling corrected. However, as I evaluated many other judicial irregularities and the inordinate examples of Judge Evans' failure to enforce the law, I realized our problems were far more serious than an innocent improper ruling. I was informed that the ruling of January 21, 1999 was actually invalid and void, having the appearance of more than a judicial error.

Ever since the filing of my Appeal on December 3, 1998 of the Modification of the Order of Protection incorporating custody, Judge Evans, the trial judge, did not have jurisdiction over custody. All subsequent custody determinations were under the jurisdiction of the Appellate Court. Yet, Judge Evans and the attorneys were proceeding as though the issue of custody remained under the jurisdiction of the Trial Court.

I was also puzzled that Judge Evans based his determination to transfer David and Marc away from me on the information obtained from Dr. Chapman's testimony of November 2nd and November 9th. Yet, on November 25th, Judge Evans granted me temporary custody of David and Marc in the Modified Order of Protection. I asked my counsel how is it that Judge Evans could rule on January

21, 1999 to remove David and Marc from my custody, based on information that he obtained prior to his recent reassignment of their temporary custody to me?

Additionally, the ruling of January 21, 1999 established that Lew was not an eligible candidate for legal custody of our children because of his abuse to our children, as per the Domestic Violence Act. The ruling also disclosed that the children needed closure because the litigation compromised them. So, I wondered how and why the Court was willing to allow Lew to proceed with a custody trial over the following months, given that the Court acknowledged it was unable to award custody to Lew today.

Even more distressing to me was how the Court could subject my compromised children to further litigation, when it was recognized that the litigation was the source of their distress. No matter where they lived, their lives remained in turmoil and they would be subjected to further polarization and the inherent damages of a custody dispute. Why would the Court *enable* further emotional destruction to abused children? My counsel did not like my questions, and I did not like that there were no answers.

*   *   *

On February 1st, the day the transfer was scheduled, I approached the Court with a Petition for Substitution of Judge Evans for Cause in which I set forth all of the judicial irregularities to date and disclosed the financial conflict of interest. Lew's counsel approached the Court with a Pleading which John Lietzau called "the race card." Their Pleading requested that I have my phone conversations with the boys tape recorded, because Marc had called Judge Evans a "nigger" at Lew's home, in his fury over the plan to be removed from me.

Neither Pleading could be heard in front of Judge Evans, so we were referred out to another court. My Petition to Substitute Judge Evans for Cause was transferred to three different courtrooms. John said, "The Courts are passing the case around like a hot potato." Unfortunately, Judge Evans was the Presiding Judge in the district and the judges under him, hearing my request for substitution, refused to recognize the merits of my Pleading.

Our Petition was ultimately heard by Judge Jacobius, an outwardly sensitive man to our cause though also under Judge Evans. Lew's counsel argued to dismiss my Petition on the basis of form and proper court protocol. After I jumped through the hoops of proper form, Lew's counsel declared that I had prior knowledge of Judge Evans' conflict of interest. Their argument confirmed my assertion of there being a conflict of interest.

To support their position, Ms. Feinberg secured an Affidavit from my prior counsel David Hopkins, in which it stated, "Judge Evans called attention to a theoretical conflict of interest related to his wife's employment as a physician and Mrs. Blumenthal's husband's employment." However, I was never informed of Dr. Evans' employment until I read about it in the Judge's Statement of Economic Interest.

I was only informed of the fact that she was a physician and may have "crossed paths" with Lew in their training over a decade ago. Even this was objectionable to me at the time, but my counsel insisted that we have Judge Evans preside over the case. He claimed that the Judge's knowledge of Lew's abuse to me and the children would benefit us in the long run. No one disclosed the Judge's real conflict of interest; to the contrary, I was led to believe it did not exist.

In our legal back and forth, Judge Jacobius held up a book entitled *Judicial Disqualification*, and pointed out that this book contained the proper procedure for disqualifying a judge. At the time, John said, "Look, he is trying to help you." John noted, "The Judge is showing you where to go to do this properly." I recognized that Judge Jacobius was telling me the legal cause and correct course for my action. Judge Jacobius even made a comment that I could obtain this book, and believed that I would be able to understand how judge disqualification is done properly. I wasn't sure what to make of it at the time, because I felt overwhelmed with a sense of futility in the face of the contradiction I had observed. I felt Judge Jacobius' empathy toward my predicament, yet I observed his unwillingness to rule against Judge Evans, his superior.

The Hearing closed with Lew's attorney saying, "Now we've got the kids." Hours later, David and Marc were intercepted on the way home from school by Marlene's husband, Joe Mann. Joe approached Marc in his car and Marc ran down the street. Marc was picked up and forced into Joe Mann's car with David and they were not allowed to come home. Initially, we were denied phone access to one another.

My heart ached, as I knew my children were unlawfully kidnapped under the guise of legitimate judicial authority, compounded by Judge Evans' failure to follow the law. I knew how disruptive this was going to be to their already tenuous lives. They longed for closure for the purpose of stability. Now they had lost it all; their home, their neighborhood, their easy access to their friends, their close proximity to their school, their animals, their daily contact with me and the comfort and security that they came to rely on and treasure under my care.

*   *   *

I was determined to bring my boys back home. My counsel filed Pleadings with the Appellate Court, concerning the unlawful ruling involving the transfer of custody to a non-parent third party. The Appellate Court responded favorably and wanted to review the case. All parties were given through February 17, 1999 to respond with the Appellate Court.

In the interim, Lew's counsel petitioned the Court for an Emergency Ex-Parte Order of Protection against me. Petitions for Orders of Protection require hearings to be obtained; but when they are petitioned "ex-parte," they are requests of the Court reflecting the interest of one side only. The basis for the Order of Protection against me alleged that the children's unfulfilled desire to contact me, live with me and have me in their lives, described as my wishes, was "to the detriment and emotional destruction of our children."

The boys were terribly unhappy at Marlene's house, and they longed to be with me. Lew's Affidavit, drafted to provide justification for his Petition for an Order of Protection against me stated:

On February 7, 1999 "Marlene advised me that Marc screamed to his mother, 'I'll kill myself. I will take a knife and stab myself in the heart if I have to live with Aunt Mar." It pointed out that my child was pleading with me on the phone to come home to me. Subsequently, "Marc ran away." After being dropped off for Hebrew School, "Marc ran 2 1/2 miles to the marital residence and broke in." (February 10, 1999)

Lew's Affidavit also referenced Brad's reaching out to be with me as cause for the protective order. Specifically, it noted that on February 8, 1999 Brad became desperate to see his mother on her birthday and said to his Dad:

"I've got to see her on her birthday! I've bought flowers for her. She needs me. She hasn't seen me in seven weeks because you prevented her from seeing me. You always prevent her from seeing me!" In Brad's determination, as Lew's Affidavit stated, "Brad left in a cab."

It was clear that Lew and Marlene were faced with the children's conflict around this transfer and their being denied contact with me. The children appeared to fight back, by rejecting Lew's authority and Marlene's direction. Lew's Affidavit further alleged that the "children had been programmed to act out in order to be capable of charging Lew with abuse, so that I am now placed into a position of having little ability to control them." Lew could not manage the boys and needed to blame me for his ineffectiveness.

Lew's inability to control the children and the boys reaching out to me became Lew's cause to restrict their access to me. His Petition for an Order of Protection against me requested that I be prohibited from "harassment" and directed to stay away from my children. It proposed to award me two hours per week of supervised visitation and 10 minutes, two times per week of supervised telephone contact.

I knew my boys were deteriorating, and it wasn't going to get better. I could see that their reaching out to me and their distress around being denied access to me became Lew's cause to further sever their contact with me. To maximize Lew's control over the children, it appeared he had to isolate them from me even more. It seemed much like the isolation he had fostered around me in the years that he actively and passionately controlled my daily life.

I was informed that the Illinois Domestic Violence Act prohibits mutual Orders of Protection pursuant to 750 ILCS 60/215 of the Illinois Domestic Violence Act as it "undermines the purposes of the act." I told my counsel I knew the law did not provide for multiple orders of protection and asked that he respond to Lew's Petition by bringing this information before the Court.

My counsel was unwilling to submit a Response to Lew's request for the Order of Protection against me. I realized that Lew was trying to turn me into being the "abuser," but I didn't know why he was taking this position and why my attorney refused to assist in my defense. I suspected that Lew's posturing and my counsel's willingness to enable this had something to do with the Judge's previous failure to follow the law. It took months for me to grasp how the Court needed to protect itself. I was drowning in the same cycle of battering, only with different players – and now the stakes were higher.

Themes Common to Family and Judicial Abuse

- Perpetrator projects Dr. Jekyll/Mr. Hyde Personality.

- Perpetrator isolates victim from all sources of support.

- Violations and altercations evolve out of abuser's vulnerability.

- Abuser exudes self-righteousness and conveys this to the victim and to spectators, though he/she may privately know otherwise.

- Abuser claims being victimized to evidence excuse for battering and camouflage cause for maintaining the abuse dynamic.

- Victim has unrealistic, wishful thinking about abuser changing.

- Victim assumes responsibility for changing or fixing the perpetrator's unpredictable, abusive behavior.

- Perpetrator is perceived by victim as "omnipotent."

- Victim demonstrates "learned helplessness," "traumatic bonding" and entrapment.

- Victim vacillates between acts of self-preservation and gestures of frustration, hopelessness and defeat.

- The abuse dynamic is cyclic and self-sustaining. It is maintained through the 3 phases of the Cycle of Violence:Tension-Building; Acute Episode; and the Calm with Kind and Contrite Overtures.

- "Denial" is the mechanism of defense employed by both abuser and victim, enabling the continuation of the cycle of violence.

- "Victim Blaming" is the social mechanism for maintaining the abuse dynamic. Outsiders assume victim should be able to change the behavior of the perpetrator. When victim does not do so, outsiders condone perpetrator's abusive actions as being appropriate or deserved.

CHAPTER 26

Cover the Error; Protect the Court

Making Movies: The Media and Community Interest

The Cobra Perpetrator

Witnesses See Judge's Bias, Prejudice and Partiality

Record Clarification and Request for Ruling Correction

Judge's Disqualification Notice

Reversal of Ruling and of Roles in Abuse Dynamic

Marc's Runaways and Self-Mutilation

I knew my Counsel heard me but could not acknowledge my wishes, just as the Court refused to listen to him when he spoke on behalf of my interests. It all felt so hopeless. I knew my court representative was folding. Recalling my initial expectation of Steve when I re-engaged him helped me put things into perspective. This led to my opening myself up for other sources of support, and much came to me.

There were court watchers, community legal support, television talk show hosts, a producer of a local TV show, an author on judicial injustice in divorce court, our New York investigative reporter, inquiries from 60 Minutes, an FBI consultant, head staff from domestic violence agencies, students who had seen my first video in their graduate academic study, and specialists in domestic violence, pointing out what I could not see. These people helped me gain perspective from which I drew strength to carry me for the next four months.

Chana Bernstein, producer of Community Focus TV Show, invited Evelyn, John and I to tell my story on a live talk show. Participating in the show had a healing effect for me. I gained significant perspective in response to the questions and insights shared in the group discussion. The information was initially numbing. Ultimately, my understanding ignited my desire to make a difference for others by sharing what I had learned.

John's expertise in domestic violence became apparent to me on a different level. Instead of primarily being a supporter and ally, he also was an excellent educator on domestic violence and its implications for our community. He brought forth a wealth of information on the abuse dynamic which I had not recognized earlier. John illustrated the parallel of a battering cycle within my litigation in relation to the withholding of funds for child support and legal resources. He showed how, month-to-month, I rode the roller coaster of the cyclic phases of battering from the tension-building phase to the acute battering incident to the kindness and contrite, loving behavior. It was very clear how the cycle had reinforced my hanging on and had also wore me down.

The tension-building phase encompassed the build up of walking on eggshells, with fear-provoking manipulations around my securing funds. The acute battering phase was the final failure to follow through and the litigation consequences created by the withholding of funds. The kindness and contrite, loving behavior was the many promises to access the marital estate, as the law provides, and the hope for justice on the horizon.

Both Evelyn and John pointed out numerous nuances of the domestic violence syndrome and the social factors contributing to its maintenance. They brought to the viewer's attention the laws regulating the reporting of child abuse. Each professional that witnessed evidence of child abuse over the years had a professional responsibility to report the abuse to the appropriate protective agencies. This had not been done before the 1994 police report in conjunction with Lew's arrest for domestic battery of Bradley.

John and Evelyn found it most disturbing that the doctors with this knowledge had a professional relationship with Lew, Michael Reese Hospital and the Judge's wife's employment. They shed significant light on how society aids in the social problem of domestic violence by maintaining the silent shield around abusive behavior. They recognized the political and judicial influence now contributing to this shied, and saw how my litigation nightmare was protecting many people from public disclosure and scrutiny.

The producer entitled our show *Court-Sanctioned Domestic Violence* and aired it on local cable TV for several months. A sequel to the show featured numerous experts in the domestic violence field, including: Dr. James Dugo, a psychologist specializing in the treatment of perpetrators; Dr. Susan London, a psychologist specializing in the treatment of victims; Evelyn Delmar, representing the position of a children's rights advocate, and Greg Adamski and his partner, two attorneys familiar with the judicial process in divorce court.

Dr. James Dugo described the profiles of the two different types of perpetrators. His descriptions appeared to be based on the conceptualization provided by Drs. Neil Jacobson and John Gottman in their book, *When Men Batter Women.* When Dr. Dugo described the perpetrator characterized as the "cobra type," chills went down my spine. The description fit Lew.

A cobra is impulsive, pleasure seeking and self-centered. He wants what he wants when he wants it, and he controls his victim in his effort to insure the fulfillment of his selfish narcissistic interests. Cobras typically come from a violent home in which there was trauma during their childhood.

Their violence toward their spouses is extraordinarily severe and encompasses significant emotional abuse. They convince their victims that they are worthless without them, and use control and intimidation to terrify their wives into submission.

Drs. Jacobson and Gottman use the term "cobra" to describe this type of batterer because these batterers showed "lowered heart rates during aggressive arguments, though looked, sounded and acted aggressive, internally they were calming down." The name "cobra" was selected because, "like the cobra who becomes quite still and focused just before striking its victim at more than 100 miles an hour, these men were calming themselves internally and focusing their attention, while striking swiftly at their wives with vicious aggression." (1998, p. 29)

Their means for maintaining control can be extremely cruel, vicious and lethal. They are unpredictable, dangerous and volatile. Yet, on the exterior they project charisma, charm and sensitivity. They learn their victim's weak spots and prey on those particular vulnerabilities. They are extremely effective at manipulating their spouses, at persuading authority and in exploiting the system. They can easily fool therapists, doctors, judges, prosecutors and police officers.

I recalled a conversation Dr. Dugo and I had in which he said, "Your husband sounds like the 'cobra,' which is the most dangerous type." Knowing his opinion of my husband's profile and watching his obvious expertise on the subject during the filming of this show, left me with feelings of internal terror along with remnants of my learned helplessness. I was in the audience with numerous other victims of domestic violence and/or litigation abuse. My whole demeanor was one of shyness, impotence and fear. In the months following the show, I sought counsel with Dr. London and began to recognize my options as a victim of abuse.

*   *   *

The making of the *Court-Sanctioned Domestic Violence* videos also impacted the other participants, on the panel and in the audience, as well as numerous viewers of the TV show. Chana, John and Evelyn all recognized the evidence of collusion among my counsel, Lew's counsel, the children's counsel, the court-appointed custody evaluator and the Judge.

Chana directed me to the attorney who appeared on the second show. In my initial meeting with him, he proposed to assist in taking the proper legal measures toward disqualifying Judge Evans. However, his communications with Lew's attorney were followed by a change in his thinking. We all realized that challenging the Court posed a conflict of interest for any counsel whose bread and butter depended on his or her operation within that particular court structure.

The book, *Judicial Disqualification,* brought to our attention by Judge Jacobius, was given to me by another interested and concerned party. It was suggested that I proceed on the matter on my own. In reviewing this book I learned the standards set forth, according to Supreme Court Rules and Illinois Law, for judicial conduct. According to the Supreme Court Rules, Judge Evans was in violation of:

Rule 63, Canon 3: "A Judge Should Perform the Duties of Judicial Office Impartially and Diligently"

The "appearance of bias, prejudice and partiality" was the legal basis for the disqualification of Judge Evans. The legal procedure required a Notice of Disqualification with attached Affidavits in support of the Judge's appearance of bias, prejudice and partiality.

At this point we had many witnesses of Judge Evans' conduct, because as the public learned of our predicament, several people came forward to be court watchers.

We had noticed that when witnesses were in Judge Evans' Courtroom, the Judge was far more cautious in making any rulings. This appeared to slow down the train. However, the public's confrontation of the judicial irregularities and the misconduct of the court agents appeared to speed up the crash in which the Judge's bias became even more self-evident.

The court watchers and community legal support provided me with Affidavits, documenting their observations of numerous judicial irregularities and the appearance of Judge Evans' bias and partiality toward Lew and his counsel. Five Affidavits were presented to me. One Affidavit was provided by Bob Johnson, an individual who reviewed the Court Record. Mr. Johnson challenged Judge Evans' "subject-matter jurisdiction," which is the authority of the court to hear and make a determination in a court action. His Affidavit included case law showing that the Judge's failure to follow the law deprives him of subject-matter jurisdiction, and thereby legal authority in our case. Additionally, Mr. Johnson questioned Judge Evans' having jurisdiction from the beginning, based on the subtleties of the law and the Judge's financial conflict of interest.

Mr. Johnson's Affidavit expanded at length on numerous examples illustrating Judge Evans' bias, prejudice and partiality. He cited the violation of my rights to due process and equal protection of the law under the Illinois Constitution and under the U.S. Constitution. He referenced the Judge allowing only one party access to income from the marital estate, while restricting the other, contrary to the "leveling of the playing field" law. He noted the bias exemplified in the Judge's failing to promptly hear one party's motions, while promptly hearing the other party's motions. He cited that Judge Evans' restricting me from presenting evidence to the Court, while not restricting Lew, further evidenced his prejudice and partiality. Reference was made to the Judge's failure to fulfill his legal duty to report the misconduct of attorneys of which numerous incidents were presented to him throughout the proceedings.

Mr. Johnson showed how the Judge's wife, Dr. Selma Evans, posed a pecuniary interest (that is a financial interest) in "covering up the abusal nature of Dr. Lewis Blumenthal." He states:

> "I believe that Dr. Evans has an interest in the fact that Dr. Lewis Blumenthal is a child abuser and a wife abuser, and that the disclosure of such information to the public would be detrimental to her and to Michael Reese Hospital."

> Mr. Johnson further points out that "an inspection of the record of this case presents uncontrovertible evidence that Judge Evans has known of the child abuse and the wife abuse by Dr. Lewis Blumenthal, and has been, and is therefore, personally an 'enabler' in such abuse." (February 16, 1999, p. 5)

Witnesses sitting in the courtroom during the proceedings came to the same conclusions as Mr. Johnson. Three individuals who sat through numerous court hearings during our proceedings provided Affidavits detailing their observations evidencing Judge Evans' bias, prejudice and his appearance of partiality. These people included: John Lietzau, Marci Weber and Tyrone Cefalu. John enumerated in his Affidavit a multitude of examples of how "the dynamics of the domestic violence syndrome have continued and manifested them-selves in the form of litigation abuse." He pointed out: "The only difference is that the brutality has shifted from the home to the courtroom and is still going on."

The Affidavits of Mr. Tyrone Cefalu and Ms. Marci Weber addressed the negligence of Mr. David Wessel to represent the interests of the minor children to the Court and his failure to protect the children from further endangerment, trauma and abuse. These witnesses also pointed out numerous examples of the Court's failure to follow the law and perform in a manner consistent with civil procedures and codes of ethics. Additional Affidavits were obtained, substantiating the same observations as those contained in the above written testimonials. The Affidavits were complied and attached to an Emergency Notice of the Disqualification of Judge Timothy Evans, presented to the Court on February 17, 1999.

*   *   *

Before this effort to disqualify Judge Evans was brought to the Court's attention, numerous other events took place. In retrospect, it appears that the accumulated efforts by my supporters and myself to interrupt the cycle of battering served instead, to enable it further and with greater fury.

On February 16, 1999, the day before our court effort to disqualify the Judge, Chana Bernstein sent a letter to Judge Evans' superior, Judge Donald O'Connell. She wrote this letter as president of FAIR, Family Advocacy, Information & Resources. Chana, acting as a concerned advocate, brought to his attention the "vicious physical and emotional abuse" of Lew, whom she identified as a "documented abuser," and Lew's denial of guilt and failure to reform. Then she pointed out how the case had been mismanaged, with rulings made that were in violation of case law. Ms. Bernstein referenced the failure of the court agents to protect the children and identified the Court's "horrific violations of the children's human rights." Her lettered closed with a threat to "turn this case and the vast documentation that comes with it to CBS to be examined by both 60 Minutes and 48 Hours."

Chana alluded to some ongoing "negotiations with CBS" regarding our case. I was unaware of Chana's letter when it was submitted. I saw the closing threat in her letter as similar to Mr. Johnson's assertion in his Affidavit that the information contained in his Affidavit "is now being prepared for publishing on the Internet for the public to see." Intuitively, I knew that this attack toward the current source of abuse to us could backfire, as had been the course of the cyclic litigation battering over the last four years.

*   *   *

While the help that came to me had elements of an offensive strategy, I continued my own strategy of defense. My efforts primarily consisted of seeking remedy for the ongoing family and litigation violations by keeping the Court Record straight. It was a consuming and, at times, overwhelming task in and of itself. On February 16, 1999, I filed my Response to Lew's Petition for Order of Protection, clarifying for the record that I was the victim of abuse, not the abuser. By filing this Pleading, much of the testimonial evidence of Lew's history of abuse to me and the children along with key points in our psychological evaluations became official court record. This included:

- the explicit information provided in our Evidentiary Hearing; Lew's domestic battery arrest, police records, the history of violence to the children with photographs and references to injuries shown to third parties

- Lew's twenty-year use of illegal substances

- Lew's ongoing physical abuse to me throughout the marriage

- Lew's admission of his abuse to us by virtue of his expressed agreement to enter into psychiatric treatment for his problem with abuse and subsequent failure to follow through

- the court sequence of events in obtaining our Orders of Protection and extending them, to date

- the Illinois Law prohibiting mutual Orders of Protection

- the numerous court references citing that there had been no evidence of endangerment by me to my children entered into the record, nor demonstrated in any way

I learned that neither defense, confrontation, nor attack served to interrupt the litigation abuse to me and my children. To the contrary, these efforts inflamed it. For example, in response to my Pleading and effort to keep the record straight, my attorney said, "You're messing up the record." These strategies were followed by an exponential growth in the legal domestic assaults. Hours after I submitted my Response to Lew's request for an Order of Protection against me, I received a Pleading from Ms. Feinberg, entitled Emergency Motion to Reconsider.

This Pleading was a request of the Court to re-evaluate the Ruling of January 21, 1999. It acknowledged opposing counsel's knowledge of the ruling not following the law, and proposed a possible "oversight" of the Court to have given me supervised visitation without there being an abuse finding. Ms. Feinberg's suggestion to remedy these judicial errors was first to take the children back from Marlene Mann, as non-parent custody was "not in comport with the law," and to give me an abuse finding *so* my boys would not be sent back to me.

Instead of simply reversing the ruling and returning David and Marc to me, Ms. Feinberg was posturing the Court to merely hand David and Marc over to Lew. The strategy for doing this was first, to allege that Judge Evans had "unlimited jurisdiction" encompassing Juvenile Court matters and, then, to give me an abuse finding. However, the law states that the Trial Court has "limited jurisdiction"; and there was no factual evidence of abuse or endangerment by me to my children.

Since there was no evidence of abuse by me in the Court Record, and I had never endangered my children, Ms. Feinberg stated in her Pleading, "Lew believes that the missing FINDING was merely an oversight and not the true intention of the Court." It was outrageous that counsel would attempt to back me into an "abuse finding" in order justify a judicial remedy restricting my visitation. It was obvious that giving this finding improperly served to protect the Court. It was like putting someone in jail and then proceeding to establish that they committed a crime. The abuse of process was so flagrant and offensive that I could not witness anymore of it. This was the last Pleading of Joy Feinberg's that I could read. All further pleadings had to be read to me by others.

*   *   *

On February 17, 1999 I presented my Notice of Disqualification of Judge Evans with five Affidavits attached testifying to Judge Evans' bias, prejudice and the appearance of partiality. This effort to disqualify Judge Evans was no more successful than the first attempt. The only positive that came out of it was that it allowed me full expression of the sequence of litigation abuses to me and my children over the full course of the proceedings. While I was keenly aware of my composure and respectful demeanor during my presentation, my disclosures did not bring us remedy.

Instead, my court watchers and I were escorted by all counsel directly into Judge Evans' Courtroom, which I had come to know as the "lion's den." It was after 5:00 PM, and I wondered what was the hurry for ushering us in for the deliverance of the next court blow, after hours. At the time, I didn't realize that any further action by Judge Evans had to occur before the end of the day on February 17, 1999. This was the last day for Lew to respond to the Appellate Court's request, stemming from our appealing Judge Evans' Ruling of January 21, 1999. Consequently, this after hour court session blocked the last window of opportunity for the potential of Appellate Court remedy for the Judge's action and intervention to assist in our plight. Why, because the Judge used this time to ostensibly correct his unlawful ruling.

What amazed me was how the Court was willing to fulfill Ms. Feinberg's wishes, irrespective of the law. On January 21, 1999 the Judge said he could not give temporary custody of David and Marc to Lew. This decision was based on the law and Lew's failure to overcome the rebuttable presumption that it is not in the best interest of the children to be placed in the custody of someone who has been found to abuse them. Yet on February 17, 1999, the Court gave temporary custody of David and Marc to Lew, **without any** further evidence presented to the Court showing rehabilitation by Lew to warrant his newly established eligibility for being the temporary custodial parent.

The abuse finding given to me was based on the allegation of the "stress of the litigation" being communicated to the children. Though there was no factual evidence concerning any communications with the children, it was assumed that the stress to me endangered the children. The most absurd part of the abuse finding was that the source of the stress originated from the people, that is Lew and his legal team, who were backing me into its ramifications. Dr. Susan London described it well, when she said that "**Your children have been kidnaaaaaaaaaaaaped over four years**, not in a brief few hours." We recognized that Lew and his use of the judicial system created the stress, and then they set out to punish me for it.

The finding of abuse by me and transfer of the boys to Lew was outrageous from a practical as well as a legal perspective. The Court's admission that it failed to follow the law established its status of lost jurisdiction. Illinois law states:

"Whenever any judge fails to follow the procedure established by law, the judge automatically loses jurisdiction

(Flake v. Pretzel, 381 Ill. 498, 46 N.E. 2d 375-1943)."
(Citizens' Rights Advocate citing case law)

The Judge's ruling to transfer the boys to Lew, when he had no standing to receive them and after the Court admitted to its failure to follow the law, set forth the basis for a void order. And, as I am told, each court order that Judge Evans issued thereafter is also invalid and void.

I recognized that the entire proceeding was a sham, as numerous people and witnesses had been telling me. It did not matter who or what I was, nor what Lew had done to me and our children. We were spending our estate to protect Lew and bury Jeanne, at the expense of our children. The Trial Court had allowed our family to utilize over a million dollars to conceal the evidence of Lew's wife and child abuse, and all efforts were vested in establishing that I was the faulty parent because of my commitment to protect my children and their attachment to me.

I had exhausted all outside options in halting this process. The court watchers, the court and child advocates, the community legal support groups, and our notification to the Appellate Court merely maintained the battering spiral of the Trial Court protecting itself, in response to our efforts to address its resistance and refusal to follow the law.

We even issued a letter firing Mr. Wessel, before David and Marc's in-camera session with the lawyers and the Judge, with the hope to subsequently obtain counsel to represent the children's interests and their innocent unheard voices. The Court refused to let Mr. Wessel go. The children's letter, signed by them, was ignored and the boys were not allowed any other representation. Their voices remained as muffled as mine. It was like screaming in a vacuum.

There was no more of my denying the litigation abuse. There was no hope for our justice in this process, at least not in Cook County and, possibly not, in the State of Illinois. It was time for me to see it for what it had become: a continuation of the domestic violence in the courtroom. Individuals familiar with the practices evidenced in our case called it "legal domestic abuse," and attorneys called it "abuse of process" by the trial court and its agents.

*   *   *

David and Marc were transferred from Marlene's residence to Lew's home in Glencoe, Illinois, and our nightmare continued. Within the first week of the children's move to Lew's home on February 18, 1999, Marc ran away several times. He rode his bike after dark in areas he was not allowed to ride in the day, in his desperate effort to come home to me. He was determined to get out from under Bradley and Lew's vengeance.

I watched Marc vacillate from being a courageous survivor to being a wounded child. One evening on the phone he said. "The Judge said he was going to take all my troubles off my shoulders, but he has put all the troubles on my shoulders." As the days worn on in which Lew denied him direct access to me, Marc became severely depressed and his despair escalated.

On February 24, 1999, he fell apart on the phone and said to me, "I am going to cut a line in my chest for every day that I can't see you."

My child was really in trouble. He said that the cuts were bleeding and hurting as he made them deeper. He cried and so did I.

I could feel his pain, and it became mine. I felt so helpless in knowing that I had been rendered legally impotent and there was nothing I could do. I put all my energy in talking Marc out of hurting himself. He told me he had carved the Judge's name in his chest, because he didn't know what else to do. He was so angry and so hurt. I could see that the litigation abuse had led to my child's self-mutilation. I promised him that I was doing everything I could to see him and made him promise me that he would stop cutting and carving his chest.

The Two Types of Batterers

Cobras	Pit Bulls
abused as children by their parents	their fathers battered their mothers
hedonistic; impulsive; antisocial; con-artist; exploits & manipulates others	immature; unpredictable; unrelenting; demanding changes from their victims
use of or dependence on illegal drugs	more likely to abuse alcohol
personal commitments are superficial	emotionally dependent on their wives
does not fear abandonment; but they will not be controlled	need to control and dominate partner; motivated by fear of abandonment
severely abuse their wives to insure getting what they want when the want it	extreme fear of abandonment produces jealous rage and need to control wife's life
internally calm when they strike	highly aroused when they strike
very frightening, yet captivating to wives	wives are enraged and feel entrapped
harder to leave, and are more dangerous after leaving in the short-run	easier to leave, and are more dangerous after leaving in the long-run
capable of severe assault and murder	capable of severe assault and murder

Conceptualized in N. Jacobson and J. Gottman, *When Men Batter Women*, 1998.

PART THREE

Abuse Is A Choice
for Adults Only

CHAPTER 27

Silencing the Victims

Restricting Contact and Blocking Intimacy

Association for Family Conciliation Courts

Supervisors Serve as Silent Seal Around Abuse

Jenevieve Delk: Supervisor, Witness and Reality Check

Lew's Baby-Sitter Discloses the Inside Story

Marc Plans His Indiana Runaway

Unlawful Interference with Visitations

I held out waiting for protection in family court the same way I had held out hoping Lew would change. Unfortunately, in both cases, I waited too long. My children and I were not going to get our justice in Cook County, and now we couldn't flee to another state. Our access to one another was cut off.

I was caught between a rock and a hard place. It did not feel right talking my children into accepting what I knew was unhealthy for them. Yet it seemed cruel to pull them into a tug of war, only to create more psychological destruction. The divorce and custody litigation was committed to supporting the dysfunction in the family, not protecting the innocent. As Evelyn pointed out in her correspondence to the authorities, "The court has silenced the victims and given a voice to the perpetrator of abuse."

I was overwhelmed with grieving about the absence of my children; I felt like I was being yanked apart. I spent my evenings alone, crying. When the boys and I were in contact, I became the sounding board for their pain. The more the children spoke, the more Lew tightened up the avenues of our communication. At first I perceived his interference with our contact as an abuse to me, and then I witnessed it as abusive to the children. The severing of parent-child contact is, indeed, a violation of human rights.

This violation, like all the others appeared to stem from a vulnerability that came from those infringing on our rights. Our having access to one another seemed to pose a threat to Lew and the Court. Restricting our contact served to prevent the ongoing battering in Lew's home from leaking out, and the potential of my truth concerning what was happening from spilling in. It also appeared to serve to prevent me and the boys from seeking our justice out of state.

Initially my children talked to me and ran away, anyway. What I heard and saw was most disturbing. There was no denying that the abuse was alive and growing in Lew's home. David and Marc were being hit, kicked, punched, pushed, dragged, tormented and brutalized routinely. At first, I reached out to Steve for assistance but, as before, there was none. Talking to Steve about my boy's plight was as productive as David and Marc's crying out to me. Steve and I had both been rendered legally impotent in protecting my children or my parental rights through the Cook County Divorce Court.

Steve encouraged me to give up, and asked me to let him go. He informed me that it would now cost $43,000 to obtain Dr. Galatzer-Levy's report. There was no explanation for why Dr. Galatzer-Levy's $16,000 report, which was held out of our Court Record for one year, was currently priced at an additional $27,000. I had no doubt that this Doctor's report was never intended to be forthcoming.

*   *   *

In my despair, I turned to Evelyn. Her interest in our case was growing as I was losing strength, so I drew from her momentum. Evelyn had been involved in collaborating with a New York investigative reporter to expose divorce court abuse and its implications to victims of domestic violence. The reporter was negotiating with a national network to do a show in which they proposed to include our case.

Evelyn's investment in our case stemmed from her recognition of a national pattern of violations to abused children in divorce court. Evelyn believed that our case illustrated gross court agent transgressions compromising American children. She remained committed to me because my case was so well-documented.

In our work together, we discovered an organization called the Association of Family Conciliation Courts (AFCC) and other tax exempt corporations that linked the parties in our case together. We were informed that the AFCC served as an umbrella operation that was not purely inter-professional support; it also provided for litigation promotion and unfortunate family destruction. The organization consists of Judges, Lawyers, Court-Appointed Mental Health Care Professionals, Court Administrators, Supervised Visitation Centers, as well as Seminars in how to fabricate the classic "Parental Alienation Syndrome," among many other psychiatric syndromes designed to sever children from a parent.

The AFCC in our state is a tax exempt Illinois corporation. Evelyn and the investigative reporter thought this organization may mirror the Association of Family Conciliation Courts of California, which was and may still be under investigation by the media. It was obvious to me that Evelyn and the New York reporter did not like what was discovered in the investigations.

I was so consumed in my own crisis and the difficulties of my children that I could not fully grasp the workings of the AFCC. What I did observe was that the supervisors who were acceptable to the Court, when there was a furious effort to limit my contact with my children, were members of the AFCC. This appeared to be a requirement for acceptance by the Court. It was clearly a red flag to me, given the history of supervisors permitted in our case over the last four years.

It took a couple of weeks to actually line up one of the supervisors made available to me. Once done, my relationship with my children was as though it had been suddenly placed in a jail environment. I felt it, and so did they. One evening at the close of a visit with David and Marc, the children and I were giving one another good-bye hugs and kisses. The supervisor was sitting in the back seat of the car. Marc wanted to share something of concern to him privately with me. The lady refused to allow Marc this liberty and Marc lost it.

He became hysterical, screaming, "You are getting in the way of my relationship with my Mom." Marc cried, "My Mom does not need a supervisor."

Marc refused to get out of the car and insisted on the supervisor giving him the space to talk to me. There was something he desperately wanted and needed me to know. He leaned over close to speak to me, and the supervisor interrupted our contact. Marc grabbed the seat belt nearest him, wrapped it around his neck and pulled it tightly, while crying on and on. The woman sat there watching Marc and refused to allow me to comfort or get near my distressed child.

This supervisor and her partners from Sheehy, Cohen and Associates were incredibly intrusive and forbid me private contact with my children. A kiss or a comforting caress was met with a bodyguard standing, literally, two inches from me and my child. The absurdity of this intrusion was disgraceful to both me and all three of my children. The boys were all keenly aware of the irony of the fact that their Dad had beaten us, but his supervisors were often in another room during his supervised visitation with the them. They questioned why Mommy, who had never hurt us, cannot kiss or love us without someone crowding in. I, too, knew how ridiculous this was, and it was truly painful for me.

We were denied intimacy by individuals acting like policeman and treating me as though I was the criminal. Yet when Lew actually had a criminal arrest and an abuse finding by the state child protective agency and the local court, his overnight supervisor did not serve to sever the children's contact with their father. Lew's weekend supervisor, appointed by the Court, was a woman named Yolanda, who was Mr. Wessel's personal baby-sitter for his own children. I was informed that Yolanda participated in the visitation as a casual guest, sitting in a corner or eating in another room, while Lew and the boys went off alone. What amazed me was that this was permitted for a full year, when the Court Order detailing Lew's supervisor's role read that she was to be "an ear and an eye shot away" at all times during their visits.

I tried to explain to the supervisors what was going on in our case, but my communications were to no avail. In reviewing these supervisors resumes, I noted that they were members of the AFCC. I learned about the cooperative efforts of individuals in this organization and realized that a significant portion of this supervisory business' income came from court referrals. Then I knew why my concerns were not heard.

*   *   *

I soon recognized that my supervisors served to assist in keeping a silent seal around the ongoing violence to David and Marc. Since words couldn't be spoken, actions finally told the story. On March 24, 1999, I pulled up to Lew's house to pick up the children for their visitation, and Maureen Sheehy, the supervisor, came to my car. The screaming inside Lew's house was so loud, we could hear it from the driveway. We went to the door and David was crying and saying, "I want to kill myself." Bradley was violently beating David, uncontrollably and the live-in baby-sitter, Dennis, was incredibly distressed.

Dennis is a young man in his late 20's, about 5'8'' tall, medium build and with a dark complexion. He is a warm, caring and loving human being. Dennis told us how Brad was fighting with his brothers, hitting them daily. He said the physical violence had been escalating over the last few weeks and Brad refused to take responsibility for any of it. Dennis explained that there were "no limits, no boundaries and no accountability." He said it was continuous berating, belittling, bullying and battering. He was concerned that someone was going to get hurt.

During our visitation on March 24, 1999, Marc let his hair down. Instead of insisting on talking to me alone, he spoke to the supervisor and me together.

He said, "Brad is hitting me everyday, and I am also getting hit by my Dad." Marc added, "There's no point in living, if I'm going to get hit all the time like this."

I comforted Marc telling him I was doing everything I could to bring an end to the hitting, yet I could see Marc's frustration in his knowing that it was only getting worse. After we brought the children home, Ms. Sheehy recommended that I seek assistance from a domestic violence specialist and gave me a name to call from the Northwestern University Family Institute. After making this referral, I asked her to document the evenings events, but she refused to put it in writing.

In another supervised visit with the children, I recognized the other function served by the supervisor was to keep my impression of violence and our predicament to myself. I realized this one evening while driving in my car with the three children and the supervisor. Bradley was picking on Marc. I informed Brad that hitting and being verbally mean to others was not acceptable, and I was not going to tolerate his doing so in my presence. He broke lose, swung over the seat and slugged Marc as I was driving. Then a comment was made about "Mom talking about the divorce." From that moment, I recognized the issue of abuse was synonymous with the divorce from the children's perspective.

My children were being told by their father that this type of communication about honoring one another and why it is wrong to abuse each other or violate others was "Mommy talking about the divorce." They were told these communications were bad for them. They were informed that the supervisor was there to protect them from being exposed to Mom's comments which "endangered" them. My children were being groomed to believe that cycles of violence were normal and that challenging abuse was inappropriate. They were also being insulated from expressing their sadness around our being torn apart and from hearing, feeling or seeing my pain from the same.

In my opinion, this was no cause for supervised visitation. The fury I felt around this led me to seek another supervisor, unrelated to the courts. Lew, Ms. Feinberg and Mr. Wessel refused to allow me to use a friend, relative or acquaintance to serve in this capacity. They insisted that I engage someone they selected or an individual who had an affiliation with the courts.

I called Jenevieve Delk, a woman from a list entitled "Available Supervisors for the Blumenthal Children," issued to the Court on February 17, 1999 by Lew's counsel. Jenevieve was referred by Lew's sister. She was half the cost, knew nothing of the case and had the appearance of being impartial, even though she came to us through Lew's family. In meeting her, I felt her integrity and decided to employ her. She was a bright sensitive, compassionate middle-aged woman. Jenny was slender, solid and had the appearance of being street wise; and indeed she was. She was direct, kind and honest. Had it not have been for Jenny, I don't know how I would have survived the next two months.

She accompanied me on four or five visitations, beginning April 5, 1999. In contrast to the other supervisors, she was a delight on visitation. While the boys and I would have preferred being alone, her presence was gentle, playful, caring and respectful. It didn't take long for Jenny to realize what was going on in our family. The violence spoke for itself, and Lew's emotional abuse to me and the children in severing our contact was quite clear to Jenny. She was keenly aware of the boys' rage at being entrapped by Lew and the battering in their father's house. She predicted something dangerous and devastating to emerge from Lew's home with the boys.

*   *   *

On Jenny's first visitation with us, the children disclosed that Dennis, the live-in baby-sitter and housekeeper, had quit. I sensed it coming, based on the last encounter in front of their house. I could see he was reaching his limit. After the visit, I called Dennis to find out why he left and what he observed about my boys.

He said, "The kids have a lot of anger, hate and violence." Dennis revealed, "I left because the fighting got to me." "Things were out of control and it was constant, going from one fight to the next, everyday."

I maintained contact with Dennis over the week, and he informed me of numerous episodes of violence in Lew's home. He spoke of many altercations, typically beginning with Brad bullying, bossing and berating David or Marc. He said:

> "Then, David and Marc would try to defend themselves and Brad would start fighting with them, getting violent. Brad would keep going on them, slapping, hitting and tormenting them – like he was going to beat them up, until David and Marc would draw into a crouched position in terror. They would get scared of him. Then, Brad seemed to enjoy that. This would happen everyday."

Dennis gave numerous examples of altercations, resulting in David gasping for breath, wishing he was dead; hard objects flown throughout the house at one another; the younger children hurt and Brad seeing their distress as "funny." Dennis noted that Lew's efforts to correct the fighting were futile, and it appeared that Lew diminished, ignored or condoned the violence in their home.

Dennis gave me examples in which Lew lost control and became abusive with the boys. There was one evening in which Marc didn't want to go to bed, because he wanted to watch the Simpsons. Dennis said:

> "Lew pulled Marc by the ear and dragged him to his room. Marc was screaming and crying, 'My ear hurts, my ear hurts'." (Affidavit of Dennis Santeliz, April 19, 1999, p. 2)

Dennis said that the boys each told him they "can't stand their living situation...Bradley hates Lew and David hates Brad." Dennis said, "The anger, the fighting and violence was too much. It was overwhelming." Dennis felt really bad for the boys. He wanted to help them because he believed they were in trouble. He submitted a four page Affidavit, including the above quotes, and much additional information detailing his observations of abuse and violence in Lew's home.

Since I had been denied the right to have an expert witness provide testimony concerning my boys predicament, I elected to submit Dennis' Affidavit into the Court Record, so the Judge would be apprised of what was going on after the transfer of the boys residence to Lew's home. I was also advised to submit Dennis' Affidavit to the police in Lew's community, in hopes that the local law enforcement would assist in protecting the children. Once again, both of these efforts backfired.

*　　　*　　　*

Initially, the police expressed significant concern regarding the endangerment to the children and even offered to help. However, after speaking to David Wessel, there was no more assistance for the children. I had become accustomed to this kind of interruption by

Mr. Wessel. The child advocates and I referred to Mr. Wessel's impact on potential helpers as being "Wesselized." Invariably, promising supporters or helpers exhibited a "change-of-heart" following discussions with Mr. Wessel. It happened every time someone in the community stepped in to assist me or my children.

Lew seemed to have the same effect on potential support for the children and myself as Mr. Wessel. I was informed by Marc that he called 911 on four separate occasions requesting police help, but Lew managed to convince the officers that it was a prank call and circumvented their intervention. In Lew's effort to defend himself, he told the police that my concerns regarding my children were a custody ploy. Subsequently, the police lost interest in stopping the abuse in the Blumenthal family.

On Saturday, April 10, 1999, my mother came to Chicago to visit. I took David and Marc out to dinner with Grandma Audree. Jenny accompanied us on this visitation. Marc pleaded with Grandma Audree to let him come live with her. He told her about his being hit in Lew's house. He said the courts would not let him live with his Mom and that he could not stand to live with his Dad. I could see that Grandma Audree wanted to help comfort him, but she too was helpless.

As Marc spoke of their horrific living situation in his Dad's house, David cried and cried. I held him, stroked his hair and heard myself comforting him with the unfilled promises of the last five years. I said, "Mommy is doing everything to stop the violence in the family." It made me sick to hear myself say it again, because I saw my own impotence. We regained composure in the boys by shifting the attention to planning for Marc's birthday. Grandma Audree purchased a red motorized scooter for Marc's upcoming birthday, and we shared in the excitement of his receiving this desired gift.

The next day Marc spent much of our visitation on the telephone at my house. He was orchestrating the logistics of a runaway. He had obtained information on the train routes and schedules, and had created a fictitious name for travel. David and I played games in the house much of this time. At the end of the visitation, Marc pleaded with me to give him over $50.00, which was more money than was customary for him to receive. I knew something was up, but didn't realize how much work he had done on his mission at this juncture. My paralysis, which evolved from my fear that I would be penalized further by the courts for assisting him, prevented me from partaking in his phone work and giving him the money.

I was incredibly split over wanting my child to exercise his ingenuity toward his self-preservation, yet I didn't want him to place himself at risk for any danger to himself in doing so. I called Lisa and asked her if she would accompany Marc, in the event that he decided to flee. We talked about it at length, and she was fearful that Lew and his attorneys would charge her with being an accomplice to a kidnapping. She said, "Dr. King, I would have helped you run with the children before, but now I see what these people can do and there is no telling what they will try next." We spent hours trying to figure out how to assist Marc without causing further trouble.

In the interim, my mother informed me that Marc had called her to discuss his plans to go to Indiana by train. After consulting with her attorney, she was advised that she would not be able to keep Marc, without being implicated in kidnapping. She proposed to be of assistance to her grandchild through the courts, but I knew this was of no avail.

The next day Marc went to school and told Ms. McCabe that he was going to run away to Indiana to go live with Grandma Audree. He informed Ms. McCabe that he was being hit and hurt at his father's home and he adamantly refused to go back there. Ms. McCabe called me on the phone and said:

"Marc is here with me and he is all upset. He is insisting on running away, because he says he is getting hit by his father and brother."

I wanted to talk to my child. She told me to come to school and help him calm down. I got ready in a matter of minutes and, as I was walking out of the door, Ms McCabe called me and told me she was in contact with Lew and he instructed her not to allow me to come to the school.

She told me, "Your husband says you need a supervisor and cannot come to the school." She promised me that she would call Department of Children and Family Services on Marc's behalf to report the danger in his home. In my innocence, I embraced her apparent commitment to help my child and hoped that DCFS would do for him what the courts refused to do: protect my child from abuse. I was wrong.

Within the hour, Marc had run away from the school grounds. He took off running down the street on his own. Dr. Duke, the school principle, chased after him, but evidently Marc outran Dr. Duke. The police were called in to retrieve Marc and bring him back to the school. Once captured, the adults consoled Marc by promising to bring in "helpers" to hear his concerns. However, Lew showed up at the school and somehow the commitment to help Marc dwindled.

That evening during my visitation with the children, Marc informed Jenny and me that Lew and Ms. McCabe went into a room and closed the door. Marc said he stood at the door and heard his Dad tell Ms. McCabe that "his Mom was psycho." Lew also communicated to Ms. McCabe that Marc was fine and there was no hitting in his home.

In Marc's despair he complained, "*No one will help me*, because Dad has told Ms. McCabe not to believe me and not to trust you."

I felt Marc's frustration and knew my limitations. The children and I hugged tenderly and conveyed words of wishing and hope at the end of our visitation. At the time, I didn't know this was the last time I would see David. Had I have know it, I would have embraced him and said good-bye in a way to hold us over for years.

*   *   *

On my next scheduled visitation, I pulled up to Lew's house with Jenny and no one was home. We waited for almost an hour and then went to the police station in Glencoe where Lew resided. I filed charges against Lew for "unlawful interference with visitation." Bev Cooper, a TV producer for a local Talk Show called "Cooper's Corner," met us there to provide support in making this complaint.

Bev was a middle-aged, vivacious and articulate woman with a personal commitment to cleaning up court corruption and legal injustice. She learned of my case through our earlier outreach and from discussions with Evelyn. Prior to this incident, Bev hosted a TV show entitled *Who Will Save Our Children?* in which I was a featured guest. My story was presented and augmented with insight from Evelyn and Dr. Dugo.

Bev offered the strength I could no longer bring forward in this meeting with the police. She insisted that the officers review the documentation from our case, which had been previously submitted to the police department. The officer taking the report came back into the room where he had been taking a statement from Jenny and myself, and his face turned white, contorted with shocking surprise. He was holding the Court Order giving me supervised visitation and my current Order of Protection against Lew with the children and I as the protected parties.

"These are two conflicting Orders," the officer said. *"Something is wrong here!!"*

I broke into tears, then stood up and started pacing. I could hardly contain myself.

The officer comforted me and said he wanted to seek assistance for us. He placed a call to the State's Attorney and explained our peculiar predicament. He said that the State's Attorney wanted me to obtain the full Court Record of all the Orders for them to review. Bev and I recognized that this gesture was more likely another dead end.

The next day, on April 25, 1999, Jenny and I arrived at Lew's house to pick up the children for their Sunday visitation with me. Once again, no one was home. After waiting for 45 minutes, we went to the police station again and Bev met us there. It was a replay of yesterday, but this time the police resisted filing the second complaint. With Bev's persistence, the officer issued the second "unlawful interference of visitation" complaint. I was informed that three of these "unlawful interference with visitation" complaints elevated the action from a quasi-criminal matter to a criminal action, resulting in six months imprisonment.

Bev escorted me to the local police of the community in which I resided to report the complaints. The interference with my visitation violated my Order of Protection, because our visitation schedule was contained within the Order of Protection. We were informed that my Order of Protection was no longer active, according to their records. Bev and I knew that this was not correct and didn't know what to make of this information.

That evening Bev and I were regrouping at my home. We heard a crashing sound at the front door. Bev and I rushed to the door. It was Marc, banging on the door pleading to come in. Behind him was Vlad, Lew's new live-in baby-sitter, pulling Marc away from my door. They struggled in front of my home, Marc screaming with Vlad trying to restrain him. Bev called the police.

The police arrived and we informed them of what had occurred. They took a statement from Vlad and Marc. Vlad, age 21, was unaware of the family history. He told the police that he was running an errand with Marc and Marc convinced him to go down my street. As they approached my house, Marc asked him to stop the car so he could look at the house and Marc jumped out of Vlad's car. Marc relayed the same story to the police and added, as indicated in the police report:

"He wasn't going back to his Dad' house, as he was denied visitation rights to see his mother this weekend, and he is repeatedly battered and abused while he stays there, and his father told him he is never going to see his mother again." (Domestic Disturbance, Case No. 9906998, April 25, 1999)

Marc held onto to me and refused to let go. The police called DCFS in Springfield, and were advised that Marc should remain with me for the evening due to the risk of harm to the child, and said they would investigate it further the next day. However, Mr. Wessel was contacted and informed the police that I was not cooperating with the court-ordered counseling, had fired my attorney and the court-ordered supervisors. Mr. Wessel strongly advised to have Marc returned to his father's home. Lew went to the police station supporting Mr. Wessel's story. After re-evaluating the Blumenthal family situation, the police came back to my house. They took Marc out of his bed in which he was sleeping at 3:00 AM to return him to his father's home. I didn't know, in awaking my child with the police at the door, that we were having our last kiss.

The Role of Learned Helplessness in Sustaining
the Cycle of Violence

Entanglement in the cycle of violence fosters victimization, which can become a self-perpetuating cycle that ultimately results in the psychological paralysis of "learned helplessness." Learned helplessness, a term coined by experimental psychologist, Dr. Martin Seligman, is a behavioral apathy and lack of response that evolves out of perceived impotence.

If a voluntary response impacts our environment, we repeat it and believe we have control over our situation. If we expect a certain outcome to occur when we make a response and it does not, we assume we have no control over the outcome and we cease to respond. Laboratory experiments show that if an animal experiences situations which it can not control, the animal's motivation to respond to the events – as aversive as they may be – becomes impaired. Compliance, passivity and submissiveness are exhibited in the face of the adversity.

Chronic abuse diminishes a victim's motivation to respond because their cognitive ability to perceive success is changed and passivity sets in. This behavioral apathy is observed in both battered women and abused children. As Dr. Walker states, "the battered woman does not believe anything she does will alter any outcome...She says, 'No matter what I do, I have no influence.' She can not think of alternatives" (1979, p. 50). Similarly, parental abuse undercuts a child's sense of mastery and control of his fate. Ultimately, as Dr. Dutton notes, "it wears down the child's defenses so that strategies to reduce the negative feelings seem beyond his will" (1995, p. 125).

Outward measures to effect change in the victim's predicament fall out of their repertoire of options. Learned helplessness is both the result of victimization and the psycho-behavioral mechanism that serves to sustain entrapment in the battering cycle.

D. Dutton, *The Batterer: A Psychological Profile*, 1995; L. Walker, *The Battered Woman*, 1979; J. King, *Domestic Violence Transformed into Litigation Abuse*, 1998.

CHAPTER 28

The Slander Weapon

Lew Threatens the Witness

The Four Year Plan to Get Rid of Mommy

The Forceful Fart

Terminating My Visitation

Getting Rid of Jenny

Feinberg's Slander Strategy

Community Colored by Magic Bullet

Our justice appeared further and further away as more people came aboard to assist in preventing our protection. The Court reached out to the community to aid in keeping our evidence hidden, while enabling the perpetuation of the battering cycle we lived. This gave the appearance of:

A) Lew can do no wrong, and can even make bench decisions.
B) The Court's justice is subjective but, nonetheless, rules.
C) Jeanne and the boys are just four more folks falling through the cracks of the system.

I recognized that many individuals in the community knew our truth, but this knowledge was not enough to help make a difference. We continued to be re-victimized by the process.

Dennis' Affidavit of April 19, 1999, detailing the abuse and violence he witnessed in Lew's home was not well received by Lew and his legal team. During the weekend that I was denied visitation with the children, Lew began calling Dennis, threatening and harassing him for providing such explicit information. Dennis pleaded with Lew to leave him alone, but Lew persisted. Between April 26 and May 1, 1999 Lew called Dennis and his family five times.

On May 1, 1999 Dennis became frightened and called me. I remained on conference call as support while Dennis returned Lew's call.

Lew said, "We have an emergency!! There is a document saying that there was a lot of fighting in my house, and that I pulled Marc by the ear, which is obviously child abuse, and obviously did not occur."

Dennis told Lew it was true, as he saw it, yet Lew claimed he "never touched Marc's ear," and he "never hit the children." Lew tore into Dennis, viciously.

"You're alleging a criminal action," Lew said, "and we are going to have a number of interactions on this." "We're going to get the kids on the stand. It's going to be ugly."

Lew threatened to bring all of Dennis' history out in the open. Dennis was puzzled because he said he was not ashamed of his history. Lew continued threatening, harassing and intimating Dennis, telling him he was now a part of a "legal procedure" which would prove he was "lying," and thus result in Dennis "going to jail."

Dennis did his best to hold his own and maintain his convictions. He was unwavering in what he saw and knew as the truth.

Lew said, "If you stand by the things you wrote about, it will be a problem and big trouble for you."

"Lew, do what you need to do," Dennis replied.

In a state of calculated fury, Lew responded, "I am doing what I have to do, and it started four years ago. Nothing is going to get in my way and you're not going to get in my way. You can take that to the bank!!!"

Dennis was quite distressed by Lew's threats and intimidation, so we went to the police in Dennis' community and filed a complaint for harassment.

In further communications with Dennis, I recognized what Lew meant by his statement, "I'm doing what I have to do and it started four years ago." Dennis disclosed that Lew, Lew's sisters (Marlene and Ingrid), and Lew's girlfriend (Ellen) had been telling Dennis throughout his employment that they needed to *"get rid of the children's Mom,"* because *"she lies and makes up stories about Lew."* Dennis informed me that they repeatedly blamed me for the boys failure to listen in Lew's home, claiming I had "brainwashed" the boys and that I was "crazy."

In another Affidavit, Dennis noted his observations during his employment:

"If Jeanne was such a bad mother, why do David and Marc want to go back to her so badly? Why are they so happy to see her? Why do they hug her and kiss her, and they don't do this with Lew?" (May 3, 1999, p. 2)

Dennis recognized that the grown-ups in the children's lives were assisting Lew in his mission to "get rid of Mommy." He believed if Lew was the good father he purported to be, "he would not push the children's mother out of their lives," and "wouldn't be hurting them the way he is."

In Dennis' effort to assist the children, he submitted two additional Affidavits, detailing Lew's harassment to him in response to his disclosures of the abuse in Lew's home; and Lew's statements evidencing his plotting "to get rid of the children's mother." This, too, was filed in the Court Record.

*   *   *

I realized that the four year legal nightmare I had been living was all an effort to protect Lew. The mission to push Mommy out of the children's lives eliminated Lew's concern for the continued disclosure of his being a wife and child abuser. I recognized that the courts assisted this mission by transferring the children's "temporary custody" to Lew before, and instead of, giving me a trial. The proceedings were actually a gross manipulation and an "abuse of process," preventing me and my children the liberty of having a trial.

I also realized that Lew was not a "reformed" abuser, he was still a batterer, as evidenced by the way he dealt with Dennis. Lew was vulnerable to Dennis' disclosures, and his method of recourse was to strike Dennis to re-empower himself. Lew's denial of his abuse to his family and his insistence that the children's mother lies and makes up stories about him proved to me that Lew remained in denial about his abuse to us.

*   *   *

Long ago, I had given up in trying to change Lew. What was most distressing for me now was the reality that the courts and the community were assisting in giving Lew liberty to abuse his family. It is abusive to sever a child from a parent with no real cause other than to carry out the vendetta of the other parent and to protect court parties serving this agenda. This is what our case had become.

As Dennis' observations were surfacing, Lew's counsel submitted a Pleading before the Court to terminate my visitation and phone contact with the children. The most compelling cause for this request was a statement provided by Maureen Sheehy, claiming that Marc "passed gas on her," and "Jeanne did nothing." The Pleading expanded on how I was endangering my child by not giving him proper consequences for this hideous action of farting on the supervisor.

I showed this Petition to Bev Cooper, and she was absolutely outraged. She insisted that we show it to the first police officer that issued the "unlawful violation of visitation" citation. The officer was speechless. All he could say was, "You must take this to your attorney." I saw the Pleading as the same type of meritless unfounded petition set forth by Ms. Joy Feinberg over the last four years in order to wrestle custody.

At the time I did not have an attorney, so the officer's recommendation was not an option, not that it would have mattered anyway at this juncture. I had fired Steve Stern on April 2, 1999, by submitting a Notice of Termination of his services, filed with the Court and issued to all parties April 5, 1999. This was done when I recognized that Steve was both unwilling and unable to assist me in representing my interests or in helping me protect my children. There was absolutely no effort from Steve to help me assist my boys in their struggle after the transfer from Marlene's home to Lew's residence. Instead, he aided opposing counsel by drafting an Order on February 26, 1999, rekindling the threat of barring my expert witnesses from the final trial and further limiting my visitation in the interim.

Since the filing of the Notice to Disqualify Judge Evans, Steve was no longer able to represent me. He had a Motion before the Court to Withdraw as my counsel on February 10, 1999. I was informed that Mr. Stern could not represent me, because according to the Code of Professional Conduct, an attorney's first commitment is to the Court; not to the client. So instead of holding my hand while we went down, it appeared he began to push me off the cliff. I could not tolerate these actions anymore.

As I write this book and review the court orders, I realize that the Order of February 17, 1999 was co-drafted by Joy Feinberg and Steve Stern, and the portion alleging the evidence of Lew's rehabilitation and my assumed abuse to my children was in Steve Stern's handwriting. How could Steve write in the Trial Court an Order which completely contradicted his Petition in the Appellate Court?

He had just filed Pleadings with the Appellate Court, asserting that there was no evidence before the Trial Court showing Lew's rehabilitation, nor was there any evidence of me endangering or abusing my children.

It was even more bizarre that, after I had fired Steve Stern, he continued to issue Pleadings concerning his Motion to Withdraw and participate in the proceedings receiving opposing counsels' pleadings, acting as though he was my counsel. On April 27, 1999, Mr. Stern faxed a letter to my home notifying me that his Petition to Withdraw was continued until April 29, 1999. His letter also stated that we would be hearing Lew's Motion to further sever my contact with my children as well as Lew's Motion to remove me from my home. What amazed me about Steve's continuing to act as my counsel was both he and the Court refused to acknowledge that I fired him weeks ago. My voice with respect to my counsel's employment by me was not heard, any more than my children's voice with respect to theirs. Steve was acting as the *court-appointed* attorney for the litigant going down.

*   *   *

On April 26, 1999, during the gap in which I had fired my counsel, even though the Court was holding him in place, Lew's counsel, Mr. Wessel and Mr. Stern appeared before the Court and terminated my visitation with my children, on the alleged basis that I had fired my supervisors or they had quit. First of all, I was legally without counsel and not present for the litigation to proceed; so this proceeding and this Order were orchestrated unlawfully. Secondly, my supervisor, Jenny, was with me on this very day at Lew's house to accompany me while visiting with my children; but again, we were denied our visitation.

Jenny prepared an Affidavit, which was submitted to the Court, in which she detailed her involvement in our case and her observations. She made it quite clear that she was picked by Lew and was aware of her being on Lew's counsel's list of "Supervisors Available for the Blumenthal Children." Her name was also listed in the Court Order of February 17, 1999, designating supervisors for me to employ. She pointed out that Lew had personally acknowledged her employment as my supervisor, beginning April 5, 1999 and paid her by personal check for these services covering 80 percent of four separate visitations in April, as per the Court Order designating our respective obligation for the supervisor's payment.

She reported that Dr. Blumenthal called her home mid-April to inquire how the visitations were going. She said, "The visits were going very well." Jenny stated she believed Lew wanted her to side with him. However, she was unwilling to do so, and this was unacceptable to Lew. As she stated in her Affidavit:

"I feel like if I had taken sides with him and said negative things about Ms. King, he would have accepted that and I would have been okay."

Concluding her Affidavit, Jenny pointed out, "I did not quit. I was terminated by Dr. Blumenthal on April 26, 1999 and by the Court on April 29, 1999." (May 12, 1999, p. 2)

*　　　*　　　*

The Court's actions on April 26, 1999, showed me a pattern that I had come to know very well with Lew over the years: the classic battering cycle. The Court did not intend to follow the law anymore than Lew intended to stop abusing me. Lew had been committed to or addicted to battering me, and the Judge had been accustomed to not following the law throughout the course of our proceedings. As one of my support associates said, "They are not practicing law in Judge Evans' Courtroom." I was advised not to wait for it. I was told that I was fooling myself, just as I had been fooling myself with Lew.

The Order evolving out of the April 26, 1999 proceeding terminating my visitation with my children was invalid, as were the Court Orders giving my children to non-parent custody and then "temporary custody" to Lew. All these Orders were unlawful. Judge Evans did not have jurisdiction over custody January 21, 1999, as it was vested in the Appellate Court. Then, after his non-parent custody ruling on this day, he lost jurisdiction in our case by virtue of his admitted failure to follow the law in his January 21, 1999 ruling; thereby, making the Order of February 17, 1999 void. Compounding the unlawful aspect of the last Order was the fact that I had fired my attorney. Legally, they could not proceed with Mr. Stern acting as my counsel; much less, proceed at all. The Judge could not release Steve, unless I was present in court. Technically, we were at a stalemate.

My unwillingness to go to court was because I could not take any further abuse by the Court. I expected my not showing up to merely buy me some time, to regroup and hopefully emerge with another strategy. I had been working on one with a non-profit legal assistance group. When I saw an Order produced out of the proceeding on April 26, 1999, particularly one that unlawfully cut me off from my children, I realized that the Court was capable of any infraction. I recognized that it was as **unpredictable** as Lew.

Knowing this, I elected to present myself to the Court along with Jenny on April 29, 1999. I did this against the advice of the non-profit organization. The gentleman of this organization did not want me to go to court, because he was working on a plan to have Judge Evans removed from the bench. This man was delighted over the fact that he could demonstrate Judge Evans' failure to follow the law in numerous cases, and believed my case was the catch to bring closure to this judge's conduct. Unfortunately, the gentleman was busy with other court matters, and estimated it would be a couple of months before he could give attention to the plan.

I knew that in the meantime, while waiting for his vision to move forward, I could be out on the street even though it was unlawful to evict me from my home. Lew had a Motion to remove me from my home before the Court on April 29, 1999. The basis of his Motion was that it would be best for the children to live in the marital residence, and his landlord had sold the house he was renting and so he needed to move. However, property laws in Illinois legally prevented my being removed from the residence in which my name was on the title. But Judge Evans had already shown me that he was capable of ordering just about anything, irrespective of the law.

Additionally, the Court professed to require to "personally meet with Jenny to approve her for my visitation" on April 29, 1999. Yielding to this was foolish of me, because I suspected what would evolve was a formal opportunity to get rid of Jenny. This is exactly what happened, along with the Court using this Hearing to let go of Steve, and to conclude the mission of "getting rid of Mommy." I now see that the house ploy served to get me into court in order to "reinstate" the "formal" proceeding, which had been stagnate since my firing Steve prior to this court date.

*   *   *

In retrospect, I see that this court date, as many others, was completely staged. All parties were present; but this time, both sides had court watchers. Lew's legal team invited the investigator of the Department of Children and Family Services and a representative from the Glencoe Police Department. I knew something was up when they were there as *court watchers*, rather than as witnesses to give testimony.

Jenny presented herself to the Court. She was articulate, professional, poised and respectful. None of this mattered, as we weren't there to evaluate her, rather we in the process of disqualifying her as an eligible supervisor. Lew's attorney established that Jenny was not qualified to supervise my visitations because she was not a "mental health professional." But neither was Yolanda, Mr. Wessel's baby-sitter, that supervised for Lew's visitations.

This sudden requirement limited my having visitation with my children to supervised visits with a "court-approved psychiatrist" in his office for $150 per each 45-minute visit. The basis for this "requirement" evolved out of Ms. Feinberg assuming the role of diagnostic psychiatrist for the purpose of this Hearing. In this role, she purported that I had a "Borderline Personality Disorder," necessitating more skilled intervention during my visitations with my children.

There had been no testimony entered into the record by anyone, other than Ms. Joy Feinberg and Lew, making allegations asserting a psychiatric diagnosis of any kind for me. In fact, to the contrary, my psychological evaluation by Dr. Kredow, the psychologist in Dr. Chapman's office stated:

"Overall it appears that Dr. Jeanne King Blumenthal is functioning in a predictably normal fashion, with no clinical diagnosis provided at this time." (October 23, 1995, p. 5)

Dr. Chapman even held back in making false psychiatric diagnosis in the record, as was boldly done by Lew's attorney. In Dr. Chapman's November 2, 1998 testimony to the Court, he said that he couldn't give me a diagnosis. He stated:

"I'm not able to go forward diagnostically with her to that extent. She is not cooperating. There is no reason for me to believe that she would answer questions, diagnostic questions accurately. So I can't say." (Report of Proceedings, November 2, 1998, p. 41)

I was disgusted with Ms. Feinberg's presentation of a fraudulent fabricated psychiatric disorder and the slanderous nature of her doing so. Representing myself, I approached the bench.

"Your Honor," I said, "Ms. Feinberg has placed before the Court a fabricated psychiatric label to distort matters and mislead the Court, and I object to this liable, slanderous action."

Ms. Feinberg went from dancing around the courtroom flinging psychiatric diagnoses, like a court psychiatrist, to a rapid retreat into her chair. This was the last time Ms. Feinberg attempted to play doctor with me, but the damage had already been done.

*   *   *

Up to this point, Ms. Joy Feinberg had flooded the Court Record with Pleadings asking the Court to order that I be sent for psychiatric treatment for a Borderline Personality Disorder. Initially, I was offended by Ms. Feinberg's misrepresentation and effort to pollute the Court with a false impression of my mental health. My counsel of record advised that I not get angered by this, as she was just trying to "yank my cord," and showing anger would buy into her ploy.

I took it upon myself to correct her false statements regarding my mental health in my own Pleadings, but she continued her psychiatric labeling. Eventually, I stopped giving thought to this harassment, because I knew it was as underhanded and inaccurate as all of her other allegations over the last four years. On some level, I become immune to her name calling and, basically, tuned her out. But when I saw how this fraudulent practice of psychiatry under the guise of practicing law was being used to sever my contact with my children, I was livid.

Earlier in the litigation, Ms. Feinberg had used one of Dr. Chapman's depositions to create this legal psychiatric bullet. This was done in a deposition in which Ms. Feinberg acted as though she was the only attorney in the room. Ms. Feinberg held the criteria for Borderline Personality Disorder in her hands – one out of hundreds of possible diagnoses – which she happened to have in her possession for her opening questions of *her* deposition with Dr.

Chapman. Ms. Feinberg read the criteria for this diagnosis, line by line, to the Doctor while refusing to allow my counsel to object to the obvious leading questioning. It angered my counsel so much that he left the deposition following Ms. Feinberg's refusal to allow him to object, which he was legally entitled to do and was professionally obligated to provide for me. We were aware that this was a staged legal psychiatric ploy, and counsel assured me it would go no further. He was right in that Dr. Chapman would not formally place his license on the line and enter a fabricated diagnosis into the record; but Ms. Feinberg was willing to do so.

It was interesting that, as I heard Ms. Feinberg walking Dr. Chapman through the diagnostic criteria, I knew it was not describing me, but rather I saw Lew in the profile. Reference was made to personality characteristics, such as:

- unstable interpersonal relationships, characterized by alternating between extremes of over-idealization and devaluation.
- frantic efforts to avoid real or imagined abandonment
- chronic feelings of emptiness or boredom
- inappropriate intense anger or lack of control of anger

The list was looking more like what I had witnessed in my marriage, not experienced in myself. I have since learned in reviewing the family abuse literature that my hunch in that deposition may have been quite accurate. Dr. Donald Dutton's extensive work with perpetrators reveals a clear and distinct relationship between the Borderline Personality and his conceptualization of the Abusive Personality. As the author points out, both of these personalities show a cyclic constellation which mirrors the cyclic conduct of battering.

Dr. Dutton cites psychiatrist John Gunderson, author of *Borderline Personality Disorder*, stating the essential defining criteria of the borderline personality are as follows:

"(1) involvement in intense and unstable relationships in which the significant other is undermined and manipulated. (2) intolerance of being alone combined with increasing abandonment anxiety; and (3) *intense anger*, demandingness, and impulsivity, often linked to substance abuse or promiscuity." (1998, p. 61)

Dr. Dutton notes that these characteristics "sounded exactly like the husbands of the battered women I have known and those that Walker described." He further points out that the primary defense mechanisms used by the borderline personality are "projection and denial," the same defense mechanisms used by the abusive personality. The author's contribution to the psychology of the batterer adds significant perspective to my understanding of the operative dynamics in my relationship with Lew and the lawyers who became an extension of him. A thorough review of Dr. Dutton's research is available in his books *The Abusive Personality: Violence and Control in Intimate Relationships* and *The Batterer: A Psychological Profile*.

*   *   *

My attorneys and I realized that, even if Ms. Feinberg or Dr. Chapman attempted to put the staged discovery into evidence, it could not hold because there was no factual or clinical basis for attaching the diagnosis to myself. The basis for the diagnosis Ms. Feinberg wanted to assign to me was the following:

A) my inability to maintain a long-standing relationship with *my* attorneys
B) my disenchantment around Lew's actions toward myself
C) all the false, unfounded allegations in Ms. Feinberg's Pleadings throughout the proceedings, which Ms. Feinberg and Dr. Chapman called "the litigation pattern"

I was so put off by this misuse of psychiatry, I said to John, "This is crazy."

"No," he said, "This is crazy making."

John and I reaffirmed this was not me, and recognized it as legal pollution. He supported me in prayer that my wholeness, health and internal strength would carry me to the end.

Now I see that this legal psychiatric ploy was the magic bullet ultimately used to snatch my children by keeping them away from me and preventing support from coming to us. While the slander was never legally put forward in the record by a psychiatrist, it was used by Lew, Mr. Wessel and Ms. Feinberg to discredit me in the community and in the proceedings. Their painting the picture of the children's Mommy as a "nut" served to gain allies for Lew and Mr. Wessel and prevent the community network of helpers from supporting me and my children. I believe this slander served to push away the local and state support coming forward for my kids during the Spring of 1999 as the legal domestic abuse revealed itself. I had been made aware of this, indirectly through The Department of Children and Family Services and through the police.

The Department of Children and Family Services had been called in to do an investigation in response to Marc's outcry at his school and to the Northbrook police, April 1999. Mr. Charles Dorothy, the DCFS investigator, informed Dennis in their interview that he learned from the father and Mr. Wessel that the mother had mental problems. The investigator revealed his not taking the abuse allegations seriously, as the mother was not to be trusted, along with the numerous advocates reaching out on our behalf.

Dennis said that Mr. Dorothy had told him on April 29, 1999, "I guess the mother's behavior is affecting the kids." And in this third party resource investigation, Mr. Dorothy never asked Dennis anything about how Lew was with the boys. What amazed me about this failed line of inquiry was that three separate people had submitted written information concerning Dennis' report of Lew's abuse to the children directly to Mr. Dorothy for this investigation. Why would DCFS not investigate what was reported?

Then, on April 30, 1999, Mr. Dorothy issued a letter documenting that his investigation of abuse in Lew's home was "unfounded." I thought it was quite telling that this letter was written the day after the April 29, 1999 Hearing which Ms. Feinberg used to set forth false representations of me in open court, with Mr. Dorothy in the audience. It is possible that his presence on this day served to protect DCFS, given the conclusionary report that followed.

The apparent political restraints around securing protection for me and my children continued to unveil, even in my children's school community. David and Marc were met at Northbrook Elementary School by Mr. Dorothy to conduct the investigation prior to his report of April 29, 1999. The investigator met the boys at their school, because it was believed that this would serve as a neutral place for conducting the investigation. However, my children were denied the opportunity to speak privately with the investigator because Dr. Duke elected to sit in on their interview. An investigation of child abuse with the child is typically done with the child alone. This is to insure the child's comfort and candor in the interview. However, Dr. Duke acted as monitor in my children's interview. David said, "It was hard to talk to the man, because Dr. Duke was in the room."

It was suggested that this action on Dr. Duke's part may have been at the direction of the school attorney. The handling of the Blumenthal family matters was no longer at the discretion of the school personnel, who had personal knowledge of the children and a long term relationship with me, their mother. Ever since Marc's statement to Ms. McCabe in October of 1998, the school had been dragged into the litigation and interfaced with our proceedings by their counsel through Mr. Wessel. Unfortunately, the school's hands appeared to be tied behind their back and their actions mirrored Mr. Wessel's agenda in concealing and diminishing abuse in Lew's home. I do not believe the school personnel who were involved were acting in a vindictive way. I feel they truly cared about the children, but they had limitations imposed by the lawyers and the politics which emerged.

Even police appeared to have adopted the same perspective as DCFS and the school after their discussions with Lew and Mr. Wessel. On April 24, 1999, I was informed by the Northbrook Police Department that my Order of Protection had expired. Yet, when I went to Highland Park, a suburb north of Northbrook, I was informed that indeed I did have an active Order of Protection in their computer. In speaking with the Illinois Sheriff's Department, I learned all the police departments had the exact same information in each department computer, as this is the only way to tract Orders of Protection throughout the state.

Bev and I recognized the Northbrook police probably communicated that my Order of Protection was expired, because they no longer wanted to entertain the filing of a violation of my Order of Protection. What we didn't know was why this was being done. Was it because I was now being viewed as a suspicious individual, based on the latest fictitious characterization of myself, or was it due to inter-department restrictions stemming from the larger politics in the law enforcement network?

We believed politics were working here, as much if not more than slander concerning myself throughout the community. Bev thought the Police in Glencoe resisted writing up our second "unlawful violation of visitation" complaint, and had refused to write up the third complaint because they were given direction from higher-up not to create any more paper work on the Blumenthal case. It appeared that more complaints would position a State's Attorney in confrontation with the actions of Judge Evans. So it seemed best from their perspective to play it down and blow us off.

The Police Department was holding out writing up the third incident on April 26, 1999, claiming to be waiting for a "court order" which Lew promised to hand deliver. However, direction to turn us away came from the police, without any documentation from the Court, but rather a memo from the Chief of the Police Department, saying that "my visitation had been terminated due to there being no approved supervisors for me." Of course, Jenny and I both knew she was legally still in place as my supervisor at that point in time. When Jenny and I saw and heard this, her eyes rolled back into her head. We both recognized that the Glencoe Police Department was no longer in a position to assist us, yet they knew of the history of abuse and the blatant judicial irregularities.

Our suspicions of "playing the Blumenthal case down" were confirmed on May 19, 1999 when the State's Attorney refused to take the two "unlawful interference of visitation" complaints before the Judge in the Criminal Court House where the complaints were scheduled to be heard. At first, the State's Attorney was going to take the matter before the Court, but then she refused to do so after communications with the Glencoe Police. I was told to take the complaints to the Domestic Relations Court, as it was part of our "private matter in divorce court" and could not be dealt with as a criminal matter irrespective of the fact that it was a law enforcement issue of the criminal court.

I was not surprised by the 180 degree change I witnessed in the potential for criminal processing of the matters related to the Blumenthal family. It became quite clear that the public protection structures held a higher interest in protecting the Domestic Relations Court from scrutiny than it did from protecting the Blumenthal wife and children from abuse. I knew this, because we still had a violation of our Order of Protection against Lew for the earlier reckless conduct and endangerment of Marc dangling before the court in both courthouses, Criminal and Divorce, and no one wanted to take action.

Some lawyers use "scorched earth" tactics, a term used to describe a strategy employed in the Civil War that involved burning down "everything" in sight to win the military objective. Many of these lawyers go all out in their effort to overpower or undermine the opposition. Often the strategy begins with a campaign to wear the wife down and starve her out. They attempt to outspend the wife by obstructing the proceedings and delaying any agreement "until she finally runs out of money and patience and gives up." When this does not work, the divorce lawyer tries to "destroy the wife's credibility." (Winner, *Divorced From Justice*, 1996, p. 58)

The Role of the Dr. Jekyll/ Mr. Hyde Personality in Maintaining the Cycle of Violence

The Dr. Jekyll/Mr. Hyde dual personality is a term used to describe an individual who projects two completely opposite images, which is characteristic of batterers. On the one hand, the person is – or can be – charming, attractive, courteous, thoughtful and even has the appearance of being easy going and romantically loving his spouse. Yet, on the other hand, behind closed doors this same person is moody, controlling, domineering, intrusive, possessive, oppressive, cruel, aggressive and brutal. An outsider may not recognize the controlling much less the dangerous abusive nature of the person.

Even the insider, that being his victim, can be confused by his "mixed signals," and his ongoing contradictions. One minute his spouse is a "rotten wife," a "psycho-wife," an "unattractive or stupid wife," and the next minute she is so important that he is willing to go to extremes to insure that no one threatens his place as the primary focus of her life. Or he might flood her with loving gestures, romantic letters and words of vulnerability interspersed between punches, pushes, shoves and kicks, depending on where the couple is in the cycle of violence (Scott, 1988; Weldon, 1999).

It can also be misleading to the outsider, because the qualities outwardly projected by the batterer to the public are seen as socially desirable. As an abused woman said in *Battered Women: Living with the Enemy*: "You would love him if you met him. To people outside, he was nice, he was in control, he seemed strong, and the type we respect in our society" (Kosof cited in Snow, 1997, p. 220-221).

As Captain Robert Snow and numerous other authors point out the abusers assets become the battering couple's liabilities. Many abusers are highly skilled at manipulating and coning police officers, therapists, clergy, lawyers and judges. In so doing, he engages a community **cloak of concealment** around his abuse, thereby enabling its continuation and more often than not its escalation.

C. Scott, *Breaking the Cycle of Abuse,* 1988; M. Weldon, *I Closed My Eyes,* 1999; R. Snow, *Family Abuse: Tough Solutions to Stop the Violence*, 1997.

CHAPTER 29

Being Abused Is a Choice

My De-Slander Effort

"The Most Severe Spousal Abuse..."

The Experts, Mom and My Inner Voice

Who's Paying for This Litigation?

Holocaust Decision and Solomon Judgment

My Exit and the Body Attachment

And the day came...
when the desire to remain the same,
was more painful than the risk
... to grow. (Anaire Nin)

It didn't matter what I presented to the Court. Our case had nothing to do with applying the law to protect victims; it was about twisting the law to enable the abuse of process. It wasn't even about "he said – she said." There was nothing I could say, do or show that would make a difference. I could not change the efforts of Lew's legal team any more than I could change Lew. My fighting against it only exasperated the conflict, demanding more struggle on my behalf to hold my own. I suddenly realized that the only way to stop the fight was to stop fighting.

I knew there was nothing I could do about the politics governing my case, however I believed that I, at least, owed it to myself to clarify the slander issue. This was my last effort to reach out to individuals who had been a party to our case or involved in our lives over the years. I compiled and organized a volume of text consisting of: Letters submitted to various political parties by Advocacy Groups; Affidavits of witnesses; Court Orders and relevant Pleadings from the Court Record; Police Reports of domestic violence and violations of our Order of Protection; and various other documents. The compiled manuscript of documentation showed how our case was turned around to where the abuser became the victim and I became the villain. I hand delivered this text to the school, and prepared two more copies for the police departments. Delivering the one to the school was so painful that I could not bring myself to give anything further to other members of the community.

The hurt I felt on the day I brought my self-assimilated manuscript to the school goes beyond any words I can find within me at this moment. I carried this volume in like I used to carry my babies in diapers when we'd visit my other children for activities at the school. I recalled dozens of times of me carrying David, while we visited Bradley for numerous school functions. I saw myself carrying Marc, as we visited Bradley for his performances and accomplishments at the school and my carrying Marc as we participated in David's school events, as well.

I had such warm and loving memories of my involvement at Meadowbrook Elementary School; from the children's plays, musicals, holiday parties, field trips, parent's conferences, and ice cream socials to birthday celebrations for each child every year. Somehow I could not reconcile the gross contradiction between all this fondness I felt and the book I was holding, much less the fact that the school was ordered to participate in the campaign to keep me away from my children.

*   *   *

I wanted to pull back from all my legal mess, but the court advocacy groups continued to reach out to me, still rearing to go. Bev wanted to tell the last of our story on her live television talk show the first week in May. She was so outraged by the community's failure to come through for the children. She recognized their limitations due to the politics impacting each group – the school, the police and the Department of Children and Family Services. Even with this understanding, she was livid about the school having been manipulated by Mr. Wessel and the courts. The school's impotence and inability to protect the children resonated old personal memories for Bev with respect to her own children. Her compassion was compelling and her empathy was authentic.

Bev invited the Director from a Safe Place, a local domestic violence shelter, to join us on the show. The woman sat next to me and watched Bev tell my story, while drawing the salient parts out from me. The Safe Place Director was stunned, as she watched the story unfold. Her contribution on the show concerning the occurrence of domestic violence in our communities was, basically, her belief that domestic violence is a "community issue." She believed that its interruption required assistance from the community, and was rarely resolved as a "private matter."

After the show, she gave me feedback that was like a dart hitting me between the eyes. She said, *"This is the most severe spousal abuse I have ever seen in the many years I have worked with battered women."* She noted that Lew was trying to destroy me, and he was using our children. She felt it was being done this way because my children meant so much to me. She encouraged me to consult an attorney out-of-state to assist in our plight.

I was not looking to get back in the ring again, in fact I had hoped to find a way to get out. I called her referral anyway, just to see what he would say about my predicament. He was a lawyer in New Orleans, Louisiana who specialized in litigation for abuse victims. He traveled throughout the country, lecturing on legal domestic abuse toward battered women, and represented victims nationwide.

He told me that the way he would approach my case was with two strategies which he would employ simultaneously: a legal TORT action against Lew for abusing our children and the custody dispute to bring my boys home. He saw my case as an extreme "abuse of process," and we also discussed a TORT action for this. He estimated the cost for his services to exceed $100,000 due to, as he said, "the involvement of Lew's attorney." Ms. Feinberg was the current president of the American Matrimonial Association. Did this impact a Louisiana attorney as well, or did the excessive figure have more to do with the politics between opposing counsel and the Judge?

His price made his representing me out of the question. I already had nearly $200,000 debt from my effort to remain in the litigation, and feared bankruptcy ahead. However, what I learned from him led me to reconsider proceeding in the fight on my own. I consulted with experts in judge disqualification and psychiatry to see if I could move the case forward. I was informed that the only way I could insure getting a fair and impartial trial would be to have Judge Evans disqualified from our case. After two attempts at this, I was discouraged over the likelihood of succeeding at disqualifying Judge Evans. Unfortunately, no attorney licensed and fed in the State of Illinois would entertain such a judicial attack at this juncture.

*   *   *

While gathering information on the legal and judicial aspect of the case, I also secured significant understanding about the psychiatric component. From a psychometric perspective the case was quite viable and completely in my favor. A psychologist at Great Lakes Psychological Services, a psychological testing service in Chicago, provided me with literature on the profiling of MMPI scores and the use of the MMPI as a diagnostic tool in clinical and court settings.

During the proceedings, his agency did a blind (without my name) interpretive evaluation of the raw scores of my MMPI. Based on these results and the criteria for clinical pathology, the psychologist gave me the facts to evidence to the Court that my scores did not resemble a Borderline Personality Disorder. All sub-scales of my testing were in the normal range, as had also been documented in the psychologist's interpretative report from Dr. Chapman's office.

I revisited the expert in domestic violence to bring forward factual data from the literature to evidence the classic psychiatric battering component that prevailed in the case. The domestic violence expert saw Lew as an "over-controlled, instrumental" abuser. He said this type is cold, calculating and extremely vicious. He pointed out how these perpetrators maintain tunnel vision around their mission to destroy their victims. He explained how this was the most dangerous type of batterer. The Doctor's knowledge of what was before me, from his observations of Lew over the years, concerned him. I knew from my reading and discussions with other domestic violence specialists that abusers in this category are capable of spousal homicide.

The psychologists' input helped me realize, once again, that being on the right side of "justice," with the normal psychological profile and the law in our favor for domestic violence cases was not enough. It became quite clear that proceeding with further litigation set me up for Lew's longed-for destruction of me. I wasn't sure how it would come, I only felt it was inevitable.

I spent much time thinking about whether I was willing to proceed in what would allow Lew and his legal team further abuse to me, which could potentially destroy me. I knew of another case in which Mr. Wessel severed a father from his three daughters, forbidding the man contact with his children as he threw custody to the wife, who evidently had control over the family finances and the political advantage. As part of the strategy for the case, the poor man was set up for criminal charges concerning a violation of an Order of Protection that he didn't even know was issued. When the man appeared to defend himself, the Judge said he was not mentally fit to offer his own defense. He was denied this basic liberty and, instead was placed in a state mental hospital for two years. I knew this man well. He was not a candidate for a psychiatric hospital, rather he was severely victimized by the system.

I learned of another women's horrific and disgraceful misfortune. She was a practicing physician in Chicago who was also a battered wife. She lost her freedom fighting for sole custody of her children who were abused by their father. The strategy for re-victimizing this women was to orchestrate a criminal process in which she was wrongfully convicted and imprisoned. She has been in jail now for three years. Her story was documented in a film produced locally in Chicago.

The rational mind says, "Oh no, this cannot happen in a house of justice," but it does. In the same way that abused children are placed into the hands of their abuser, innocent people can be victimized by the judicial system. Not that it always happens, but when it does it is real.

*   *   *

To reconcile the disparity between my burning desire to be with my boys and the realities of the judicial process before me, I called my mother. Mom had always been a good sounding board, and I wanted her opinion. I went to Kinko's copy store where I spent almost as much time as I did in my own home. I poured a cup of coffee and pulled up a chair next to a pay phone. Mom and I had many "heart-to-hearts" like this during the month of May, 1999. At one point she said to me, "You sound exhausted. You could go on one of your health retreats, get your strength and come back and be abused again." I almost spilled the coffee.

The thought of her comment made me sick. Throughout the course of my marriage, following my 1988 cervical spine injury and for the full course of the divorce proceedings, I made a habit of pulling back every six to twelve months for mental and physical rejuvenation through days of silence and yoga. I grew to cherish these days of personal solace and renewal. This practice contributed to my ability to maintain balance in the face of severe and prolonged adversity. But the thought of regaining my strength to come back to the hell I was living was out of the question. I explained to my mother that I felt like I was in a third world country and I no longer wanted the strength to stay. I recognized my ability to refuel was serving as my liability, not as an asset, in the family abuse dynamic. Mother encouraged me to follow my heart. She, too, saw danger coming.

After talking to my Mom and the "experts," those that knew what I was dealing with and those that had been there, I consulted with my own expert inner voice. I knew I had weathered enough. I recalled last Fall sitting in Temple for the Jewish High Holy Holidays. The Rabbi had directed the congregation in silent meditation. In the quiet moment of my prayer, tears came rushing down my checks. Marc was sitting next to me and asked, "Mommy, what's wrong?" I was praying, "Please, let us go." I was asking God to make them let us go. I remember not having the words to convey the pain I felt in that moment, even to myself much less to my child.

Then I was flooded with memories of intense anguish engendered by the legal nightmare and I knew it was destroying me. I recalled the day John and I walked out of court following Ms. Murphy's sham exit, after she buried my case and left me on the threshold of trial, helpless and defenseless. As John and I left the courthouse, we walked down the street and I started screaming, "I want out!!" I burst into tears and said, "Give me my life back...or kill me." He walked me into a sandwich shop and he tried to help me get a hold of myself. I told John that I absolutely couldn't go on with being abused by the proceedings, nor could I continue in court with the million-dollar-plus "legal muffler" which had been placed over me during the last three years.

Reflecting on where I had been and the prospect of what was ahead made my inner answers clear to me. I needed my life back; they had taken everything from me, except my soul. From here the answers came clearly and convincingly. First, I realized I wanted my life back. Second, I knew I wanted to be alive, with my health, sanity and freedom when my boys outgrew Lew's control. Finally, I recognized I needed to accept that pushing against the legal domestic abuse directed at me and my children enabled it to continue, inflaming it more and more. The insidious and exponential growth of the abuse cycle made my long term desires, concerning my health and commitment to my children, both impossible.

*   *   *

I realized my belief that I could impact the delivery of justice for me and my children was as unrealistic as my prior belief and commitment to changing Lew. I was not responsible for what they were doing, nor was it my job or within my means to fix it. Earlier in the litigation, I had become immune to Lew's strategy of "starve her out" and "say she's crazy," and simply saw it as a ploy to harass me in his effort to push me out of our children's lives. I grew to recognize that his actions were part of the pathology of an abuser, and all my counsel supported this as being true. My counsel repeatedly assured me that these actions were to taunt me, but would not result in the children being removed from my custody.

However, the "getting rid of Mommy" began to have the appearance of being driven by more than Lew. It seemed to protect Judge Evans and all those involved in the court crimes that were being perpetuated and exposed. I believe the lawyers wanted me to remain quiet while I was starved out, denied my civil liberties, and through the destruction of my professional practice from the inside out, as well as the compromising of my children's emotional health with one legal psychiatric ploy after another. This was acceptable conduct to the Court. It was suggested that I was to remain quiet while they emptied Lew's purse. Then, as I was told, they would let us go. It was explained that this is how it sometimes works when you combine the perpetrator pathology and the divorce industry at its worst.

But Lew's purse was not emptying. He had fed over four court agents for four years. In the third year of this massive legal spending, I realized Lew was going through more money than he earned and more than what we and our families had combined. In calculating the legal expenditures, it appears Lew spent roughly one million dollars *more* than what he had available from personal or family resources. The advocates wondered where Lew was getting the money.

Throughout the litigation, Lew's counsel resisted disclosure of his legal spending on the basis that it was "confidential." I wondered how and why the Judge accepted this position, contrary to the Illinois Laws requiring full financial disclosure. I was threatened with court sanctions and a Default Judgment for not being able to present documents no longer in my possession, while Lew was privileged to keep the funding for his legal representation a secret.

It was suggested that the litigation was being funded by a purse beyond Lew's control. When the Judge's connection to the hospital came out, it was suspected that Lew was being protected by the same source that the Judge was protecting. Or was the additional $1,000,000 of legal services, beyond the Blumenthal family re-sources, provided pro bono by counsel? This, too, is a possibility, given the interest in protecting the Court and the lawyers following the litany of legal malpractice and professional transgressions during the course of the litigation.

This endless funding or infinite legal resources, coupled with the Court's evidencing its unwillingness to change by following one unlawful ruling with a fraudulent one, helped me see the reality of my predicament. The Court had established that Lew was a wife and child abuser; but when it was time to reverse the unlawful ruling of non-parent temporary custody, Judge Evans showed he had a greater investment in protecting the Court than my boys. Once the Judge's conflict of interest was exposed, I suspect he could not and would not admit his need to protect the Court and/or its agents from further scrutiny.

His correcting the unlawful ruling with a fraudulent ruling, establishing Lew's newly founded "rehabilitation" and me as the "abuser," – *before and without a hearing* – insured the Court's maintaining **control**. Denying my rights for due process had become the court norm in our proceedings. It is possible that my confronting the Judge's conflict of interest evidenced my loss of faith in my seeking our justice there. My natural next step probably would have been to flee to secure judicial protection elsewhere for me and my children. I suspect they expected this, and did what was necessary to prevent it, irrespective of the law.

Now that the second unlawful ruling had been issued, the Court began to give the appearance of seeking legal justification for their actions. If this was their need, their natural next step would have been to make me the unfit parent or person, giving me a criminal or psychiatric record, to substantiate the Judge's last ruling.

Whatever the motives, it was clear Lew was not my only perpetrator and my salvation was not being delivered in divorce court. I had to cut my ties with the Cook County Court system and find salvation from within. There had been a time during the litigation when I felt safe with Lew battering me through the courts. I convinced myself if he could do it this way, he wouldn't have to do it on the streets. I recognized judicial violence can be as destructive as domestic or street violence. I no longer wanted any part of it.

*   *   *

Ultimately, it became a Holocaust survivor decision for me to pull out. It was not humanly possible to handle my grieving the loss of contact with my boys, being kicked out of my home, making ends meet at my no-profit practice, and fighting by myself against three to four attorneys who were rigorously and relentlessly compromising my liberties; and all of this simultaneously. I knew if my body didn't deteriorate in this litigation nightmare, the Court was capable of making determinations that would destroy my life.

I was not willing to remain in the abuse dynamic any longer with anyone. I needed to look toward salvaging my life and pray I would reunite with my children on the other side of this injustice. At first I could not deal with the idea of "turning my back" on my children. So I held on, as did my boys. For over a month, Lew denied me contact with the children. The pain of our longing for one another, both theirs and mine, tormented me so much that the decision made itself. The agony, hollowing, screaming, and crying on the phone to see Mommy was excruciatingly painful for them and unbearable for me as a witness and a party to maintaining it. I saw that my staying in the fight would further enable what was tormenting and abusing all of us.

My reaching out to my children brought up for both them and me an intense desire to be together. I knew this was healthy. I also knew Lew's efforts to use this longing as a vehicle to further sever our tie was extremely destructive to my children. Lew was trying to manipulate the boys into believing their attachment to me was not good for them and their contact with me was unhealthy and endangering them. This became Lew's justification to the boys for recording our telephone conversations, which was degrading for me and uncomfortable for them. From my perspective, Lew was attempting to dismantle half of my children's foundation, and I could not allow him to do this.

Lew's legal team asserted to want to proceed with custody litigation. However a custody dispute at this juncture, under the care of their father, set the boys up for further polarization. Lew's effort to secure the children as allies for the custody battle involved emotional manipulation and brainwashing to convince them that the abuse to us was either imagined or appropriate. I recognized that doing this would unravel the values I spent twelve years instilling in my children. Their knowledge of the difference between honoring and violating others deserved to remain intact. To me this foundation is essential to their making healthy responsible choices as young adults.

I could no longer commit to a process that I knew was designed to destroy my sons from the inside out. I wanted them to use whatever resources remained within them to maintain their integrity, and I recognized they, too, could take no more. It became a Solomon Judgment to allow my children their wholeness and trust in their inner strength.

I endured such mental anguish in coming to grips with my options and the reality of my predicament that I became physically sick. When my mind resisted letting go, my body demanded my doing so. I developed a severe upper respiratory infection, resulting in my loosing my voice. After several days, I broke down and went to my internist, Dr. James Sheinin, for an exam to determine if the infection had gone into my lungs. He suggested that I rest for a few days and provided me with a note recommending that I not participate in the court proceedings until May 26, 1999. One of my court advocates filed my doctor's note in the Court Record. I was really too sick to go anywhere, much less court.

*   *   *

Lew and his attorneys wanted to proceed May 24, 1999 on their Motion to remove me from my home, bar my expert witnesses for the trial and then prepare for the final trial. What I had envisioned started to unfold. They actually expected me to participate in a trial against Lew's two paid law firms, denying me any possibility for paid legal representation or expert witnesses. They expected me to proceed in this cruel abusive litigation after being evicted from my home, pushed out of my children's lives, and depleted of all my resources. Basically, they wanted to bury me along with all of our favorable evidence and have me fight my way out.

They purported to conduct this legal warfare while I submit to a psychiatric intervention for a condition that I did not have; and if I resisted, they threatened to hold me in contempt of court. I refused to allow Lew and his legal team to walk me into wearing a psychiatric label that was not mine or wear a straight jacket that I did not deserve. And I refused to pay criminal penalties for my unwillingness to further enable this legal psychiatric ploy.

They had railroaded me enough; I needed my life back. My children had suffered beyond repair, and I could not witness or enable anymore damage to my boys. I kept reminding myself that now my oldest son weighs as much as me, and if Lew hits him, Brad will soon be able to strike back. I put my energy into finding a place to live because I knew I would be out on the street. I moved June 1, 1999 and learned that Lew's counsel asked the Court to place a "body attachment" on me, because they wanted me back in court.

So now Lew had my children, my home, my savings and my professional practice. I wondered what more did they need from me to be calling me back to the court. It appears they needed to continue the litigation, even though Lew remained in the legal ring fighting himself. For over a half a year Lew's attorneys mailed Pleadings to my mother's home, requesting further production of financial documents and more discovery. Lew was holding out paying Steve Stern, and apparently did not want to bring the case to closure.

Why Victims Leave Abusive Relationships

Abuse victims leave their batterers when they experience a sudden breakthrough that changes their connection to the abuse dynamic. It evolves spontaneously, yet gradually, by reaching a clear and dramatic intra-psychic shift. The breakthrough surfaces in a manner similar to the "snapping-out" phenomenon wherein someone abruptly comes out of a trance-like state induced by a controlling religious cult. A new perspective emerges in which the victim emphatically says, *"That's it. No More!"* The precipitating causes that lead to the inner shift and final break include:

"Fear of Staying"
Believing your abuser might kill you or cause permanent physical damage

"Loss of Hope for Change"
The realization that there is nothing you can do to change your situation or circumstances

"Hitting 'Rock Bottom'"
Reaching your limit, crashing to your rock bottom like an alcoholic

"Positive External Influences"
Gaining a new perspective on the abusive relationship through an informed objective viewer; Receiving strong encouragement and positive visions of finding a comfortable life without the abuser

"Tipping the Scales of Hope and Fear"
Increased fear after an intolerable escalation of abuse or victimization and a heightened awareness of its danger; Complete loss of hope for change from the abuser; Increased faith in a good life without the batter; Diminished fear of life without the abuser

---

Citing G. NiCarthy, *The Ones Who Got Away: Women Who Left Abusive Partners*, 1987.

CHAPTER 30

The Thinning Thread

Brad's Run Away, Hospitalization and Payment

Dexter Is Dead, Says Lew's Girlfriend

Grandma Denied Contact with Her Grandchildren

The Federal Attorney

The Dwindling E-Mail and Telephone Connection

My Mending and Recovery

The first month after my departure was one of picking up the pieces. There were many adjustments ahead for all of us. Days after my leaving, Bradley ran away from Lew's home. He fled and hid for a week, until he was picked up at a friend's house. Then Lew placed him in an in-patient psychiatric hospital. From Bradley's perspective, he was hospitalized as a punishment for running away. He said he fled to attempt to look for me. It angered Lew very much, and he used all of Brad's savings from his Bar Mitzvah to pay for Brad's hospitalization. This infuriated Brad. Following the hospitalization, Brad was placed at Marlene's for part of the summer.

David had a similar experience of maltreatment, with the details being much different. When the boys moved back into the marital residence, David wanted his dog Dexter to live with him again. I knew the boys would want Dexter, so I placed him in a kennel before my departure and indirectly notified the children where they could pick up their dog. David called the kennel daily, yet Lew refused to pick up Dexter. A message was left on my voice mail to call the kennel.

The lady in charge at the kennel notified me that a woman named Ellen called her and vehemently ordered her to "tell David that the dog is dead." The lady at the kennel said, "I am not going to lie to the child." She said she felt so badly for David because he kept calling and crying for his dog. A sword went through my heart, hearing that Lew's girlfriend, Ellen, would attempt to sever my child from another of his most precious attachments. I could not understand how this woman, who has a dog of her own, would do this to my child. I supported the kennel in being honest with David, and insisted that we do all that was necessary to get Dexter to David. Weeks later, David received Dexter.

In the interim, I was flooded with memories of my last attempted contact with the boys on April 26, 1999. This was the day Jenny and I went to Lew's house to pick up the children, in accordance with my visitation schedule, but for the third time, we were denied visitation. Ellen came to the front door when we arrived and forbid the children to come out of the house. Marc ran out anyway and rushed over to embrace me. He wanted a hug, and I opened my arms to receive my child. Ellen screamed, "Jean," (the name Lew insisted on calling me – the name given to me by Joy Feinberg in the court proceedings) *"Don't torment the child!!!"* I was shocked that she perceived a mother's loving gesture as "tormenting" a child.

I realized that communicating to my children that their dog was dead was not too much different for Ellen than trying to sever their attachment to their natural mother. I was certain she was merely carrying out Lew's orders. My children saw the "other side" of Ellen. Privately, I had hoped that she would take my place in becoming Lew's victim.

My children reached out to my mother, and she continued to be available to them. However, in a matter of one week, this too was interrupted. Lew's attorney, Ms. Feinberg, called my mother at her home and viciously yelled at her, saying she could not call or talk to her grandchildren without a supervisor. There was nothing in the Court Record from the Judge ordering an interference of the children's contact with their innocent grandmother, whom they love and longed to be near. Ms. Feinberg was now making "bench decisions," as Lew did in April and thereafter. It was obvious, even to my children, that Lew and his counsel had walled them off from their maternal family. Doing so caused significant distress to my boys, my mother and to me.

*   *   *

Even though I had secured some protection by removing myself from the jurisdiction of the Cook County Court, my nightmare was not over. I had filed all of the proper Pleadings responding to Lew's efforts to sever me from my children and evict me from my home. But the distance and setting the record straight was not enough. The war continued inside of me as it did for my boys. Psychologically, I could not let go of my children and they would not let go of me.

I called a federal attorney to vent my frustrations. The attorney told me that I could have proceeded with the litigation on a federal level in a Diversity Action for Child Abuse. He said the case would have evidenced to the higher court how the local divorce court buried the real issue of abuse through distortion and manipulation of the litigation process. I told him of my children's efforts to flee the abuse, and I was informed that my boys and I could have been protected under the "Uniform Child Custody Act" if we had pursued our rights in another state.

Initially, I was angered that I had allowed myself to buy into the fear-provoking strategy of the Chicago divorce attorneys around my children and me leaving the state. I was disgusted with myself for believing that leaving with my children was kidnapping. For God's sake, I was the parent with legal custody. We were the victims with the Order of Protection, and we continued to be abused. I realized that we may have been saved in a higher court with this legal action.

At this juncture, I did not have the resources to proceed with further litigation. I did not have the financial means, the physical strength or emotional resilience to weather any further legal combat. I had been litigated to the hilt, ad nauseam, with four years of pre-trial railroading through the system, and had reached a point where I could not even look at a pleading without it turning my stomach. The attorney had suggested that I compile the record, but there was no way I could bring myself to do this at that juncture. Instead, I recognized it was time to mend, but I wasn't quite sure how I was going to do this either.

*   *   *

My children were denied direct access to me, and our heartache expressed itself in our telephone conversations. As we grieved, Lew used our symptoms of pain and longing for one another to diminish the thread between us even more. It became very clear that this was being done to insure the silent seal around the abuse in their home and keep my truth out. It is also possible that it was done intentionally to prevent us from seeking any remedy outside of the control and influence of Lew and the lower court. The federal attorney predicted this would happen. He pointed out, as the children remain with Lew, they will be manipulated to conceal the abuse and fight against themselves. The attorney was correct. In the months to follow, I saw my children progressively more entrapped, and me pushed further and further out of their lives.

Many of my letters were "lost." My phone messages on Lew's voice mail to the boys were ignored, and my e-mail was sifted and sorted and, some, rejected. In spite of Lew's efforts to keep the children and me apart, we continued reaching out to each other by phone and e-mail. All three of my sons, Bradley now 15 years, David 12 years and Marc 10 years, tell me they are miserable. They know the battering is still present and is particularly apparent to David and Marc. My sons feel entrapped, imprisoned and robbed of their personal freedoms. Intense anger festers in each of them, having been denied contact with me. It is clear that they love and miss me ever so much, and they want to see me, be near me and live with me. I know they know what happened, in spite of what their father tells them.

My children have expressed their truth in over 20 e-mails, and the more candor they put in their correspondence the less Lew allowed them to write. It first tapered off by Lew demanding to read their letters before they were sent out to me, and always insisting to read the letters I sent to them. Lew apparently needed to override the boys expressing their love for and desire to be with me, as well as any disclosures of their unhappiness or discussion of violence in their home.

Seven months after our last time together, Marc said in an e-mail:

"I'm just tearing apart from not seeing you. We have to find a way to let us see each other without dad noing (knowing) that we are..."

In another e-mail, October 24, 1999, Marc writes:

"Dear Mom: I got the pictures that you sent me ...please tell me give me a number that I can call so you can tell me so dad won't here (hear). I will go to my friend Adams house so I can call you..He wants to help us get back together son (soon) send this message with answers please. love Marc."

David's e-mail also expressed his love, his longing and his anger. On November 11, 1999, David wrote:

"Dear Mom, I love you so much. I am so angry that I can't see you. My dad was on the phone listening to our conversation this Tues. He came upstairs and ripped the phone from me and hung it up because he couldn't stop our talking even know (though) he was talking real loud. My dad is now going to take me off of A. O. L. just so I can't talk to you. I am so angry at him. I hope I can find another way to talk to you. Love your son David"

David was really concerned he was going to lose this contact. In his next e-mail he wrote:

"Mom, I will keep in contact as often as possible with you. I was so scared that I would not be able to talk with you anymore. I really want to thank you for E-mailing me so often. Whenever I check my mail there is always an e-mail from you. I'm very sorry if you are not getting alot from me. For now on I'm going to write whenever I have a chance no matter what. I love you soooooooo much, Mom, and hope to see you soon. Hugs and kisses. Love you son. David Brian King (Blumenthal)"

I could see the backfire of Lew's actions by the way David signed his name. Then on November 21, 1999, David wrote:

"Mom, I would have alot better life if I lived with you...I can't take it any more..I love you and miss you so much."

During Hanukkah, David sent an e-mail saying:

"Dear Mom, ...Happy Hanukkah! I'm so angry I can't open gifts and light candles with you this year. I am going to make a Hanukkah wish to be with you. I love you so much........I love you always, Your son David"

Bradley's e-mail reflected his understanding and his wishes as well. During the summer he wrote to my brother and said:

"Things could be a hell of a lot better...I am very angry with my dad because I blame him mostly for her (referring to me) *leaving."*

In an e-mail to me the day after Thanksgiving, Brad wrote:

"We had a pretty dull Thanksgiving dinner. We went around the table and said what we were Thankful for this year and nothing very important came to mind. My health could be one thing, I guess, but there is so much more that I just don't have to be thankful for. I guess you can say I'm thankful for e-mail because we can communicate like this.....I look at the pictures you gave me everyday and I think about all the fun times we used to have together. I can't wait until we have fun together again....Love always, Brad."

This holiday contact, Thanksgiving and Hanukkah, was the end of the end. To interrupt our correspondence, my e-mail address was blocked completely and my letters were not going through to them. My e-mail came back with an AOL message saying: "NOT ACCEPTING MAIL FROM THIS SENDER." I attempted to circumvent this with a new e-mail address, but then the boys were denied access to the computer. The children informed me that they were "grounded" from the computer, a consequence unrelated to their behavior. It was obvious to them that this was done to prevent our writing to one another.

Before our being cut off from e-mail, I was able to send 58 e-mail letters and greeting cards to my children, oozing with my love and affection. Repeatedly, I kept telling the boys they are in my heart, in my thoughts and in my prayers, everyday. I let them know how much I love and miss them. I kept reassuring them that "I am your Mom always," and "no one can take Mom's love away."

*   *   *

I have spent more time on this section concerning our dwindling e-mail and phone contact than I have on whole chapters in this book. I guess it is a sign that I have not fully come to grips with losing this last thread of connection with my sons. The absurdity and insanity of our communications being severed by Lew is that he has been spreading rumors that I abandoned my boys and have not attempted to contact them. On November 12, 1999, my mother sent me an e-mail, saying she heard through my cousin that Lew told her I have abandoned my children and that I "have made no attempt to contact the kids."

We have maintained phone contact, but this too has been difficult. At first, Marc spoke spontaneously, expressing his anger and his fear. In one of our first conversations he said, "*The Judge has ruined my life.*" Then, he cried and cried. At one point, he told me that if he were to say anything about his being hit in his Dad's house, he would be put in a "foster home."

On another occasion, Marc and I were on the phone talking, and his father picked up the phone and refused to get off. Marc pleaded with Lew to hang up the phone so he could speak with me, but Lew refused. The firmer Lew was, the more frightened Marc became. Marc was concerned about Lew's having contact with me, and in a panic Marc said, "Mom, hurry, hurry hang up the phone."

At some point, I decided it was ridiculous for me to be frightened, because Lew was on the phone. I was talking to David, and Lew interrupted our conversation. David begged him to get off the phone, and again Lew refused. This time, I continued talking with David. Lew became angry and said to me, "Stay on the phone and I will have this call traced." I recognized that he was threatening me, because David was saying things that Lew didn't want me to hear.

To protect himself, he threatened me. I saw the dynamic, and it turned my stomach.

We continue to have some telephone contact now, but always with Lew tape recording the conversation and having either himself or his baby-sitter, Vlad, on the phone while the children and I speak. Brad knows exactly what is going on, and David is well aware of it too. I remain proud of my sons' commitment to knowing their truth, in spite of being told lies. David said his father told him he has to live with his Dad because *"Your Mom will prevent me from seeing you if you live with her."* David is outraged knowing the absurdity of this statement, as he knows I always wanted him to have full access to both of his parents, and it is his father that is preventing him access to me. All I could say to my son was, "Actions speak louder than words."

*   *   *

The boys have told me they feel like they are in jail, particularly because of the way Lew refuses to allow us any phone contact without the live monitoring. Marc explained that his Dad said this was being done because, *"Your Mom did not go to the doctor and get fixed."* Marc added that his father explained, *"Dad went to the doctor and got fixed."* This seemed confusing to Marc.

I am not allowed to tell the boys how I feel about what is being done, though I am sure David and Brad know because they share the same truth. In one conversation with David, in which Lew was on the phone, I tried to tell David that I did not want to speak with his Dad on the phone. I suggested we pick another time. I told him I believed it was "not right" that someone was listening while we were on the phone.

Lew broke into the conversation and said, "If you tell them this is *not* right, I'm going to have to take away this privilege too."

I wondered who's *privilege* was it, theirs or mine. I could not participate in the dialogue with Lew and merely told David, I love him and to call me another time.

During this conversation, it occurred to me that I was playing Russian roulette with an abuser who bought the court. I backed off, as I knew telling my children how I felt about being pushed out of their lives could result in my not hearing their voices or their not hearing mine until they are 18 years old. I was unwilling to take that risk.

On Valentine's Day, Marc was crying on the phone, pleading with me, "Mom, take it to a higher court." He begged me to come back and said, "Your hiding out in another state *is making it* so we can't see you." Marc said, "If you don't come back, Dad will get full custody and we will never see you again."

I heard his pain and felt my own. I found it telling that months ago he wanted to hurry me off the phone when Lew came on, because Marc knew Lew posed a threat to me. I wondered if Marc had forgotten that Lew was not allowing me to see him when I was living in our house, and had been denying us contact since April, 1999. It appeared that Marc had been told he isn't seeing me because I wished it that way, and now he was beginning to believe it.

My children being given incorrect information about why we aren't together is what originally fueled my momentum to write this book. I was concerned that they might internalize and adopt the false information given to them in my absence. I wanted so badly to tell Marc my truth about why I left. *I wanted him to know I did not leave him, but rather I was pushed out of his life.* **I was abused out of his life; I was abused out of all three of my children's lives.** Of course, everything is being monitored so I can not speak as I wish. I don't know what this false information will do to my youngest child, but it does not look good to me. I feel Marc is confused.

I believe it is a horrific violation to all three of my sons to be denied their right to have access to me, their mother. My boys are locked in child abuse; emotional, psychological and physical. I have been prevented from assisting them, at least through the lower courts. Today, I am fearful of returning to Chicago, as I expect doing so will re-engage me in the abuse dynamic with Lew and the Cook County Divorce Court. I cannot allow this to happen. This remains unfinished in my nightmare. My children and I have a relationship that goes beyond Lew's rage and his use of the courts to chase me out of their lives.

To comfort Marc, as I am sorting through what my next step will be, I consoled him like one does when someone has died. I told him, "Mommy is still in the bigger picture. I am with you in heart and in spirit, and you can keep me with you in your heart and in your thoughts." I explained that he was in charge of his thinking and he could enjoy memories of us being together. I painted pictures of activities we did together and said, "When you're riding your bike, feel Mommy's presence riding behind you." I told him to eat foods that we liked eating together. I reassured him that he would always be my baby and no one would take that place. Then, I hung up the phone and I cried.

*   *   *

My life, since I left, has been about hanging on to the thinning threads connecting me to my children, healing my wounds, recovering from Lew's abusing me and our sons, dealing with my being re-victimized by the lawyers and court agents and regaining my strength, integrity and wholeness. Each month has moved me further along.

I spent June and July grieving significantly, vacillating between being afraid of my own shadow to drowning in my own tears. I felt wounded and raw. Seeing a child in public made me both livid and sad. I avoided large segments of community, simply not to feel my own remorse, resentment and pain. To divert the flow of mental anguish and emotional discomfort, I directed my energy to making a little home for myself. I recognized that I had been robbed of the experience of one's own sanctuary.

August and September were months of repair and renewal. I focused on getting my body back in shape, regaining strength I had forgotten was in me. My muscle tone came back, and my weight went from 107 to 117 pounds. Eating became a pleasurable event that served to refuel and revitalize me. My body began to assimilate what I ate, and I gravitated to foods that enriched me. There was no more sluggishness and indigestion following a meal, but rather a feeling of invigoration and well-being. My elimination became regular and normal, something I had only known following a yoga retreat or a body cleanse. I began to sleep soundly and in perfect peace, with windows of awareness letting in wisdom of my unconscious.

With my newly found physical stamina and mental alertness, I longed to ease my heart. I taught myself everything I could get my hands on concerning forgiveness, and learned a path to emotional freedom. I discovered that *forgiveness is for the one forgiving*, and no one else. I recognized that my experience gave me something beyond my prior professional skills to offer humanity. I became committed to making a difference in the world of domestic violence and the self-empowerment and recovery of victims of abuse. From here, I directed my energy toward writing *All But My Soul*. I have learned that writing unites matter with spirit and reading connects the minds of many.

Since writing this book, my experience of myself in relation to Lew is different. I no longer shake when I hear his voice, though I still perceive him as unpredictable and volatile. My communications with my children remain direct from my heart, and I have a knowing that we will reunite. When I see children and adolescents, I am available, open and interested. The words justice and injustice no longer pierce my inner being with pain. My vision is broader and more expanded, encompassing all that is. I continue longing passionately to be with my children and look forward to the day that this, too, will come. Often, I fantasize about some magical shift occurring that brings us together now. I don't know how long it will take for my boys to outgrow their father's control, and I don't expect Lew to change.

Everyday, I think of my children. I miss seeing their shinning faces and hearing their natural spontaneous voices. I am not sure how I will reconcile that I am no longer in the daily picture to clean their ears, sing to them as they fall asleep, hold ice to their sports injuries, nourish their bodies, stimulate their minds, comfort them in their moments of sadness, share in their pleasures, hopes and dreams, be a part of their challenges, melt in pride over their accomplishments, teach them right from wrong, show them cause and effect, and live with them naturally as we are entitled. I was their mother, teacher, coach, guide, minister, confidant, comforter, protector and friend. Today I am their mother, pushed out of their lives and they are my sons, denied contact with me.

March 15, 2000

My Personal Lessons

Marc asked me "Why did God do this to us?" I did not have a meaningful answer to his question when it was asked. Now I recognize the growing pains of the last sixteen years have provided me with profound lessons. Each lesson came to me as a blessing, a nugget of wisdom embracing my entire being. In closing, I offer them to you and to my dearest sons.

1) The abuse dynamic is a dysfunctional attachment between a perpetrator and a victim.

2) It takes two to maintain an abuse dynamic.

3) Violation evolves out of vulnerability in both the batterer and the victim.

4) Battering is impotence longing omnipotence.

5) Being victimized is denial of inner-self and the surrendering of oneself to another.

6) Violence erupts out of vulnerability, not power.

7) Sustained fear is psychologically self-imposed.

8) Changing the status of a perpetrator and/or a victim occurs from within.

9) I can not change a perpetrator from being abusive.

10) No one, but me, can rescue me from being a victim.

11) I am responsible for my own actions, feelings and beliefs.

12) Others are responsible for their actions, feelings and beliefs.

13) Abuse can be maintained in divorce court when the batterer controls the funding or aligns with the politics.

14) My relationship with my children is not a legal matter; it is a parent-child connection.

15) My bond with my children is not a function of their father's desire; it is a human attachment that has a life of its own.

16) Children are their own people, no matter what anyone else wants for them.

17) Mind matters, and what we think we create.

18) We choose our experience.

19) What we focus on and engender experientially expands and attracts more of it onto itself.

20) It is not what happens to you in life, it is what you do with it that matters most.

21) Forgiveness frees oneself, serving the one forgiving.

22) Pure expression expunges wounds from the mind, body and soul.

23) Effortless writing is divinely driven.

24) Divinity abounds and awaits to be let in.

25) Invitation and surrender are the keys to communion.

Locked In Child Abuse

On March 28, 2000, Brad ran away from Lew's home, once again. This time he fled by train to California. He reached out to the members of my immediate family for assistance in his effort to stay away from Lew. It appears that he wanted to live on his own until he was of age to live with me. He remained in hiding for one full month.

His communications brought much of what was being concealed in Lew's home to the foreground. Bradley said he fled because, over the last few months, his father had been threatening to lock him up in a mental institution. Brad had been taunted with the details of how this institutionalization would occur. He was informed of the ambulance company that would take him away on a stretcher. He was convinced that his father had made all the necessary preparations for payment, as well as the nuances of the locked room in which he would lose his freedom.

My family was limited in their ability to help my child, because Lew demanded Bradley's return to him. Lew showed my family that he would evoke "custodial interference laws" if they assisted Bradley while on the run. So my oldest brother, Lou King, attempted some inter-family negotiations between Bradley, Lew and me. Bradley said he would surface if he could live with me. My brother approached Lew with Brad's wishes, to get him off the streets, however Lew refused to allow my child to come to me. Lew expressed his preference to have Brad remain running the streets of southern California over living in my protective care.

Equally astounding was Lew's rationale for this preference. He informed my brother that I could not see my children because of a Court Order forbidding our contact. When asked how this Order got entered, Lew said, "She is not healthy. She went through eleven attorneys." Lew told my brother, "Jeanne can't see the children until she comes back to Chicago." He insisted that I had some issues to resolve there, but refused to identify them.

My family recognized that Lew was more interested in his battle with me than he was in the immediate protective care of Bradley. I found it numbing that Lew took this position in light of his recognition of Brad's distress prior to his leaving. Lew informed my brother that Brad had been depressed for months before his departure over not seeing me. Lew relayed Brad's saying how he was "forgetting what his mother looked like," and how this was distressing and depressing him. Lew said there was significant and regular fighting between Brad and his brothers. I was informed the fighting was so severe and continuous that the boys were not allowed to be together without an adult in the room. Brad claimed there was also excessive, intense and violent fighting between himself and his father and the baby-sitter, Vlad.

Marc told me that Brad left because, "he could not take the stress." In the same conversation, Marc pleaded with me to come back to Chicago. There was an air of belligerence in his tone and blame directed at me for our not being together. My next worst nightmare was coming true. He appeared to be "identifying with the aggressor." While I know this is common and even understand how it happens, I was hurt by his demeanor. I felt the anger he directed at me and also sensed the pain he harbored. He said Lew's sister and girlfriend have been telling him that he would be able to see his Mom if she had stayed to *"fight"* for him, and if she had *"listened"* to the Court and went to the doctor.

What they didn't tell my child is that I had been standing in a battlefield, fighting for him for four years, with four guns shooting at me, and each time I picked up a gun it, too, was aimed at me.

Further, my child was not informed that as we approached the last round of court war, I was being backed into psychiatric chains put on my legs that would have caused bruises for the rest of my life and would have impeded my ever being able to stand up for us. And all of this was to occur while I enable and witness my compromised sons torn in half. Of course, I could not tell my child this; he is too young to understand. I couldn't even give him an age appropriate explanation because our conversation was being monitored and tape-recorded, and I would have been penalized with court sanctions for revealing my truth.

From my perspective, it looks as though our family pattern remains the same. While I am quite different internally, our outward circumstances are not that much different. My children are locked in an abuse dynamic concealed by Lew, and my family and I remain intimidated by Lew's ability to use the system to get his way and carry out his vengeance. So in some way we, too, are engaged in the dynamic – apparently the tension-building phase of the cycle of violence.

I wanted so badly to intercept my runaway child and protect him from his nightmare, but I was informed that attempting this would result in criminal charges against me and more abusive litigation instigated by Lew. My mother believed Lew wanted me to intercept Bradley to give him cause to arrest me. I suspected this, as well, because a similar set of circumstances occurred during the course of the proceedings in which this seemed to be the case. Had it just been Lew and I at war, I may have gone looking to capture Brad despite the Court Order to forbid me contact with him; but the last year proved otherwise. I recognized that the Court's prior abuse to me served to paralyze my natural instinct to retrieve my child or secretly attempt to flee underground with him.

I recalled my earlier conversations with the federal attorney concerning federal laws to protect abused children, specifically the Unified Child Custody Act. I was told that my efforts to evoke this act for Brad's protection would require a Petition by me for the transfer of his custody. However, I then learned that the matter would be transferred to the home state, because the culture of the courts is to defer to the jurisdiction of the home state. In my hopes to circumvent this, it was suggested if I could demonstrate that our rights had been violated in Illinois, our case might be heard in the state where I reside. In a matter of days, I compiled the entire four year Court Record and submitted it for an independent legal analysis in preparation for a court's review.

I learned that, indeed, our record reflects gross denial of "due process" to me – and, from where I stand, this means my children as well. The attorney said:

> The most grievous interference of my due process rights was when my children went from Lew's sister, Marlene, to Lew *without* a Hearing. He explained that after the Judge reversed his non-parent ruling, I should have had a Hearing **before** any other placement was made. In a mere reversal of the ruling, the boys would have been given back to me. The attorney further explained I was, therefore, the custodial parent at this time and that any assignment of custody deviating from that would necessitate a Hearing. By not giving me a Hearing, at this juncture, **my children were improperly removed and illegally kept from me**.

As I was attempting to secure legal protection for my son, my family and I maintained contact with him as much as possible without falling prey to Lew's wrath. Communications occurred daily to be assured of Brad's safety. Everyday was like a week. Much transpired and things moved rapidly. At one point I thought there would be remedy for Brad, but before it could happen he was picked up and returned to his father. While the King family did all that could be done to assist Bradley without subjecting anyone to Lew's threat of court ramifications, we were unable to protect my child from his being returned to the Blumenthal abuse tradition. Brad's entire maternal family has truly become impotent in helping him escape abuse, whereas Lew and his family remain blind to the abuse.

* * *

I am sickened with facing, once again, Lew and his use of the courts to deny me the right to protect my child. It is a primal violation to both Bradley and to me. I am keenly aware of the fact that my recoiling from the "threat-of-Lew's-use-of-the-court" was because I knew Judge Evans' Court was capable of anything. Judge Evans acted as though he was beyond the law; and he was. Earlier on I recognized my attachment to my children would resonate with an alignment to abuse as long as the Court re-invested control in Lew, which had been done months after they had established that he was an abuser in May 1995. I suspect this is the reason many states prohibit batterers from fighting for custody, because allowing them to do so merely enables the abuse dynamic and further entraps all the family members into abuse and violence indefinitely.

My son's runaway and what it brought out has rekindled my desire to "right the wrong" and remedy the legal infractions done to me and my children. The only question is that I don't know how I would proceed with such a venture. I do not have the financial resources to pursue my children's protection and our rights in a court of law – *at least not one manipulated by a perpetrator* – nor have I found counsel willing and able to confront the injustices to me and my children.

Still, it is not that financial resources are not there; rather the family money is to serve Lew and his wishes only. Last month Lew's attorneys sent an *un-filed* Pleading to my mother's home requesting that $72,000, which he claims is *my* portion of *our* remaining pension, be secured by Lew as my contribution to child support. Further, the Pleading purposed that I be charged the tax penalty for his withdrawal of these resources. I have been informed that an assignment of this tax liability to me is in violation of federal tax law. The resources that could have served my children's interests by paying for my expert witness report finally have been located, and again it remains beyond my reach to use these funds to protect my boys.

Everyday I pray for my children's protection and our justice. I recognize my limitations and try my best not to beat myself up for being boxed in the corner – held in checkmate – while failing in my ability to protect my boys. I am practicing seeing my children as whole and ultimately having the wisdom to remember our truth and empower themselves.

I struggle in my anxiety for Bradley and my grieving the loss of years with all three of my sons. I don't know how I will convince myself, much less convince them, that we accept our waiting for their emancipation until we can resume our normal contact with one another. It might be that we accept it because it *is*, not because it is right. Then the question for me is, *how do I deal with the pain of not being with my children;* and the question for my boys is, *how do they fix the injury of their mother torn out of their lives.*

June 10, 2000

Identification with the Aggressor is a term coined by Anna Freud describing an attachment to, and emulating of, the aggressiveness of a stronger and more powerful person who imposes severe and random punishments on his/her victim. The weaker more helpless individual comes to identify with the controlling perpetrator in order to ward off danger and "avert violence against themselves." It is an effort to see the world from the eyes of the dangerous individual in the victim's desperation to control or "restore some predictability" in their own lives. (Dutton, 1998, p 140)

Statistics on Family Violence

- Four million women are abused in a single year. (*The First Comprehensive National Health Survey of American Women* cited in Campbell, et. al. 1997)

- The American Medical Association reported that 1 in 3 women will be assaulted by an intimate partner in her lifetime. (*Time, July 4, 1994*, cited On-line)

- Every 15 seconds a women is battered by a partner who "tells her he loves her." (cited in Wilson, 1997)

- Abuse by husbands and partners is the leading cause of injury to women ages 15 to 44. (*U. S. Surgeon General Report*, cited in Torr, Eds, 1999)

- Over two-thirds of violent victimizations against women were committed by someone known to them. (*U.S. Department of Justice Bureau of Justice Statistics*, 1994)

- One out of every four men will use violence against an intimate partner at some point in their relationship. (M. Paymar, *Violent No More*, 1993, cited On-line)

- Approximately one-third of men counseled for battering are professional men (doctors, psychologists, lawyers, ministers and business executives) who are well respected in their jobs and communities. (*Massachusetts Coalition of Battered Women Service Groups*, cited On-line)

- Fifty percent of all women are battered during marriage. (cited in Walker, 1979)

- Twenty-five percent of all victims of domestic violence are pregnant women. (cited in Gondolf, 1985)

- Forty percent of assaults on women by their domestic partners began during the first pregnancy. It is estimated that pregnant women are at twice the risk of battery. (Martins, et al., 1992, cited On-line)

- Violence is the reason stated for divorce in 22 percent of middle-class marriages. (*EAP Digest*, 1991, cited On-line)

- Battered women are at a 75 percent greater risk for homicide by their ex-intimate partners after they leave the relationship. (*National Coalition Against Domestic Violence*, 1988)

- Over 80 percent of all women murdered by their male partners had called for police help one to five times prior to being killed. (cited in Walker, 1979)

- In the first seven months of 1992, seventeen women were murdered in Massachusetts; ten of these women had orders of protection. (cited in Jones, 1994)

- Ninety percent of all family violence defendants are never prosecuted, and one-third of the cases that would be considered felonies if committed by strangers are filed as misdemeanors. (*News from U.S. Senator Barbara Boxer*, 1993, cited On-line)

- One study showed 59 percent of fathers who won custody physically abused their wives and 36 percent kidnapped the children. (cited in Jones, 1994)

- Experts estimate that 70 percent of men who abuse their female partners also abuse their children. (cited in Jones, 1994)

- Approximately 3.3 million children in the United States between the ages of 3 and 17 are at risk of exposure to family violence. (cited in Wilson, 1997)

- More children die at the hands of their parents than in car accidents, house fires, falls, drowning or any other accident. Every year 18,000 children are permanently disabled, and 142,000 seriously injured through abuse and neglect. (cited in Snow, 1997)

- An estimated seven million children are beaten by a sibling within a single year. (cited in Martin, 1977)

- Seventy-nine percent of violent children have witnessed violence between their parents. (*Family Prevention Fund*, 1991, cited On-line)

- Sixty-three percent of young men between the ages of 11 and 20 who are serving time for homicide have killed their mother's abuser. (*March of Dimes*, 1992, cited On-line)

- Ninety percent of hard core criminals, especially perpetrators of violence, were abused as children. (cited in Sandberg, 1989)

- Eighty percent of all men in American prisons were abused children. (cited in Gondolf, 1985)

- Fifty-seven percent of respondents in the Time/CNN poll of 1995 said that they personally knew a victim of domestic violence. (cited in Campbell, et al., 1997)

- Two out of three Americans who reported knowing a victim of domestic violence had nevertheless admittedly "failed to even talk to her about the abuse." (cited in Campbell, et al., 1997)

- Fifty-three percent of 143 accredited medical schools in the United States and Canada do not require medical students to receive educational training in family violence. (cited in Wilson, 1997)

- Each year medical expenses from domestic violence total at least $3 to $5 billion and costs businesses another $100 million in lost wages, sick leave, absenteeism and non-productivity. (*Colorado Domestic Violence Coalition,* 1991, cited On-line)

- Every five years, the death toll of individuals killed by family members and acquaintances equals that of the entire Vietnam War. (cited in Gondolf, 1985)

Cycle of Violence

The Cycle of Violence is a sequence of cyclic phases of battering behavior, identified by Dr. Lenore Walker in *The Battered Woman*. This battering cycle explains how battered women become victimized and resort to patterns of learned helplessness, and why they do not try to escape their batterers. Augmenting Dr. Walker's conceptualization with insights from Dr. Donald Dutton's *The Batterer: A Psychological Profile* shows the contribution of both the abuser and victim in the establishment and maintenance of the cycle of violence.

Tension-Building Stage: Less lethal forms of battering incidents occur involving; psychological, emotional and more minor physical altercations. The battering is done primarily to rebuild the batterer's fragile sense of self. He exhibits a heightening of uncomfortable feelings, which Dr. Dutton identifies as "aversive arousal." It is a state of agitation, tension and irritability, which manifests in his being "a little moody" or "a bit tense" for no apparent reason. Battered women note that the escalating verbal and physical attacks are unrelated to current circumstances. Batterers "don't merely react to events, but create a different view of the world in which emotional bumps become earthquakes." As Dr. Dutton explains, "Small issues assume great importance, as if he were caught inside them and couldn't see their limits." (1995, p. 42)

The battered woman attempts to calm the batterer by nurturing, compliance or staying out of his way. This inadvertently gives the batterer the message that "she accepts his abusiveness as *legitimately* directed toward herself." She does not believe she deserves to be abused, but assumes that her actions will prevent the batterer's anger from escalating. She thus has become an accomplice in the battering by assuming responsibility for the battering behavior.

She does not get angry at the batterer, instead she resorts to denial around her being unjustly hurt psychologically or injured physically. She internalizes the batterer's faulty reasoning that she is responsible for his actions and/or blames outside factors to assist in her maintaining her own denial. Her denial keeps both her and her batterer in check, as she knows he is capable of far more danger.

The batterer is aware that his abusive behavior is inappropriate, but does not admit it. Instead the batterer harbors more internal fear of his wife abandoning him, and thereby becomes more possessive, jealous and oppressive. His intrusiveness and brutality are his means of keeping her captive. This phase can maintain at a constant level for weeks, months and in many cases years.

The battering incidents become more frequent and the resulting anger becomes undeniable and lasts for longer periods of time. It becomes more difficult for the victim to recover from the pain and torture evoked by the battering. Exhaustion sets in and she withdraws from the batterer. The batterer's internal discomfort escalates and the delicate balance can no longer be maintained.

The Acute Battering Incident: The second phase of the battering cycle consists of an uncontrollable discharge and release of the tension built up in phase one. It is distinguished from phase one by the enormity of destructiveness and lack of control in and around the altercation. The trigger for moving into this phase is typically an external event or the internal state of the batterer. The perpetrator ruminates on his victim's malevolence, escalating his arousal and fury higher and higher.

The batterer's rage is so severe that it blinds his control over his behavior. It is impossible to predicate the type or extent of violence that will occur during this phase. Generally it is quite brutal and results in an injury. Both the batterer and the victim evidence a disassociation: a "red out" and loss of control of the escalating violence for the abuser, and an escape or self-anesthetizing for the victim. The altercations escalate into harder and faster blows until the perpetrator reaches exhaustion or faces depletion in himself or his weapon.

The acute attack is immediately followed with initial shock and disbelief around the severity and seriousness of the altercation, by both parties. Victims often do not seek help at this juncture unless the injury requires immediate medical attention. Phase two generally lasts from two to twenty four hours.

Kindness and Contrite Loving Phase: The kind loving phase is the calm after the explosion occurs and the tension is released. It generally lasts longer than phase two, but is shorter than phase one. The abuser may completely deny what has happened or attempt to atone and promise reform. The abuser in denial will mentally reconstruct the act, blaming the victim for provoking his aggressions. He may minimize the severity and/or frequency of his violence and deny any personal accountability for his aggressive behavior.

If, on the other hand, he recognizes he has gone too far, he will seek atonement and may convince himself, his victim and others that he will stop his abusive conduct. He re-engages his victim by showering her with gifts, flowers, cars, jewelry, and loving words of endearment. The real hook for many victims is the batterer's playing on her sense of guilt, amidst all these loving gestures. Often he will enlist both family and community to convince her that she is vital to his getting better and responsible for keeping the family and/or marriage together. In her "ownership" of these obligations, her victimization becomes complete.

The changes of the perpetrator seeking help are minimal if his battered wife stays with him. Whether she recognizes this or not she becomes so enamored by his charming loving promise that she reinvests in a fantasy, rekindling her original romance. She convinces herself that his loving side is the "real" man she loves. Her reward for accepting his abusive violence is the rekindling of calm, kindness and love.

This generally being the time that "helpers" see her confuses and confounds the battering couple's troubles. He looks so right and she's so willing. Hope, honeymoon and tolerance ensue and separation is off. This is the phase in which she will drop the charges, renege on the divorce and often sees the frailty and insecurity of her batterer.

She clings to the loving phase hoping the other two phases will cease. However if she has been through several cycles of violence, she realizes that she is trading her safety for this temporary dream. This selling herself out results in self induced embarrassment and self-hatred. She becomes an accomplice to her own battering. The perpetrator begins rebuilding his ego at the victim's expense and the battering cycle begins again. As the cycle of violence ensues, the battering and severity of violence typically escalates into dangerous, life-threatening proportions.

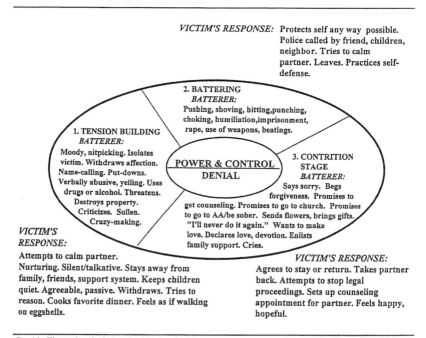

Graphic Illustration depicting the "Cycle of Violence" from D. Dutton, *The Abusive Personality: Violence and Control in Intimate Relationships.* © 1998 Copyright by The Guilford Press. Reprinted with permission.

Myths and Facts about Family Violence

Myth 1: Men who abuse their partners are uneducated, socially inept and outwardly aggressive.

Fact: Batterers, like battered women, are rich, poor, educated and uneducated. They are of all origins, races, religions, ages and sizes. Some are fat, some are thin, and some are even unmanly and fragile. Their expression of violence has little to do with their outward physical stature, and more to do with their need to control.

There are those who are less polished socially and many more who are charming and socially sophisticated. In general, they are typically well adept at interfacing socially in order to manipulate matters to their liking.

Some intimate abusers are outwardly aggressive, but more often they are not. Their family aggression characteristically occurs "behind closed doors" and is an expression of the flip side they project to the outside world. This Dr. Jekyll/Mr. Hyde aspect of their personality is what camouflages batterers. In *When Violence Begins at Home*, Dr. Wilson notes that the batterer's Dr. Jekyll/Mr. Hyde Personality creates are "air of doubt" when their victims disclose their controlling brutality and violence. (For an elaboration of the Role of the Dr. Jekyll/Mr. Hyde Personality in Maintaining the Cycle of Violence, see Chapter 28, Information Insert.)

Myth 2: Women often provoke men into battering them and deserve to be beaten.

Fact: Men initiate violence independently of what their partners say or do. As noted by Drs. Lenore Walker and Donald Dutton in their respective work on battered women and batterers, an acute battering incident is a release of built-up internal tension within the batterer. It is an explosion of violent rage that accumulates within the batterer during the tension building phase of the cycle of violence.

The term "provocation" implies that the victim got what she deserved; but there is no justification for beating another human being. Violent responses are only appropriate as self-defense. One can not "provoke" another to chose violence; there are always other options in an interaction. Violence has a life of its own and is fully within the responsibility of the one perpetrating it. As Michele Weldon, journalist and former victim of domestic violence, poetically notes:

> "Violence, I learned, is illogical and unforgiving. Like a fire, it spreads where there is air and space and where it is allowed. It is consuming and it is deadly, and it will defy boundaries even if you aren't the one who lit the match. Violence in the home is an encompassing, ruthless intruder. It will burn you and your children, and *it has little to do with provocation*. It rages past you and through you no matter how you try to pacify it, no matter how much water you throw in its path. It can never be enough. It feeds on itself. And it can kill you." (emphasis added, Weldon, 1999, p. 47)

Myth 3: Battered women could stop abusive behavior by changing their own behavior.

Fact: Implied in this myth is that battering can be or should be controlled by someone other than the batterer. However, the batterer is the only one responsible for and in control of the battering behavior, As Drs. Jacobson and Gottman note in *When Men Batter Women*:

"...battering cannot be changed through actions on the part of the victim. Battering has little to do with what the women do or don't do, what they say or don't say. It is the batterer's responsibility." (1998, p. 53)

The authors' examination of battering incidents shows that not only are there no triggers leading to violent episodes, but there are *no switches for turning it off*. This misconception of battering behavior is not only shared by outsiders but also by the battering couple. More often than not battered women believe it is their "job" to stop their husband's violence. This form of personal ownership in "fixing" it serves to perpetuate the cycle of violence and never remedies it, because the batterer is the only one who can change his behavior.

Myth 4: Alcohol and drug abuse cause abusive behavior.

Fact: Substance abuse does not cause abusive behavior, though it often exacerbates an already existing tendency toward violence. The two conditions are quite separate, yet both are considered to be addictions. Substance abuse is an addiction to drugs and/or alcohol; whereas battering is an addiction to brutality. The violent, abusive behavior actually serves to maintain the personality of a batterer; it maintains the abuser's sense of feeling whole. As Dr. Dutton points out in *The Batterer: A Psychological Profile:*

"Abusiveness is not, however, just a copied behavior but rather a learned means of self-maintenance. The abusive man is addicted to brutality to keep his shaky self-concept intact. The only time he feels powerful and whole is when he is engaged in violence" (1995, p. xi).

Myth 5: Batterers cannot control their anger.

Fact: Battering is usually voluntary. Behavior that is voluntary involves a choice, and the outcome one seeks determines the choice one makes. Battering is a choice in the same way that all other voluntary actions are chosen. Drs. Jacobson and Gottman's research with batterers reveals that the "Cobra" batterer's physiological response to conflict supports increased concentration and focused attention. These batterers show a lowering in their heart rates during aggressive arguments. The researchers purport that the batterer's self-imposed internal state of lowered arousal functions to "focus their attention, to maximize the impact of their aggression." These abusers are not only in control of their aggressive behavior, "but they use their control over their physiology to strike more effectively" (1998, p. 42).

Following an altercation, batteres remembered their aggression; but either minimized its significance or denied responsibility for their actions. In some cases, they deny that the violence even occurred. The researchers interpret this denial as the batterers merely lying, which serves to extend their control over their victims.

Myth 6: Women who stay in abusive relationships are crazy; they must enjoy being abused, otherwise they would leave.

Fact: Battered women do not enjoy being abused, nor are they crazy. They remain with their abusive partners for a number of reasons, many of which are related to fear of leaving and unrealistic hopes for change. The research on battering couples shows that the risk of harm to the victim increases significantly after leaving the relationship, and battered women know this before their departure. They are inundated with threats of what will happen after they leave, and often this binds them to the relationship long after they have given up. As Drs. Jacobson and Gottman note, "It is easier to get into an abusive relationship than it is to get out of one" (1998, p. 49). What entraps victims, long before they reach the point of having serious thoughts of breaking away from their abusive partners, is an unconscious programming that is a by-product of the dynamics of the cycle of violence. Victims are mesmerized by the sweet seductiveness of the contrition phase of the cycle of violence. They cling to this phase, and it becomes the source for rekindling their faith and commitment to the relationship. It is suspected that it works as a strong reinforcer because it is delivered on an intermittent and random reinforcement schedule – just like the slot machine. It is random to the victim by virtue of the fact that it follows an acute episode of violence; an event in which the onset and termination is beyond their knowledge and control.

Entanglement in the cycle of violence conditions victims in their own victimization. I call this "in-trance" victimization, because that is how I experienced it. Dr. Dutton identifies the bonds that bind abuse victims to their tormentors as "traumatic bonding." He suggests that it stems from one person holding more power than the other, intermittent and random abuse, and intermittent reinforcement to keep coming back for more. Recognizing the factors that bind victims to their batterers, Dr. Dutton points out:

"There is no special deficit in a battered woman's personality that makes her susceptible to getting trapped in an abusive relationship. To the contrary, the features of the relationship itself are sufficient to account for the trapping" (1995, p. 57).

While in-trance and gripped in the bondage of their perpetrators, victim's survival behaviors do appear unusual and even bizarre. Dr. Wilson, a former victim of domestic violence, points out that these behaviors have earned battered women the mislabeling of being "crazy." However, as she notes, the dynamics and intensity of the abusive relationship pose a constant threat that affects how these women think, feel and act. Their "survival strategies" are an adaptation to a threatening situation, which helps keep them "safe and in control of their environment" (1997, p. 14).

Myth 7: It is better for children to have their father at home, even if he is violent.

Fact: While it is true that having both parents living in the home with their children is ideal, when there is violence in the home it is not. As Dr. Walker notes in *The Battered Woman,* children who formally lived in a violent home universally express a tremendous relief in living with a single parent in a nonviolent home.

Despite some family traditions, violence is not beneficial to children. To the contrary, the child development and the family violence literature consistently show that children witnessing or experiencing abuse has adverse and detrimental effects on their emotional, psychological, social and behavioral health and development. As Dr. Judith Herman, author of *Trauma and Recovery*, states, "repeated trauma in childhood forms and deforms the personality" (1992, p. 96).

Abuse to a child is experienced as a trauma, in which there is a significant trauma reaction, that has both an immediate and long standing impact on the child's well-being. In *The Batterer: A Psychological Profile* Dr. Dutton points out that the abuser, to the child receiving or witnessing violence, is uncontrollable and has "all the power." The child feels utterly and completely powerless, and is placed in a state of learned helplessness. The child knows that expressing the rage, sadness or pain he experiences in response to the abuse will result in further punishment, so he is "forced to swallow his rage toward the perpetrator and experiences sham at his own impotence. This further undermines his sense of self" (1995, p. 125). He becomes a prisoner in his own family. He may cope through passive withdrawal and dissociation, though ultimately he learns to model abusiveness for dealing with conflict and frustration, and as a means for releasing his internal aversive arousal.

In the long run, parental abuse to children impacts their basic self-esteem, erodes their sense of "self," impairs their capacity to trust, and hinders their ability to maintain healthy intimate relationships in adulthood. Child abuse is also often associated with the onset of adolescent delinquency, substance abuse, chemical, social and behavioral addictions, chronic medical disorders, varied mental health disturbances, and the classic traits and characteristics of an offender profile in adulthood. There is no doubt that **violence begets violence** – violence onto oneself and/or violence onto another.

(For an elaboration of the relationship between child abuse and delinquency see *The Child Abuse-Delinquency Connection*, by David Sandberg; and for an a review of the relationship between child abuse and addiction development see *No Safe Place*, by Christina Crawford.)

Myth 8: Battering is a more significant problem for lower class women because it is harder for them to seek help and secure assistance in leaving.

Fact: Upper middle class women have even less options than middle and lower-class women, especially women whose wealth is dispensed at the discretion of abusive husbands. Usually the more the money in the family and the wider the disparity of income between partners, the greater the likelihood of the battering husband to maintain full control over the family's financial resources. Dr. Richard Gelles, Director of a Family Violence Research Program at the University of Rhode Island, has pointed out that these women's situation is clearly worse than most battered women. Dr. Gelles states:

"The upper-class woman married to the nice Jewish doctor gets zero social services, and the support system in the US is not designed for her." Imagine her checking into a shelter, where she's has to share the third mattress from the left. Instead she could go to a motel, but the American Express card is probably in her husband's name. So as soon as the monthly statement comes, her batterer knows where she is. (cited in A. L. Bell in Torr (Eds) 1999, p. 33)

Myth 9: Psychotherapy is a more effective intervention than prison for batterers.

Fact: Most psychotherapy programs are unlikely to stop violence and even less likely to end emotional abuse. More often, psychotherapy enables and reinforces battering by giving the batterer an opportunity to manipulate, control and exploit the process.

For example, individual therapy by its nature tends to be a supportive environment; and thus, the therapist may end up colluding with the abuser and supporting the patient's justifications and continued use of power. In *Ending Men's Violence Against Their Partners*, authors Stordeur and Stille point out that "correcting intrapsychic problems is not likely to decrease the violence if the batterer is still being rewarded for abusive behavior and continues to gain compliance from his victim through his violence" (1989, p. 56).

Marital or couples therapy and family therapy, which is derived from a family systems perspective, does not address the violent behavior of the abuser as the main problem either. This treatment approach equalizes the responsibility for the abuse dynamic between the batterer and his partner. Practitioners note that couples therapy exacerbates the batterer's tendency toward externalization and supports his thwarting off of personal accountability for and ownership of his battering behavior. Consequently, the intervention more often supports the maintenance of the abuse syndrome (Stordeur & Stille, 1989; Jacobson & Gottman, 1998, Dutton, 1995).

The pioneers of the innovative psycho-educational intervention for batterers report a greater success rate than any other psychological treatment for battering. The general consensus among these practitioners is that treatment effectiveness first necessities the batterer's assuming responsibility for his abusive behavior. The professional literature addresses the importance of support from the judicial system to hold batterers accountable for their abusive behavior. Authors consistently agree that this is best done when domestic violence is treated as a crime with appropriate criminal action. The judicial system's use of psychotherapy gives the message that assault is not a crime when it occurs in the family. This message merely enables battering through passive consent (Jacobson & Gottman, 1998; Snow, 1997).

Myth 10: Our social structures and judicial system provide remedy for family domestic abuse.

Fact: Society has long allowed battered women and abused children to be victims of abuse by treating domestic violence as a "family matter," rather than as a crime. The police are reluctant to arrest batterers, and the courts give light sentences to those that are arrested or often none at all. Ann Jones, journalist and author of *Next Time She'll Be Dead: Battering and How to Stop It*, points out that states do not prosecute domestic violence cases because the state will then have the responsibility of the perpetrator's wife and children. Dr. Dutton notes that police do not arrest domestic battery offenders because they know judges rarely send them to prison – so why bother. He points out that the judge's reticence is not only economically driven, but also a concern for the potential of retaliatory violence after release. Unfortunately, the lax intervention or the doing nothing remedy is *more likely* to contribute to the exacerbation of the abuse syndrome. Why, because escalation is the only direction in which family abuse goes, and the batterer learns he can get away with it.

Battered women learn that the social and judicial "helpers" provide them with little support, relative to their needs, to help them escape their abusers (cited in Torr, Eds., 1999). Dr. Walker says, "Women who have been battered state that they feel no one can protect them from their men's violence. They frequently comment that they feel their batterers are beyond the grasp of the law" (1979, p. 64). It is no wonder that battered women feel this way; it is the fact of our law enforcement. Legal scholars have pointed out, "...the law effectively abets the batterer ... and turns a deaf ear to the battered woman" (cited in Jones, 1994, p. 27). Not only are these women ignored, even more devastating is the fact that "these crime victims are often being re-victimized by the criminal justice system" (cited in Davis, 1998, p. 113).

Myth 11: Battered wives could just get a divorce and end the domestic violence.

Fact: Divorcing a batterer does not necessarily put a stop to the family abuse. More often than not, it continues in one form or another, particularly when children are involved. As illustrated in *All But My Soul*, divorce court is a fertile ground for the transformation of domestic violence into litigation abuse. Battered women – abused wives and often the protective parents – on their way out of their abusive relationships, via divorce court, are eligible candidates for losing their children, their homes, their jobs, reputations, health, freedom, and their lives. Ann Jones notes "many men use child custody suits as one more weapon to punish and control a woman who is trying to get free" (cited in Jones, 1994, p. 31).

If a battered woman, or mother of abused children, takes the matter of protecting herself and/or her children into her own hands, she increases the likelihood of losing custody to the father. She may be charged with kidnapping and deprived of her parental rights while custody is turned over to the "nonoffending" father. A strategy often employed by abusive men to secure sole custody of their children is *"to abuse and terrify their mother until she has no choice but to run,"* either with or without the children. Ms. Jones points out, "the more abusive and violent a man is, the more likely he is to get sole custody of his children"(emphasis added, cited in Jones, 1994, p.33).

Child custody disputes by batterers serves to engage the family in endless family domestic abuse and perpetuates indefinite re-victimization of the victims. Our social and judicial systems enable family violence beyond what most people realize or could even imagine, and everyone suffers. In *The Hostage Child*, authors Rosenthal and Etlin cite a case in which there was well-documented sexual abuse of a young boy by his father and the paternal family. A custody battle evolved out of the mother's efforts to protect her son and the father was awarded custody. The mother continued seeking assistance from social services to come to the aid of her abused child, until the mother and father shot one another. The paternal grandfather was also wounded in the shooting. The father is now dead and the mother is in jail for murder. Domestic homicide, whether by the family abuser or the victim, is not an act of passion; but rather the out-growth of an un-arrested, long standing problem of family abuse.

Myth 12: Increased public awareness about domestic violence has facilitated protection for victims.

Fact: While it is true that there is considerable political and media attention given to the epidemic of domestic violence in our commu-nities today, the growing incidence of family abuse continues. And silence appears to be the leading culprit. Marissa Ghez of the Family Violence Prevention Fund says:

"Domestic violence continues to flourish because of silence, and the subtle but pervasive ways that American society implicitly accepts and condones disrespect of and violence against women." Our society's "patriarchal cultural bias" along with the ongoing belief that domestic violence is a "private, and not a public," concern leaves battered women and children at the mercy of their perpetrators. The cultural climate in this country, today, is one in which people say that domestic violence is *wrong*, but in which they nevertheless *look the other way* from the problem. In so doing, our society supports family abuse by subtly reinforcing its continuation through disrespect and devaluation of women. (cited in Torr (Eds.), 1999, p. 203)

Journalist Ann Jones suggests the silence and continued incidence of domestic violence, in spite of the efforts of the battered women's movement and rising community attention, may have more to do with the intrinsic value that battered women hold for society. Ms. Jones proposes:

"In the aggregate, battered women are to sexism what the poor are to capitalism – always with us. They are a source of cheap labor and sexual service to those with the power to buy and control them, a 'problem' for the righteous to lament, a topic to provide employment for academic researchers, a sponge to soak up the surplus violence of men, a conduit to carry off the political energy of other women who must care for them, an exemplum of what awaits all women who don't behave as prescribed, and a pariah group to amplify by contrast our good opinion of ourselves. And for all their social utility, they remain largely, and conveniently, invisible." (1994, p. 205)

I suspect that the problem of domestic violence today is a function of many factors, including: the intra-psychodynamics of the batterer, the victim and *all* who are a party to the abuse dynamic (those who admit it and those who do not); the inter-relationship dynamics of the cycle of violence; as well as the myriad of social, cultural, judicial and political influences supporting domestic violations. Until change occurs across all of these facets of humanity, batterers will batter, victims will be victimized and family abuse will continue.

Author's Final Note

Our family story, my understanding of family and legal abuse and my knowledge of today's social resources has helped me see the multitude of pieces to this human puzzle of social domestic abuse. It is clear to me that there is much that supports domestic violence in America today. From here, I envision avenues for addressing family violence through education, healthcare, law enforcement and legislation. I am dedicating my future professional servitude to the implementation of the visions I have today.

If you are interested in contributing to breaking the cycle of violence in family, in court and in our communities, please contact me at Dr.King@AllButMySoul.net

References

Barnett, Ola and LaViolette. (1993). *It Could Happen to Anyone: Why Battered Women Stay.* Newbury Park, CA: Sage Publications, Inc.

Bender, David and Bruno, Leone. (Eds.) (1994). *Child Abuse: Opposing Viewpoints.* San Diego, CA: Greenhaven Press, Inc.

Besharov, Douglas J. (1990). *Recognizing Child Abuse: A Guide for the Concerned.* New York, NY: The Free Press.

Betancourt, Marian. (1997). *What to Do When Love Turns Violent: A Practical Resource for Women in Abusive Relationships.* New York, NY: HarperCollins.

Brown, Larry and Francis, Paul. (1994). *Juice: The O.J. Simpson Tragedy.* Los Angeles, CA: Globe Books and Princeton Publishing West, Inc.

Campbell, Jacquelyn, et.al. (1997). *Ending Domestic Violence: Changing Public Perceptions/Halting the Epidemic.* Hohusand Oaks, CA: Sage Publications. Inc.

Clawar, Stanley and Rivlin, Brynne. (1991). *Children Held Hostage: Dealing with Programmed and Brainwashed Children.* Chicago, IL: American Bar Association.

Crawford, Christina. (1994). *No Safe Place: The Legacy of Family Violence.* Barrington, NY: Station Hill Press, Inc.

Davis, Richard. L. (1998) *Domestic Violence: Fact and Fallacies.* Westport, CN: Praeger.

Dutton, Donald G. and Golant, Susan K. (1995). *The Batterer: A Psychological Profile.* New York, NY: Basic Books.

Dutton, Donald G. (1998). *The Abusive Personality: Violence and Control in Intimate Relationships.* New York: The Guilford Press.

Engeldinger, Eugene. (1986). *Spousal Abuse: An Annotated Bibliography of Violence between Mates.* Metuchen, NJ: The Scare crow Press, Inc.

Garbarino, James and Eckenrode, John. (1997) *Understanding Abusive Families: An Ecological Approach to Theory and Practic.* San Franciso, CA: Jossey-Bass Publishers.

Gill, David. (1977). *Violence Against Children: Physical Child Abuse in the United States.* Cambridge, MA: Harvard University Press.

Gondolf, Edward W. (1985). *Men Who Batter: An Integrated Approach for Stopping Wife Abuse.* Holms Beach, FL: Learning Publications, Inc.

Hagen, Margaret A. (1997). *Whores of the Court: The Fraud of Psychiatric Testimony and Rape of American Justice.* New York, NY: HarperCollins Publishers, Inc.

Herman, Judith L. (1992). *Trauma and Recovery: The Aftermath of Violence from Domestic Abuse to Political Terror.* New York, NY: BasicBooks.

Helfer, Ray and Kempe, Henry (Eds.). (1974). *The Battered Child.* Chicago, IL: The University of Chicago Press.

Jacobson, Neil S. and Gottman, John M. (1998). *When Men Batter Women: New Insights to Ending Abusive Relationships.* New York, NY: Simon & Schuster.

Johnson, Scott A. (1993). *When "I Love You" Turns Violent: Emotional & Physical Abuse in Dating Relationships.* Far Hills, NJ: New Horizon Press.

Jones, Ann. (1994). *Next Time She'll Be Dead: Battering and How to Stop It.* Boston, MA: Beacon Press.

King, Jeanne I. (1998). *Domestic Violence Transformed into Litigation Abuse: A Chronology of Correspondence.* Chicago, IL: Jeanne King, Ph.D.

Kushner, Harold S. (1981). *When Bad Things Happen To Good People.* NY: Avon Books.

Magid, Ken and McKelvey. (1987). *High Risk: Children Without a Conscience.* New York, NY: Bantam Books.

Martin, Del. (1977). *Battered Wives.* New York, NY: Pocket Books.

Miller, Mary S. (1995). *No Visible Wounds: Identifying Nonphysical Abuse of Women by Their Men.* New York, NY: Ballantine Books.

Murphy-Milano, Susan. (1996). *Defending Our Lives: Getting Away from Domestic Violence and Staying Away.* New York, NY: Anchor Books.

Nelson, Noelle. (1997). *Dangerous Relationships: How to Stop Domestic Violence Before It Stops You.* New York, NY: Insight Books.

NiCarthy, Ginny. (1987). *The Ones Who Got Away: Women Who Left Abusive Partners.* Seattle, WA: Seal Press.

Ochberg, Frank M. (Ed.). (1988). *Post-Traumatic Therapy and Victims of Violence.* New York, NY: Brunner/Mazel, Publishers.

Quinn, Phil E. (1994). *From Victim to Victory: Prescriptions from a Child Abuse Survivor.* Nashville, TN: Abingdon Press.

Rosen, Leora and Etlin, Michelle. (1996). *The Hostage Child.* Bloomington, IN: Indiana University Press.

Sandberg, David N. (1989). *The Child Abuse-Delinquency Connection.* Lexington, MA: Lexington Books.

Savina, Lydia. (1971). *Help for the Battered Woman.* South Plainfield, NJ: Bridge Publishing, Inc.

Scott, Cathrine L. (1988). *Breaking the Cycle of Abuse: A Biblical Approach to Recognizing and Responding to Domestic Violence.* Elgin, IL: Accent Books.

Seligman, Martin E. (1975). *Helplessness: On Depression, Development and Death.* San Francisco, CA: W. H. Freeman.

Snow, Robert L. (1997). *Family Abuse: Tough Solutions to Stop the Violence.* New York, NY: Plenum Press.

Stordeur, Richard and Stille, Richard. (1989). *Ending Men's Violence Against Their Partners: One Road to Peace.* Newbury Park, CA: Sage Publications, Inc.

Sugarman, Alan (Ed.). (1996). *Victims of Abuse: The Emotional Impact of Child and Adult Trauma.* Madison, CN: International Universities Press, Inc.

Torr, James and Swisher, Karin (Eds.). (1999) *Violence Against Women.* San Diego, CA: Greenhaven Press, Inc.

Walker, Lenore E. (1979). *The Battered Woman.* New York, NY: Harper & Row, Publishers, Inc.

Wallace, Harvey. (1996). *Family Violence: Legal, Medical, and Social Perspectives.* Boston, MA: Allyn and Bacon.

Weldon, Michele. (1999). *I Closed My Eyes: Revelations of a Battered Woman.* Center City, MN: Hazelden.

Wilson, Debra J. (1995). *The Complete Book of Victims' Rights.* Highland Ranch, CO: ProSe Association, Inc.

Wilson, K.J. (1997). *When Violence Begins at Home: A Comprehensive Guide to Understanding and Ending Domestic Violence.* Alameda, CA: Hunter House Inc.

Winner, Karen. (1996). *Divorced form Justice: The Abuse of Women and Children by Divorce Lawyers and Judges.* New York, NY: HarperCollins Publishers, Inc.

World Wide Web – On-line References

Domestic Violence: The Facts. On-line World Wide Web.
    <http://www.cybergrrl.com/dv/book/toc.html>

Domestic Violence Statistics. On-line World Wide Web.
    <http://www.home.cybergrrl.com/dv/stats.html>

Mental Health Effects of Family Violence. On-line World Wide
    Web.<http:/www.ama-assn.org/public/releases/assault/fv-
    guide.htm>

About the Author

J eanne I. King, Ph.D. earned her doctorate degree in Counseling
Psychology from Northwestern University in 1979. She is a
psychologist, consultant and author. Dr. King has provided clinical
psychotherapy for over 20 years. Her primary specialty has been the
treatment of pain, stress, trauma and anxiety disorders. She designed
and developed the Biofeedback and Stress Reduction Program,
which she conducted in hospitals and with hundreds of patients at
the Chicago Center for the Treatment of Pain and Stress.

Jeanne King is the proud mother of three sons, whom she loves
and remains connected to beyond words and with whom she has
been severed by acts of gross family and legal abuse. Currently she
thrives on memories and prayers of her boys as their father, her exhusband and perpetrator, has completely pushed her out of their
abused children's lives.

Since last seeing her children April 1999, she has directed her energies toward *All But My Soul: Abuse Beyond Control* and the Foundation of Inner Sanctuary, a non-profit foundation dedicated to breaking the cycle of violence. Dr. King is devoted to re-uniting with her sons and making a difference in interrupting the cycle of violence in family, through the judicial process and in our communities at large.

*   *   *

Dr. Jeanne King welcomes your letters, invitations to give seminars and your personal and professional contributions to breaking the cycle of violence. To contact Dr. King, please visit her Website at: **www.AllButMySoul.net**